"The divinity and greatness of Jesus for a secular age, Carroll asserts, are not to be found in miracles ascribed to Him, nor in the grandeur of His elevation by millennia of Christian theology. Carroll argues, finally, that the appeal of Christ to the contemporary faithful has much less to do with creed, and more to do with our ability to imitate Him in his unwavering acceptance of love for the brokenness of human beings."

—*The Washington Post*

"Carroll's own reading of Jesus, at once stunningly original and strangely familiar, is a testament to the power of a critical, creative faith."

—*The Boston Globe*

"Written in the brisk, argumentative style that has won James Carroll a broad popular readership, *Christ Actually* avoids the interminable maundering of academic prose, even as its extensive footnotes indicate attention to advanced, if radical, scholarship. Conservative Christians may well be shocked and annoyed at Carroll's configuration of Jesus. Nevertheless, for its pushback against the boundaries of conventional interpretations and, above all, for its passionate presentation of the sinfulness of Christian anti-Semitism, his book deserves serious attention."

—*Commonweal*

"It's the book's greatest virtue that Carroll can present all these real-world possibilities for Christ alongside his lifetime's work in theology, historical research, and biblical criticism. . . . But for all this historical fidelity, Carroll's writing is also thoroughly modern and devotional. His notion of Christ for today depends on taking seriously the possibility that ours is now a 'religionless world.' . . . Believers like Bonhoeffer and, later, Day, whose very lives opposed the infernality of war, groped for words that might give Christ some meaning amid the ruins of Christendom. Carroll gropes too and well. But there are no words as powerful as our human lives. Carroll knows this. It is his final word. And for Christians, he concludes, the fullness of their lives remains Christ's only hope." —*Los Angeles Times*

"With well-researched clarity, Carroll explores the question posed by anti-Nazi Lutheran pastor and martyr Dietrich Bonhoeffer: who actually is Christ for us today? . . . Because Christ actually is meaningful in some way to a billion Christians around the globe, this heartfelt investigation is of interest to many." —*Publishers Weekly*

"Carroll . . . strives to reconceive Christ for a secular, post-Holocaust, post-Hiroshima era. . . . Readers seeking a faith responsive to the zeitgeist will find it here." —*Booklist*

"Compelling." —Todd Gitlin, *The Tablet*

PENGUIN BOOKS

CHRIST ACTUALLY

James Carroll is the author of eleven novels and seven works of nonfiction. His memoir, *An American Requiem: God, My Father, and the War that Came Between Us*, received the 1996 National Book Award in nonfiction. His book *Constantine's Sword: The Church and the Jews: A History* was a *New York Times* bestseller and was honored as a Best Book of 2001 by the *Los Angeles Times*, the *Christian Science Monitor*, and others. Carroll is a columnist for the *Boston Globe*, and Distinguished Writer-in-Residence at New York University. He is married to the novelist Alexandra Marshall.

Also by James Carroll

FICTION

Madonna Red
Mortal Friends
Fault Lines
Family Trade
Prince of Peace
Supply of Heroes
Firebird
Memorial Bridge
The City Below
Secret Father
Warburg in Rome

NONFICTION

An American Requiem
Constantine's Sword
Toward a New Catholic Church
Crusade
House of War
Practicing Catholic
Jerusalem, Jerusalem

James Carroll

Christ Actually

*Reimagining Faith
in the Modern Age*

PENGUIN BOOKS

PENGUIN BOOKS

An imprint of Penguin Random House LLC

375 Hudson Street

New York, New York 10014

penguin.com

First published in the United States by Viking Penguin,
a member of Penguin Group (USA) LLC, 2014
Published in Penguin Books 2015

Grateful acknowledgment is made for permission to reprint excerpts from the following copyrighted works:

"Christmas Trees" from *New and Collected Poems 1952–1992* by Geoffrey Hill. Copyright © 1994 by Geoffrey Hill. Reprinted by permission of Houghton Mifflin Harcourt Publishing Company and the author. All rights reserved.

The Jewish Gospels: The Story of the Jewish Christ by Daniel Boyarin. Copyright © 2012 by Daniel Boyarin. Reprinted by permission of The New Press.

"Triduum" from *A Little Book of Hours* by John F. Deane (Manchester, England: Carcanet, 2008). By permission of the author.

The Scripture citations in this book are from the Revised Standard Version, unless otherwise noted.

THE LIBRARY OF CONGRESS HAS CATALOGED THE
HARDCOVER EDITION AS FOLLOWS:

Carroll, James, 1943–
Christ actually : the son of God for the secular age / James Carroll.
pages cm
Includes bibliographical references and index.
ISBN 978-0-670-78603-9 (hc.)
ISBN 978-0-14-312784-0 (pbk.)
1. Jesus Christ—Person and offices.   I. Title.
BT203.C365 2014
232—dc22   2014022328

Printed in the United States of America
1 3 5 7 9 10 8 6 4 2

Set in Adobe Jenson Pro
Designed by Francesca Belanger

For Annie

The present life of man, O King, seems to me like to the swift flight of a sparrow through the great mead-hall wherein you sit at supper in winter, with the warm fire ablaze, whilst the storms of rain and snow prevail abroad; the sparrow, I say, flying in at one door, and immediately out at another, once more into the dark winter.

So this life of man appears for a little while, but of what went before, or what is to follow, we are utterly ignorant. If, therefore, this new teaching contains something more certain, it seems justly deserving to be followed.

—A chief counselor to Anglo-Saxon king Edwin in 627[1]

Contents

Christ Actually

Christ Actually

Against wild reasons of the state
His words are quiet but not too quiet.
We hear too late or not too late.

—Geoffrey Hill[1]

Operation Spark

In Germany, early in 1943, things got serious with "Operation Spark," the anti-Nazi conspiracy to assassinate Adolf Hitler. In March, two bomb attempts were made on Hitler's life. They failed, but in early April a number of the conspirators were arrested by the Gestapo. One of these was a young Lutheran theologian named Dietrich Bonhoeffer. For two years, he was imprisoned—first at Tegel military prison, in Berlin, and ultimately at Buchenwald and Flossenbürg concentration camps. A committed pacifist entangled in a plot to kill a tyrant, he wrote, "The ultimate question for a responsible man to ask is not how he is to extricate himself heroically from the affair, but how the coming generation shall continue to live."[2]

Bonhoeffer was executed three weeks before the war ended, before the horrors of 1945 were fully laid bare. Yet there is a hint in his statement that, in the thick of the evil, he had grasped what was now at stake: nothing less than the moral self-destruction, and perhaps the physical self-extinction, of the human species; its "continuing to live." He did not survive to articulate the meaning of what he'd come to, but in subsequent years the fragments of thought he left flashed through Christian theology like crystal shards through a darkened

1

conscience. That was especially so once Auschwitz was paired with Hiroshima—absolute evil absolutely armed: the death camp and the genocidal weapon all at once bracketing the human future. The mad nuclear competition that followed then made the problem of human survival literal.

Initiating a project for belief that has yet to be accomplished, Bonhoeffer declared himself in a letter to his student and friend Eberhard Bethge: "What keeps gnawing at me is the question, . . . who is Christ actually for us today?" That line, written in a Nazi cell, is a shorthand proclamation of Bonhoeffer's penetration to the deepest question about the human condition, which raised, for a serious Christian, an equally grave question about Jesus Christ and the tradition that takes its name from him.

I, too, have found something "gnawing at me," if in far shallower ways than the martyred German. As it happens, I was born precisely as Operation Spark was launched. The son of committed Irish Catholics, I fully embraced that legacy and came of age with Jesus Christ at the center of my identity. But as I grew older, tectonic shifts in culture, religion, politics, and structures of thought cracked the foundation of Christ's meaning—even for me. Among the many factors that have contributed to that dislocation, none looms larger, I see now, than the still unreckoned-with moral catastrophe faced by Bonhoeffer. He was a first witness to the apocalyptic fervor of the Third Reich, the millennial character of the crisis—and the fact that "Christendom," a culture in place since Charlemagne and nearly the sole context within which Jesus Christ had been understood, was mortally undermined by racist Nazi imperialism. And Bonhoeffer was one of the first to grasp how the ethical shattering of Christendom extended to the keystone of Christian faith—to Jesus himself.

I begin this grappling with the new actuality of Jesus Christ by recalling Bonhoeffer not just because I associate with his hinted-at intuition that we need a radically reimagined Jesus, but because his undeveloped and rudimentary inquiry was sparked—"Operation Spark" indeed—by that brutal confrontation with what has shown itself to be the double-barreled moral problem of our age. The bottomless pit that opened in southern Poland, and into which Bonhoeffer was already staring, was only one chamber of an abyss into which humanity had been plunged also by the devastation of a city in Japan. It was not the scale of bloodshed in these two manifestations that made Auschwitz and Hiroshima historic—other genocides and mass bombings compare, from Stalin and Pol Pot on one side to Curtis LeMay and Bomber Harris on another. Rather, it was the character of Auschwitz and Hiroshima as related revelations about the past and future: the anti-Jewish heart of Western civilization, and the vulnerability of the human species to suicide.

I grew up during the Cold War on bases of the United States Air Force, where my father, an Air Force general, served as a member of America's nuclear priesthood. My otherwise mundane Oedipal reckoning unfolded in the shadow of nuclear Armageddon.[3] It was eventually impossible for me to avoid the harsh reality that, taken together, Auschwitz and Hiroshima had changed everything—except human ways of thinking and believing.[4] A transcendent shift in moral meaning had occurred. Christians regard what the tradition calls the Incarnation as an interruption in history. But so was 1945. Looking back across the decades, it has finally become clear to me how the actualities of that year forced the question: Who is Christ actually?

Religionlessness

Here is Bonhoeffer's full statement to Bethge:

> What might surprise or perhaps even worry you would be my theological thoughts and where they are leading, and here is where I really miss you very much . . . What keeps gnawing at me

is the question, What is Christianity, or who is Christ actually for us today? The age when we could tell people that with words—whether with theological or pious words—is past, as is the age of inwardness and conscience, and that means the age of religion altogether. We are approaching a completely religionless age; people as they are now simply can't be religious anymore.... If eventually we must judge even the Western form of Christianity to be only a preliminary stage of a complete absence of religion, what kind of situation emerges for us, for the Church? How can Christ become the Lord of the religionless as well?... The question to be answered would be, What does a Church, a congregation, a liturgy, a sermon, a Christian life mean in a religionless world? How do we talk about God without religion?... Christ would then no longer be the object of religion, but something else entirely, truly the Lord of the world. But what does that mean?... I hope you understand more or less what I mean, and that it's not boring you.... Goodbye for now. Yours, as ever. I think about you very much. Dietrich.[5]

Existentialist philosophy, psychoanalysis, modernist literature, political engagement for the sake of justice—such movements coming to a head after World War II salted the religious self-understanding of Christians, especially in nations bracketing the North Atlantic. Fully developed theologies flourished with figures like Protestants Karl Barth, Reinhold Niebuhr, and Paul Tillich; Orthodox figures like Alexander Schmemann, dean of St. Vladimir's Seminary, in New York; and Catholics of the Second Vatican Council[6] like Karl Rahner, Hans Küng, and John Courtney Murray. Compared with the decades-long contributions of such thinkers, all of whom were implicitly responding to crises engendered by the genocidal violence of the century's wars, Bonhoeffer's sketchy intuitions, offered most significantly in his *Letters and Papers from Prison*, read like picture captions. But the picture he holds up shows the deep truth of an unprecedented circumstance. It is clear from the passage cited above that the traumatized German was groping for words to express what remained an *unspeakable* experience. The groping itself is his legacy and challenge.

Paul Tillich, a German Lutheran twenty years Bonhoeffer's senior, lived to carry on the postwar inquiry—mainly because, unlike Bonhoeffer, Tillich responded to Hitler's coming to power by taking up a life in exile in New York. Tillich had been dismissed from his Frankfurt professorship by the Nazis, and he, too, found the crisis of Nazism at the center of his reflections. Like Bonhoeffer, he saw a consequent religionlessness as somehow necessary—but also as revelatory. Indeed, it formed the basis of his existentialist theology, which came to fruition in his postwar reflections, especially in the books *The Courage to Be* (1952) and *Dynamics of Faith* (1957). Here, in slightly more abstract language, is Tillich's echo of what Bonhoeffer wrote in the letter to Bethge:

> The relation of man to the ultimate undergoes changes. Contents of ultimate concern vanish or are replaced by others... Symbols which for a certain period, or in a certain place, expressed the truth of faith for a certain group now only remind of the faith of the past. They have lost their truth, and it is an open question whether dead symbols can be revived. Probably not for those to whom they have died.[7]

The most important symbol that had lost its truth for Tillich was the symbol of God Himself, which, after Hitler, had been irrevocably undermined. In *The Courage to Be*, he wrote,

> God appears as the invincible tyrant, the being in contrast with whom all other beings are without freedom and subjectivity. He is equated with the recent tyrants who with the help of terror try to transform everything into a mere object, a thing among things,

a cog in a machine they control. He becomes the model of everything against which Existentialism revolted. This is the God Nietzsche said had to be killed because nobody can tolerate being made into a mere object of absolute knowledge and absolute control. This is the deepest root of atheism. It is an atheism which is justified as the reaction against theological theism and its disturbing implications.[8]

In the 1960s, Bonhoeffer was posthumously conscripted into the briefly voguish Death of God movement in Britain and America, which made watchwords of his nascent notions of "religionless Christianity" and "man come fully of age."[9] Whether obsequies for "theological theism" are a function of maturity is debatable, to say the least, yet Bonhoeffer's seemed an uncanny anticipation of Europe's postwar exodus from religion, with the resulting mass redundancy of church buildings and the muting of the voices of clergy. Today, apart from the hollow formalism of royalty-ruled churches in Britain and Scandinavia, institutional religion has entirely vacated the public realm of Europe—and, in some places, the private conscience, too.[10] In America, the decline of mainstream religion was slower in coming, but the Death of God presented itself as a theological problem more in the United States than anywhere.

As figures of wide influence, there were no successors on either side of the Atlantic to Tillich, Niebuhr, Schmemann, Küng, or Murray. Eventually, with salvos from pop culture, screen technologies, and hyperlinks of the Internet, with "all talk, all the time" draining words of weight and impact—universally at the expense of contemplative reading—the devastation of inwardness itself could also seem a fulfillment of Bonhoeffer's prophecy. "The history of faith," as Tillich put it, "is a permanent fight with the corruption of faith." The fight, all at once, seemed lost. The claim of faith was "exposed to the continuous test of history."[11] And for many, it seemed to fail. The late-twentieth-century arrival of a broadly unchurched culture in the North Atlantic nations, with an apparent legion readily dispensing with theism, especially among educated elites and younger people, seemed to suggest that the Death of God theologians had been grappling with something real. "God has hidden his face from the world," as one Jewish Holocaust writer put it, "and delivered mankind over to his own savage urges and instincts."[12]

Bonhoeffer's focus was on the delivering *humans* had done, not God, but the "absence of religion" he predicted turned out not to be "complete."[13] The "Secular Age" might have dawned in most of Europe and parts of North America—regions of the Enlightenment legacy—but even there, assumptions of an earlier age held fast among many. The twenty-first century's so-called new atheism had its answer in a new fundamentalism, whose leaders, notably in the United States, enlisted on the reactionary side of the culture war being fought over flash points like abortion and gay rights.[14] On questions ranging from "family values" to the "war on terror" to the corporate ethos of retail giants, overt appeals to religion, in fact, defined large segments of American society more than ever.[15] "Today, one of the most glaring refutations of the case that religion has vanished from public life," as the critic Terry Eagleton puts it, "is known as the United States."[16] And not just the U.S. Across the globe, religious true belief has solidified identity in a sea of uncertainty.

Negatively, religion spawned world-historic acts of violence—from the 1995 murder in Israel of Yitzhak Rabin by a Jewish zealot to the perversion of *Allahu Akbar* over Manhattan, the Pennsylvania countryside, and the Pentagon in September of 2001 to the God-ordained orgy of killing in Norway in 2011 by a Christian supremacist. One wants to separate such killer-nihilism from "true religion," yet jihadist and crusader impulses do have underpinnings in authentic faith. We will investigate that connection in this book.

But the power of contemporary religion has been showing itself positively, too. Essential to the civil rights, human rights, and peace movements in the West, faith was also key to the nonviolent grassroots revolution that brought down the Soviet Union in the 1980s. Religion was a pillar of the inchoate Muslim awakening to democracy, so hopefully begun in the Arab Spring of 2011.[17] Indeed, independent of politics, religion remains a source of consolation and strength—of inwardness and conscience—for global multitudes, decisively including impoverished masses to whom material structures of meaning are simply unavailable.

So was Bonhoeffer wrong? Did religion in fact survive intact, if altered? Did he misconstrue the nature of religionlessness? For that matter, what is religionlessness? I locate this question, first, not in poll numbers or philosophical debates but in a deeply personal problem: having myself absorbed—and learned to take for granted—basic assumptions of the so-called Secular Age, what of my own religious inheritance can I believe without being dishonest? I am no fundamentalist, and the limits of religion, even its perversity, are fully apparent to me. If the faith continues to impose itself as a primal option, it does so in my case despite—or is it because of?—the crises of 1945. What happens when traditional belief slams into the wall of the Holocaust? When it plunges into the abyss of Hiroshima? Those questions are what draw me to Bonhoeffer and his crucial intuition that religion and Jesus Christ are not identical. Because Hiroshima had not happened when he was writing, the potential suicide of the human species was not an *actual* prospect for Bonhoeffer. Yet the "continuation" of human life had surfaced as an overriding moral problem, and I, a nuclear warrior's son, live to be haunted by it to this day. In Buchenwald, Bonhoeffer may well have had a foretaste of the full horror of Auschwitz, but that particular death camp's meaning as an epiphany of radical evil remained implicit. For me, though, its meaning as an obliteration of inherited religious absolutes could not be more explicit. The point is that Bonhoeffer, in all of this, sensed that some pin had been removed from the ordered mechanism of civilization, and I know with personal certainty that he was not wrong. How had the jailed German pastor come to such knowledge? Decisively, the answer involved what he saw befalling the Jews.

In April 1933, a newly empowered Hitler tipped his hand when he ordered the Nazi boycott of Jewish businesses, prompting a Germany-wide display of anti-Semitism. For several days, Jewish businesses, synagogues, institutions, and individuals were subject to insult and even attack—a dress rehearsal for the violent assaults against Jews that would escalate across the decade. Right at the outset of the Nazi campaign, raising a rare voice of protest in that first year, Bonhoeffer published the essay "The Church and the Jewish Question." He called on his fellow Christians to stand with Jews against their persecution by the Third Reich. The Church should be prepared, he wrote, "not only to help the victims who have fallen under the wheel, but," if necessary to stop the murderous careening, the Church should be prepared "to fall into the spokes of the wheel itself."[18]

Bonhoeffer might not have been aware of it, but such a grasp of an absolute moral mandate to oppose assaults on innocent Jews had to undermine, however gradually, the sanctified religious anti-Judaism on which such an anti-Semitic campaign depended—a religious anti-Judaism to which Bonhoeffer himself still subscribed. In 1933, Bonhoeffer opposed Hitler-friendly Church leaders who, in line with Nazi racism, wanted to bar all non-Aryans from ordination in the ministry, but, at least in that early period, he still saw conversion to Christ as the Jewish destiny. Jewish *religion* had no reason to continue. That Bonhoeffer was a Christian supersessionist is probably what accounts for the fact that he has never been named a "Righteous Gentile" by Yad Vashem, the Jerusalem Holocaust museum.

The main point, though, is that an authentic rejection of racial anti-Semitism *had* to lead, however indirectly, to a rejection of religious anti-Judaism. Here Bonhoeffer was putting his ethical insight

ahead of his theological conviction. This elevation of ethics over theology is what made him a religious revolutionary. Few Christians saw
it yet, but wicked hatred of Jewish persons and doctrinal denigration
of Jewish religion were joined as a grenade is to its pin. Bonhoeffer,
simply by taking in what was in fact happening all around him, even
as most Germans averted their eyes, found himself set on a course of
personal and religious change.[19]

By 1938, when the Nazi onslaught climaxed in the blatant violence
of assaults on Jews everywhere in Germany and Austria, Bonhoeffer's
understanding of the relationship between Church and Synagogue
had evolved—an at least implicit abandonment of supersessionism—
to the point that he saw them as equal "children of the covenant." In
the margin of his Bible, next to Psalm 74, Bonhoeffer wrote, "November 10, 1938"—the date of what came to be known as *Kristallnacht*.[20]
The adjacent verses read, "They set thy sanctuary on fire, to the ground
they desecrated the dwelling place of thy name . . . How long, O God,
is the foe to scoff? . . . Why dost thou hold back thy hand?" The attacks on Jews had become a matter of religious revelation. "Crystal
Night" took its name from glass being shattered all over Germany—
Jewish businesses, homes, and places of worship being ransacked and
torched. All at once, the Lutheran pastor's own Martin Luther had to
look different: "To save our souls from the Jews, that is, from the devil
and from eternal death," Luther had written long before, "my advice
is, first, that their synagogues be burned down, and that all who are
able toss sulphur and pitch; it would be good if someone could also
throw in some hellfire. Second, that all their books—their prayer
books, their talmudic writings, also the entire Bible—be taken from
them, not leaving them one leaf."[21] This was a Luther with whom
Bonhoeffer could have nothing further to do.

By the time of his *Ethics*, written in Berlin between 1940 and
1943, Bonhoeffer began to see the theological meaning of the political horror unfolding in Germany, and his simple insight amounted

by then to a personal revolution: "An expulsion of the Jews from the West," he wrote, "must necessarily bring with it the expulsion of Christ. For Jesus Christ was a Jew."[22] We will see how this assertion is not as obvious as it seems in the twenty-first century; in the first half of the twentieth century in Europe, home of the Aryan Christ, it was revolutionary.[23] The expulsion of Jews meant the expulsion of Jesus—full stop. Only a realization of such magnitude could have then prompted the pacifist pastor's enlistment in the conspiracy to assassinate Hitler: "For Jesus Christ was a Jew."

Note that Bonhoeffer does not say, as Martin Luther did in the title of the first of his two tracts about Jews, "That Jesus Christ Was Born a Jew." Luther's emphasis belongs on "was born," since the whole point of the Gospel narrative, once "the Jews" rejected Christ's teaching and sponsored his crucifixion, is that Jesus became something else—"the firstborn of the new Creation," the first Christian.[24] Bonhoeffer's life-changing insight, in envisioning Jesus as one of those expelled—*"Juden raus!"*—is surely what gave rise to the great question he then asked from prison: Who *actually* is Christ for us today? He had already provided the beginning of the answer. Jesus Christ was a Jew.

Bonhoeffer's personal reckoning sparks mine. I have outgrown a childish faith in Jesus, but he remains the one to whom my heart first opened when I became aware. What I grasped of him on my small knees before the crucifix in St. Mary's Church, stripped by now of the dross of dogmatism, remains the pulse of my faith. This book is my attempt to say why Jesus has this hold on me, but the attempt requires a certain historical sweep, a theological scope. I will return to the New Testament, but, fully attuned to our contemporary struggles, I will read those texts through the lens of centuries of total war and corrupted power, trying to see how violence, contempt for women, and, above all, hatred of Jews distorted the faith of the Church I still love.

Yet Jesus is elusive. If he were not, he would be useless to us. An ultimate paradox lies at the heart of Christian belief: Jesus is fully human; Jesus is fully divine. Best to say frankly right here at the outset: *Jesus as God* and *Jesus as man* are the brackets within which this inquiry will unfold. It will look at Jesus, the Scriptures, and tradition in the contexts of both history and theology. It will ask how the texts about Jesus were written at the start, how they were interpreted early on, and how they can be understood today. That means keeping in mind at least three distinct time frames—the lifetime of Jesus, the era some decades later in which the Gospels were composed, and the present Secular Age, when faith in Jesus *and* in the Gospels has become a problem unto itself.

Jesus is fully divine? What can that mean now? Before dismissing such a claim, or diluting it with literary-critical revision to the point of meaninglessness, I post a kind of cautionary declaration against which every assertion in this book must be measured: if Jesus were not regarded as God almost from the start of his movement, he would be of no interest to us. We would never have heard of him. Nothing but his divinity accounts for his place in Western culture—or in my heart: not his ethic, which was admirable but hardly uncommon; not his preaching, which was firmly in line with Jewish proclamation; not his heroic suffering, which was typical of many anti-Roman Jewish resisters; not his wonder working, which was attributed to all kinds of charismatic figures in the ancient world. Nothing but a two-thousand-year-old divinity claim puts Jesus before us today.

And more: if a faith in Jesus as Son of God—a present self-disclosure of God's fatherly and forgiving disposition, an "incarnation"—does not survive the critically minded, scientifically responsible, properly "secular" inquiry of the kind I aim to undertake, however imperfectly, then Jesus will surely drop back into the crowd of history's heroes, ultimately to be forgotten.

The God/man affirmation, in other words, need not condemn

this pursuit to irrationality or absurdity—or to a separate "non-overlapping magisterium" where normal rules of logic do not apply.[25] It can, instead, sponsor a retrieval of the light, depth, and beauty of Christian tradition at its best, even while offering a new way—appropriate to a less credulous time—to say that Jesus is Christ; that Jesus Christ is God. Speaking quite personally, nothing matters more to me than that. For no other reason would I take up this work.

But the words "Jesus" and "Christ" bring us back to Bonhoeffer, for whom, under the pressure of history, the key was Jewishness. For while "Jesus" can be routinely understood as a Jew, "Christ" is taken to be the claim that cuts him off from Jewishness. In fact, on the hinge of this contradiction, as Bonhoeffer saw, turns every question—both those that close off inquiry and those that open into new understanding.

Jesus a Jew[26]

That "Jesus" was Jewish can seem an obvious statement today, but in fact, the idea has barely penetrated the shallow surface of Christian theology.[27] And we are not just talking here about grossly anachronistic distortions of Jesus into something alien—like the blue-eyed, flowing-haired Northern European who appeared in the picture Bibles, holy cards, and altar murals of modernity.[28] No, the anti-Jewish distorting goes deeper than race, ethnicity, or cultural milieu. Lessons of the Holocaust notwithstanding, it perverts the religious imagination of the West to this day.

Christian anti-Judaism springs from the Gospel construct, dating to the late first century, that pits Jesus against "the Jews" during his Passion and death, which occurred early in that century. That construct led to the "Christ killer" slander, which many Christians have declined to repeat since World War II.[29] A transformation of mainstream Christian theology, centered in the Roman Catholic reforms of the Second Vatican Council, has mostly transformed the age-old "teaching of contempt" for Jews into a "teaching of respect." Most Christians routinely, and authentically, renounce anti-Semitism. Christian scholars and religious leaders find in Jews creative and open-minded partners in the momentous project of interfaith dialogue; Jewish scholars and leaders reciprocate.[30] Nevertheless, a chasm separates Jewish and Christian perspectives, and the slow plumbing of this chasm will be a main project of this book. The separating gulf begins not at the beginning, but not long after the beginning, with the portrait first drawn of Jesus and then, across time, reified by the Church.

Among Christians, and therefore among everyone else, thinking about Jesus has not really changed much, because, even beyond the most troubling verses ("His blood be on us and on our children," for example[31]), the *entire* structure of the Gospel imagination assumes a cosmic conflict between Jesus and his own people such that, despite the narrative's taking pains to place Jesus in the line of David, he was hardly portrayed as authentically Jewish at all. This is more than, say, Mark's pitting him against Pharisees in Galilee and against high priests in Jerusalem; more than the libels of the Passion. As the Christian memory overwhelmingly shapes the story, Jesus is opposed not just to particular antagonists but to the whole culture into which he was born.

In the Prologue to John's Gospel, we find the theme struck with power: "He came to his own home, and his own people received him not."[32] It's a basic rule of narrative, older than Aristotle: every story needs a conflict. In history—in about the year 30, the first of our three time frames—the mortal conflict faced by Jesus, like every Jew in occupied Palestine, was with Rome. But the Gospels—dating to that *second* time frame, between 70 and 100—do not tell it that way. As various historians and theologians point out today,[33] the virtues of Jesus (openness, compassion, egalitarianism) are constantly displayed in the Gospels precisely by contrast with his corrupt Jewish milieu, which is rendered as exclusivist, unloving, legalistic, and mercilessly hierarchical. "Jesus" is the name of the manual laborer from Nazareth. Once he began to see himself, or be seen by others, as the exalted "Christ" (from the Greek for "anointed" and meaning "Messiah"), Jesus began to be understood as other than Jewish, even if his declared identity was as a fulfillment of *Jewish* messianic expectation. His being "Christ," that is, worked against his being "Jesus," because his elevation up the pyramid of what scholars call "high Christology"— from peasant Galilean to anointed Christ; then to apocalyptic Son of Man; then to favored Son of God; then to preexisting *Logos*, or "Word"; ultimately to second person of the Trinity, and "True God of True God"—had the practical effect of obliterating the single most cogent note of his identity as a man.

Judaism, after all, is a religion—a form of mediation between humans and God. Such mediation is necessary because, by definition, humans cannot have direct access to God. If it were otherwise, there would be no need of religion. But because Jesus as the Word of God ("In the beginning was the Word, and the Word was with God, and the Word was God. . . . And the Word became flesh and dwelt among us"[34]) was understood as fully participating in the Godhead, in immediate mystical union ("I and the Father are one"[35]), the Gospel writer makes it clear that Jesus had no real need of the mediation of religion. He had no real need, that is, of the Jewish rituals of sacrifice, Temple observance, salvation history, metaphors, memory, Book, Law, peoplehood. Jesus underwent the paradigmatically Jewish initiation of circumcision, yes, but early Christians obsessively invented non-Jewish reasons for him to have done so.[36] Christian theology, since at least the Council of Chalcedon, in 451, has insisted on the true humanity of Jesus, but by deleting the religious significance of this main fact of his particular human condition, theology has simultaneously undercut his humanity. Belief in the divinity of Jesus as usually propounded, that is, makes his authentic Jewishness not just unnecessary but impossible.

Since well before Bonhoeffer, Christian scholars have known there is a problem here. But ever since Bonhoeffer—and the crisis of the war—theologically minded historians, together with historically attuned theologians, have been driven to do heroic work in addressing that problem. We will see that. But scholarship aside, a complete transformation of popular consciousness and faith has yet to occur. If our reach is toward such a transformation here, still our reckoning with the full Jewishness of Jesus Christ will mark only the start of the story, not its end point. Taking my own case as typical, I thought years ago that I understood the meaning of the Jewishness of Jesus, having been ambushed one afternoon in the Art Institute of Chicago, for example, by the sight of the French-Jewish artist Marc Chagall's *White Crucifixion*, a large painting of the crucified one draped not with the familiar loincloth but with a Jewish prayer shawl. The cross rises up from a lit menorah, and the figure is surrounded by fugitives dressed in recognizably Jewish garb, terrorized by raging fires. I read, presumably on the artwork's posted identity card, that Chagall had painted the work in 1938, in response to Kristallnacht. *Jesus was a Jewish victim!* But that recognition came to me in the tumultuous 1960s, when it seemed the most natural thing in the world to see Jesus, even more dramatically, as a kind of Che Guevara Jew, in rebellion against the corruptions of most fellow Jews and a Jewish establishment that saw to his killing. That perception was a block to what Chagall revealed. *Who the victim?* The line from Sophocles came to me, first, in this connection: "Who is the slayer, who the victim? Speak!"

The so-called Dead Sea Scrolls marked the start of a scholarly transformation and ultimately, in my case, a personal one—a decisive illumination of the context within which Jesus lived. Having been discovered beginning not long after the end of World War II,[37] the ancient texts produced whole libraries of studies demonstrating that in the time of Jesus, there was not one "Judaism," but a multiplicity of Judaisms. Various Jewish groups of that ancient era vied with one another, sometimes violently, over such questions as: Who is the "true Israel"? What is the Temple's place? How is the Law to be kept? Given such a context, it can now be seen that Jesus in conflict with fellow Jews over just such questions was not anomalous, but typical. If he was a rebel, it was for the cause of his people. His participation in intra-Jewish disputation—arguing with Pharisees, for example, over what was permitted on the Sabbath—underscored his integrity as a *defender* of Israel, not its opponent. The Christian mistake— mine—has been to miss that context of intra-Jewish tension. Even today, what is more Jewish than the argument over what it is to be a faithful Jew?

In other words, the post-Holocaust task, deriving from Dietrich Bonhoeffer's rudimentary insight, is to make the Jewishness of Jesus the first lens through which to view him. This means, perhaps, put- ting aside for a time—and this is rarely done—the viewfinders of the four Gospels, all of which are usually read to locate the heart of his conflict with "the Jews" in his rejection of Jewish cult and Law. Our view of Jesus must come into focus around a new organizing prin- ciple: nothing we say or believe about "Christ actually" can be allowed to exclude the authenticity of his profound and permanent participa- tion in the life of Israel.

Twice a day, Jesus pronounced the Shema.[38] Every Sabbath, he read the Torah—or, if he was illiterate,[39] was present for its reading. He believed that God's Torah was given to God's people, *Am*, to be brought to life in God's land, *aretz*.[40] As regularly as he breathed in oxygen, he took in God's saving history. At least once a year, at Pass- over, his attention turned to the Temple in Jerusalem, for the burnt offerings of animals while Psalms were sung. He observed purity and revered the Temple. And if, as most Jesus historians still assume, he enacted a "cleansing" demonstration of some kind there, it was less likely an attack on the purity system of the Temple, as the story is usually read, than a defense of it. We will see more of that.

Jesus must not be imagined, in sum, as a pretend Jew, any more than he can be regarded as having been a pretend human being. If he preached the good news of love; of the trustworthiness of God, who is like a father; of the Kingdom of God[41] present here and now, he did so from *within* Judaism, not against it. He preached not a New Testament God (of love) in opposition to an Old Testament God (of judgment),[42] but *one* God: the God of Israel, pure and simple.

But for Christians to actually accommodate such an adjustment in their view of Jesus, they would first have to confront the indictment of their own most sacred tradition that is made explicit in the catastrophe of Christian anti-Semitism. Here is why the extensive postwar revisions by scholars—historians and theologians both— have had so little impact on the minds of ordinary Christians. Here is why, in the Catholic context, the theological transformation conceived at Vatican II was all but stillborn.[43] This failure to reckon with an essential Christian failure about the Jews, for that matter, is at least part of why the spirit bled from mainstream Protestant denominations in the decades after the failure showed itself. And it is why the only form of Christian belief to actually grow in these years— evangelical fundamentalism—is a faith dedicated to the restoration of the very biblical literalism that put "Christ killer" Jews at risk in the first place. To *actually* change their understanding of Jesus Christ, that is, Christians would have to far more fully confront the Church's own ancient and ongoing betrayal of Jesus, the one that makes such change necessary.

It is curious that Christians should find it so difficult to imagine that both ordinary members and consecrated leaders of the Protestant and Catholic churches alike should have grievously let their Lord

down in the twentieth century's Nazi era, since the Gospels emphasize that, in the first century, the entire inner circle of Jesus' followers
abandoned him in his hour of need. Over time, the ubiquity of such
failure by "the faithful" was de-emphasized to the point of being forgotten as the Church developed its mechanisms of self-canonization.
But, because of sand thrown by history, those mechanisms are stuck.

The history in question, of course, includes not just failures of the
followers of Jesus, early and late, but also the counterbalancing glories of sustained intellectual inquiry. That project—faith seeking
understanding—steadily promoted new levels of human wisdom,
but ultimately, with the coming of rationalism at the time of the Enlightenment, it also undermined traditional notions of nature and
the supernatural, a development that had to affect understandings of
Jesus. So this book, about belief in the Secular Age—like any work
on the topic—has necessarily been provoked by challenges arising
from science, but that is not its primary stimulus. Far more gravely,
this reflection aims to reckon, for the sake of faith, with the tragic
compulsions of human behavior.

There are, to be sure, intellectual obstacles to traditional faith,
but many otherwise "modern" believers have accommodated those, if
only by leaving critical reflection and historical-mindedness outside
when they pass through the door of the church. Yet in the twenty-
first century, *ethical* obstacles to belief have become increasingly difficult to ignore. Moral anarchy has shown itself in sanctuary after
sanctuary, whether one considers the descent of strains of Eastern
Orthodox religion into Islamophobic brute nationalism (think of the
recent Balkans wars, in which genocidal attacks on Bosnian Muslims
by Orthodox Serbs were religiously justified); or the ongoing Roman
Catholic blasphemy of a power structure protecting priestly child
abusers instead of their abused victims; or the evangelical Protestant
embrace in America of know-nothing bigotry against immigrants.

Whatever Christ is preached by such churches, what Christ can actually be *seen* through them?

But perhaps the palpable readiness of the faithful to confront this dark character of Christian religion—and abandon it in droves[44]—does indeed flow, if only unconsciously, from the prior moral trauma that initiated this period of accountability. Bonhoeffer's death-row recognition was simple, and may yet prove timeless: if Jesus had been remembered across most of two thousand years as the Jew he was, the history of those millennia—and their climax in the crimes of the Thousand-Year Reich—would be very different.

Our search for a believable Jesus necessarily assumes a fresh encounter with the Gospels and the epistles of Paul. Our reading will be informed by a firm grasp of the historical forces to which those writings were responses. Roman violence against Jews overwhelmingly generated those forces, and we will see how. It's enough here to note that all the writers of the New Testament sought to give their readers the message—and the figure—they sorely needed, just at the time of their writing. The Gospel themes of suffering endured, violence rejected, failure forgiven, and discipleship maintained were directly addressed to the conditions that would surely have defined the experience *just then* of those who clung to the memory of Jesus. Archetypical were Peter, who, by betraying Jesus, became the exemplar of the forgiven one; Paul, who invented a transforming understanding of Jesus; and "Mark," the first and paradigmatic Gospel writer. We will see how all of the first Jesus interpreters, working in the second of our three time frames, presented with remarkable freedom the oral and written material that had come to them across the years since the life and death of Jesus. And we will take special note of how this remembering, interpreting, and, finally, writing were all tied to "the Scriptures," which, of course, meant for those early Jesus people the *Hebrew* Scriptures.

We will take for granted the largely invented character of the narrative that came of all of this, how it was shaped from various elements, only one of which had a connection to what we might call the historical record. Against the assumption of most Christians today, the Gospel writers aimed less at facticity than meaning. We twenty-first-century readers of sacred texts about Jesus could usefully take this interpretive and presentational freedom as license for our own interpretations, even if by now Paul, "Mark," and the others are to us what they were not to themselves—which is Bible.

Many of the questions asked by modern believers—and many of the notes of faith dismissed by modern skeptics—lose their bite when it is acknowledged that they were neither questions nor notes of faith for Jesus and his first interpreters. For example, our contemporary way of seeing is bifocal, based on the supposition that all reality is oppositional. To see a thing wholly, for us, is to see its foil, too. Existentially, this can be understood as generated by Descartes: isolated self against all else. Socially and politically, the pattern is associated with Hegel: thesis against antithesis. Our minds are constantly slicing perception, and joining its halves, whether explicitly or not, with the hyphen word "versus": religion versus politics; natural versus supernatural; faith versus reason; meaning versus fact; now versus then; ethical present versus apocalyptic future; Gospel versus history; fiction versus truth; metaphorical versus metaphysical.

This divided-mindedness may have come into its own in modernity, but it pervades our story, reaching all the way back nearly to the start. For one factor to rise, another must fall. Such a dynamic, in fact, long ago overwhelmed the Christian imagination, which, as we shall see, took its final form from an extreme conflict—not the contentions of doctrinal dispute, but the savagery of violence—that was inflicted on believers, extreme conflict that ultimately set the Church against the Synagogue: the primordial oppositionalism.

But what happens when a mind openly in the grip of such habitual dichotomizing encounters the experience of long-dead strangers who were at first not given to thinking this way? To acknowledge essential ignorance about how precisely those strangers took in reality, and expressed themselves about it, is the beginning of a new sort of understanding. That returns us to our initial and greatest oppositional set: the paradox of Jesus the human who is Christ the divine.

As war in the twentieth century gives us our starting point, war in the first and second centuries will give this account its largest shape. The Gospel writers had an intuition, and it was shared by their readers, that only within the context of meaning provided by Jesus Christ could the extreme disruptive experiences they were undergoing make sense, or be survived. Jesus—as first made available in the drama of his usurping a rival, or mentor, named John the Baptist; and then in the other dramas that brought him to Jerusalem and the "place of the skull," Golgotha—was the key to the meaning of God's covenant in the new context of violent strife. Jesus, that is, was the figure in whom the *in extremis* fulfillment of God's promise could be seen. God was faithful to Jesus, up to and through death. The Gospel readers, at the mercy of war, desperately needed to know of that faithfulness, and to find it on offer to them.

But God's "faithfulness," as the essence of good news, was later replaced in the heart of belief by the "faith" of the Church, as defined by the loyalty oath of creeds. Modern readers of the sacred texts have attempted to enter that distant world of implication with the "doctrinal" Christ at the threshold, but twentieth-century incredulity about doctrine itself slammed that door for many. At another, once promising threshold stood a figure deemed to be the "historical Jesus," but the impossibility of getting reliably behind the sources kept the academics bickering, and the meaning of Jesus seemed more elusive than ever. And why shouldn't most laypeople remain indifferent to the contentious work of Jesus scholars?

Yet in an inquiry like this, scholarship must be key. Indeed, modern theologians and historians have laid the path for us, and, despite the squabbling, what a golden road that work opens up. The historian Diarmaid MacCulloch calls Jesus scholarship of the past two centuries "perhaps the most thoroughgoing and sophisticated analysis of any set of texts in the history of human thought."[45] Informed by such scholarship, I am attempting an instance of faith submitted to reason, which, in this era, means doctrine rescued from all that is doctrinaire. Therefore, the beloved Creed must be criticized. Its every word, the theologian Hans Küng writes, "must be translated into the post-Copernican, post-Kantian, indeed post-Darwinian and post-Einsteinian world, just as former generations, too, had to understand the same Creed anew at decisive shifts of historical epoch."[46] History shapes faith, which might seem the most banal of observations, yet in a tradition that long ago set itself against history, it is revolutionary. But the current epoch—shaped not only by Copernicus and company but by the moral challenge of which Bonhoeffer is an avatar—has forced the question anew. Critical belief is the only humane belief, a simple fact that follows from the endowments of mind with which our Creator showers us.

So theologians and historians do indeed center this work, but the interpretation offered here draws on witnesses, too—mostly, in my case, the silent witness of the fellow believers with whom I rub elbows in the Communion line on Sundays. With them, I routinely submit reason to faith, knowing that the endowments of mind are insufficient to account for themselves. At Mass, fortunately, there is a place for mental vacancy, too—the quiet contemplation that is not the enemy of critical thought, but its trustworthy companion. My fellows in the pew sustain my faith. With them, I stand to hear the Gospel read, and they help me to pay attention.

The Gospel writers had what we might call a theological concern, but they were not doing theology. They had reference to received data from the past, but they were not doing history. The closest we can come to what those ancient authors were up to is simply to say that

they were telling a story. Against all that is doctrinaire and histori-
cist, the intuition that drives the present work is that the simple story
of Jesus—whatever the history behind the story—offers a necessary
structure of meaning, and perhaps even a mode of survival. Stories
exist to be taken, first, at face value, even if, second, they demand to
be read in light of theological reflection and historical criticism. Stories deserve to be thought about, yes—but mostly to be taken in.

So creeds, doctrines, and the scientific method of textual analysis
all give expression to the meaning of the Gospel—but they are not
the Gospel. The Gospel is the story. What this work is doing, between the brackets of theology and history, is returning to the story.
We are doing so if only because, as story, the Gospel of Jesus Christ
has braced the human imagination in a way far surpassing any other
artistic or intellectual creation. Its meaning for culture, its primacy
in Western civilization, would be enough. Yet more than culture is at
stake here.

Culture, of course, shapes this inquiry—shapes me. I am a Catholic, informed by the Catholic tradition, but the enforcers of Catholic
orthodoxy are not sitting on my shoulder. The only authority I assert
is the authority of what I think. I make no claim to objectivity. Indeed, my entire point is subjective, however much the writing aims to
be critically informed. The wonder of the way God works in history
lies in the fact that the core proclamation of what's called good news
powerfully arises out of what is time-bound, as well as out of the
thicket of failure so vividly on display in what precedes and follows.
Human fallibility marks the story at hand as much in its first century
as in its twenty-first.

But unlike the work of theologians and historians, this work also
asks whether the story of Jesus should be the starting point at all.
"Jesus is the answer" is scrawled on the walls of tenements and prison
cells, but sometimes, just below it, one also reads the addendum
"What is the question?" After Auschwitz and Hiroshima, the true

gateposts of the Secular Age, the question is not the survival of belief as much as the survival of the human species itself. As this reflection begins in Dietrich Bonhoeffer's cell, and in my own youthful faith, it will move through the harshest of challenges, including the unrelenting darkness of war and its resulting ideology of oppositionalism, to find a pragmatic way forward in the world as it is. The faith we seek, the Jesus Christ we aim to retrieve, is the key to a new meaning of redemption, which is, for the first time in history, nothing less than the literal possibility of a human future. We look again for Jesus Christ because we need a reason *now* for hope. The end of this book is not threat, but promise.

CHAPTER ONE
Personal Jesus

Jesus Christ, with His divine understanding of every cranny of our human nature, understood that not all men were called to the religious life, that by far the vast majority were forced to live in the world, and, to a certain extent, for the world.

—James Joyce[1]

Where Is God?

The word "genocide" and I are exactly the same age. It is, perhaps, outrageously narcissistic of me to strike an autobiographical note in relation to the historic crime that, until then, had no name, yet the coincidence of timing somehow explains the obsessiveness of my Catholic preoccupation with the fate of Jews. So yes, "genocide" was coined the year I was born.[2] It was the year that Los Alamos opened and the year Auschwitz became a true killing factory.[3] The arc of the years since then defines the curve of the recognitions that shape this book. Awareness of the moral legacy of the Shoah and a felt sense of the radical contingency of life under the threat of the genocidal weapon have largely altered understandings of the human condition itself. The premise of this book is that those recognitions should therefore by now have equally changed the way Jesus Christ is thought of, by believers and nonbelievers alike. No such transformation has taken place. Yet Jesus has become a problem across the boundaries of faith and skepticism, the problem with which this book wrestles.

In my case, the change began with the paired witnesses Anne

Frank and Elie Wiesel, whose testimonies overlapped. In 1960, I saw the filmed version of *The Diary of a Young Girl* as a high school senior at the U.S. Air Force base theater in Wiesbaden, Germany. Holocaust denial was a broad cultural motif everywhere, but in Germany proper, the murdered ones remained—as ghosts. While unacknowledged, the disappeared were nevertheless a felt presence. Our American enclave, for example, was a river town, an easy boat ride up the Rhine from Koblenz, which, we'd heard, was near Hinzert, one of the notorious "night and fog" concentration camps, part of the death network administered from Buchenwald. We sons and daughters of the American occupiers had whispered of such places, wondering what the Germans we encountered knew of them. Yet we were unable to actually imagine the horrors.

Suddenly, with the on-screen dramatization of the Frank family's plight, the death camps were less unreal. The movie (like the play) ends with Anne's sweet voice declaring, "In spite of everything, I still believe that people are really good at heart." But I wondered. I left the movie theater feeling more shaken than I'd ever been by a film. I immediately read Anne Frank's book, and felt implicated by it. Yes, she wrote those affirming words—but that was before she was taken off to Auschwitz. If she could have spoken from the grave—or the pit— what would she have said, actually? That question was the beginning of my inquiry.[4]

Anne's was a real face for the horror, a girl with whom to identify. Many stateside Americans had this reaction to her, I knew, yet on Wiesbaden's Biebricher Allee, where my Air Force family lived, I was all at once aware of Jews—former neighbors who were simply no longer there. Ghosts indeed. The film and book turned the abstraction of the "displaced persons," as Jewish victims were still referred to, into a deeply felt anguish. On *my* street, Jews had been rounded up. Yet what I felt was less empathy than perplexity. I knew better than to assume that, had I been in Amsterdam, I myself would have been at risk in an annex room, like the Franks. No, I would not have been a victim. Then what? Sophocles again.

Elie Wiesel, whose *Night* I read only a year or two later, just as I was embarking on the religious life as a young seminarian, was another sufferer whose fate troubled me. The book describes the cramped dormitory where young Eliezer slept on the narrow upper berth of a bunk bed, a detail with which I unexpectedly identified, since my own childhood bed had been a shelflike upper bunk above the bed below. It seems wrong now to have made any comparison, yet I did. Under my bunk had been my brother Joe's bed. Two years my senior, he had been stricken with childhood polio, and the disease, after numerous surgeries, left his legs twisted and shorn of muscle. Sometimes in the night, across the years that took me into adolescence, I would crane over the edge of my bunk to look down at my sleeping brother, expecting that he had kicked his blankets off. I would stare at his skeletal thighs and shinbones, bruised and gnarly with scar tissue. Under Eliezer, in that rancid death-camp dormitory, was not a disease-tortured brother, but his dying father. Eliezer, too, was powerless to help.

A shallow sort of empathy for Wiesel—even if my brother's suffering went deep—yet I felt it. But that was as far as this recognition could take me. As a young seminarian anxious to prove my faith, I was troubled by the outrageous challenge to God around which *Night* organizes its narrative. Whatever my sympathy for Wiesel, it could not outweigh the scandal I took from his book's climactic blasphemy— that, after such death as Auschwitz inflicted on the chosen people, God himself was dead.

In response to a fellow inmate's called-out prayer at Auschwitz, Wiesel replied, "Blessed be God's name? Why, but why would I bless Him? Every fiber in me rebelled. Because He caused thousands of children to burn in His mass graves? Because He kept six crematoria working day and night . . . ? How could I say to Him: Blessed be

Thou, Almighty Master of the Universe, who chose us among all nations to be tortured day and night, to watch as our fathers, our mothers, our brothers end up in the furnaces?" Then Wiesel reports that a man asked, "Where is God? Where is He?"

In a well-known passage, Wiesel recounts an incident that occurred at Auschwitz. Prisoners were forced by the Nazi guards to stand before the gallows and watch as a child hung from a noose,

> struggling between life and death, dying in slow agony under our eyes. And we had to look him full in the face. He was still alive when I passed in front of him. . . .
>
> Behind me, I heard the same man asking:
> "Where is God now?"
> And I heard a voice within me answer him:
> "Where is He? Here He is—He is hanging here on this gallows."[5]

For Wiesel, this moment epitomizes the death of God, an end of faith that equates, as negating revelation, with the theophany on Mount Sinai. Indeed, Auschwitz was the opposite of theophany—the manifestation of nothingness. Yet it transformed the imagination of many Jews, with history trumping religion as a defining note of identity—history perceived from the point of view of its climax in the Shoah.[6]

But I did not read the gallows passage as divine abandonment. For me, the vision evoked by Elie Wiesel at Auschwitz was a manifestation—and I would not see for years what a perversion this was—of the depth of God's longing for human beings, God's readiness to take their suffering as His own. Quite simply, to me, the young man whom Wiesel saw on the gallows was Jesus on the cross. His death was a replay of the great redeeming sacrifice. Jesus was the answer to suffering—to my brother's, surely, but also to Anne's and to Elie's.

Like Christians of old, I was struck that the Jewish vision—

Wiesel's vision—entirely missed the meaning of Jesus' death on the cross. In my own version of an ancient Christian surprise, I thought it obtuse of Wiesel—though I'd never have uttered such an insult—not to have recognized in his lynched campmate the agonized Christ, who alone redeems the evil of every abyss.

Enchantment

What one makes of Jesus depends, first, on how one sees the world. Though born near the middle of the twentieth century, I was initiated, like so many of my kind, into a way of thinking and believing that owed more to the Middle Ages than to modernity. I use myself as an example not because my case is special, but because it is not. My faith was grounded in a common teaching that shaped the views of most Catholics and many Christians. Fewer and fewer people in the contemporary age have experience of such a worldview, yet it was the decisive milieu in which every experience of Jesus could be had.

Religion, as I first embraced it, was less a realm apart than all of life, taken together from a certain perspective—a naive perspective, since it was not understood as such; not understood to be merely one of numerous possible vantage points. In my youth, all but unknown to me, premises of belief had supposedly been refuted decades or centuries before. Descartes, Darwin, Nietzsche, Freud, Marx, Sartre: hadn't they all done their worst—or best—already?[7] But the intact cogency of immigrant Catholicism in postwar America—and the same was true in other denominational settings—felt perennial, immune from any possible assault, including those said to have already occurred, whether from a profoundly threatening "science," depth psychology, or from the erosions of "materialism." In piety, liturgy, theology, and even metaphysics, midcentury Christian institutions were advancing conceptions of reality that had been untouched by the Enlightenment.

Intellectually, the parish in which our values and understandings were rooted was, well, parochial. But then, in our view, so was the much larger cosmos, consisting of a three-tiered geography, with Earth firmly bracketed by the up and down of heaven and hell, which were actual places to us. If space was constricted, so was time, with the *now* of this life set off from the *then* of afterlife. The realm of nature was set off from grace, the immanent from the transcendent. Yet all of these borders were porous. The natural world was under the influence of supernatural forces, which could interrupt history and alter the course of normal lives. Spiritual beings populated not just the cosmos but the air around us—saints, angels, archangels, spirits, and the devil, whose name was Lucifer. In grade school, I was instructed by the nuns to leave room in my chair for my guardian angel, ever beside me. For Catholics, the Blessed Virgin Mary was a vivid presence. Not so long before—in my mother's lifetime—Mary had appeared to children like me, albeit Portuguese shepherds in the town of Fátima.[8] Our Lady was capable of showing up anytime. Sun rays penetrating clouds to form a golden fan in the sky could itself seem an apparition. Was that her?

A Christian could participate in the economy of miracles by way of an earnest recitation of prayers. Specially blessed rosary beads were a feature of the Catholic parish. At Mass, the women absently carried them, wrapped around fists or dangling from fingers, the way office workers now display credentials on clips or chains. Sometimes, watching television from the living room floor, I would glance back at my mother and see her lips moving, only to glimpse the beads in her lap. I recall thinking that they slipped through her thumb and forefinger the way cartridges moved into the machine guns of war movies. A woman who stifled expressions of distress, Mom showed it mainly in her compulsions of devotion. Quiet supplication was her constant mode, and a wealth of aids was available in the form of relics, which she handled like pieces on a game board—the little gold pendants and boxes that enshrined bits of bone or cloth, tokens of the saints who had already overcome all woes and worries. A game board, but more than a game was in play. Relics had one function in our house, as I understood whenever I saw her touch them to my brother's withered legs. The prize of her collection was a crystal vial of holy water said to have been collected from the stream at Lourdes.[9] At night, she sprinkled Joe's bed before kissing his forehead. I was entranced by, and wholly convinced of, the efficacy of such rituals. It did not occur to me to wonder why my brother's ordeal was never lessened, or why his legs were never made whole.

All of this defines an enchanted world that was not recognized as such, perhaps, until it was declared "disenchanted" by social scientists.[10] As I came of age, eventually learning in school to name and date Copernicus, Galileo, Newton, and Darwin (although not Marx, Freud, or Sartre), Benedictine monks and Jesuits instructed me and my mates on the compatibility of science and faith (Copernicus was a priest!), helping us to avoid the common notion that descent from monkeys, say, undercuts the creed. My teachers, that is, protected the fragile middle ground between atheism and fundamentalism, the middle ground where most American Christians lived at the time, although fewer do so now. But the clerics taught these lessons with an imperative vehemence that showed that religion had things to fear in the secular progression, as Charles Taylor defines it, from living in a "cosmos" that crackles with intimations of the transcendent to being included in a "universe," which understands itself wholly in its own terms. Reformation, Renaissance, Enlightenment, science, deism, skepticism, and "a kind of galloping pluralism on the spiritual plane"[11] left traditional religion on the defensive. And instead of inviting questions, a gingerly Christian education in modern ideas discouraged them. Evolution was real, but so were Adam and Eve. Earth revolved around the sun, but it remained, nevertheless, the center of God's creation. Man was its pinnacle. Natural law reflected the

Creator's absolute presence in creation, but the laws of nature could be violated by the miracle-working Creator at will. The moral order was arranged in a "hierarchy of being" that was presided over by God, yet leveling principles of democracy were, at least in our America, to be revered. There were as many contradictions in this new cosmology as there were stars in the night sky—and they were taken in stride by chalking them up to "mystery." The night sky's galaxies seemed infinite, but—*a priori*—could not be. Only God was infinite.

And because of the sin of Adam, God was at infinite remove. Our human forebears had abused their gift of free will, and that was what accounted for the suffering that was part of every life. I saw this early. If I could not actually put myself in the place of the first two biblical ancestors who'd started the unbroken chain of human sorrow, I readily attached their bequeathed misery to my Irish grandparents. I sensed the weighted legacy I had from them—the measure of what I knew to call original sin, which might have been the first large idea I made my own. My mother's mother carried the wound of the Irish famine in her sad eyes, and my father's father displayed it in his taste for alcohol, which, early on, I recognized in the sour odor of his breath. The "ould sod" was the Eden from which my family had been sent into exile. When, at the end of every rosary recitation, we prayed as "poor banished children of Eve,"[12] I thought of green Ireland.

Punishment was a feature of the world first presented to me. As my sense of time began not with the first day of creation, but with the eaten apple, my religion began in the idea of hell. I often lay awake at night, in that narrow bunk above my scar-ridden brother, parsing definitions of the Baltimore Catechism, which made clear that "the damned will suffer in both mind and body, because both mind and body had a share in their sins." The body's suffering would consist in being "tortured in all its members and senses." Fire was the given image. Nausea choked me during those dark-night bouts of anguish, as I struggled to get my brain around "infinite pain, infinitely felt—forever." Plunging into that idea—down, down, down—was the nightmare that, when I woke just before hitting bottom, made me know why they called the sin of Adam the "Fall." My first luminous sensation of transcendence, that is, was the horror of eternal damnation. Obsessed with hellfire, I once held my hand over a candle to test the pain. I managed not to cry out, but the blister became infected.

In fact, I was a good boy, rarely punished by my parents. But I dreaded punishment all the more for that—which, no doubt, helped me to be good. The most dramatically locating experience of my childhood was initiation into the Sacrament of Penance: Confession. At age seven or so, I grasped that the confessional booth was the judgment seat of God, which was why the priest, God's representative, was seated, while we the penitents would kneel. First Confession was prerequisite to First Communion, scheduled for the next day. Ahead of the momentous rite of passage, I was instructed in the rubrics of self-scrutiny, which presented me with what I understand now as my first conscious moral dilemma. I was assured by the nuns that I was guilty of sins and that, in the darkened booth of the confessional, I was to explicitly admit them—not so much to the priest but to God, who was in there, listening. Of course, God already knew what my sins were.

My dilemma was immediate, and simple. I could not think of any "sins" I had committed. The examples offered in the preparation sessions—anger, lying, stealing, taking God's name in vain, failing to say prayers—defined actions and attitudes to which I had no known connection. Not that I assumed innocence. I was convinced that I had committed sins, but without knowing what my sins were, which was surely another lapse. So, on my knees in the darkened booth, staring at the profile of the priest, whose aroma reminded me of my grandfather, I confessed to neglecting my prayers, although, to my knowledge, I had not. I said I had disobeyed my parents, which I would never have done. I admitted having had bad thoughts, with no

clue as to what such thoughts could be. In the recitation of my scrupulously memorized Act of Contrition, I solemnly declared to God
that I was sorry for my sins less because I "dreaded the fires of hell"
than because they offended Him, who "art" all good—and that was
not true, either.[13] Avoiding the fires of hell was absolutely the point of
what I was doing. No sooner, having carefully made the sign of the
cross in sync with the priest's words of absolution, did I push out
through the velvet curtain into the shadowy church than it hit me
that, in my first Confession itself, I had lied. *Now* I had a sin—a mortal one. And God knew it! More than that, it was God to whom I had
been untruthful! As I knelt at the Communion rail to say my Hail
Mary, I stifled sobs, which the nuns took as a signal of my piety—a
further deception. My emotion was moral panic, pure and simple, a
draft of the poison of scrupulous self-loathing that can ambush me to
this day.

I know now that this was not the intended faith of the Bible, yet it
came to me with biblical potency. Oddly, perhaps, religion gave me
my first taste of despair—for, despite my youth and, yes, innocence,
despair was the distilled essence of all these feelings. I acknowledge
that I am describing here the initiation of a susceptible and vulnerable child into fear and guilt—yet this is a system of inculcation
many Christians would recognize, the mechanism of what's called
"atonement." As a system of inculcation, it strikes me now as ingenious. In the melodrama of my own recruitment into the Catholicism
of my parents and grandparents was recapitulated the central dynamic of the faith—not as it began, perhaps, but as it unfolded across
the centuries: Jesus as the answer to an impossible question.

I retraced the well-trod route: Religion made me aware of God,
but God was forbidding and judging. God presided over hell, which
was far more vivid to me than heaven, where, in any case, the sovereign was not God but God's Blessed Mother, *Regina Coeli*. God's om-
niscience boiled down to His capacity to see through to the core of

my unworthiness. So why shouldn't I have viscerally grasped the urgent need of some intermediary, someone to take my side against God and keep me safe? Not safe from Lucifer, mind you, nor from my own concupiscence, which was surely the first four-syllable word I learned, but from the Creator of the universe Himself. For such salvation to take, it had to be offered by one who could counter an *enemy* God's threat with equally stout protection, a balancing of the scale, which required nothing less than a *friend* God. And wasn't that precisely the offer coming, wondrously, from Jesus Christ, the Son of God? Jesus alone could get God the Father to change His mind about me, from damnation to redemption. So, of course, I accepted at once. I took to Jesus as one drowning takes to air.[14]

God's Legs

In the beginning, Jesus was a boy with whom to identify. A favored picture book showed him by Saint Joseph's side in the tidy carpentry shop attached to the modest house in Nazareth. Jesus, looking to be ten or eleven, used his foster father's carving tools to fashion a little bird. He was a boy like me, until . . . until . . . he breathed on the model he had made, and it came instantly to life. The bird's wings fluttered, and all at once it lifted off Jesus' hand and flew away. The boy who seemed like me was God the Creator.[15]

That Jesus grew up and accomplished the purpose of his life by suffering, as my brother, Joe, was suffering, sealed Jesus' significance. Joe is central here because, of course, his condition was the content of my guilt. I was at the mercy of dread that my sin, whatever it was, had caused his polio. The punishment due to me had been cruelly deflected onto him. My healthy legs were the precondition of the scarred blight of Joe's.

The starting point of the reflection we pursue here was Elie Wiesel's question in the face of wretched suffering, "Where is God?" Without meaning in any way to equate my bunk bed with Wiesel's, I am accounting for the answer that was given to me. When, as an altar boy, I knelt before the crucifix at St. Mary's Church, it was the battered legs of Jesus that transfixed me. God had legs like Joe's. That the monsignor refused to let Joe become an altar boy because he had the limping gait that went with such legs was my first lesson in the difference between the all-loving Lord and the Church authorities whose kindness is self-servingly selective. Somehow it had become crystal clear to me that Jesus, as God, could readily have avoided the tortured fate of crucifixion, but he'd freely taken it on—here was the nugget of my first belief—for the sake of my brother, Joe. I loved my brother, and so did Jesus. When I looked down from the top bunk, I saw one for whom God's love was absolute—absolute to the point of the cross. That love established my first sense of the moral order of the cosmos, just as the stars in the sky bespoke its physical order, and as the sure presence of a guardian angel beside me did the spiritual order. The moral order is love. Love embraced Joe. And me. Where is God? God is here, in the bunk bed with us, as love.

But love is tied to suffering. In the liturgical cycle that was the main calendar of our parish, Good Friday defined the year, just as that holy day's crucifix-centered suffering defined the depth of the Jesus God's love for us. As an altar boy, I was regularly present for the solemn veneration of the cross, the stripping of the altar, the dousing of the sanctuary lamp, the clothing of every surface with black. The Gospel account of the Lord's Passion and Death was the first true dramatic narrative that I made my own—as an Athenian boy, perhaps, would have internalized the journey of Ulysses.

As the entire dynamic of a faith that transforms God from enemy to friend had implicitly rooted me in the so-called penal atonement, so the fate of the loving Son as an appeasement of the judging Father brought me, also implicitly, into a world of contempt for Jews. To indict Jews as the instrument of Christ's suffering does not go far

enough. Jews made that suffering necessary in the first place. Following the sure logic of the salvation Jesus offered, I viscerally grasped
why those who put him on the cross—notwithstanding that it was a
Roman execution device—had to be the Jews. The matter was simplicity itself, since the enemy God from whom Jesus had come to save us
was the Jewish God, also known as the God of the Old Testament.

As the merciful, loving God of the New Testament—the "Abba"
of Jesus—began to vanquish the damning, vengeful, lawgiver God of
Moses, the Jews were naturally determined to defend their brutal deity. If that meant killing the carpenter's son from Nazareth, the Jewish God willed it. Why else were His high priests in the forefront of
the crucifixion? But Jesus triumphed. The God who was Law became
Love, with an attitude of boundless mercy for all—except, perhaps,
for the Jews who had killed His Son. The Savior saved those of us
who followed him from the very ones who had killed him—Jews. Because he did, they could not kill us. Although we never forgot that, if
they ever could, they would. Jews were the enemy, period.

So even the religious imagination of a normal Christian child was
shot through with the buried fury of anti-Judaism. In my case, as
noted, it was through openings crafted by Anne Frank and Elie Wiesel that these overheated currents first broke the surface of awareness. Ultimately, revelations tied to the Holocaust burst forth as the
steaming geysers of a late-twentieth-century moral accounting. Because of accidents of circumstance, I myself had no choice but to take
the temperature of this fever—hatred as an illness in the religion of
love.

I came of age as a Catholic priest. To my surprise, I was initially
required by my Church to continue the reckoning I'd begun with
Anne Frank. During my seminary training, Christian theology reversed itself in the matter of the "Christ killer" slander, a change
sparked just then by the Second Vatican Council, already referred to.
The council was itself an overdue attempt to respond to what had

been laid bare by the Holocaust.[16] Christian thinkers began to contemplate the possibility that Jews had not been wrong to reject the Gospel, given the ways in which it was presented to them. The Christian doctrine that the covenant God made with Israel had been "superseded" was repudiated. Christian preachers of my generation were instructed in new ways of reading Gospel texts that had previously demonized "the Jews." And a new wave of "historical Jesus" scholarship was launched, in part as an effort to purge Christian attitudes of an anti-Judaism that inevitably insulted Jesus himself, who—surprise!—was Jewish.

When I was a college chaplain in the late 1960s and early 1970s, my priesthood took root in the call to bring Jesus alive for young people, which brought him alive for me. As civil rights, peace, and social justice issues defined my ministry, I found myself emphasizing a memory of Jesus as a resister of unjust social structures and the empire that protected them. During the years of the Vietnam War, haunted by the record of a Church prostrate before the Nazi onslaught, priests like me joined the antiwar movement, however timidly. Silence in the face of a criminal war was not an option. My piety was redefined around the image of Jesus as a man of nonviolence. Indeed, far more was at stake for me than mere piety. Because I was raised to obey, not to rebel, and because my father was himself a man of war—an Air Force general with a key role in the U.S. bombing campaign that would kill more than a million Vietnamese—only the counterweight of a divine sanction could justify my open rejection of Dad's worldview.

The climax of that rejection came in a midnight jail cell in Washington, D.C., where, with other religiously motivated antiwar protesters, I joined in the singing of verses from Handel's *Messiah*. I felt fully and unexpectedly released when we came to Isaiah's resounding litany, "called Wonderful, Counselor, the Mighty God, the Everlasting Father, the Prince of Peace."[17] That Jesus was essential to this rite of passage, enabling me to claim my adult identity as a man, separating from my father, sealed my bond with him forever.

As the Catholic hierarchy began to roll back the liberalizing innovations of Vatican II, reimposing restrictions on women and reinvigorating old Catholic rejections of modern thought, I came more than ever to see in Jesus' conflict with Jewish high priests, scribes, and Pharisees a model of anti-establishment dissent—that Che Guevara figure. I did not realize that I was resuscitating an anti-Jewish motif. As a left-wing priest, I would be "marginal" to the reactionary Church and to war-making America the way Jesus was marginal to the Judaism of his day.[18] To see dissent as righteous, in our oppositional culture—also known as "counterculture"—one simply had to reject orthodoxy. The liberation theology that my kind embraced began, in its Gospel template, as liberation from an implicitly Jewish power structure. The Jews.

After five tumultuous years, I left the priesthood to claim a more spacious Christian faith, which freed me to begin a profound recasting of the meaning of Jesus Christ. Only as a former priest was I free to question the assumptions—going far deeper than ancient "Christ killer" slanders—that perpetuate, even in this ecumenical age, anti-Jewish stereotypes. Again and again, I had to confront the ways in which my own attitudes toward Jesus were stubbornly anti-Jewish. As a person in the pew, also, I regularly heard the negative-positive pairing of Old Testament against the New Testament, and the tone-deaf sermons that assumed the war between Jesus and "the Jews." I still hear such preaching at least once a month.

I staked my future on a writerly conscience, but I never abandoned my first religious insight—about God and suffering. It meant everything to me that the entire religious tradition of which I was still a part began with God's coming to Moses not because God had seen the *sin* of the people, but because He'd seen their *suffering*: "I have seen the affliction of my people who are in Egypt," He told

Moses, "and have heard their cry because of their taskmasters; I know their sufferings, and I have come down to deliver them."[19] Yet it took me decades of work on the sly mechanisms of the anti-Semitic imagination—including two books detailing the history of Christian contempt for Jews[20]—to reverse my primal identification of the gaunt-eyed Jews at barbed wire with the flayed and battered body of my Lord. Having put Auschwitz at the center of my work, I found it necessary, instead, to look at Jesus *with the death camp as a lens*—the opposite of my innate urge to see Auschwitz through the redeeming frame of Jesus' self-sacrifice. At last, I shared the recognition that Dietrich Bonhoeffer had come to in a Gestapo prison; I could see the point that Elie Wiesel had made before the Auschwitz gallows: If Jesus had been hanged there, it would not have been as the atoning Son of God, but as another Jewish victim. Period. If there is to be Christian reckoning, it must begin there.

The Search for Meaning

I have outgrown my childish faith. About time, for a man my age. I've left behind naive assumptions about reality irreparably divided between the material world and a separate spiritual world, the bifurcated realms of nature and grace, this life and afterlife. I don't think that the Enlightenment's closed system of mechanistic cause and consequence more faithfully renders reality than the spirit-filled world of miracles, but neither do I expect divine interference in history. I hold the faith not because religion can prove its claims for God, but because those claims can make a cosmos that includes self-knowing creatures more intelligible, not less. Proof is not the key; it is irrelevant.

That we know ourselves, and know that we do—there's the opening to mature belief. One can move through it even in an era when the creation is understood as the infinitely expanding cosmos, rushing madly away from an unknown center, with humanity ever more marginal, insignificant, and puny. Yet we are the puny creatures who know, who think, and who love. We will return to this idea. The point here is that, as humans go endlessly in search of meaning, we also dare to ask what is the *meaning* of meaning?

"In the beginning was Meaning, and Meaning was with God, and Meaning *was* God. . . . Meaning became one of us." That eccentric translation of the opening verse of the Gospel of John—traditionally rendered as "In the beginning was the Word . . ."—points, in an age when the quest for "meaning" has replaced the hope for "salvation," to a new sense of the relevance of the idea of God, drawing on a particular tradition of Western culture that makes God present.[21] A tradition named for Jesus Christ, who, whatever else can be said of him, was a man whose meaning captured what is essential to the meaning of every human fate. And he did this as a Jew—only a Jew, a Jew to the end.

Therefore, the most important way in which I have left behind the childish things of my religion has to do with the Jewish people, whose history remains the key to a plausible and morally responsible faith. I repudiate the hatred of Jews that courses through Christian understandings of Jesus like veins of mineral impurities through marble. "Impurity" in stone hardly defines the wickedness of this history, yet it does suggest the actual pervasiveness of the mentality, belonging, as we have already seen, as much to me as to my tradition. I have no right to judge the hatred of Jews from a place on the moral high horse.

It helps to know how that hatred perverted the story of Jesus, starting with the very human conditions within which the New Testament faith first grew, coming eventually to the apocalyptic climax of 1945, and continuing to the Christian reckoning that has been occurring since then. The long, tragic drama includes unpredicted turns of history more than any will of God. And it shows that, just as the first intimate friends of Jesus betrayed him at his hour of greatest need—all fleeing, except the women—so, too, were the second and third generations of Jesus people treasonous when, however inadvertently, they remembered him in a way that set him against his own people.

Even before that, was there perhaps betrayal when, in the phrase the Roman-Jewish historian Josephus uses of them, "those who first loved him and could not let go of their affection for him"[22] stopped proclaiming the Kingdom of God, as Jesus had, and began instead to proclaim Jesus *himself* as Lord? The primal texts are complex when it comes to this question, as we will see. But what Jesus never did—put himself in the place of God—the Church did, making his humanity deeply problematic. Twenty centuries later, the most fateful consequence of that twist in the story was made brutally clear, for Jesus' Jewishness had thereby been made problematic, too.

There's the surprise. The deep past is far more present with us than we think—not only a past that is defined by the figure of Jesus, but a past that took its shape from forces with which, despite seeming dissimilar at first, we are in fact quite familiar. The quest for meaning is never finished. It is open-ended. It is shaped by the imperfections of human perception. Seeking the truth about Jesus can lead to mistakes about Jesus. Our most well-intended efforts are marked by a propensity for error and—most dramatically, as this story will show—by impulses to run from danger. Equally, on the positive side, these efforts are marked by our enduring capacity as humans to surpass ourselves. Once we have tasted the delight of meaning discovered or invented, our thirst will not be quenched. A personal Jesus is never enough. As much as he beckons, so he withdraws at our approach. Such contingencies, for better and worse, drove the faith forward into history, and still do.

Christ actually was like us in all of this, yet for him the lasting anguish would have been, perhaps, in how *his* elevation as meaning itself, from Word of God to "God from God,"[23] ultimately drew attention away from the only One to whom he ever wanted to point. That was his Abba, the God of Love who—this must be emphasized—always was and always will be neither an "Old Testament God" nor a "New Testament God," but the God of the Jews, pure and simple.

CHAPTER TWO

The First Holocaust

Our images of God, man, and the moral order have been permanently impaired. No Jewish theology will possess even a remote degree of relevance to contemporary Jewish life if it ignores the question of God and the death camps.

—Richard Rubenstein[1]

The Jewish War

By what logic is the claim sustained that the Holocaust provokes a major re-envisioning of Jesus Christ? Among other reasons, because, startlingly enough, a version of this catastrophe happened before, with just such re-envisioning a consequence.

The Nazi genocide against the Jewish people is unique. More than six million were murdered, not merely in the normal progress of the German death machine that mauled tens of millions of others. No, Jews were singled out, hounded, rounded up, transported, bludgeoned, gassed, and cremated expressly and only for beings Jews. The murdered included more than a million children. Nothing they could have done—no conversion, no betrayal, no bribe, no willingness to support the war effort, no embrace of Aryan ideology, no renunciation of Yahweh—would have led to their being spared. Their offense consisted in having been born. This sets what Hitler ordered apart from any other tyrant's bloody decree. Other genocides have occurred, both before and since (and Joseph Stalin engaged in genocidal spasms of killing even as Hitler did), but no moral scale exists on which one group's suffering can be measured against another's.

Nor is there a competition in victimhood. Every genocide is unique, and each one is a mortal crime. Yet what happened to Jews *as Jews* in the heart of twentieth-century Europe, at the hands of members of the most highly sophisticated culture in history carrying to an extreme basic tenets of Western civilization itself, remains a watershed of horror.

But the Jewish people, *as a people*, were previously the target not just of perennial discrimination and periodic violence but—once before—of an effectively eliminationist assault that also might have succeeded: the long-ago Roman War against the Jews, which was ignited not long after the lifetime of Jesus.[2]

What the Romans called *Bellum Judaicum*, "the Jewish War," unfolded in three phases: first between the years 66 and 73, then between 115 and 117, and, finally, between 132 and 136. The scale of destruction—with perhaps millions of Jews killed,[3] with Judea and Galilee laid to waste, and with Jewish communities throughout the Mediterranean attacked—is alone enough to bear comparison to the twentieth-century barbarity. The pre-industrial Romans accomplished the killing man by man, woman by woman, child by child, not in mechanized mass-destruction factories. The mayhem, therefore, was, if anything, even more cold-blooded than what the bureaucratically minded Germans did. Yet it is true that the Romans were not motivated, as the Nazis were, by what moderns would regard as racial anti-Semitism. Romans were not operating out of an ontological or theological enmity, as twentieth-century Europe was in abetting—or ignoring—the "transport" of Jews. For Rome, the matter was one of simple imperial control, and that required submission on the part of subject peoples. Total submission, not elimination, was the purpose of total violence. A broad and consistent Jewish refusal to yield prompted levels of killing that were genocidal in effect, whatever the intent.[4] Yet viewed from below, the carnage would surely have looked the same—from the point of view of the many thousands of men hung on crosses, the untold numbers of women raped and forced into slavery, the multitude of infants whose bodies were torn apart, the experience was no doubt comparable. On the ground, annihilation is annihilation.

Rome was just being Rome. Yahweh's people were just being Yahweh's people. Unlike most others under the yoke of the empire, the people of Israel found it impossible to sustain a spirit of submission, because the impositions were simply blasphemous, grotesque insults to the Lord: the ubiquitous offering of sacrifices to gods; requirements to acknowledge the emperor as divine; the intrusions of legionaries into sanctuaries; ultimately, the occupation by pagans of Eretz Yisrael—the Land. The territory of Israel had been given as the sign of the covenant, and therefore was itself sacred. The Roman heel set loose in that land was trampling upon God.

The rule for populations conquered by Rome, however, was straightforward: Submit or die. What motivated the refusal to yield mattered not at all. In the Christian memory, Jews have always brought trouble down upon themselves, a malign trait that would show itself across the centuries as stiff-necked stubbornness. Yet "stubbornness" fails to credit the true—and heroic—distinctiveness of this resistance. Jews were motivated not only by a religious self-understanding that set them apart, but also by the conviction that the liberation of Israel from Rome was willed by none other than the God of Israel. More than that, God could reliably be counted upon to bring that liberation about—and soon.

To the modern imagination, such an expectation seems cracked. Neither its genesis nor its urgency can be grasped—yet this holy political assurance was defining for all Jews, able to be reduced to neither mere fantasy nor mad enthusiasm. Messianic hope, more than any other single factor, set this people apart. It accounts both for the Jews' survival as Jews and, equally, for the stunning reinventions—when history made them necessary—of Rabbinic Judaism and the Jesus movement.

The conflict with Rome became lethal when the strength of such belief confronted the strength of the empire's determination to squelch it. An entire people unyielding in resistance could face only elimination. And it nearly came, beginning with the prelude to Rome's *Bellum Judaicum*, a century before its actual start. In 65 B.C.E., two generations before the birth of Jesus, the legions, commanded by the Roman general Pompey—Gnaeus Pompeius Magnus—first swept into Palestine from Syria. Pompey, popularly known as "the vulture," had brought Rome's fist down on peoples from Hispania to the Caucasus, and now his armies were solidifying the empire's southeastern frontier. For most of a thousand years, Israelites had been at home in the crossroads region between Syria and Egypt, centered on David's city, Jerusalem. Though various powers had vanquished them and occupied their territory, they had survived as steady claimants of Palestine through accommodation (to a point), loose alliances, and periodic rebellions. But with Rome solidifying the borders of its sway, Eretz Yisrael's turn under a new imperial wheel had come—this time with an unprecedented totality. Sixty years before the birth of Jesus, and a century before the official Jewish War, the Romans laid siege to Jerusalem. For three months, the Jews of the holy city held out, but then it was over. "Of the Jews," writes Josephus about this first contest, "there fell twelve thousand, but of the Romans very few."[5] That was the beginning.

In subsequent decades, sporadic rebellions broke out against local Roman authorities and their client-rulers. For example, around the time of the birth of Jesus, in the power vacuum left by the death of Rome's puppet king Herod the Great, Jews rose up, first in Galilee, then in Jerusalem. The Romans promptly slammed down, burning towns and villages in the environs of Nazareth, then killing and enslaving many in Jerusalem. Josephus says that in Jerusalem alone on this occasion, two thousand Jews were crucified.[6] The Jews again submitted, but restlessly. They were waiting for openings, and for God's deliverance.

That tension surely shot through the life of Jesus: he almost certainly would have grown up hearing stories of the local Roman rampages in his neighborhood at the time of his birth. Events then would have slid, as he came of age, into the all-defining myth of Roman violence, which showed up eventually in the Gospel story of Herod's slaughter of the innocents.[7] Jesus' life span was bracketed, that is, by savage Roman violence against unyielding Jewish troublemakers—of whom, finally, he would be only one.

It was in train with this century-long experience of forced occupation[8] that the climactic Jewish rebellion—the Great Revolt—came in 66 c.e., more than three decades after the death of Jesus. Such was the heat of smoldering resentment that a local dispute over defilement of a Jewish holy place in Caesarea, a Palestinian seaport city with a sizable population of Greeks and Hellenized Jews, escalated into a Judea-wide rebellion. In Jerusalem, Jews associated with the priestly caste attacked the Roman garrison and took control of the entire inner-city plateau on which the Temple stood. As word spread of this audacious action, Jews from all over Judea and Galilee rushed to Jerusalem to join in its defense, an onslaught sufficient to drive out the puppet ruler Agrippa II. The Roman historian Tacitus puts the number of these Jewish defenders of Jerusalem at 600,000; Josephus posited one million.[9] The Roman legions regrouped, were reinforced, and were put under the command of Vespasian, conqueror of Britain. He invaded Galilee, systematically dismantled rebel defenses, destroyed towns, burned crops, and set his soldiers loose on women. Gradually, the Romans made their way to Jerusalem.

The suicide of Nero[10] in 68 sparked a brief civil war in Rome. Vespasian returned from Judea to Italy and joined the succession fight, quickly emerging as the new emperor. His son Titus took over as the head of the legions in Judea. They laid siege to Jerusalem, cutting it off from resupply and reinforcement. In the beleaguered city, the Jewish rebels fell to attacking one another, with so-called Zealots executing any Jew who advocated surrender. One should note here, and later, that the term "zealot" is not just a generic synonym for die-hard enthusiasts. Zealots in first-century Palestine were religiously motivated political partisans (or politically driven religious sectarians) who included, for example, the Sicarii, killer squads whose name meant "knife wielder." Zealots were like the Taliban, or even perhaps Al Qaeda.[11]

While the Romans patiently built ramparts for an eventual assault on the city walls, the Jerusalem defenders ran so low on food that many starved, and others began to flee. Those caught by the Romans were promptly and prominently crucified, so that the Jews could see—and, as the corpses rotted, smell—whom they were dealing with. The siege lasted most of a year, during which something like ten thousand crosses sprouted in a ring around the inner city, each with its stinking cadaver.

In May of 70, the Romans succeeded in breaching the city wall. The Zealots concentrated their forces in the Temple itself, where they made a last stand, holding out for more than two months. At the end of July, the Romans took the Temple, killed its last defenders, looted its treasury, and set it afire. Those Jews not killed were enslaved. On the Hebrew calendar, it was the ninth day of the month of Av, a date memorialized in a Jewish liturgy of mourning to this day.

Jewish resistance continued in the hills of Judea and in the Jordan Valley, high above which stood a butte—Masada—which served as the last Jewish stronghold. It took the Romans nearly three years to finish off the die-hard rebels. When the Romans finally stormed Masada, Josephus reports, they found that of the 967 resisters, 960 had killed themselves. In all, the Jewish dead in the Great Revolt numbered, according to Josephus, 1.1 million.[12]

As the Roman Empire expanded its control to the east across Asia Minor and west along the north coast of Africa, Jewish communities in various cities were loath to surrender their religious and cultural prerogatives. In the Diaspora, too, the integrity of worship of the one God, Yahweh, was at stake. It was inevitable that such smoldering religious steadfastness would become inflamed, and in the year 115, four decades after the Great Revolt, it did. The restiveness of Jews in the coastal city of Cyrene, in present-day Libya, flashed into open rebellion against newly re-established Roman authorities. The uprising was quickly imitated by Jews in various other Mediterranean cities—in Egypt, Cyprus, and Mesopotamia, in present-day Iraq. This was expressly Jewish resistance, beyond the far briefer and less potent reactions of other peoples laid low by Roman expansion.

Soon enough, Jews in Judea joined in the assaults, making this the second large revolt in half a century. Once again, Rome reacted with crushing power. In this conflict, the Roman general Lusius Quietus led the campaigns; one of his deputies was a fierce military leader named Hadrian. Hundreds of thousands of people were killed, with Jewish communities in Cyprus and Libya entirely wiped out. The violence finally ended in 117. This Mediterranean-wide sequence of Jewish uprisings is known as the Kitos War, from a corruption of the name of the Roman commander, Quietus. In Hebrew, though, the wars are known as the Rebellion of the Exile.

For the following decade or so, Jews bided their time, nurturing their faith-supported conviction that a Messiah would yet deliver them from Roman rule—and quietly preparing for the next conflict.[13] Rome, meanwhile, was beset by perennial intrigues of imperial succession. After the death of the emperor Trajan, Hadrian outmaneuvered Quietus, his former commander, to become emperor. He began a new campaign of solidifying the far-flung boundaries of Roman control. He built, for example, what we call Hadrian's Wall, which still stands in Britain. His visit to Judea in 130 occasioned his order to rebuild the Temple of Jerusalem and restore the city that still bore the scars of the Great Revolt in 70. But he gave Jerusalem a new name, Aelia Capitolina, and declared that the new temple would be dedicated to Jupiter. When Jews protested, Hadrian resolved to eliminate the unyielding people once and for all. He cut to the quick of Jewish identity by outlawing circumcision, making yet another Jewish revolt inevitable.[14]

In 132, it came. A Jewish force led by a Galilean named Simon Bar Kosiba surprised the Roman garrisons in the countryside, and then quickly wrested control of Jerusalem from the unprepared occupiers. Kosiba was proclaimed by Jews to be the longed-for Messiah, and he was given the name Bar Kokhba, "son of a star"—a reference to the messianic prophecy "A star shall come forth out of Jacob."[15] For more than two years, Bar Kokhba, centered in Jerusalem, led a powerful resistance to Rome's armies, presiding over a reclaimed, if not restored, nation. Coins were struck bearing the inscription "Freedom of Israel."[16] The revolt spread to Jewish communities under Roman control in Arabia and Syria. Those in the Mediterranean diaspora who had been subdued and enslaved during the Kitos War saw another chance. Cassius Dio, the Roman historian, writes that "Jews everywhere . . . were gathering together and giving evidence of great hostility to the Romans."

Hadrian was having trouble with vassal peoples all across the empire, from Britain to Dalmatia to the Danube, and word of the revolt in Judea spread. "The whole earth, one might almost say, was being stirred up over the matter."[17] Hadrian's hatred of Jews was one thing, but now Roman imperial hegemony itself was at stake. He ordered an unprecedented mobilization, including the emergency conscription of males throughout Italy. From as far away as Britain he summoned "his best generals," Cassius Dio reports, and dispatched them to Judea, together with six full legions and sizable parts of six others—tens of thousands of crack soldiers. They arrived with

ferocious determination and set about the plowing under of towns
and villages, the razing of cities. Jewish resistance matched the Roman ferocity, and the fighting went on for more than two years. The
Talmud says that the Romans "went on killing until their horses
were submerged in blood to their nostrils."[18]

By the time the Romans managed to suppress the revolt in the
summer of 135, according to Cassius Dio, nearly 600,000 Jews were
dead and nearly a thousand towns, villages, and cities had been
razed—most especially including, again, Jerusalem. Not just the
Temple Mount but the entire urban area was laid to waste. Still,
Hadrian was not finished. He ordered the execution of all Jewish
scholars. He outlawed Torah, halachic practice, the Jewish calendar.
He ordered the torching of Torah scrolls on the site of the former
Holy of Holies, and, in addition to a statue of Jupiter, he ordered one
of himself erected on the Temple Mount. In an unprecedented act,
Hadrian commanded that the province of Judea be renamed, now to
be known as Syria Palaestina. Jews were henceforth banished from
its capital, Aelia Capitolina—except one day a year, when they would
be permitted entrance for the sole purpose of expressing their grief
over the loss of Zion. Cassius Dio concludes, "Nearly the whole of
Judea was made desolate."[19]

As noted, the mortality figures supplied by ancient historians are
to be taken more as broad indicators than precise counts, but even so,
the picture that emerges of the cost of this Roman war is clear and
historically reliable. However much the motives of the Caesars differed from those of the Führer two millennia later, the consequences
of their assaults against the Jewish people are comparable. Hitler
killed one in three of all living Jews, a ratio the Caesars may well have
matched.[20] My purpose here is not to compare war statistics, but to
emphasize the extreme human suffering—the evil—that formed the
context within which both Christianity and Rabbinic Judaism came
into being. To read, as all Christians do, the Gospel portraits of Jesus

Christ without reference to the Roman War that raged exactly as those portraits were being composed, and first revered as Scripture, is like reading Bonhoeffer's *Letters and Papers from Prison* without reference to events unfolding outside his cell as he wrote.

The Temple in Ruins

Return to the savage destruction of the Temple in 70—the event that began the slow-motion genocide we have tracked. Nothing defines the chasm separating Jewish and Christian perspectives more sharply than the difference between Jewish and Christian responses to what befell the Temple. For Jews, its destruction stands as the defining emblem of all Jewish suffering. The white woolen prayer shawl worn by Jewish men—a tallit—is marked with black stripes said to be a sign of mourning for the Temple's destruction. The Jewish liturgical year is anchored, as noted, by the annual grief ritual Tisha B'Av, the ninth of Av—the date on the Hebrew calendar on which the Romans set fire to the Temple. In the Christian memory, that event, if it registers at all, is celebrated as a proof of Christian claims made for Jesus. That the Temple was destroyed means that Jesus was right in his claim to superiority over Jewish authorities, and Jews were wrong to reject him. The Church Triumphant rose from the ashes on the Temple Mount.

To accept the destruction of the Temple as proof of Christian claims, one has to accept a particular view of Jesus as a future-foreseeing "prophet." He is remembered in the Gospel of Matthew, for example, as having pointed to the buildings of the Temple compound and declaring, "You see all these, do you not? Truly, I say to you, there will not be left here one stone upon another, that will not be thrown down."[21] Thus, words taken to have been uttered in the year 30 or so, about an event that occurred forty years later, are registered both as proof of Jesus' power to foretell the future and as an indictment of those who "kill the prophets and stone those" who are sent from God.[22] Despite his being shown weeping at what he foresees—"Jerusalem, Jerusalem!"—Jesus allegedly *approves* the destruction. Indeed, in the Gospel of John, he taunts his antagonists by saying, "Destroy this temple, and in three days I will raise it up." That claim is promptly explained by the Gospel writer: "But he spoke of the temple of his body."[23] Jesus was himself the replacement of the Temple—precisely in the way that the Church would replace the Synagogue. On Good Friday, at the very moment of Jesus' death, Matthew, Mark, and Luke are alike in reporting that, in Matthew's language, "the curtain of the temple was torn in two, from top to bottom"—a symbolic destruction of the Temple.[24] Jesus' death means that the day of the Temple is over. An occasion not of mourning, but of celebration.

We saw earlier that meanings change when, instead of looking at Auschwitz through the lens of the cross, the cross is beheld through the lens of Auschwitz. A similar shift occurs when, instead of looking at the tribulations of Jerusalem in 70 from the vantage of "prophecies" offered by Jesus in 30, we look at the *texts* about Jesus from the vantage of the later *context* during which the texts were composed. Quite simply, when Jesus is remembered as describing in harrowing detail the events that will accompany the destruction of the Temple—"You will hear of wars and rumors of wars . . . nation will rise against nation, and kingdom against kingdom, and there will be famines and earthquakes in various places: all this is but the beginning of the birth-pangs. Then they will deliver you up to tribulation, and put you to death; and you will be hated by all nations for my name's sake. And then many will fall away, and betray one another, and hate one another"[25]—he is not foretelling an apocalyptic end of the world. Rather, almost as an eyewitness, he is offering a journalistic description of precisely what happens when the Romans smash down on the Jews and when Jews themselves turn against one

another. And "eyewitness" is to the point, of course, because, though
Jesus did not see such things, the author of the Gospel of Matthew,
and the people to whom he was writing, surely did.

It is possible, although far from certain, that in 30 or so, Jesus did
use an imagined destruction of the Temple as a metaphor, but he was
not "predicting." This is a small but urgent point; the fully human
Jesus could not and did not foresee the future. As an apocalyptic
prophet, drawing on the deep legacy of Israel's past, which had been
defined by the Temple destruction at the hands of the Babylonians in
588 B.C.E., such an image *could* have occurred to him. Jeremiah's lamentation for *that* destruction of the Temple might have come readily
to his lips. But if Jesus invoked such a nightmare scene, the past was
his point of reference, not the future—Nebuchadnezzar, not Caesar.
Like all Jews, he would have found the literal destruction of the Temple a second time unthinkable, much as Americans, even remembering, say, the apocalyptic carnage of the Civil War, would have found
unthinkable the events of September 11, 2001—until they happened, in all their horror.

Whether Jesus had in fact discussed the Temple destruction was
less the point for the Gospel writers and readers than the harsh fact
that, in their time, the Temple *had* been destroyed. We will take
up the chronology of Gospel composition below; it's enough here to
note that all four of the Gospels were written during or after the destruction in 70. The writers would have invoked Jesus, and the destruction of his death, in connection with the Temple destruction
whether he had literally made any such reference or not, precisely as
a way of finding meaning in the midst of the meaninglessness of total
violence. That the destruction *now* could be encompassed in the vision *then* of the one who was their hope made it tolerable. But such
was the extremity of their experience in the thick of Roman war that,
for a time, it was even possible to imagine these events as harbingers
of nothing less than the end of the world. That dread, too, was given

expression, transformed into hope, by the remembered Jesus; "And because wickedness is multiplied," he is remembered to have said, "most men's love will grow cold. But he who endures to the end will be saved. And this gospel of the kingdom will be preached throughout the whole world, as a testimony to all nations; and then the end will come."[26]

The Gospels are obsessed throughout with the destruction of the Temple, and why not? Recall that all four of the canonical texts define the crime for which Jesus was crucified as a crime against the Temple.[27] The content of the charge of blasphemy brought against Jesus is defined by his statement "I tell you, something greater than the temple is here."[28] Whatever actually "happened" in the lifetime of Jesus, the momentous violence of the Roman War that was being indiscriminately inflicted on Jews even as the Gospels were written was enough to force the narrative into the form that it took—now with the "Jewish" enemies of Jesus getting what they deserved for rejecting him. The point deserves emphasis: the Gospels' first purpose was to respond to the *present* crisis of those who wrote the texts and to whom the texts were addressed. The Temple dominates the story of Jesus in 30 because the Temple—in its destruction by Rome—dominated the story in 70 of those who wrote the Gospel, read the Gospel, and heard the Gospel.

Looked at from this vantage of torment decades after the death of Jesus, even the Passion narrative takes on a character unimaginable to later Christians who tell his story without reference to the Roman War. Instead of the usual way of seeing Jesus' agony and death on the cross as unique, a one-time instance of transcendent suffering extreme enough to redeem the fallen cosmos, the view from the year 70—recall the ten thousand corpses hung on crosses ringing the Temple Mount—would necessarily have seen the crucifixion of Jesus as mundane. The consolation offered by the Passion account had to be less a matter of Jesus as the *substitute* sufferer than of Jesus as the *fellow* sufferer. *What befell Jesus is befalling us!* When, at the moment of his death, according to the three Gospels, the Temple is symbolically destroyed by that torn veil, the identification of Jesus with the horrors of Roman savagery would have been taken to be complete. One could imagine surviving the Temple-destroying savagery only because Jesus had. Here, of course, is the power of the proclaimed Resurrection, the hope that evolved into conviction that survival, even of the worst fate imaginable, was a possibility—nay, a promise.

The Temple as the Cause of the Gospel

By the time of Jesus, the Temple Mount had been the historic heart of Jerusalem for at least a thousand years, and the mythic tradition of Israel pushed the date of its sanctification perhaps twice that far into the distant past. Indeed, the "mount" was first associated with Mount Moriah, to which Abraham brought his son Isaac as a ready sacrifice, obeying what he took to be God's brutal command. Abraham may or may not have existed, but if he did, he is dated to about the year 2000 B.C.E., a full millennium before King David. Abraham's altar of sacrifice—where, in the Genesis account,[29] an animal replaced a human as the preferred offering of Israel's God—became the altar to which the people, in that neverland of myth, brought their lambs and doves. The mount entered history when, precisely there, David ordered the first construction of the Temple in about 1000 B.C.E., and his son Solomon accomplished that construction. Across the subsequent centuries, the Temple would be built and built again, although the Babylonian destruction in 588 would permanently mark the difference between the First Temple, attributed to Solomon, and the Second, built by those returned from Babylon in 515, and rebuilt by their descendants.

A century and a half before the birth of Jesus, a Jewish dynasty—the Hasmoneans—restored the independence of Israel after a period of Seleucid (or Greek) domination. They marked this triumph by undertaking a massive reconstruction of the Temple. Indeed, Hanukkah, the annual Jewish festival of light, recalls the joyous rededication of the Temple after that restoration. It had walls made of huge stones and broken by five stout gates, embellished palaces, a citadel, towers, courtyards; the ritual buildings themselves occupied a plateau that was about three hundred yards square.[30] This construction repeated patterns and designs common in the Hellenized world, and the Jerusalem Temple began to loom as one of its great structures.

When the Romans, under Pompey, brought Israel's independence to an end in 67 B.C.E., skirmishes, referred to earlier, were fought by resisting Jews in Jerusalem and on the Temple Mount, but no lasting damage was done to the Temple as the dominance of Rome began. When the Roman client ruler, the quasi-Jewish Herod the Great, was elected "King of the Jews" by the Roman Senate in about 39 B.C.E., his challenge was to establish his legitimacy with a population that regarded him as an interloper. With a view to winning over his skeptical subjects—and to impressing his patrons in Rome—he undertook the project of making the Jerusalem Temple even grander. By about the year 20 B.C.E., having scrupulously commissioned more than a thousand Jewish priests as masons and carpenters, Herod had completed most of a major reconstruction, which indeed made the Temple of Jerusalem one of the most spectacular buildings in the world. Ad hoc construction on the compound would continue for another eighty years, until the catastrophe of 70 C.E., but the main redesign and renovation was accomplished quickly. Red-tiled roofs, colonnades, hundreds of pillars, grand stairways, a huge central sanctuary with looming columns, wall bridges, hundreds of finely hewn blocks, multiple courtyards, double and triple gates, porticoes—all made of gleaming gold-white Jerusalem stone and pale limestone, and positioned atop a spectacular butte visible for miles: the Temple was breathtakingly beautiful.

That the Temple magnificently enshrined the sacred precincts in which believers, gathering periodically by the hundreds of thousands, could make their joyous sacrificial offerings in petition and thanksgiving was what made the Temple precious to almost all Jews. Indeed, it was precious to non-Jews as well, with the so-called Courtyard of the Gentiles being one of the Temple's most commodious spaces— an indication of Israel's ecumenical openness that contradicts a later Christian disparagement of Judaism as exclusivist and clannish.

The glories of the Temple notwithstanding, Jews disdained Herod and his successors, and many were ambivalent about the Hellenized culture that stamped the architecture of his greatest achievement. But ambivalence drained away as they made "*aliyah*," going up to the hilltop city for religious festivals, and from the city up to its sacred plateau. Jews were devoted to the Temple not for its physical splendor but for the devotion it inspired. That it brought them into intimate contact with the Holy One, in a setting whose magnificence could make the Holy One's presence seem palpable, redoubled their love for this place. It was truly the navel of the cosmos, *axis mundi*, the house of God.

But where is God when God's house is destroyed? As would happen in the twentieth century, scattered Jewish survivors of Rome's mass violence in the year 70 were at the mercy of the dread that their God had abandoned them. Because their sanctuaries, religious symbols, and texts were destroyed in the Roman onslaught, and because they had been driven from the living center and seal of the covenant— Eretz Yisrael and its soul city, Jerusalem—the content of the Jewish religious imagination was in danger of being all but deleted.

But instead of simply disappearing, as so many peoples crushed by empire had and would again, the Jews, even as the Roman brutalizing continued intermittently for decades, retrieved from the tradition new meanings of old revelations, a fresh interpretation of the interpretations. They were able to do this only because once before,

returning from Babylon six hundred years earlier, they had reinvigo-
rated their religion around an equivalent experience of total loss. All
first-century Jews, the followers of Jesus decisively included, were
primed by an ancient tradition to transform that loss into a profound
act of religious reinvention—spawning, ultimately, both Rabbinic Judaism and the Church.

I make these observations about expressly Jewish ideas—here
and elsewhere in this book—from outside the Jewish community,
aware of the dangers that adhere in Christian readings of Jewish history and thought. If I presume to do so, it is as a Christian aware of
my own tradition's essential tie to this legacy. When the Temple was
destroyed, in sum, the sacred imagination was quickened, and something new happened between God and God's people. Even if this was
the initiating spark of Christianity as a separate religion, the phenomenon of *renewal out of loss* was Jewish to the core—because it had
brought Judaism into being in the first place.

As the twentieth-century Holocaust can be said to have been at
least analogously foreshadowed by events two millennia earlier, so
with the Roman assault on Jerusalem. It, too, was a kind of replay.
Jewish religion, after all, had its true beginning six centuries before,
when armies of Nebuchadnezzar of Babylon laid siege to Jerusalem,
destroyed the Temple, carted away the Ark of the Covenant, enslaved
the people, and carried them off to exile. The Babylonian Captivity
lasted about sixty years (597–538 b.c.e.), a period of time roughly
duplicated by the Roman-Jewish war (and, coincidentally, roughly
duplicated by the time elapsed from the liberation of Auschwitz until
today). When the Jews returned from Babylon to Jerusalem, picking
up the pieces of faith and tradition, they were—as this Christian
reads the story—a different people, with a different God.

Out of the trauma of destruction and banishment, that is, they
had created something new. Prophets, especially Ezekiel and Jeremiah, had recast the meaning of what happened—proclaiming a

God who had used belligerent Nebuchadnezzar as a purifying instrument; a God who had accompanied His people into exile; a God, therefore, whose presence was no longer seen as restricted to the Temple of Jerusalem. Where, previously, the Holy of Holies had held the Ark of the Covenant, that sacred object, whatever it was,[31] had been lost in the destruction. From now on, once the Temple was reconstructed, the Holy of Holies was to be left vacant—a numinous *non*appearance that perfectly symbolized the new understanding to which the people had come. The God of Israel was seen as transcending place. A particular sanctuary defined by absence became the sacrament of God's universal omnipresence. With that apophatic affirmation by means of negation, the imagination of Jewish religion sank its roots in paradox.

Editors and redactors, through the same experience of Babylonian exile, had recast the oral and written traditions that had long shaped the consciousness of this people—but now with a new order, a coalescence carrying a new meaning. Creation myths, ritual songs, poems, etymological tales, proverbs, parables, and narratives of memory were selected, discarded, reshaped—and *composed*. Only now did the people recognize in their rich store of tradition the collected revelation of God's Word—the Bible, or Tanakh, an acronym for "Torah, Prophets, and Writings." Returned from captivity, they became people of Torah—of the Book. And more: only now had editors arranged the revelation to begin with Genesis, a creation myth that accounted not, like others of the ancient Near East, for the origins of the tribe, but for origins of the cosmos. Genesis made the astonishing primordial claim that the God of this people, no mere local deity, was the Creator of the universe, the God of all people. Only now, that is, was the God of Israel understood to be one God, transcending not only place but time. Monolators had become monotheists.[32] Such are the radical new religious convictions that came from prophetic reflection on the first of the Temple destructions. The religion of Jews was begun.

The second destruction of the Temple, in 70, was equally decisive. It sparked an immediate crisis in the life of every surviving Jew, and that crisis is the dominant—if not necessarily only—source of the Gospel preoccupations with the Temple. All Jews were forced to ask the great questions: how could the chosen people undergo such near eradication? And, in particular—now!—what is it to be a Jew without the Temple? The Temple was the seat of the priest-led theocracy established by God Himself! What is it to be Israel without that? Without priesthood, sacrifice, the Holy of Holies—sacred ritual that had brought Israel close to God for a thousand years?

Two surviving parties of Jews offered their answers—surviving parties, by the way, that were alike in having sought and found distance from the violent rebellion of the Zealots and from those who rallied to their revolution, which had brought down the wrath of Rome. Only such distance from Zealotry, which the Jews in the thick of combat had to experience as betrayal, enabled their survival *as Jews*. Thus, in 68 or 69, as the Romans were closing in on Jerusalem and the Temple, a Pharisaic party led by Rabbi Johanan ben Zakkai petitioned the Romans to be allowed to leave the city. They were permitted to go, establishing themselves in Yavne, on the Mediterranean coast. This core would flourish as the center of a post-Temple Rabbinic Judaism. In a similar way, speaking generally, followers of Jesus decamped Jerusalem for Pella, across the Jordan, and for places in Syria, Asia Minor, and North Africa. In Palestine, the Jesus movement remained centered in Galilee, where Roman legions raised havoc, but not with the brute totality of their assault against Jerusalem. Both groups, in line with previous prophetic readings of the Temple destruction wrought by the Babylonians, saw in the Roman destruction a purification willed by God, but they differed in their views of what constituted the behavior from which God took offense.

For simplicity's sake, let's call the first group "the rabbis," attached to a party of Jewish leaders identified in the Gospels as Pharisees.

They were inclined, even before the Temple destruction, to emphasize observance of the Law and study of the Torah more than, say, the priests of the Temple, who, given their ritual role at the altar, would have placed prime emphasis on cultic sacrifice. But with the Temple gone and the priests either killed or made superfluous, the rabbis insisted that to be a Jew now was to be focused more than ever on Torah, study of texts, and close observance of the Law. Their attachment to the study-centered institution of the synagogue came into its own. When the tradition of priestly sacrifice was replaced by the metaphoric sacrifice of "a broken and contrite heart,"[33] manifest in Law observance, Rabbinic Judaism was born.

Let's call the other group "the Jesus people." They had an even more succinct answer to the question "What is it to be a Jew without the Temple?" Now, they said, *Jesus* is the Temple—"the new Temple." Here, too, cult sacrifice has entered the realm of metaphor, with Jesus having accomplished the last sacrificial offering "once and for all when he offered up himself."[34] In this the Church was born. The first group said that the Temple had been destroyed because Israel was insufficiently faithful in observing God's Law. The second said the Temple had been destroyed because Israel had rejected Jesus. The point is that both groups consisted of Jews searching for meaning in the midst of the Roman-generated catastrophe, centered on the destruction of the Temple.

These equally Jewish answers to the Jewish crisis both envisioned an *imagined* Temple and the necessary movement of sacrifice into the realm of metaphor,[35] yet the answers seemed profoundly contradictory, and, in a context in which civil war among Jewish groups was rife, those proposing these answers became fiercely antagonistic. Such competition between factions of an oppressed people was deliberately stoked by the imperial overlords—the universal practice of empires.[36] So Rome, too, is a factor in the conflict between the rabbis and the Jesus people.

Usually, the Christian story is told without reference to the fact that the approximate year of the first Gospel's composition—Mark, in 70—was the same year as the destruction of the Temple.[37] If the connection is noted by Christians today, it is assumed to be coincidence, since, in the Christian memory, the fate of the Jewish cultic center four decades after the death of Jesus could have no real bearing on Christians, who by the second century had come to regard their movement as having begun in Jesus' own repudiation of the Temple.

It may well be that when Jesus of Nazareth arrived on the scene in the year 28 or 29, it was as part of a Temple purification movement. The facts that Herod the Great, the despised Roman lackey and puppet ruler, had rebuilt the Temple, and that his structure reflected the Hellenized style of grandiose pagan temples elsewhere in the Near East, had, as we saw, discomforted some Jews. It sparked full-bore opposition from certain Jewish critics, like the Qumran sect, puritanical ascetics who lived a communal life apart from Jerusalem, centered near the Dead Sea.[38] These conscientious objectors to the moral compromises of urban life in a Hellenized world—let's call them "arch-conservatives"—may have included John the Baptist. But they would have criticized Herod's Temple in the name of God's Temple— a point we saw, in brief, before. To resist Herod's blasphemy, of course, was a mode of resisting the blasphemy of his patron, Rome. But such criticism of the Temple would have been for the Temple's sake.

Jesus might have associated with the radicals of Qumran. If they included John the Baptist, he surely did. But it seems likely that, from a certain point on, Jesus kept his distance from such purists, including John. As Jesus came into his own, it was as anything but a Zealot. Indeed, the Gospels go out of their way to show him as a man not given to puritanical repudiations. He was not an ascetic, nor did he eschew the bustle of towns and cities. Accommodation marked his style. We will see more of Jesus' difference from the Zealots below.

If we are, *a priori*, to take seriously Jesus' character as a devout Jew, then his devotion to the Temple follows, and we should be very slow to imagine him as repudiating either the Temple itself or the transactions, like money changing, that would have been germane to it.[39] There is every reason to believe that Jesus himself, as a devout Jew, was devoted to the Temple, and could not conceivably have repudiated it in total. If, as all four Gospels report, he committed a transgression there, it was more likely as a defense of the Temple than as an attack on it.[40] The main evidence for believing that Jesus revered the Temple until the day he died is that his followers then continued to devoutly worship in the Temple *as Jews* for as long as the holy place survived.

Against the notion that the Gospels began to jell as written accounts of the story of Jesus *without reference* to the destruction of the Temple and the ongoing Roman War against the Jews that were simultaneous to the writing, I argue that the destruction of the Temple, and the attendant mass violence, were precisely what created the urgent need among the Jesus people for these texts *just then*. They needed the texts *as Jews*. That the oral traditions of the story of Jesus, combining memory, myth, interpretation, and literary invention, began to find written form at this moment was no coincidence. It was an answer. And if the Gospels are read in this light—as documents dated to 70 and after, instead of as prophecies dated to 30—they take on meanings that differ decisively from what Christians usually say and are usually told. We are closing in on the actuality of origins.

The most obvious instance of this is well known by now, although its implications have yet to be fully unpacked: the way in which the Gospels are read as setting Jesus not only against the Temple but against his own people. The intra-Jewish antagonism—rabbis versus Jesus' followers—dating to the last decades of the century hugely influenced how the Gospels, describing events earlier in the century, were composed. The point is that all four canonical Gospels took

form *after* the Roman destruction of the Temple, *after* the rivalry between surviving groups of Jews began to calcify, in the deadly context
of massive war. The war with Rome sparked civil war among Jews,
and the Gospels are the literature of that civil war.[41] "The Jews" portrayed by evangelists as the mortal enemy of Jesus in about the year
30 were enemies of—if anyone—the followers of Jesus five decades
later.

The point for us, though, lies in the way in which the Temple defines the very center of this conflict. Since the Gospels were all written during the catastrophic years in which Jews were traumatized by
the loss of the Temple of Jerusalem, it would be odd if that crisis were
not reflected in how the story of Jesus was told, since the entire point
of composition just then was to put Jesus forward as the solution to
the problem of the destroyed Temple. The Jewish experience during
the savage violence of what I presume to call the first Holocaust, in
other words, could be expected, in the scales of narrative composition, to weigh as much as, if not more than, the remembered actualities of Jesus' life four decades earlier. The crisis of Temple destruction
in 70 was enough for the Jesus people to put the Temple at the center
of their explanations of his meaning—and they did. We will see
more of this.

Wartime Literature[42]

Humans are forever on the hunt for meaning, but brute experience
can force radical breakthroughs into other orders of existence. The
religious wars of sixteenth- and seventeenth-century Europe, in
which tens of millions of Protestants and Catholics slaughtered one
another in the name of God, came to the hyper-violent climax of the
Thirty Years' War (1618–1648). That paroxysm of killing, in which
something like eight million persons died, led in short order to a new
politics—distilled in the idea of the separation of church and state, a

pillar of democratic liberalism—while simultaneously advancing a new intellectual culture: the scientific revolution.[43] The total-war violence of the twentieth century's two world wars, in which more than one hundred million died, led in Europe to a Continental repudiation of narrow nationalism and a broad rejection of war as an instrument of political power—the foundational principles of the European Union.

Savage war generates, in reaction, new ideas. This principle undergirds the line of thinking here—that the Roman War against the Jews prompted radical shifts in the religious imagination of Jews. The shifts were taken as revelations from God. But this was the pattern established in the religious DNA of Israel by the Babylonian War, which, as we saw, generated the essential character of Jewish religion in the first place. In the centuries after Babylon, Israel found itself under one heel after another, a succession of oppressors—Persians, Greeks, and Hellenized Egyptians—against whom Jews launched no significant resistance. But then came the Greco-Syrian Seleucids and the next Jewish war, the so-called Maccabean Revolt (167–160 B.C.E.), resulting in the next shift in the religious imagination of Jews.

Again, the war produced wartime literature, indeed a new genre of it—the so-called apocalyptic, epitomized by the book of Daniel.[44] The author of that text, an unnamed pious Jew writing in Aramaic, presented a wildly imaginative rendering of otherworldly dreads, hopes, and expectations—redemptive interpretations of his present tribulations. In Daniel, six stories set during the Babylonian Captivity, centuries before the book was written, describe the ways in which Jews faithfully clung to their identity as God's people during that previous Jewish war. Then, in four ecstatic visions, the coming triumph of the "saints" is promised. Daniel is full of dreamlike fancies and horrors, an almost psychedelic hallucination, with figures flying through the air, men surviving a fiery furnace, the man Daniel surviving lions because "God sent his angel and shut the lions' mouths"[45]—visions so exotic as themselves to require deciphering by angels. The book of Daniel was sparked by an expression of enraged reaction to the Seleucid desecration of, yes, the Temple—"the abomination that makes desolate."[46]

But at bottom, the apocalyptic vision was a mode of turning pure destruction into creative transformation. "And there shall be a time of trouble, such as never has been since there was a nation till that time; but at that time your people shall be delivered . . . and many of those who sleep in the dust of the earth shall awake."[47] Bracing and consoling a people who, when violence flared, inevitably found themselves endangered and beleaguered, the apocalyptic vision insisted that transcendent intervention was about to occur, changing a broken and suffering world into a realm of peace and joy, with Israel at its center. "Go your way till the end; and you shall rest, and shall stand in your allotted place at the end of the days."[48] Violence would be redeemed by God's act, and hopeless military odds would be reversed by God's direct interruption of history. The vision was both realistic—acknowledging present violence—and hopeful, in that it insisted that the violence would not be vindicated in the end. The book of Daniel, usually dated to about 160 B.C.E., is *the* classic work of Jewish apocalypticism, searing the imagination of Israel across each of the two centuries before and after Jesus. Josephus, calling the figure Daniel "one of the greatest of the prophets," said the book was hugely influential among Jews in that era.[49] No surprise, therefore, that Jesus' core meaning was constructed out of materials drawn from this work. We will see more of this.

The portrait of Jesus Christ given in the Gospels grows as much out of the stresses of war as did the already defining texts of Jewish religious understanding, from Jeremiah to Daniel. Nowhere is that clearer than in the Gospel of Mark, which is reliably dated by scholars, as noted, to about the year 70—a time when, after more than two years of Roman rampage throughout Palestine, all hell broke loose in Jerusalem. Mark is the main source of, and template for, the later Gospels of Matthew and Luke. Mark's rendering of Jesus, and its proclamation of his meaning as the "Christ," are the central pillars of the Christian imagination. Yet Mark is rarely read in the context of the war raging outside the cell in which it was composed—an omission we found unthinkable in the case of Bonhoeffer's letters from prison. A foregrounding eye on the Roman War against the Jews *must* change the Christian reading.

The point to emphasize is that the author of Mark was writing as the legion's phalanxes closed in on Jerusalem, setting up the ring of crucifixes around the Temple Mount and slaughtering hundreds of thousands of Jews.[50] If in the Gospel of Mark, to start with the largest point, Jesus is portrayed as obsessed with the traumas of the End Time, it may be because, as an apocalyptic messianic figure, that was indeed the main note of his preaching when he was alive. The early sources on which the author of Mark drew seem to have emphatically interpreted Jesus within the Jewish apocalyptic genre, especially Daniel, whether that interpretation began with Jesus himself or with those who came after him.

Yet however much Mark drew on the visions of Daniel, his text could not be more different. While Jesus describes in vivid detail scenes right out of an apocalyptic End Time, he is shown doing so without a hint of hallucination—not "vision," but dead-on description. The Gospel is starkly realistic, striking for its spare, objective reportage. Taking seriously the *context* out of which this *text* emerged leads inexorably to the thought that Jesus was rendered by Mark as obsessed with End Time traumas not only—or even mainly— because of literary influences from preexistent Jewish apocalyptic genres like Daniel, but because the catastrophic End Time seemed at hand *as Mark's story was told*. The Roman assault of 70, that is, could well have felt, to those who experienced it, like the end of the world.

Mark's Apocalypse

Chapter 13 of Mark is the heart of it, and what Jesus is shown offering at great length there can be read, in fact, as an almost literal description of what was happening to the people for whom Mark was written. Horrors—not hallucination. The chapter begins with verses already referred to, the "great buildings" of the Temple thrown down, "not one stone left upon another." In fact, the Roman destruction of the Temple was by fire, not block-by-block demolition, but that takes nothing from the trauma Jesus describes. The ruination of the Holy of Holies is the point, and the factual destruction of the Temple in 70 is the historical background for the poignant advice that Jesus is shown offering to his frightened disciples, less to those in front of him than to his followers a generation later: "Take heed that no one leads you astray. Many will come in my name, saying, 'I am he!' and they will lead many astray."

Here we have reference to those war-generated disputes between and among Jews, with Zealots not hesitating to kill those they regarded as collaborators or as cowards. Self-anointed Messiahs appeared in abundance during the mayhem, and if you were not with them, they were against you. In the dominant Christian memory, these verses of antagonism are read as if the assaults are coming from "Jews" attacking the followers of Jesus as such, but the assaults at issue *actually*—that is, when Mark is written—come from two directions: from warrior Jews attacking Jews not as Jesus people, but as rejecters of the anti-Roman rebellion; and, always, assaults coming indiscriminately from Romans, who were crucifying five hundred Jews *every day*.[51]

Listen to Jesus, forewarning: "For they will deliver you up to councils; and you will be beaten in synagogues . . . Brother will deliver up brother to death, and the father his child, and children will rise against parents and have them put to death; and you will be hated by all for my name's sake. But he who endures to the end will be saved."[52]

Unlike other Gospels, Mark does not offer any account of the origins of Jesus, but is satisfied simply to announce his arrival "from Nazareth of Galilee."[53] Recall that the Roman War against the Jews began in Galilee, a rocky, mountainous region difficult to subdue. In 67 and 68, some sixty thousand legionaries killed and enslaved something like 100,000 Jews, mostly in Galilee, before moving on to the siege of Jerusalem. Scholars are divided as to where Mark was written, and to whom it was addressed. One ancient tradition locates both the author and the readership in Rome, with the Gospel taken as an account reflecting the views and experiences of Jesus' favored apostle, Peter, whose intimate friend "Mark" was taken to be.[54] That tradition nicely serves the primordial purpose of elevating Peter as the Church's mythic first leader, as if something like the papacy already existed. But the tradition does not address the contradiction embedded in Mark's overwhelmingly negative portrayal of Peter, which alone is enough to cast doubt on the idea that the Gospel represents Peter's point of view. We will see more of this below.

But, in fact, the author of Mark is necessarily anonymous, and the community for whom the text was written is uncertain.[55] The Gospel was written in Greek, but internal evidence suggests that the writer was a Palestinian Jew whose first language was Aramaic. He was probably a resident of Jerusalem. Reading the texts in the light of what was befalling Jerusalem just then, it makes sense that those being addressed were actively involved in the trauma. If one assumes that they were Jesus people clustered in Galilee, at remove from the defense of Jerusalem but still at the mercy of Roman forces as well as roving bands of Jewish Zealots, the vividness of Jesus' description of trouble takes on a compelling edge. For those people were, above all, in the tormented thick of the complications that went with both the

Roman assault and the vengeful punishment inflicted on noncombatant Jews by fellow Jews engaged in the fight.

"Alas for those who are with child and for those who give suck in those days!" Jesus laments. "For in those days there will be such tribulation as has not been from the beginning of the creation which God created until now."[56]

If the Gospel of Mark represented the point of view of Peter, it is exceedingly unlikely that it would have portrayed Peter as it does. While effectively pictured as the one on whom Jesus most depended, Peter is also rendered as vain, buffoonish, impulsive, sadly lacking in courage. Peter is honored to have been given his special name by Jesus: "Simon whom he surnamed Peter."[57] But the resounding affirmation that accompanies that name change in the later text Matthew—"You are Peter, and on this rock I will build my church"[58]—is nowhere in evidence in Mark. Peter, with James and John, is the special witness of the Transfiguration: "and there appeared to them Elijah with Moses, and they were talking to Jesus." But Mark's Peter is immediately shown to misunderstand the meaning of this fleeting epiphany, for he responds by saying, "Master . . . let us make three booths, one for you and one for Moses and one for Elijah." The author of Mark comments, "For he did not know what to say, for they were exceedingly afraid."[59]

It falls to Peter to answer the momentous question posed by Jesus: "'But who do you say that I am?' Peter answered him, 'You are the Christ.'" But no sooner has the apostle put this astounding understanding into words than he mortally offends Jesus, who has just forecast what is coming, for Jesus is soon to face suffering and persecution. Peter, who will have none of such tribulation, either denying it or wanting distance from it, "took him, and began to rebuke him. But turning and seeing his disciples, he [Jesus] rebuked Peter, and said, 'Get behind me, Satan! For you are not on the side of God, but of men.'"[60]

Then, in the thick of the suffering Peter wanted nothing to do with, he is, again with James and John, privileged, nevertheless, to be invited by Jesus to share in the moment of greatest anguish: "My soul is very sorrowful, even to death," Jesus confides, an extraordinary admission. He asks the three to "watch" with him, but then, "he came and found them sleeping, and he said to Peter, 'Simon, are you asleep? Could you not watch one hour?'" Twice more, Jesus returns to find Peter and the others sleeping. "And he came a third time, and said to them, 'Are you still sleeping and taking your rest? It is enough.'"[61]

If Peter fell asleep three times, that was nothing next to the three-fold betrayal that came then. At the Last Supper, in response to Jesus' prediction that "you will all fall away," Peter arrogantly declares, "Even though they all fall away, I will not." Jesus' response is the most drastic personal statement in the entire Gospel: "And Jesus said to him, 'Truly, I say to you, this very night, before the cock crows twice, you will deny me three times.' But he [Peter] said vehemently, 'If I must die with you, I will not deny you.'"[62] And then, of course, with exquisitely belabored detail, Mark renders the three denials of Peter—"I do not know this man of whom you speak"—as the worst blows struck against Jesus. When the cock crowed a second time, Peter "broke down and wept."[63] As a matter of narrative gravity, these denials weigh more than the betrayal by Judas.

All of the intimate friends of Jesus are portrayed in Mark as unreliable, doltish cowards. As Jesus hung on the cross, none of his chosen inner circle were present, only "women looking on from afar."[64] The Gospel of John, written three decades after Mark and in different circumstances, describes a poignant post-Resurrection reunion of the Lord with his dear friend Peter, where the threefold betrayal is reversed as Jesus asks Peter three times, "Do you love me?"—a beautiful ritual of forgiveness and reconciliation, of which we will see more. But Mark offers no such consoling denouement. Instead, Mark ends with the breach between Jesus and Peter, and the others—except for the women—entirely unhealed. This Gospel seems to have as its central subject the abject failure of the friends of Jesus to support him. What is going on here?

Mark's overwhelmingly negative portrayal of Peter has not been highlighted in a Church that subsequently mythologized Peter as a first "pope." Texts from other Gospels—especially Matthew's resounding "keys of the kingdom" commission—are preferred. When Mark's negative portrait of Peter has been directly reckoned with, the usual explanation has involved early Church rivalries, as if the Christian community based, say, in Syria and associated with the apostle John, or in Asia Minor and associated with the missionary Paul, was out to discredit the community most associated with Peter, whether Jerusalem or Rome. The denigration of Peter, in that case, would undercut the prestige of the community attached to him— rather like cities competing for the Olympics.

But if we keep our focus on the Roman War as the defining key to Jesus *actually*, there is a far simpler explanation for this frankly shocking portrait of Peter as a cowardly, unreliable man. If the Gospel of Mark was addressed to a frightened, demoralized collective of Jesus people holed up in Galilee, to people threatened on all sides by marauding Romans, revenge-seeking Jewish Zealots, or Jews associated with rabbis who insisted that acceptance of the false Messiah Jesus threatened the survival of what remained of Judaism; and if those Jesus people, additionally, bore the burden of guilt at their failure to join in the anti-Roman resistance, or were tempted to believe the accusations of cowardice hurled at them by their fellow Jews; and if they had even lost faith in their Lord, whose rescuing return had yet to come about—well, what in the world would good news look like to such people? In this context, the message of Mark was straightforward: *Do not feel guilty because you have faltered in the faith; do not feel disqualified because you have lost hope; do not count yourselves lost— because look! The most intimate friends of Jesus behaved in exactly the same way, including, especially, the exalted Peter, whose name everyone reveres. What you need to hear in this time of grotesque tribulation is that Jesus extends his call not to heroes but to cowards, who fail him. An honest reckoning with such failure is the starting point of discipleship.*[65]

In reading the Gospel of Mark, or hearing it read, such people would have had their fears transformed, for this Gospel's very subject is the flawed condition of all. Peter's rejection of the suffering and persecution that Jesus knows awaits him would have rung with pointed resonance for people who were—even as they read this text—themselves facing just such suffering and persecution, and wanting no more of it. Indeed, they would have taken special note of what Mark describes as following directly on the rebuke of Peter for his rejection of the Lord's suffering, where Jesus called "to himself the multitude with his disciples and said to them, 'If any man would come after me, let him deny himself and take up his cross and follow me.'"[66]

Recall that as this verse was written, ten thousand crosses were ringing the Temple Mount in Jerusalem. *That* is what the Christians in Galilee would have known, and *that* is what would have defined their dread. The cross was no mere religious symbol to them, as the author of Mark knew very well when he put that word in Jesus' mouth. Mark's readers were themselves already undergoing what, in the Gospel, Jesus predicts for them, and that alone would have offered consolation. Their suffering itself was a way of drawing close to their Lord—"you will be hated by all for my name's sake."[67] While such words did not relieve their suffering, the words changed its meaning.

Yet in Galilee, perhaps the violence of Rome was not what threatened most, nor was assault from parties of fellow Jews. What threatened most might have been the Jesus people's own sense of unworthiness in the face of what they suffered; how it generated disputes among themselves; and how it made undeniable the recognition that, in the terrible context of omnidirectional wars—fratricidal and imperial both—they had failed and failed again. Instead of standing up to Rome, they hid. Instead of standing up to their fellow Jews, they equivocated. Perhaps they informed on one another. Became collaborators. Ran off to caves in the desert. Or committed suicide, or helped others to do so. Perhaps they betrayed members of their own families, as Jesus himself foresaw: "Brother will deliver up brother to death, and the father his child, and children will rise against parents and have them put to death."[68]

They looked out for their own skin. They behaved as beleaguered, terrified humans always do. They were sinners, and knew it. To that condition, the Gospel spoke directly. Peter was a sinner. *And he was their hero.* The Lord knew precisely what sort of man Peter was, and chose him anyway. More than that, Jesus *loved* him. If flawed Peter could answer the call to discipleship—this was not Mark speaking, but Jesus himself—so could they.[69]

The mass violence inflicted by the Romans in 70 demanded this text. The catastrophe, centered on the destruction of the Temple, was forcing the Jesus people to look back on their memories, prayers, collected sayings, and stories in a new light. So illuminated, the people saw themselves as never before, because, as never before, they saw their Lord. Mark was first to shine that particular light on the figure of Jesus. It was light cast by the fires of war.

CHAPTER THREE

The Jewish Christ

The past is a foreign country; they do things differently there.

—L. P. Hartley[1]

Low Christology

His followers, all Jews, gathered after the death of Jesus to recall what they remembered of him. The men may have been given mostly to text study, searching their Bible for images and ideas that explained his significance. The women may have mainly given expression to lamentation, through the singing of psalms that had particular relevance to what Jesus meant to them. These resources became ritualized, and informed the composition of stories and hymns. As Jews, in a profoundly Jewish mode, they interpreted their present experience by means of past traditions.

Through all of this, slowly but surely—reinterpretations of interpretations—a new literature was created. It was a version of what Jews had done before, going right back to the primordial work of the editors and redactors who, as we saw, shaped the Bible during and after the Babylonian Captivity. Experience led to recollection, which led to story. In this quite traditional way, narrative building blocks were put into place across the years after Jesus died. That some from outside the world of Israel—called Gentiles—may have been responsive to what they knew of Jesus, and may have been brought into this process, did not take away from its Jewish character. All newcomers to the Jesus movement, whether Gentile or Jew, would have been initiated into its meaning and purpose precisely by participating in such narrative reflection and reenactment. What began as memory and interpretation became proclamation, catechesis, and instruction. Gospel.

In the form it took in the Gospel of Mark, the story builds toward, and is centered upon, the Passion narrative: the distinctive and supremely well-shaped account of Jesus' confrontation with authority in the Temple; the plot by his enemies to arrest him; the betrayal by Judas; the anguished intensification of suspense at the Last Supper, and in the garden of Gethsemane afterward; the failure of his friends; the arrest, trials, torture, and death of Jesus. That dispiriting death, above all, was the inciting incident of the Jesus movement, and finding a hopeful interpretation for it—ultimately known as the Resurrection—was the first challenge.

That the entire Passion drama is enacted through the hours of the Passover cycle of fast, vigil, sacrifice (literally, the slaughter of lambs), meal, and remembrance is the great clue to Mark's purpose. With the Last Supper clearly defined as a Passover meal, scholars now conjecture that this earliest Gospel itself began as a narrative recounting the Passover liturgy as conducted by Jesus people in the formative years of the movement. They would have done this to show how Passover, Israel's constitutive event, took on new meaning because of Jesus; or, perhaps better, how Passover's meaning *survived*, especially after the Roman War put Israel's very existence at risk. Jews were entering once again into their founding liberation—Exodus—but as an adaptation by Jews who saw in Jesus, the paschal lamb, a signal that the liberation now had an explicit meaning for *them*. The ancient ritual brackets of the blessings of bread and wine took on fresh resonance, the seed of the bread-and-wine Eucharistic liturgy. When the Jesus Jews gathered together for their paschal observance, that is, the story of Jesus, culminating in his death at Passover a few or many years before, would have formed the content of their worship at

Passover now. Jesus is Jewish. But so is the shape of the story told about him.[2]

But even scholars who mostly assume that "Jesus," and even the Jesus texts, were Jewish, take for granted that "Christ" was not. Claims made for Jesus by his followers after his death and Resurrection, that is, immediately cut him off from Jewish meaning, especially once he was proclaimed to be "divine." Supposedly, given the radical otherness of Yahweh, there was no place in the Jewish vision of the created cosmos for any "divine" reality or activity. That Jesus could be the preexisting Word of God—"In the beginning was the Word, and the Word was with God, and the Word was God"[3]—was held to be inconceivable in Jewish categories, as were claims that God could be "incarnate" in Jesus: "And the Word became flesh and dwelt among us."[4] This not only led to the rejection of Jesus as a blasphemer by those of his Jewish contemporaries portrayed as hearing him make such claims for himself—"Why do we still need witnesses? You have heard his blasphemy!"[5]—but has erected the defining barricade between Christians and Jews to this day. Contemporary Jews are too polite to put it this way, but ordinary Christian divinity claims for Jesus amount to idolatry.

Some mainstream Christian scholars, aware of the importance of fully locating Jesus in his human—and therefore Jewish—milieu, informed by post-Enlightenment critiques of anthropocentric assumptions, and aware of contemporary encounters with other religious views that undermine Christian uniqueness, have gotten around these disqualifying problems by finding in the historical research little or no textual evidence for the assertion that either Jesus himself or his first followers understood him as a divine figure. *Jesus never claimed to be God. He did not think of himself as God.* Obviously, this is vastly more important than most head-of-a-pin scholarly debates. Whether Jesus was "God," and knew himself to be, is the hinge on which all of Christian history turns—the past, of course, but, even

more decisively, the future. Will any recognizably Christian religion
survive if a straightforward belief in the divinity of Jesus is jettisoned?
This question could shatter the Church. But I raise it as one who
could himself be shattered. In a way, it is *the* problem with which this
book is reckoning. We saw the question earlier, and we will see it
again—and again.

Jesus might have been a charismatic figure, a historically unique
personality, or even the Jewish Messiah, in the understanding of historians and theologians who now debunk his divinity; but, they insist, he was not put forward as God. Deleting Christ's divinity from
Christian understanding requires nothing less than, as one scholar
put it, "a hermeneutical critique of Christological totalization, and a
religious critique of Christological idolatry."[6] This move away from
traditional affirmations helps with the contemporary queasiness one
finds in numerous academic settings about what's called "high Christology," the set of beliefs—the doctrinal school—that elevates Jesus
to equality with God. It soothes the queasiness to be able to say that
Jesus himself, and his early followers, had little or no truck with such
claims. In simple terms, Jesus was a Unitarian.

So emphasis in the skeptical scholarship is given, for example, to
the fact that Jesus often called himself "Son of Man"—more than
sixty times in the Gospels. Rarely, if ever, did he refer to himself as
"Son of God." Those titles—one centered on "man," the other on
"God"—are taken as defining the difference between *low* Christology
and *high*. Speaking generally, the former emphasizes the humanity of
Jesus, while the latter emphasizes his divinity. The low preference of
much recent historical Jesus scholarship offers a way of protecting
the historical (Jewish) Jesus from the mystical (ultimately Aryan)
Christ. Thus, low Christology scholars emphasize that the Greek
term rendered in English as "Son of Man" is better translated as "the
human being." Indeed, some contemporary versions of the New Testament offer that phrase in translation—as if Jesus was decidedly

affirming his simple humanity by so referring to himself. The fathers of the Church understood "Son of Man" in just this way—as an affirmation of humanness.[7]

Much is made, in this argument, of the climax in Mark when the high priest asks Jesus, "Are you the Christ, the Son of the Blessed?" Jesus replies in the affirmative but immediately, as it were, corrects the high priest's title mistake: "And Jesus said, 'I am; and you will see the Son of man sitting at the right hand of Power, and coming with the clouds of heaven.'"[8] When, in the Gospel of Luke, the interrogator puts to Jesus the question "Are you the Son of God, then?" he pointedly refuses to accept the title, replying instead, "You say that I am."[9]

As the Jesus movement spread across the Mediterranean region in its first decades, so the reasoning goes, the relatively narrow worldview of the Palestinian villagers, and even of the Jerusalem urbanites who first embraced the movement, was challenged and expanded by encounters with Greek thought, which had strongly influenced Diaspora Judaism. This so-called Hellenization was especially important as ideas about Jesus developed, with the introduction of Greek philosophical categories infused with God talk and divinity claims. High Christology was the native language of the Hellenized Jesus movement.

We will presently look more closely at the question of whether these sharp distinctions between "Hebrew" and "Greek" classifications do justice to ancient understandings: what did Jews and Greeks actually mean by "God" anyway? The point for us here is to note how a contemporary near consensus has developed among Jesus experts that ideas about Jesus underwent a more radical shift the farther they traveled from Palestine.

Historical Jesus scholars show how a Galilean Jew, with his followers on the move, morphed into a supra-historical cosmic figure more at home in a Greek milieu than a Hebrew one. Metaphysics trumped metaphor, and soon enough the human Jesus was lost in the

divine Savior. Jews and Christians, who disagreed about so much
else, agreed from then on that high Christology—*Christ is God*—
destroyed any tie to the Jewishness of "Jesus Christ." Jews derided
"Christ" as idolatry, while Christians celebrated "Christ's" distance
from Judaism. In subsequent Christological debates across the centuries, Christian heresies that denied or subordinated Jesus' true human nature were condemned, but thrived anyway. High Christology
went through the ecclesial roof. In the Christian imagination, from
early on right down to today, the divine Jesus is definitively understood, as I described earlier by means of quickened model birds, to
have been a pretend human being.[10]

Thus, whatever one made of Jesus of Nazareth, "Christ" could not
be Jewish,[11] and the Incarnation-proclaiming Jesus movement was
necessarily cut off from what remained of "Israel" just at the point—
the war in 70—when Judaism had to find a new self-understanding.
Much emphasis is given, in this line of reasoning, to the fact that in
the New Testament, the "highest" Christology—that dual equation
of "the Word" with Jesus *and* with God—comes in the latest book,
the Gospel of John, dated to after 100.

Indeed, the idea itself of "Word," from the Hellenized *Logos*, is a
name for the divine first used by Heraclitus (535–475 B.C.E.), and
then by the Stoics, and as such is taken to be far removed from any
Hebrew reference. Never mind that throughout the Mediterranean
world before and after the time of Jesus, Hellenized Jews accustomed
to think in Greek categories readily applied them to their own texts.
To take only one example, the great Jewish sage of Alexandria, Philo
(30 B.C.E.–50 C.E.), whose lifetime overlapped with both Jesus and
Paul, elaborated a doctrine of the *Logos* as a "second God," which
might have been controversial, or even meaningless, to illiterate rural
Jews of Galilee or their rabbis. Philo's *Logos* nevertheless found a se-
cure place in the intellectual history of Diaspora Judaism.[12]

A Foreign Country

The ancient world is a foreign country, as L. P. Hartley reminds us; they did things—and, I would add, they thought—differently there. Very differently, and nothing makes the point more powerfully than the question of the "divinity" of Jesus. If that was the blade that cut Jews off from Christians, removing Jesus from his own people once he was proclaimed as godly "Christ," it makes sense to start with this larger question of ancient understandings. And the best figure with whom to begin that inquiry is, indeed, the Hellenized Philo.

Those who assume a sharp division between Hebrew categories (the Yahweh of Moses) and Greek (the unmoved mover of Aristotle) ignore that vast population of ancient Jews, perhaps a majority, living in Palestine as well as in the Diaspora, who were, in fact, thoroughly Hellenized. Also missing from such analysis is that sizable population of Gentiles who associated with Jews and Jewish cult, as admirers and even devotees—the "proselytes" and "God fearers."[13] The single largest obstacle to our authentic reimagining of Jesus Christ is the inability of contemporary thinkers to be at home in the truly foreign landscape of the ancient intellect—Greek and Hebrew, but also Babylonian, Egyptian, Sumerian, Canaanite, and the general intermingling of all these. Biblical and other sacred texts reflect such multiple influences to varying degrees—and can therefore never be fully understood by readers today as they were understood by those who wrote them, first read them, or heard them proclaimed.

In general, the ancients saw a three-tiered universe: Earth bracketed by the dome-like firmament of the stars above and the unplumbed underworld below. Some saw in the blue of the sky a signal of a vast overhead ocean. Earth was broadly taken to be flat, with four corners. Unseen worlds had as much reality as the seen. The native language of ancient cosmology was myth; its diction was metaphor. Yet moderns make a mistake by dismissing the long-ago-conjured images of space, time, origins, personified forces, and fate as mere naïveté. An assumption of the superiority of our more critically considered worldview may lead us to miss the ingenious character of the old imaginings as sensitive penetrations to an impressive depth of the perennial mysteries of existence.

Having insisted that the past is different, however, one must equally reckon with the way in which humans are united across eras and cultures. The sublimity of the cosmos, perceived with the naked eye or through the Hubble telescope, generates responses in mind and heart that in one place and time can give rise to religion, and in others can give rise to a secular sense of transcendent value that, while making no reference to a deity, still reaches toward what can only be called, despite itself, the supernatural. This is true of the beautiful and of the horrible—the glorious sunset and the devastating earthquake; good and evil. There is nature, and there is what is beyond nature. "To know that what is impenetrable to us really exists," the atheist Albert Einstein wrote, "manifesting itself as the highest wisdom and the most radiant beauty which our dull faculties can comprehend only in their most primitive forms—this knowledge, this feeling, is at the center of true religiousness."[14]

The point is that, compared with the impenetrables in the universe that generate awe and stir moral feeling, *all* human faculties are dull—whether ancient or contemporary, credulous or atheist, religious or scientific. If the creation myths, three-tiered cosmologies, and sky-god faiths of long ago—including the biblical—are now taken to be "primitive forms," so are the myths, cosmologies, and faiths of a metaphysics that reduces everything to the "facts" of, well, physics. "It was Einstein's faith that some transcendental and objective value permeates the universe," as the scholar Ronald Dworkin commented, "value that is neither a natural phenomenon nor a subjective reaction to natural phenomena."[15] Naturalism, as even an unbelieving Einstein promoted it, points beyond itself to something else, even if the word "supernaturalism" is rejected as a definition for it. That "something else," while ultimately inexpressible, arises not just from the wondrous facts of nature but from the supremely wondrous enchantment of *nature rising above itself* by being, in human consciousness, self-aware.

So the very "unmodern" theologies and mythologies of the ancient world are responses to demands and values that endure, and that is why we still measure wisdom by the ancients, even as we insist on their otherness.[16] A more or less realistic view of the physical world dates back, among the Greeks, to five centuries before Christ. Ancients were careful observers of the movement of heavenly bodies, studying the relationship of those movements to life-and-death matters of rainfall, river tides, and cycles of the calendar. It may not be too much to say that natural science began with those observations, especially as Greeks began to calibrate their calculations and conclusions. But these profoundly *material* preoccupations led into an elaborated idea of an *immaterial* consciousness—and consciousness became the all-trumping point as awareness became aware of itself. Observations led into systems of belief not only about nature, but about deities under whose influence nature operates.

Aristotle's natural philosophy assumed the movement of spheres and took for granted that a spherical Earth was at their center. Beyond the moon, he imagined the unchanging perfection of a celestial realm, a First Heaven, home to an unchanging and radically other Supreme Being. For Aristotle, following Plato, the movement of the unmoved mover consisted essentially in contemplation, with the ideas of that divine mindfulness expressing themselves in the "created" forms of all that exists. The human capacity for mimetic contemplation, going from the form of things to the substance of their ideal, is what enables humans not just to imitate divine being but to participate in it. Mindfulness is holy. But transcendent ideas were embodied not only in humans but in the gods, whose participation in divine being was elevated above that of mere mortals. The Greek pantheon, in Aristotle's time and after, was populated with a bevy of primordial deities, immortals, Olympians, Titans, sea deities, earth deities, and personified influences.

Such a plethora of divinities mystifies the modern mind—the gods at play on Mount Olympus?—and leaves us wondering how such otherwise brilliant people (Aristotle, Sophocles, Plato, Aristophanes, Homer) could have taken such a worldview "literally." But did they? That the gods were conceived of so anthropomorphically suggests a profound demystification. The impoverished literalism of modern thought is suggested by nothing so much as its inability to imagine other meanings than the *literal*, which is a consequence of the conviction that the "real" can be reduced to scientifically provable "fact." Once, with the Enlightenment, "God" was perceived as such a "fact," having "existence" in "Himself," it followed that a laboratory standard of "truth" would be applied to "Him." Mount Olympus could not meet the standard, and neither could Yahweh. The Secular Age followed.[17] But if an ancient were asked if he really believed in all those gods, the answer would probably come back, "What do you mean, 'really'?[18] What is this 'fact' you keep talking about? And, by the way—just asking—what is this 'believe'?"

Among myth-happy Greeks, the line between an astrology of divinities and a more strictly observed astronomy of heavenly bodies was made sharper with the work of Claudius Ptolemy, a Greek-Roman who lived in Egypt and whose lifetime (90–168 C.E.) coincided with the jelling of both Christian and Rabbinic self-understandings. Ptolemy's vision refined Aristotle's, projecting the universe as an order of nested spheres, with Earth at the center—a vision that defined the worldview of the West until the vindications of Copernicus and Galileo. It was then that humans moved, in Charles Taylor's distinction, from the cosmos to the universe.[19]

The One God?

After the destruction of the Temple, the emergent rabbis and Jesus people were alike in searching for ways to express, in Einstein's terms, "the highest wisdom and the most radiant beauty," which their "dull faculties [could] comprehend only in their most primitive forms." In saying that "God" was present in the *practices* of Law observance and Torah study, or that "God" was present in the person of Jesus Christ,[20] the confusion begins not with Law or Jesus, but with "God." What did those who thought in these divergent ways about keeping faith with Israel think when they thought about "God"?

Consider the great affirmation, recited twice a day by observant Jews from the time of Deuteronomy: "Shema Yisreal: Hear, O Israel: The Lord is our God! The Lord is One!" Jesus recites the Shema in the Gospel of Mark.[21] This eloquent declaration comes to the modern ear as the essence of monotheism, the idea that there is no divine being except Israel's God. That is why Paul's adaptation of the Shema in his first letter to the church at Corinth seems to define the necessary conflict between Jewish tradition and belief in Jesus: "For us there is one God, the Father, from whom are all things and for whom we exist." But when Paul, seeming to posit equality, goes on to say in the same verse, "and one Lord, Jesus Christ, through whom are all things and through whom we exist," monotheism seems contradicted.[22] Jesus seems to be put forward as a second divine being, and what monotheistic Jew would not have trouble with that?

But if subtleties of ancient polytheism as described above elude the literal-mindedness of modernity, the same is true of the "monotheism" of Shema. Indeed, as the *-ism* suffix suggests, the word was coined only in the Enlightenment era, and the idea of *mono*, emphasizing a numerical value, may entirely miss the actual meaning, in the ancient mind, of God's "oneness." In the verse running up to that just cited from his letter to Corinth, Paul says, "For although there may

be so-called gods in heaven or on earth—as indeed there are many
'gods' and many 'lords'—yet for us there is one God."[23] In the Letter
to the Ephesians, Paul offers an even more pointed litany of higher
beings. Not only does the devil rank above humanity, but so do a
host of others: "For we are not contending against flesh and blood,
but against the principalities, against the powers, against the world
rulers of this present darkness, against the spiritual hosts of wickedness in the heavenly places."[24]

Christians rush past these words of Paul because what they quite
specifically imply—a pantheon of at least semi-divine beings of varied ranks—does not fit with the modern idea of God in heaven alone.
The post-Enlightenment "disenchantment" of which Weber speaks
has mainly excluded, even for many believers, the lesser beings like
angels and a personal Satan—along with the places in which, formerly, they were thought to live. But Paul's world was still quite
charged with the consoling and threatening energies of such super-
agents. If he seems to assume "many 'gods' and many 'lords,'" a host of
beings with some attributes of the Godhead, no wonder he can attribute Lordship—which implies divinity—to Jesus. Was the cost of
that attribution, though, precisely what disqualified Jesus as a Jew?

But what if the oneness of Israel's God was a function of the Lord's
supremacy as the "High God," not of his isolation in a cosmic sphere
devoid of lesser deities? The Old Testament, in many passages, affirms
the existence—the reality—of other gods, even while claiming the supremacy of Israel's God and the requirement to worship Israel's God
alone. Indeed, the biblical notion of the supremacy of Yahweh grew out
of his mortal combat with the gods Baal and El, who could be labeled
"false gods" without denying their reality.[25] To be sure, the Bible rejects
the crude idolatry of figurines, but it still assumes the existence of the
transcendent powers, even deities, for which the figurines stand.[26]

The stereotype that pagans "worshipped" their little carved statu-
ettes is crude. It is far more likely that such objects were revered

because they made God present not in themselves but in the minds of those who beheld them. God's presence *to the mind* was the point. Thus, throughout the Bible, other gods—divinities of diverse tribes, supernatural beings with varied functions, some enemies of the Lord, some the Lord's servants—are taken for granted.[27] Many texts assume a High God, coexisting with a kind of deputy God whose business is to serve as an intermediary with human beings.

Philo, the Jewish contemporary of Paul and Jesus, can confidently be assumed to have been a Shema-proclaiming "monotheist," yet, as noted, he posited the *Logos* as a second God, and in another place he spoke of "the most holy dwelling place of the manifest and visible gods."[28] Such language is not exceptional, but typical. The Jewish scholar Paula Fredriksen, whose work especially informs me here, has proposed that because "multiple divine personalities are native to ancient monotheism," the word "monotheism" itself, taken by moderns to deny such a host of beings, has not been usefully applied to, in her phrase, "the study of Christian origins." Jews take for granted that divinity claims for Jesus contradict monotheism, while Christians have twisted themselves—and their thought—into knots explaining why such claims do no such thing. Fredriksen is a leading advocate of a return to a full appreciation of the permanent Jewishness of Jesus, and that is what leads her to question this basic obstacle to such an understanding. If, as Fredriksen quite boldly states, "ancient monotheists were polytheists,"[29] where does that leave the Jewish-Christian dispute over claims made for Jesus? Where, for that matter, does it leave ancient and contemporary Christian assumptions about the unique intervention God has made in Christ?

The Son of Man

A bishop in Sardis, in what is today Turkey, charged the Jewish people with the crime of murdering God. That bishop's name was

Melito, and the year was 167. The lethal indictment made Jews "the deicide people," but it showed that Jesus was by then fully regarded as divine, at least by some Christians. Soon enough, that tenet defined the faith of the whole Church, with a thoroughly Hellenized Christology articulated in the fourth-century Nicene Creed:

> We believe in one Lord, Jesus Christ, the only Son of God, eternally begotten of the Father, God from God, Light from Light, true God from true God, begotten, not made, of one Being with the Father. Through him all things were made.

By thus making Jesus Christ and God the Father wholly equal, Christians put a definitive end to any possible further affirmation of Jesus by Jews. But when, actually, was this obstacle constructed? When, that is, was Jesus irrevocably taken to be "God"? And what did that mean for his followers, his critics—and what does it mean for us?

By the time of the Gospel of John, in around 100, Jesus had quite explicitly begun to be spoken of as God—that *Logos* language. John has Jesus say, quite baldly, "I and the Father are one."[30] Even before that, Saint Paul, whose letters date to between 50 and 60, saw in Jesus the one who was "in the form of God [yet] did not count equality with God a thing to be clung to." When Paul declares that "everyone who calls upon the name of the Lord will be saved," he is applying to Christ the name reserved for Yahweh in the text he is echoing.[31] Paul draws on hymns, "enthronement psalms," and traditions that precede him, suggesting that Jesus was taken to be divine even earlier. It is not out of the question that Jesus *might have understood himself* to be in some way God. Is that what broke him from his Jewish identification?

In recent years, a set of unexpected investigations into the historical Jesus, conducted by Jewish scholars as well as Christian, have upended what had become a conventional historians' position—that Jesus "of Nazareth" can be understood as Jewish, while Jesus "Christ" cannot.[32] That consensus had depended, though, on the narrow reading of Jewish "monotheism" that we have already criticized. Such low-high debate about Jesus can seem to take place in an academic echo chamber, but for a Christian believer looking to retrieve some meaning of traditional faith in Jesus the Son of God, it can come as a bracing revelation to learn that early Jesus-proclaiming Jews—those who had traveled with him—saw no conflict between their Shema affirmation of the one God and the conviction that Jesus, as "Christ," shared in God's divinity.

It is clear, in fact, that not long after the followers of the murdered Jesus began gathering in his memory, they took to calling "on the name of our Lord Jesus Christ."[33] Was this "acclamation," a kind of lifting up of Jesus as an inspiration? Or was it "prayer," an addressing to Jesus appeals that a Jew would formerly have addressed only to God? If it was the latter, the Jesus people, in a decisive recasting of the identity of their deceased peasant leader, might have been "involved," in one scholar's phrase, "in a mutation of Second Temple Jewish monotheism."[34] My exploration of this question does indeed assume a "mutation" in Jewish self-understanding, but so far I have located it in the change-producing trauma of 70, with the destruction of the Temple. Now I am asking whether it occurred much before that. If so, how much of a break with the past was it, and were there precedents in Jewish tradition that made it less radical than supposed? Does the word "mutation" really apply?

The term "Lord" might, in itself, have indicated a move toward an understanding of Jesus as divine, since Hellenized Jews were accustomed to Greek versions of the Hebrew Scriptures that used that word for God. We saw an instance of that from Paul, above. But those same Jews would have been familiar with a common usage of the title "Lord" that applied it to human figures, like the emperor.[35] So the use of the term "Lord," in itself, confuses as much as it clarifies.

Certainly there were early disputes among Jews about Jesus; the personal biography of Paul attests to that. By his own account, he zealously pursued the followers of Jesus and "persecuted" them— presumably in the years immediately following the crucifixion. But was that a matter of combating blasphemous divinity claims, or a lesser dispute over the question of whether Jesus was the awaited Messiah of Israel—an exalted figure, to be sure, but not divine? If Jesus were a "false Messiah," that could have been reason enough to try to stamp out his movement, drawing fire from fiercely committed figures like Paul. Less mystically, Jews under the ongoing threat of Roman crackdown might well have opposed the Jesus people simply on the grounds that their enthusiasm for the crucified one, however described, could have once again brought the Roman hammer down on what remained of Israel. Whether Jesus was "God" or not might have had nothing to do with it.

These intra-Jewish disputes, coming to a head after the destruction of the Temple, were eventually, if only slowly, resolved when Jews and Christians embraced the settled and separate identities that keep them apart to this day.[36] The divinity of Jesus, as the Son of God equal to and "of one being with the Father," was and is the border marker. That is why having Jewish scholars side by side with Christians today in explorations of the origins of that sharp boundary *within Judaism* is so intriguing. And it is why the engagement with these questions on the part of one scholar in particular has been momentous.

Daniel Boyarin, an Orthodox Jew born in 1946, is one of the most respected talmudic scholars in the world, with unassailable credentials to speak as a Jew, and for Jews. He has published significant books on Paul and on the points of dispute between Judaism and Christianity.[37] But in 2012, Boyarin published *The Jewish Gospels: The Story of the Jewish Christ*, a book that, as the title suggests, raises the dispute to a new level by stoutly affirming the Jewishness not just of the historical "Jesus," but of the exalted "Christ." Or, as Boyarin himself puts it, "I wish us to see that Christ too—the divine Messiah—is a Jew."[38] With careful analysis of New Testament texts, Hebrew texts, and the broader Jewish culture, Boyarin shows that Jews *as Jews*—perhaps including Jesus himself[39]—were quite well prepared *by their own tradition* to understand him not only as Messiah but as, in some way, God. This sounds radical—for a Jew, blasphemous—but Boyarin insists it is not:

> While by now almost everyone, Christian and non-Christian, is happy enough to refer to Jesus, the human, as a Jew, I want to go a step beyond that. I wish us to see that Christ too—the divine Messiah—is a Jew. . . . Many Israelites at the time of Jesus were expecting a Messiah who would be divine and come to earth in the form of a human. Thus the basic underlying thoughts from which both the Trinity and the Incarnation grew are there in the very world into which Jesus was born and in which he was first written about in the Gospels of Mark and John.[40]

Because of Boyarin's scholarly authority, his assertion cannot be readily dismissed. Still, if accepted by Jews and Christians alike, a Jewish origin of belief in the "Word made flesh" and "the triune God" would upset centuries of tradition. At the very least, it would require a change in the way Rabbinic Judaism and Christianity see their origins. It's more likely that Boyarin's thesis would be rejected, precisely because there is something slippery about the idea of Jewish sources for distinctively Christian notes of faith in Jesus. If such notes come, as Boyarin suggests, from their own book of Daniel, why don't Jews accept them? Are we back to supersessionism and the question of whether Jews betrayed themselves in not accepting Jesus? That is, of course, a nightmare question—not only for a devout Jew like Boyarin, but for a Christian seeking to undo centuries of religious contempt.[41]

Not only Jews might object here. The Christian expert on Judaism Peter Schäfer dismisses Boyarin's "breathtaking hypothesis." His book "leaves the reader irritated and sad," Schäfer says, and is "wildly speculative and highly idiosyncratic."[42] The distinguished Christian scholar Larry Hurtado weighs in on the dispute in favor of Schäfer, yet Schäfer's criticism is brushed off by others as a "vicious attack."[43]

This is more than an academic dispute. When Boyarin points out that "for centuries after Jesus' death, there were people who believed in Jesus' divinity as the Incarnate Messiah, but who also insisted that in order to be saved they must eat only Kosher, keep the Sabbath as other Jews do, and circumcise their sons,"[44] he is reminding us that ancient categories of Jewish-Christian division were not nearly so cut-and-dried as contemporary scholarly polemic—not to mention Church pronouncement—assumes. We are back to Bonhoeffer and his implicit grasp of the fundamental issue showing itself in Germany during the Nazi years: Christians, Bonhoeffer insisted, must find whole new ways of taking seriously that "Jesus *Christ* was a Jew." That insight pushes to the heart of the question—and this was inchoate in Bonhoeffer, too—of whether, and how, Jesus was also God.

Against mainstream assumptions of Christians and Jews both, we find ourselves confronted with the very real possibility that the longed-for Messiah figure was *expected within Israel* to be in some way divine. Here is another way to say it: some belief in Jesus' divine status, far from coming much later in the world of Hellenism, began not with the first followers of Jesus, or even with Jesus himself, but with hopes that had already seized the Jewish imagination before Jesus was born. "Many ancient Jews simply accepted Jesus as God," Boyarin writes, "and they did so because their beliefs and expectations had led them there."[45]

The story of Jesus, as Christians usually recount it, begins with the angel's announcement to the Virgin Mary that she has been "overshadowed" by the Holy Spirit—presumably marking the narrative's beginning at about nine months before the child's birth. The nativity[46] is the happening that sets the action of the Gospel in motion, with the included detail about Herod's slaughter of the innocents a good example of how a story's end can efficiently be foretold at the start. Jesus is the infant who escapes the slaughter, yet the fate of all those little boys who are killed because of him causes a chilling shadow to fall across the entire Gospel. This will be a story about brutal, unjust death—and it tells you so right at the outset.

Yet Matthew's account of the slaughter of the innocents, an echo perhaps of that more or less simultaneous crucifixion of a thousand Jewish rebels around the time of Jesus' birth, points far back into Jewish history, to a different starting point. Matthew writes,

> Then was fulfilled what was spoken by the prophet Jeremiah: "A voice was heard in Ramah, wailing and loud lamentation, Rachel weeping for her children; she refused to be consoled, because they were no more."[47]

Jeremiah's lamentation is the point of the entire infant-slaughter episode, and it establishes the context within which the story of Jesus is set, for the prophet Jeremiah's distress was prompted centuries earlier by the defining catastrophe of the people Israel—which was, as we saw, the destruction of Jerusalem by the armies of Babylon. We are back to the central influence of war, and war's function as the spark of innovation in religious imagining. Jewish survival of war and Jewish resistance to war-making oppressors make up the background for the Gospel.

It is in that context that Daniel Boyarin's argument unfolds, for it depends on a close analysis of the title applied to Jesus that we have already considered: the "Son of Man." We have seen how those disinclined to regard Jesus as divine prefer that title to "Son of God," because they read it to mean "human being," emphasizing the humanity of Jesus over any conceivable divinity of "Christ." But Boyarin, in his reading of Jewish Scriptures in which both titles are found, sees exactly opposite meanings in the two phrases. "When Mark in the very beginning of his Gospel writes, 'The Beginning of the Gospel of Jesus Christ, the Son of God,'" Boyarin declares, "the Son of God means the human Messiah, using the old title for the king of the House of David. When, on the other hand, Mark refers to him in the second chapter of the Gospel as the 'Son of Man,' he is pointing to the divine nature of the Christ."[48] When the voice of God is heard declaring to Jesus, after his baptism, "Thou art my beloved Son; in Thee I am well pleased," Mark's readers would have detected the echo of the psalm in which God said to the *whole of Israel*, "You are my Son, today I have begotten you."[49] When Christians stopped reading the text with a Jewish eye, especially once a "sonship" theology of the Trinity developed later, these "Son of God" references were taken as signals of divinity. But a return to a Jewish reading of these verses brings the surprising flip: "Son of God" means human; "Son of Man" means God.

How can that be? The key lies in a particular Jewish text, one to which we have already referred. The "beliefs and expectations" that led Jews to anticipate a Messiah who was divine were rooted in the "Son of Man" figure presented in the book of Daniel, which, as we saw, pointed back six centuries to the Babylonian War but was composed during the brute violence of the Seleucid pogroms and the Maccabean Revolt, two centuries before Christ. And, as we saw, the book of Daniel had wide circulation among Jews before and after Jesus' birth, profoundly influencing the Jewish religious imagination. The story of Jesus, in other words, drawn from images and motifs of such texts, had its deep origins in those two wars (Babylonian and Maccabean) that had traumatized Israel—and reshaped its understandings—long before his birth. But the story does not come into its own *as story* until the full-bore Roman War, several decades after Jesus. Wars define.

As we saw, the Gospel of Mark can be read as having been sparked by, and as an attempt to make sense of, the catastrophic destruction of the Temple in 70. It should not surprise, then, that central to the Gospel's portrait of Jesus, drawn from traditions that went back in all likelihood to Jesus himself, is the single most important image of hope that Israel's contested past had produced. In Israel's texts and traditions, the title "Messiah," referring mainly to one restoring the royal line of David's kingship, pointed therefore to a human being like David himself. Now we can appreciate why the book of Daniel—so little known to most Christians—carries such weight in our investigation. Written between 167 and 164 B.C.E., in the thick of rebellion, Daniel looks forward to *one whose kingship is eternal*. It looks forward, that is, to a Messiah who transcends David, transforms the hope of Israel—and is somehow divine.[50]

Daniel's ecstatic rendition of this personage is quite explicit: "I saw in the night visions, and behold, with the clouds of heaven there came one like a Son of Man, and he came to the Ancient of Days and was presented before him." The "Ancient of Days" referred to here is the enthroned figure, aged and sovereign, who becomes lodged in the religious imagination of Jews, and ultimately Christians, as the Father in heaven, the High God. He will one day be pictured paradigmatically by Michelangelo on the ceiling of the Sistine Chapel—flowing white beard and all. But the lesser "Son of Man," also showing up in this vision, has a divine character, too. He is, in effect, the second God, younger but also enthroned. "This is the vision," Boyarin comments, "that will become in the fullness of time the story of the Father and the Son." The High God and that God's divine viceroy fulfill the dual human needs for belief in an all-controlling, if distant, ruler and in a more immediate source of personal care. A judging God must be paired with a God of mercy. That the relationship between the two in Daniel is clearly one of Supreme Being to subordinate divine agent protects the principle of God's "oneness."[51]

That Daniel evokes the "clouds of heaven" is the great clue, for the image of one "coming in clouds" appears seventy times in the Hebrew Scriptures, and it *always* connotes a divine figure.[52] Unlike King David, whose long-anticipated messianic restoration promised sovereignty over a time-and-place-bound Israel, the Son of Man's rule will be universal and forever. "And to him was given dominion and glory and kingdom, that all peoples, nations, and languages should serve him; his dominion is an everlasting dominion, which shall not pass away, and his kingdom one that shall not be destroyed."[53]

Thus, when Jesus is shown referring to himself as Son of Man, the last thing he should be understood as saying—and this contradicts a dominant trend of much historical Jesus scholarship—is that he is just another human being. At the very beginning of his public ministry, as Mark recounts it, Jesus takes pains to insert himself precisely into this current of Daniel's vision. Mark's scene has Jesus encountering a paralyzed man. When Jesus announces that the man's sins are forgiven, he senses the skepticism of the witnesses. Jesus asks them:

> "Why do you question thus in your hearts? Which is easier, to say to the paralytic, 'Your sins are forgiven,' or to say, 'Rise, take up your pallet and walk'? But that you may know that the Son of Man has authority on earth to forgive sins"—he said to the paralytic—"I say to you, rise, take up your pallet and go home." And he rose, and immediately took up the pallet and went out before them all; so that they were all amazed and glorified God, saying, "We never saw anything like this!"[54]

The later and climactic "Son of Man" scene in Mark, already noted as coming on the eve of the Passion and commonly taken as an affirmation of Jesus' humanity—is transformed when read in its proper context, the book of Daniel: "Again the high priest asked him, 'Are you the Christ, the Son of the Blessed?' And Jesus said, 'I am.'"

Yes, there is an implication of Yahweh's "I AM WHO I AM" in that reply,[55] but, aware that verses from the book of Daniel would have been in the forefront of every Jewish mind just then, what Jesus goes on to say moves beyond implication to something quite explicit: "And you will see the Son of Man seated at the right hand of Power, and coming with the clouds of heaven." Jesus is a Jew in these texts, and—here is the momentous point for faith—he is God.

Mark is offering, in other words, a crystal-clear repetition of a passage in Daniel that is itself a clear proposal of a somehow divine Messiah. And now look at the reaction this statement by Jesus drew: "And the high priest tore his garments, and said, 'Why do we still need witnesses? You have heard his blasphemy. What is your decision?' And they all condemned him as deserving death."[56]

Against the way this priestly condemnation is usually read, the offense here was not that Jesus was proposing an unthinkable human claim to divinity, but that he was claiming for himself the role of the somehow divine Messiah that was already and broadly a feature of Jewish expectation just then. *The divine one in the clouds*, Jesus was saying, *is no longer a figment of future expectation, but is right here in front of you.* That was the blasphemy. Similarly, to Jews, there was no shock in the idea that the divine Messiah would be Lord of *all* people—this notion would prompt Paul's "mission to the Gentiles." The shock, as Boyarin points out, was in the claim by this peasant nobody from Galilee that *he* was the Son of Man.

But for us, the most important point—in Bonhoeffer's context, the momentous point—is that the disciples rallied to Jesus not because he represented a transcendent break, or mutation, with a moribund, corrupt Jewish tradition, but because he so fully lived up to the vital and creative function that had been at the center of Jewish hope for most of two centuries. There might have been dispute about whether Jesus of Nazareth embodied that hope, but not about whether the hope was true to the covenant with Israel. Bonhoeffer

may have only incidentally included the word "Christ" in his propo-
sition that "Jesus Christ was a Jew," but that word goes to the heart of
the malign idea, shared eventually by Jews and Christians alike, that
there was an ontological, theological barrier between Jesus and his
own true people. There was no such barrier. Instead of *against* the
Jewish context, Jesus could be taken as "Christ" *within* it, and that
truth removes a pillar of the cosmic hatred that developed between
the Church and the Synagogue. Against the overwhelming weight
of much historical Jesus scholarship, it was not that "Hellenized"
followers of Jesus, coming long after him, invented a new idea of
divinity—"Christ"—and shoehorned the Galilean peasant into it,
but that, as "Jesus," his story naturally fell into the tropes and rhythms
of a profoundly Jewish narrative, as "Christ," that had been there to
be embodied before he came along.

Recognizing this should mark the end of the debates between
those who see "Jesus" as human (and Jewish) and those who see
"Christ" as divine (and universal). The understanding of Jesus as a
somehow divine Messiah figure, the man-God already firmly rooted
in Jewish thought, almost certainly marked those who responded to
him at the start. Jesus himself, sharing their worldview as a Jew of his
time, could quite readily have understood himself in these terms as
well. The End Time is here. And so is the Son of Man.

This revised understanding should mark, also, the beginning of
the end of the idea that the split between Christians and Jews was the
result of some action of God's. That does not mean opening the door
to some kind of religious reunion or reconciliation between Judaism
and Christianity, because, given the tragic arc of history, that always
assumes a Jewish embrace of claims made for Jesus. It is conceivable
that Jews could find in Jesus a figure of religious relevance, perhaps in
the tradition of the prophets, but beyond that, nothing. The split is
properly irreversible—Jews *as Jews* cannot and should not accept the

faith of the Church[57]—but what makes the split irreversible today is what caused it in the first place: accidents of history, especially the violence of war, not God's will.

Your Resurrection

All of this raises the question of what Jesus and his contemporaries, in the foreign country of the past, meant by the word "divine." We will take up that question presently, and fresh reflections on the mystery of the human-divine can, perhaps, move the entire discussion of differences between Judaism and Christianity to a new level, which could model, for that matter, a similar shift in the split between the religious and the secular. Christians celebrate human divinity while Jews banish it, but what if each group means something entirely different by the concepts expressed in this language? What, finally, is the content of *any* faith in God?

But our focus now is on how the question of the divinity of Jesus, and the theological inevitability of the break with Israel, derive with equal power from the proclamation that Jesus was "raised from the dead"—the other article of Christian faith that is understood to have caused the near-immediate break between the Church and the Synagogue. But did it?

"Do not be amazed," the young man in white said. "You seek Jesus of Nazareth, who was crucified. He has risen, he is not here."[58] As belief in the divinity of Christ has been thought to be a general Christian "mutation" breaking absolutely with Judaism, necessarily capping and calcifying Jesus' conflict with his Jewish milieu and preparing the Church for its positive-negative opposition to the Synagogue, so with the Resurrection of Jesus on the third day. That miracle is taken to be a particular—and heightened—form of the radical break with Judaism. Christians from the start have seemed to define the

Resurrection as the defining act of God the Father's intervention in favor of His Son, an act decisively against the Son's enemies, especially "the Jews" who had seen to his death.

This inquiry animates much expressly Jewish scholarship focused on the meaning of Jesus Christ, in a Jewish context. Jon D. Levenson is a Jewish scholar who wrote the groundbreaking *Death and Resurrection of the Beloved Son*, which laid bare the Jewish roots of basic Christian ideas—including even the claim by the Church that it had superseded the Synagogue.[59] Now Levenson has joined with his Harvard colleague the Christian scholar Kevin J. Madigan to write *Resurrection: The Power of God for Christians and Jews*, a book that informs my observations here. The authors observe that, for Christians, Jewish rejection of the Resurrection is a signal of the Jewish faith's timeless irrelevance, its inability to reckon with mortality— the single most tragic fact facing humankind. Jewish shallowness in the face of dying means that the sting of death remains. For Christians, without the Resurrection there is no meaning. "If Christ has not been raised," Saint Paul insisted, "then our preaching is in vain, and your faith is in vain."[60]

For their part, Jews, early and late, right down to the present, have seen the Resurrection of Jesus and its promise of resurrection for all who call upon him as an obliterating break with the tradition of Israel. "Christian belief in resurrection," Levenson and Madigan write, "has often served in Jewish minds to fuel a contrast between an otherworldly and superstitious Christianity, on the one hand, and a thisworldly, socially responsible and progressive Judaism, on the other."[61]

But what if, as with the general question of Christ's divinity, the Resurrection of Jesus—what finally elevates him to "the right hand of God"[62]—is rooted in the very heart of ancient Jewish belief and expectation? For Christians, this is a dangerous question, since a wholly miraculous, unexpected, and religiously unique Resurrection is the foundation stone of Christianity's claim of being a religion from above. All other religions, however value-laden, are from below—generated by human longing for transcendence, as opposed to by God's astounding intervention on the third day.

The problem with this notion of the Resurrection's having come down to us out of the blue, as an until-then inconceivable turn in the story of Jesus, is there to be seen in the central Christian statement of belief. The Nicene Creed, already noted as dating to the fourth century, plainly says, "On the third day he rose again in accordance with the Scriptures"—in accordance, that is, with categories, images, expectations, and theologies already extant in Jewish life. The Gospels include passages that are read after the fact as Jesus' "prophecies" of his Resurrection ("Destroy this temple, and in three days . . ."[63]), but, as we saw, those words describing the unthinkable were likely put in Jesus' mouth *after* the Temple destruction, and *after* the Easter experience had shaped Christian understanding.

In fact, when it comes to the Resurrection of Jesus, the "Scriptures" in question are centered on the text that we have already identified as central to the meaning of Jesus as "Christ"—the book of Daniel. As that apocalyptic vision spawned the lively Jewish hope for a divine Messiah, shaping the way Jesus was understood—or understood himself—as "Son of Man," so Daniel proposes "the first transparent and indisputable prediction of the resurrection of the dead in the Hebrew Bible."[64] As an essentially Jewish vision of the resurrection of the dead, verses of the book of Daniel gave the first followers of Jesus precisely the language and the theological precedent they needed to accomplish the tour de force act of interpretation that changed forever the meaning of the crucifixion.

"And many of those who sleep in the dust of the earth shall awake." Daniel's proclamation promises an overturning of the primordial curse of death, and while the text speaks of "many," there is more here than a forecast of generalized continuity of a people. The promised life beyond death is particular, attached to individuals. The community lives on only because its members do, each one being reckoned with according to life choices she or he has personally made. Thus, upon being raised, all will be dispatched, "some to everlasting life, and some to shame and everlasting contempt. And those who are wise shall shine like the brightness of the firmament; and those who turn many to righteousness, like the stars for ever and ever."[65]

There had been intimations of resurrection in other, older texts in the Hebrew Bible—notably in Ezekiel, whose interest for us lies in the prophet's having lived and written during the all-important Babylonian War and exile, what first gave Judaism its bite as the religion we know. Ezekiel, whoever he was, looked out over the war-torn valley and saw a vast litter of dry bones, a legion of the war dead. "There was a noise, and behold, a rattling, and the bones came together . . . and the breath came into them, and they lived and stood upon their feet, an exceedingly great host."

"Host" is the point here, since Ezekiel's vision, although one of resurrection, refers to resurrection of the people. While this being raised is universal, it is decidedly not particular—or singular. Indeed, the prophet is explicitly told by the Lord, "These bones are the whole house of Israel."[66] God's promise to Israel is reliably vindicated, and, yes, Israel is enabled *as a people* to return to Jerusalem and recover the Temple. That is the story of what happened at and after Babylon. The chosen people not only survived but came into their own, as a religiously mature people of the Book. But this says nothing about the throng of *individuals*: those dead in battles one by one; tortured in slavery a scream at a time; lost in exile, but not soon forgotten by some bereaved person or other. The fates of such persons considered singly are not addressed in the vision of Ezekiel. The Resurrection is not for them.

As we learn from Madigan and Levenson, there are other such instances of *corporate* rescue from death in the Hebrew Bible. In Isaiah, the cry goes out, "Thy dead shall live, their bodies shall rise. O dwellers in the dust, awake and sing for joy!"[67] But this jubilation is for the restoration of God to His throne, the gathering back of tribes, the End Time triumph—*of Israel*. The individuals sublimate their hope in the broader fate of the nation. There is no more promise of personal resurrection in the dust than in the valley of bones.

There are instances when individuals *are* brought back to life in the Hebrew Bible, but only temporarily. The prophet Eli'sha, for example, stretches his body out on the cold corpse of a child. "The child sneezed seven times, and the child opened his eyes."[68] But that child—like Lazarus, brought back to life by Jesus—would die again. This resuscitation is not resurrection. It is being brought back from the dead, but only for a moment.

These precedents are what make the book of Daniel transformational, for with its overturning of death comes the permanent state of "everlasting life," also translated as "eternal life." As Madigan and Levenson explain, this phrase in Daniel—which, "for all its frequency in later Jewish literature, occurs nowhere else in the Hebrew Bible"[69]—is key. Eternal life means that those resurrected will never die again. But whether their standing in such a state is blissful or tormented—brightness or shame—entirely depends on a postmortem adjudication of them as individuals. This is first the fate of persons, only secondarily of a people.

One readily imagines how such a prophecy came to be, thinking of the extremities confronting the Jews under the heel of the Seleucid oppressors, and of those who gave their lives in rebellion, or those who loved the deceased victims. This promise of individual judgment would have redeemed the absurd and crushing circumstance of people in conflict with an unjust enemy and, as is always true in such situations, in conflict with one another—a sure reward for those who kept faith with Israel, and punishment for those who betrayed her.

But recall that Daniel's vision is of an apocalyptic End Time. Whether Jesus described himself by drawing on the imagery and religious meaning of Jewish apocalypse is disputed by scholars, but it is clear that Jesus was understood from an early date in such terms by his followers.[70] We cannot know with certainty how Jesus understood himself: we will see more of this later when we take up the contrast between Jesus and the apocalyptically minded John the Baptist.[71]

Apocalyptic motifs followed naturally from the traumas of the year 70, when the climactic horrors of the last days must actually have seemed to be occurring. This plausibly accounted for Mark's emphatically apocalyptic portrait of Jesus, composed exactly then. But consider now the year 30, when, for the followers of Jesus, the trauma, however crushing, was narrower. In 70, there were ten thousand crucifixions; in 30, there was only one that counted. For those who loved Jesus, that one was enough.

And look at what the Jesus people did. They drew again on the vision in which, with Jesus, they were already steeped. Apocalyptic thinking, in one scholar's phrase, was "everywhere in the air."[72] Because the End Time into which Jesus had promised to usher them was, as they *still* believed, near at hand, it was the most natural thing in the world to turn, again, to Daniel, to find in its forecast of the resurrection of the dead a solution to the momentous problem of the brutal death of Jesus. The vision Daniel offered, that is, had a coherence and a totality that led their thinking forward. Not only was Jesus "Son of Man," favored of God—and perhaps, even, in some way God Himself. He was also the agent of God's wondrous intervention in history, bringing it to a climax. This was larger than the Davidic restoration of the kingdom of Israel, a political victory over Rome under a militant Christ. It was a decisive completion of a cosmic destiny, transcending politics and making of Rome a side story. To conceive of Jesus as the zealous revolutionary, a figure favored by Jesus historians, is to profoundly underestimate his meaning in this new context. Indeed, according to this other vision, his purpose was the renewal of the human condition itself, the fulfillment of the life principle that beats in every human heart. Such an outcome could be signified only by Jesus' personal victory over death, which could only take the form of *his personal Resurrection*. To follow the lead of the book of Daniel was to follow a chain of logic that led directly to the empty tomb. That, in turn, was a renewal of the promise that the End Time was near. Very near.

The Gospel of Mark, unlike the other Gospels, is exceedingly spare in its description of the Resurrection, and there is a major clue in that for us. In fact, "description" is the wrong word, for Mark simply asserts, in the voice of a young man dressed in white, addressing the three women, "He has risen, he is not here." The text makes no attempt to define the Resurrection, or to embellish it with anecdotes of "appearances." The Gospel abruptly ends, with the women rushing from the tomb, "for trembling and astonishment had come upon them; and they said nothing to any one, for they were afraid."[73]

Scholars debate the significance of this ending, so unlike the endings of the other Gospels, which offer elaborate accounts of Jesus' post-Resurrection manifestations. By comparison, Mark's simple assertion, almost mundane in its eschewing of the wondrous, amounts to a refusal to offer any evidence for its extraordinary claim. Mark's place as the earliest Gospel makes this failure to elaborate the miracle doubly troubling for those who take the post-Easter wonders as defining proofs of Christian claims. Indeed, that lacuna in Mark worried early Jesus people and made the physical Resurrection less credible. Some modern scholars speculate that additional verses that might have more traditionally filled out the accounts of the appearances were lost. Others propose that the author of Mark surely intended to expand on the Resurrection miracle but died before completing his Gospel. Mark's spare conclusion seems to have troubled ancient readers in these ways, too: some of them adjusted it. One amended version, attached to the end of Mark in the middle of the second century, added another dozen verses, with more appearances, including those to Mary of Magdala, to two walkers on the road, and finally to the eleven disciples.[74]

But in our reading, the abrupt ending of the Gospel, with its bald but unelaborated declaration that "He has risen, he is not here," is full of implication. The verses efficiently make the connection to the vision of Daniel. That the story seems unfinished is fitting, since the finishing was going to happen not on the page, but in the lives of the followers of Jesus. The point was: his being raised rang the bell on the new day, the last day. As the followers of Jesus, while he was alive, expected to be led by him into the fulfillment of God's restored realm, so, at his Resurrection, was that same expectation renewed. The abrupt ending serves a purpose. For the author of Mark, the scale of killing and destruction that the Romans were just then wreaking on Jerusalem and against God's chosen people was itself a revelation. With the world falling around him as he wrote, he could not have more eloquently conveyed the urgency of his conviction that into this cauldron Jesus himself, resurrected and victorious, was somehow about to step. "He has risen, he is not here," period. The period was the point.

In effect, the Gospel of Mark concludes the way it began—with Galilee. Recall that, unlike the other three Gospels, Mark offers no account of the origins of Jesus but is satisfied, in the opening chapter, simply to announce his arrival "from Nazareth of Galilee."[75] And note now that the young man in white, having announced, "He has risen, he is not here," goes on to say, "Tell his disciples and Peter that he is going before you to Galilee. There you will see him." Galilee. Beginning of story; end of story. We saw that Mark is plausibly understood as being addressed to troubled Jesus people in war-torn Galilee, and here the plausibility is redoubled. *The Resurrection of Jesus*, the author of Mark is telling his readers, *will be manifest in you.*

Precious Disappointment

Disappointed expectation is the single largest experience that shaped the religious imagination of Jesus people—and it did so not once, or twice, but constantly, across the decades after Jesus died. And that experience is uniformly overlooked by believers today as we try to understand where our faith came from. If Jesus was an apocalyptic preacher, announcing the approach of the last day, when God's unbroken commitment to Israel would be vindicated, imagine what a blow it was when, before that vindication was accomplished, Jesus suffered that ignominious death on the cross. It was this disappointment that the subsequent three Gospels, each with its consoling adjustment, sought to more completely reverse, but the disappointment was compelling all along.

When, by an ingenious—and profoundly Jewish—act of interpretation "in accordance with the Scriptures," the lifting up of Jesus on the hill at Golgotha was transformed into the lifting up of Jesus in the glory of Easter,[76] expectation was renewed. The followers of Jesus came quickly—and intensely—to believe that he was soon to return, to bring about the resurrection of all, according to the promise found in the handbook of Jewish self-understanding just then, the book of Daniel. As the first expectation was disappointed by the Roman execution, in 30 C.E., the second expectation was disappointed by the passage of time. A decade after the death of Jesus, in about the year 40, his failure to have returned by then in glory was the source of a demoralizing crisis of faith among Jesus people. They feared that only those who were alive when Jesus came back would participate in his triumph, but some of the most devoted had died already, and others would be dying soon. Many began to doubt that the return of Jesus was near. *Where is he?*

These preoccupations were addressed by the very first words

written in what became, once various texts were collected and "canonized," the New Testament. Its oldest text, dated to about 51, is Paul's First Letter to the Thessalonians. Paul's overriding purpose was to soothe the anguish of those whose loved ones had already died without having been exalted by the Lord's return: "And the dead in Christ will rise first," he wrote, an announcement of the primacy that would belong to the ones already being mourned. Only then did he attend to the others: "then we who are alive, who are left, shall be caught up together with them in the clouds to meet the Lord in the air." Note the explicit reference to the image from Daniel: the Son of Man riding on clouds. And the promise is not of a temporary resuscitation, but of eternal life: "and so we shall always be with the Lord. Therefore comfort one another with these words."[77] Paul was convinced that he and most others would still be alive when Jesus returned. Indeed, a decade later, by the time of his last letter, written in around 60 to the community in Rome, he was still feverishly insisting on it: "You know what hour it is, how it is full time now for you to wake from sleep. For salvation is nearer to us now than when we first believed; the night is far gone, the day is at hand."[78]

But where is he? By the time the author of Mark writes his account of the life of Jesus in 70, Paul, the tribune of imminence, is himself dead. And so are many others whose faith in the pending return of a glorified Jesus had been crushingly disappointed. Indeed, one can assume that such disappointment—and the ongoing absence of Jesus— was essential to whatever motivated the writing of the Gospel of Mark just then. Exactly as the first disappointment, the crucifixion, was overcome by an act of interpretation—Jesus understood to have been raised from the dead—so was the second disappointment transformed. The meaning of the problematic failure of Jesus to return was changed by finding a presence of Jesus in the community of those gathered to tell and hear his story. *Where is he? He is here, in the Gospel itself.*

Accomplished during the time of catastrophic war, this earliest iteration of the Gospel impulse was a version, again, of what the Jewish people, in their prophets, and in the editors, redactors, and authors of the Hebrew Bible, had done during the Babylonian War and exile. Returning to Jerusalem from exile, they found that the raided and wrecked Holy of Holies had been stripped vacant. God's house, the Temple, was unoccupied. In that absence, by means of an ingenious reinterpretation, the people found a new sense of intimacy with God, nurtured now by the whole *story* of the people, from Abraham and Moses forward—the Bible. The Word of God became a mode of God's presence.

The Gospel of Mark pulls off an astonishing—one wants almost to call it "trick." Drawing on Daniel, Mark portrays Jesus as a fevered apocalyptic, proclaiming the nearness of the reign of the Lord. But the Gospel does so *four decades after the fact,* inevitably changing the meaning of "nearness." Mark's readers and hearers knew very well that those who had heard Jesus preach were disappointed by his crucifixion, and that those who had preceded them in faith in the Resurrection were disappointed when the Kingdom did not come. Their deceased parents in the movement had been cheated of what they'd been promised. Mark's readers felt the bite of those disappointments themselves.

The Gospel invited them to change if not what they believed, then what it meant. And the Gospel did this not from outside the experience of those beleaguered Jesus people, but from within it. Mark was not an intervention, but a realization. After all, assuming that Mark's readers were stressed "followers of the Way" in Galilee, they had faithfully maintained some kind of expectation of Jesus through decades of adversity—adversity just now coming to a terrible head in war and civil war. They had done so through their gatherings, memories, and rituals—especially through some form of the breaking of the bread, an activity recalled as having rooted the interactions of

Jesus himself during his lifetime. In effect, the new form of Gospel narrative—a summing up of Jesus' life and meaning—gave expression to what had already turned out to be true for those who could not let go of their affection for him: that in their memorial gatherings themselves, over time, they sensed his presence. The Jesus people, that is, had already been living as though what they saw in Jesus of God were true. And reflecting on that experience, they began to come to the recognition that the way to make Jesus present, and God's realm actual, is to live as though it *were* true. As though the Kingdom, long expected there and then, were, in fact, here and now. *The absence of Jesus is the mode of his presence.*

The Gospel of Mark did not invent this mode, and did not complete it. The meaning of such a recognition had dawned upon believers only slowly. And that meaning would continue to show itself. Mark is, in effect, a marker. Matthew and Luke, Acts, and John would elaborate the recognition, and reinterpret it. But this new form—Gospel—was giving expression to the adaptation that Jesus people, drawing on their Jewish habit of mind, had already been making.

The letters of Paul, written one and two decades before Mark, are the prime example of that adaptation—a crucial, painstaking, slowly evolving reckoning with the first raw fact of the Jesus movement *as movement*: his failure to return. By helping his companions (a word derived from the Latin for "breaking bread with") deal with their disappointment in the failure of Jesus to return, Paul, in effect, prepared for the invention of Gospel, which brought about the return of Jesus *in language*.

In the New Testament, thirteen letters—"epistles"—bear Paul's name; at least seven can be attributed to him with certainty, and it is clear that among early Christians, these writings were circulated, read aloud, and made the centerpieces of gatherings. Without them, and without the transformed spirituality the writings both proposed and enabled, the Jesus movement, in light of the failure of its leader to fulfill expectations, might well have disappeared. Given the prime importance of Paul, we will return to him in a subsequent chapter.

But the irony in Paul's accomplishment is large, for even while he himself was insisting on the imminent return of the Lord, he was, in his brilliant and eloquent reflections on the Lord's meaning, equipping the believers for a life without that return. He was preaching the Resurrection, yes, but Paul offered a way of seeing the cross itself, without a resurrected victim, as a source of hope. Usually, Paul's interpretation of the crucifixion is explained in terms of Jesus' voluntary sacrifice that atoned for sins—a ransom, some mechanism that triggered a change in God's attitude toward a fallen creation. Jesus was the new Adam, whose saving act reversed the Fall of the old Adam—saving the baptized from the merciless judgment of God. Paul's rationales for the positive significance of the monstrous ignominy of the way Jesus died are nothing short of ingenious. But at bottom, they amount to Paul's version of the broader understanding to which the followers of Jesus came during the decades after his death. The courage, steadfast faith, and radical trust that defined how Jesus had died—and every account strikes those notes—brought into the open the full meaning of how he had lived. Only in the way his death enabled his followers to recognize something new in his life was it somehow "saving." All at once (an "instant" that might have taken years to unfold), the way Jesus died brought out the meaning of the way he'd lived. That meaning defined the Resurrection, and, as Paul insisted, without the Resurrection, the faith of Christians was in vain.

Emphasizing baptism, and the presence of the Spirit of God among the baptized, Paul gave a first expression to the spirituality of Christ's wholly unphysical presence in the community. He put into words the nascent experience of those who could not let go of Jesus. The way to make the longed-for Jesus present, and the way to make real the Kingdom of God Jesus preached, was to live *as though it were true*—here and now!

If forgiveness was God's attitude, it should also be the attitude of those forgiven. The truest sanctuary of God's love was the love of the members for one another. That love imbued every creature with dignity. Ethics, in Paul's vision, preceded doctrine, for only in the behavior of the baptized could the truth of the faith be seen. Thus, Paul established the moral standard against which members had to measure themselves, for they were members of nothing less than Christ, alive in the here and now of their presence with one another. This moral standard was more than a cult of the good deed; it was goodness itself, a sure sign of God's presence "in Christ." The disciples had seen that goodness not so much in what Jesus "did" as in the attitude he struck in every situation—and Paul, who never laid eyes on Jesus, *experienced* that attitude in his encounters with those who preceded him, and then accompanied him, in the movement. Taken, down through the centuries, as the great champion of the resurrected *physical* body of Jesus, Paul was, far more significantly, the author of the theologically more potent idea of the *mystical* body of Christ. "May your spirit and soul and body," he wrote, "be kept sound and blameless at the coming of our Lord Jesus Christ." Convinced of that eschatological coming in the short run, that is, Paul nevertheless invented ways of thinking and believing for the ever-postponed long run. Against all that invited them to lose heart, Paul helped the followers of Jesus to believe that "he who calls you is faithful."[79]

The Gospel writers may or may not have been intimately familiar with the specific letters of Paul, but they were surely influenced by the transformational attitudes reflected in those letters. The Gospel of Mark and subsequent Gospels built on such adaptation and changed meaning in the broad world of the Jesus communities. Bit by bit, people's understanding of the meaning of their faith—of their attachment to Jesus—was changing. How could it be otherwise? No matter who or where they were, it was simply no longer credible, de-cades on, to ask Jesus people to maintain an urgent expectation of apocalyptic deliverance, any day now.

The highly charged vision of Mark's apocalyptic Jesus owed more to the crisis unfolding in 70 than it did to any conviction the author of Mark could have had about the historical Jesus in the period be-fore and after 30, which had so clearly proven *not* to be the End Time. And one can plausibly propose that the point of the abrupt ending of Mark's Gospel, with the risen Jesus undefined in every way except by his destination, was that the actualities and troubles of Galilee were themselves, in 70, the boundaries of the Kingdom of God, *now* being ushered in.

Instead of merely longing for a fulfilling (and peaceful) future, Christians were called on to find the reign of God in the present (even tormented) moment. They were encouraged to shift their gaze, from the other world to this one. Eternal life is not what happens *then*, but what happens *now*. "Afterlife" and *this* life are inextricably intertwined. Such rejection of temporal oppositionalism—then ver-sus now—amounts to a transformation of the meaning of time. "Eternity" is an opening of *human perception*, not an endless stretch of hours, days, eras, and eons. Eternity is not time without end; it is not "time" at all. A vertical conception here overtakes a horizontal one. The call is to find the sacred in the *depth* of life, not the breadth or length of it.

The apocalyptic dualism that readily divided the good from the evil, typified by the preaching of John the Baptist, is nowhere in evi-dence in the Jesus of the Gospels, who associates with sinners and affirms the delights of ordinary life. Indeed, the break between Jesus and John the Baptist, which all four Gospels report, may be the great clue to what kind of apocalyptic figure Jesus was and what kind of Kingdom he preached.[80] We shall see more of the tension between John and Jesus below.

By the time the Gospels of Matthew and Luke are written, a decade or more after Mark, Jesus is still shown preaching the Kingdom of God, but he explicitly proclaims it as the living reality already present to those who have eyes to see: "The kingdom of God is not coming with signs to be observed; nor will they say, 'Lo, here it is!' or 'There!' for behold, the kingdom of God is in the midst of you."[81]

"The time is fulfilled," he declares, in effect, in both Matthew and Luke. The End Time has broken into present time. "Blessed are your eyes, for they see; and your ears, for they hear. Truly, I say to you, many prophets and righteous men longed to see what you see, and did not see it."[82]

So what we are tracking is an adjustment in the apocalyptic character of Jesus, which takes its original form from the book of Daniel. What began, perhaps with the historical Jesus himself, as a radical rejection of the present world in favor of a transformed world to be established by the history-ending act of God, had evolved across time—*because of time*—into an embrace of the present world as the realm to which God comes, not through an otherworldly divine intervention, but through the attitude taken by God's people, and through the faithful and compassionate acts that attitude inspires. However accounted for, this marks, in the words of the scholar James D. G. Dunn, "a decisive break with the apocalypticism of Jesus' time."[83] But it was a break made by Jews, in Jewish ways.

CHAPTER FOUR

Gospel Truth

Homo sapiens is the species that invents symbols in which to invest passion and authority, then forgets that symbols are inventions.

—Joyce Carol Oates[1]

The Meanings of Jesus

Skepticism flourishes less because science has been so good at debunking religion than because religion has declined to embrace scientific insight. Yet the famous conflict between science and religion need not have arisen. Arguments about the nature of evidence, and the modern use of the so-called scientific method as a weapon with which to bludgeon faith, spawned an inevitable defensiveness in believers, since evidence can never define the whole of belief. Science, meanwhile, seemed to insist that evidence was all. Religious people themselves, though, confused myth and fact in the way they read their scriptures, and they, too, began to insist on proofs with a literal-mindedness more appropriate to the laboratory than the sanctuary. Because of this muddle, those devoted to Jesus of Galilee ultimately made an unnecessary enemy of one whose very name most eloquently honors him: Galileo Galilei. The work at hand has been aiming at repair, in part by seeking to embody—for the sake of belief—the critical but self-transcending consciousness into which Galileo, a believer to the day he died, ushered the world.

Historical-mindedness—if you will, realism—is the case in point, defining the archaeology of faith we have undertaken here. One of the goals of digging into the past is to construct a satisfying faith that complies with modern history and science. The rational cosmology within which we all live is one reason for doing this, but—with Bonhoeffer's question as our fixed point—so is morality. There are *moral* consequences to the way we look at the world, and the catastrophes of the twentieth century warn us to be aware of that. How people live out what they claim to believe—that constitutes, for religion, the evidence that matters most.

Historical consciousness is, generally speaking, a modern phenomenon, even if its roots were in the linear notion of time that defined the biblical worldview. Once salvation history, from Genesis forward, came to be presented as a march of epochs, each one centered on one main covenant with God (Adam, Noah, Abraham, Jacob, Moses), and once that march was understood as aiming at an End Time culmination, the seeds of the historical mind-set were sown. The harvest came, though, in the eighteenth and nineteenth centuries, when history itself was understood as the realm in which all human meaning resides.[2]

Historical consciousness is distinguished from the so-called classicist worldview in its very attitude toward the character of human experience.[3] The former takes for granted that change through time is constant, contingent, and random; the latter assumes that the world is complete, ordered, and in harmony with God's unchanging purpose. Historical-mindedness begins with the situated, and seeks meaning; classicist thinking starts with abstract principles and applies them to situations.

The point here is not to track the conflict between two philosophical camps, but to see how the movement from classicism to historicism, unfolding in the West across the past three centuries, has only intermittently influenced religious awareness. That is the taproot of our faith problem today. The assumption of this work is that the Holocaust was an interruption in history, forcing Jews and Christians, in different ways, to reckon with a revolution in transcendental imagination. *History did this.* For Christians, the Roman Catholic Church's Second Vatican Council, referred to earlier, marks perhaps the defining moment in the change in consciousness—when mutations in Catholic and Christian theology began to occur.[4] The difference was succinctly caught by the Vatican II–era Jesuit Bernard Lonergan, writing in his study of Jesus Christ, "Where earlier history was a matter of believing testimony, contemporary history is a matter of understanding evidence."[5] Most blatantly, historic evidence of Christian anti-Semitism led to reexaminations of believing testimony that had undercut, for example, the Jewishness of Jesus Christ. The present work is an instance of that reexamination.

Among Jews, the distinction between past and present worldviews is equally decisive, and though this shift gained momentum through the nineteenth century, it, too, was pushed to mandatory climax by the Holocaust. "The emergence of historical consciousness in modern Judaism," as a leading Jewish thinker writes, "comprises a fundamental change in mentality . . . Historical thinking facilitated the urgent and agonizing effort to rethink the nature of Judaism."[6] This revolution in consciousness, actually, should not be so startling for Christianity and Judaism, since, unlike many religions tethered to myth, both are rooted in history itself. Israel and Jesus *happened*. Therefore, precisely in upholding those beliefs for a new era, both traditions should welcome investigations of history as what they have become in the modern era: a scientific discipline. The instruments of measuring history may lack the precision of those in, say, physics or biology, yet assertions about the past can be tested—and they must be. That does not mean that texts of bygone eras are to be read literally, as both fundamentalist believers and rationalist debunkers like to do—the one to shore up, the other to tear down. Text must always be in context, which necessarily implies more than the investigating eye can see. Even while submitting to science, that is, faith also takes for granted that, in Pascal's famous words, "the heart has its reasons which reason does not know. We feel it in a thousand things."[7] There is evidence to be tested, but in accounting for belief, there is also testimony that comes with its own authority. As science knows very well yet often forgets, every truth is partial.

The main idea of this book is an analogy, and it is rooted, finally, in history: if the Nazi war against the Jews is the second hinge on which a contemporary understanding of Jesus Christ must turn, the Roman War against the Jews, which killed Jesus, is the first. This is not to reduce genocide against the Jewish people to a mere symbol or marker in time; the Holocaust, like the Roman War long before it, was no mere metaphor. It was real, with real men, women, and children suffering excruciating pain—millions of them, yet each one as an individual. That harsh fact of history must remain the ground of our reflection, even as we drop back in time from the Holocaust to the Roman War, searching out meanings and confronting consequences. Meanings and consequences for the faith.

To review, in brief: The earliest traditions about Jesus, collections of his sayings, memories of his acts, and accounts of his meaning were all stimulated by the shock of his disappearance. "Those who had in the first place come to love him," as Josephus put it, "did not give up their affection for him."[8] They gathered to speak about him. Soon, and over decades, traditions thickened, layer building upon layer. The layers consisted of narratives drawn from the Hebrew Bible and applied to Jesus; hymns and ritualized confessions of faith; and, perhaps, a first written document known as "Q," dating to the 50s but now lost. Such were multifaceted *Jewish* responses to Jesus' failure to return.

Those who loved him began to acclaim him, and, perhaps, to pray to him. The Gospels, beginning with Mark, were fuller acts of memory and imagination that used those earlier adaptations as raw material in responding to yet another stage in the developing significance of Jesus. The main notes of that new situation were, as we saw, the crisis of Rome's brute escalation of violence beginning in the late 60s; the destruction of the Temple in 70; the related civil wars among Jews; and, compounding all of this, the fact that those who, "in the first place," had known and loved Jesus were dying off, or already dead.

Those war traumas are our useful focusing lens through which to watch how the Jesus people, across a vast geography, reached the point where the central event of faith was not Jesus of Nazareth but Jesus of the Gospel. We start with Jesus as historical figure, tracking forward to Jesus as "Christ" of Israel, to Jesus as somehow divine, to Jesus as "raised" by God "in accordance with the Scriptures," to the invention of a narrative form—Gospel—that made real a community of the baptized, which itself embodied an intensified presence of the one known by then as Jesus the Lord. The "Jesus of history" remains essential, but this "process of history"—call it a development of doctrine[9]—is the only way those of us coming later, and much later, can know Jesus. And we have emphasized how all of this, against common Christian assumptions, had a *Jewish* character. The Gospel, expressing Jewish understanding and hope, was a Jewish invention.

The movement found its primal incitement in the *apocalypse soon* vision of Daniel, perhaps first given expression by Jesus of Nazareth himself, at least in the time he associated with the firmly apocalyptic John the Baptist. Then, imminent End Time fervor stamped the disciples of Jesus, especially Paul, whose knowledge of Jesus was mediated and mystical, not direct. There was always continuity between the historical Jesus and the interpreted Jesus, but the figures were not the same and occupied different places in time.

Then, this unfolding exercise of Jewish religious imagination came to crisis with the catastrophic Roman assault on Jerusalem. Because that destruction, centered on the torching of the Temple, was destruction of the very order of Jewish meaning, it absolutely required a response from surviving Jews. That was especially true among the Jesus people—still ostensibly Jewish—whose faith in the return of Jesus their Lord was inevitably shaken. For them, it is plausible to assert, the Rome-inflicted disaster was what called forth *just then* the first Gospel, with its renewed apocalyptic emphasis. *He is coming!*

This ingenious response to a contingent historical event, ironically, might—I'm now speculating, but still with plausibility—have rescued the Jesus movement altogether, precisely by forcing a wholly original interpretation of what apocalypse actually entails. It gave the movement a distinct identity. Successive *re*interpretations, each generated by new situations, required adaptations in the meanings of Jesus: rabbi, prophet, Son of Man, Son of God, Christ, God. These meanings overlapped, coexisted, or competed in the varied communities where Jesus people found themselves, but they uniformly required further adjustments in the meanings of what it was to be Jewish, to be a human being, to be bound by time, to imagine the transcendent, and to live in hope.

This complex, drawn-out amalgamation of experiences, both received and created, makes available, to repeat, not Jesus of Nazareth but the Jesus of the Gospel. It seems certain from historical research that Jesus of Nazareth preached the Kingdom of God, and it is almost certain that he did so as some kind of eschatological apocalyptist, proclaiming that God's End Time intervention in history for the restoration of Israel was near at hand. But once Jesus was gone, every passing day on which that divine intervention did not occur added weight to the pressures that brought about a new interpretation.

And as the Jesus movement spread out from war-torn Judea and Galilee, borne by men and women who felt compelled to tell his hopeful story, conditions in a wide variety of locations around the Mediterranean shaped the consciousness of Jesus people in different ways. This led diverse communities to give emphasis to different aspects of his meaning: Rome in Italy, Corinth in Greece, Alexandria in Egypt, Caesarea in Palestine, Antioch in Syria—a constellation of particular human experiences. The itinerants and migrants in the faith, circumstantially so different and far from "one Church" at this point, were nevertheless bound by a surpassing unity tied to the remembered Nazarene. Always, the core of Jesus' proclamation of the Kingdom was retained: that God wills an end to suffering, and God's power can be trusted to bring that end about within our span of history. No wonder the preaching took hold wherever humans suffered.

If, by the year 70, the meaning of Jesus' original preaching of the Kingdom had necessarily changed, by 100, when the Gospel of John was composed, it had changed again. Other texts were being composed about Jesus beyond those that were eventually collected as the New Testament "canon."[10] The retrieval of a sustainable faith for *our* time and place—the aim of this book—must reckon with the prime fact that the times and places of the early Jesus people are what shaped *their* faith. Twenty-first-century Christians, therefore, make our first mistake when we go in search of the meaning of Jesus Christ, because there are *meanings*.

The second mistake, in reading the invented meanings of Jesus, is forgetting that *they are invented*. The largest point is that the empirically identifiable Jesus, focus of historians' quest, and the interpreted Jesus of the Gospels, focus of theologians' contemplation, are *not the same Jesus*. Historical consciousness and theological awareness both acknowledge the fact that the Gospels (post–death and Resurrection, post–failure to return, post–Temple destruction, and post–dispersal from Palestine) attributed meanings to Jesus that he simply could not have embraced himself. Furthermore, later readers of the Gospels, not intimately acquainted with the Gospels' mode of composition, went on to attribute meanings *to the Gospels* that the Gospel writers did not intend.

This is because, through history and the imaginative adaptations it required, the faith had entered the realm of *literary* meaning. "It is proper to a literary classic," as the scholar Jack Miles writes, "that it touch readers generation after generation, century after century, in ways that transcend the intentions of the originating author."[11] The Gospels, taken together as the Gospel, constitute just such a literary classic—for better and for worse. As literature, the Gospel's relation to historical "fact" is transformed, a departure after which "evidence" properly weighs less than "testimony."

The single most obvious—and damaging—instance of this sort of transformed meaning across generations is the portrait of Jesus, drawn in the thick of intra-Jewish civil war, as a man in religious, and even ontological, conflict with "the Jews," as if he were not one of them. In keeping one eye on that distortion, and the moral imperative to correct it, we keep the other eye on the recovery of a disarmed faith, a usable Jesus, Christ actually.

Symbol of God

We have already emphasized that populations of the past—itself a foreign country—had mind-sets, worldviews, and assumptions about existence that profoundly differed from ours—and modern awareness of that, what we are calling historical consciousness, may itself be the prime difference that sets us apart from them. Those who wrote the Christian creeds in the third and fourth centuries probably had little understanding of the ways in which the sacred texts before them were composed, and scant notion of the varied situations out of which the texts came. This is not to say that the first Christians, or their ancient successors, were readily fooled in ways we are not; nor is it to denigrate their intelligence or native wisdom. After all, those who assembled the canon of the New Testament apparently were not troubled by the clear and numerous ways the four Gospels factually contradict one another. So "fact" was not necessarily a more determinative criterion of Gospel truth for them than it is for us.

But the first followers of Jesus, like Jesus himself, took for granted the pre-Copernican cosmos, with Earth at its center, and the human person as the moral and physical pinnacle of creation. In this overarching worldview, we see the *religious* meaning of the pre-historical mind-set. Jesus and his followers assumed that the world had been made in a matter of days in the not so distant past, and that humans descended from a single man and a single woman, whose moral choice was decisive for all of history. Indeed, that choice—the Fall—meant that the Creator God was thereafter required to become a Savior God, to redeem the world that had removed itself from His favor. In this project of redemption, God was opposed by personified forces of evil—Satan and his legions—who not only seduced humans into sin, but caused illness and psychological pathology, to say nothing of the havoc continually wreaked on God's chosen ones by successive imperial oppressors.

Ancient people, on the other hand, were at home with what we call metaphor in ways that we moderns (or postmoderns) are not. To be sure, we value poetry today, the native terrain of metaphor, but as something apart—and, frankly, as something of, at most, ornamental value.[12] We know the benefits of living after Copernicus and Galileo, but here, surely, is an impoverishment. The most casual visit to any American university or perusal of any government budget will lay bare the stepchild status of the creative arts, and, lately, of the humanities themselves. The post-Enlightenment concentration on discernible fact, empirical evidence, and the reductionist methods of rationalism have hollowed out the imagination in all sorts of ways. A naive belief in supernatural powers has been dispelled, thankfully, but scientific naturalism has proven incapable of accounting for a whole range of human experiences, from simple self-awareness to love.

Momentously for our purposes, this disenchantment hinders our capacities either to enter into the actual world of the Gospel or, once there, to understand its language as addressed meaningfully to the historically minded. While the writers and first readers of the New Testament texts knew what was "real" as well as humans ever do, they took for granted the way in which "reality" was spacious enough to accommodate what we would call the symbolic. The "real" and the "symbolic," that is, were neither contradictory nor condemned to exist in different—oppositional—orders.

Thus, those who crucially portrayed Jesus, with images drawn from the book of Daniel, as flying through the air, a figure coming and going on clouds, knew very well that the realm into which Jesus had been "lifted up" was not "the sky." They might not have known Newton's law, but the effects of gravity were as fixed in the deep past as they are now. If I am certain—and I am—that the pull of gravity on Earth is absolute in my own time, I know with certainty that the pull of gravity was absolute in the time of Jesus. It was the same Earth, spinning on its axis, at the mercy of the same laws of nature. Son of Man or not, Jesus did not come and go on clouds. If he was said to have done so, then those doing the saying meant something else.[13] So, too, with their use of apocalyptic images. They might have anticipated some kind of restoration of the temporal power of the kingdom of Israel, but, in contrast to common twenty-first-century associations with the apocalypse, "there is virtually no evidence that Jews were expecting the end of the space-time universe,"[14] as the scholar N. T. Wright asserted. Consistent with their worldview, the ancients were as at home in the realm of creative expression as we are, or more so. To use Wright's phrase, they "knew a good metaphor when they saw one."[15] But how they thought of the images they used, like the relationship of those images to sense perception, is impossible for us to know precisely.

Narratives might have developed fairly soon after the death of

Jesus that were centered on accounts of his resurrected bodily appearances, and even argued for their bodiliness, as in the "doubting Thomas" story.[16] But the significance of these accounts adheres more in narrative than in bodiliness. The meaning, not the metaphysics, much less the physics, was the point. Whether the Resurrection was "historical" or not, there is no doubt that those who followed Jesus had a historical experience of his being raised from the dead by God. What that was, we cannot know, even if, taking our own scientific worldview seriously, we can be certain that it was not bodily *resuscitation*. This principle of modesty applies to all biblical apparitions, from the "going through" the Red Sea to the "going up" from the tomb. The question is: what is the "something else" to which these images point?

The upward agility of unwinged creatures was, as it still is, symbolic language, but for ancients, assuming the classicist worldview, its being symbolic was no denigration. The question of whether to take "literally" the description of Jesus in flight, token of what makes him "Christ," is a decidedly modern one. The assumption that "real" means "literal" is rooted in a post-Enlightenment valuing of the measured over the immeasurable, of physics over metaphysics, and of everything over metaphor. When the literary realm and the historical realm overlap, how images are used and understood changes through time. Thus, it is the most natural thing in the world for a twenty-first-century reader to take images and incidents differently from readers in the nineteenth century, the fifteenth, the eighth, the third, or, for that matter, the first. Even if Saint Paul took the images he used "literally"—and it is not clear that he did—that does not mean we must.

Stretching toward an appreciation of the ancient mind-set reminds us not to take for granted, or leave unexamined, our modern modes of interpretation. They are not as cut-and-dried as we usually think. The contemporary impoverishment of excessive literalism, for example, can belong as much to religious zealots as to antireligious scientists. The Catholic novelist Flannery O'Connor famously said of the "real presence" of Christ in the consecrated bread of the Eucharist, "Well, if it's a symbol, to hell with it."[17] "Mere" symbol is what she meant. O'Connor, in offering an account of her statement, describes the "very shaky voice" with which she made her profession of faith in the *literal* character of the real presence of Christ in the bread. The shakiness may be revealing, because O'Connor, a genius fiction writer, had to know of the radical *reality* of her fictions. In fact, O'Connor's dismissal of the symbolic was a response to the prior dismissal of her conversant, a lapsed Catholic who had used the term "symbolic" in the reductionist, modern way. The point, though, is that even a highly sensitive believer, whose very métier was metaphor, could be trapped in this denigration of metaphor. Symbol and metaphor, which are equivalent terms in this context, define the only language that can be used of God, who is beyond all "literalist," and certainly scientific, expression.

Reflecting a historically minded view, the contemporary Jesuit theologian Roger Haight tellingly entitled his major work of Christology *Jesus: Symbol of God*. He later wrote, "Some may prefer the term 'sacrament' over 'symbol.' I take them as equivalent in the religious domain."[18] All religious language is symbolic language. A symbol is not identical to the thing symbolized, but neither is it apart from it. A symbol both is and is not what it points to—a complexity of relatedness familiar to Catholics whose religious imaginations glory in sacramental symbols. Flannery O'Connor could not conceivably have said of the Eucharist, "Well, if it's a sacrament, to hell with it." No one who receives Communion—the body of Christ—imagines for a moment that chewing the consecrated bread is chewing the flesh of a human being. Catholicism is not cannibalism. By definition, the communicant has entered the realm of symbol. And that is true, equally by definition, of those who read the New Testament accounts of the miracles of Jesus. Consecrated bread both is and is not the body of Christ. The miracles Jesus performed both did and did not "happen." These are paradoxes, not contradictions, and they are products of the analogical imagination, like, well, parables. Indeed, one scholar explicitly sees the Gospel miracle accounts as "screaming parable," and takes them as parables rather than as historical events.[19] For example, the two stories known as the feeding of the multitudes are an obvious call by Jesus for the community to feed the hungry.[20]

The point, for a modern reader, is not to debunk miracles, but to enter into their meaning. Enlightenment thinkers—typified, say, by David Hume, who did gleefully debunk miracles[21]—held that the material world is a closed system in which every measurable occurrence is explained by another measurable occurrence. Only sense data can be credited as real. Everything that happens must occur within the laws of nature. But, against the Enlightenment's own cardinal rule, such assertions come not from evidence, but from a prior metaphysics of materialism, which is rife with unexamined assumptions about "nature." One needn't be a supernaturalist to regard this as a shallow reduction of the spacious world of human experience, which can include, for example, untestable psychological influences on physical occurrences.[22] It is possible to defend many of the reported miracles of Jesus by appealing to such subjective, merely mental assessments, as if the "curing" Jesus did is better understood as "healing." Not that he actually made the blind to see, but that he enabled the blind, and the social surround, to feel better—less guilty, less condemning—about the infirmity.[23]

But this, too, misses the point of New Testament miracle accounts. It is fruitless and misleading to measure them against *any* kind of scientific standard. The miracles live in the realm of poetry, not of science. The main mistake Christians make, though, is in clinging to Jesus as some kind of wonder worker, with his capacity to

break the "laws of nature" being *proof of divinity*. Divinity had nothing to do with it. Ancient Jewish cosmology allowed for the attribution to some charismatic but wholly human figures of the power to
heal and work wonders. For such figures, miracle working was not
exceptional, but typical. Once again, Christian amnesia on this point
wrongly separates Jesus from his Jewish milieu.[24]

It is impossible for us, bound by a very different cosmology, to
know what kinds of events lay behind reports of such activity, and it
misleads us to obsess about "miracles" as essential to the meaning of
Jesus. Instead of focusing on his working of wonders, a contemporary
person does better to keep the emphasis where Jesus himself put it:
on his resistance to suffering. "The blind receive their sight and the
lame walk . . . the poor have good news preached to them."[25] Jesus'
acts of healing and curing, whatever else they were, were signals of
the kind of God he was preaching, a God who opposes misery and,
ultimately, will end it. The "miracles," therefore, were important not
in themselves but as symbols. Every symbol points beyond itself.
More important, the symbols of religion—and here is what skeptics
and zealots alike miss—participate in the transcendent reality of
what they point to. Meaning is itself an opening to God.

In thinking of Jesus, perhaps the retrieval most urgently needed,
for that matter, is of the fact that, in his lifetime, Jesus pointed to
God, not to himself. What little is known for certain of the historical
Jesus is based on this: he obsessively proclaimed the One whom he
called Father. As the power of Jesus' witness took hold and a link was
drawn between him and the One whom he preached, Jesus would be
moved to the center of the faith of his followers. Jesus-centeredness
has defined the essence of Christian piety for most of two millennia,
with innumerable benefits. But it was not that way at first.

Whatever the complications of text and the difficulty of getting
behind them to the historical Jesus, the God whom Jesus preached
comes through in the Gospels loud and clear. Jesus preached a God

at home with human complexity, a God undefeated by death, a God whose love for creation is prodigal. Asked to describe the Holy One, Jesus told the story of the father whose bond with his son, no matter the son's unworthiness, was unbreakable. The story was an echo of the prophets' account, again and again, of Yahweh's refusal to allow an unfaithful Israel to walk away from the covenant. Of all ties, this tie is unbreakable. The entire story of Jesus—not just its images and parables—is symbolic of this mystery. A profoundly Jewish mystery.

The life and death of Jesus are not the *mechanism* of redemption at last attained, but the *signal* that redemption is the permanent ground of being. No mechanism of change is necessary. The Gospels, taking written form, again, beginning in about 70, represent the overt recognition of what had already been true for some time—that the one being awaited in the future is already here in the present. The story of Jesus is told to reflect not what it was in 30, but what remains with us. And what Jesus lays bare in this story is revelation about God—about the way God has always been. God is the prodigal Father whose love was never withdrawn from the wayward son, despite the son's certainty that the father's love was long gone.

Humans are ever like the son, imagining their doom only because, in strict justice, they deserve it. Justice is an essential element of the divine economy; otherwise, we would be too easily reconciled to the human capacity for betrayal, and even atrocity. But justice is not the whole story, or even the main one. What humans cannot imagine is that, to the merciful God, just deserts are not the point. God is the father forever prepared to rush out in greeting, with the fatted calf prepared for the feast. It is not God's mind that needs to be changed, therefore, but the self-condemning human being's. Salvation, Jesus says, is the recognition of this God as the only God. The favor of the God who created us in the first place is unchanged. Creation is all the redemption we need. Because this recognition happens *now*, hope moves from the future to the present.

Because Jesus' purpose is to reveal that salvation has always already happened, Jesus' *not returning* is essential to his revelation. If he had come back in glory, it would be *his* glory we would see, when what he wants us to see is *ours*. We are repeating here the ancient pattern of Jews finding in God's absence God's presence. When, at last, the revelation takes and, in the mess of our apparently unredeemed lives, we see the love of God for the permanent redemption it is, we see in the same moment that, *in this,* Jesus is present. This is the return that matters.

Such is the content of an eschatology that has been "realized." The followers of Jesus came to the recognition only gradually, by remembering how he lived but also by seeing the continuity between how he lived and how he died. All accounts agree that in his last days and hours Jesus took on a courage, a calm, a trust, and a love. The accounts agree, too, that even from a distance, his quite agitated followers saw it—the grandeur of attitude. This demeanor of Jesus as he faced death is the one undisputed "fact" that can be assumed from the various conflicting accounts and interpretations of his Passion.[26] His followers' memory of Jesus so conducting himself in a plight of such extremity enabled them to behold afresh the courage, calm, trust, and love that had marked him throughout the entire time he was with them in Galilee and Judea. Only in that recognition of its wholeness—the promise of wholeness to all—was his death, for them, salvific.

Not only did the brutality of the crucifixion, against every Roman expectation, *not* undo the meaning of Jesus' life; his death on the cross brought that meaning to consummation. The rescue of *meaning* was the unimagined reversal. The new life that came to the Jesus people went far beyond the trick of a physical resuscitation. We saw that Saint Paul wrote that the faith is vain unless Jesus is raised.[27] Whatever that meant to Paul, it means to us that Jesus had made God present as salvation—by how he lived and how he died. The Resurrection is the symbol for that momentous recognition.

The Gospel writers gave expression to this recognition "in accordance with the Scriptures," drawing on the images, especially, of the book of Daniel. In Boyarin's account, "A people had been for centuries talking about, thinking about and reading about a new king, a son of David, who would come to redeem them from Seleucid and then Roman oppression, and they had come to think of that king as a second, younger, divine figure on the basis of the book of Daniel's reflection of that very ancient tradition. So they were persuaded to see in Jesus of Nazareth the one whom they had expected to come: the Messiah, the Christ."[28] His death, instead of obliterating this conviction, confirmed it. A man who might have been forgotten, even if he were an exceptional man and wonder worker, was acclaimed as more than that.

The first-century air was full of Jewish harmonies that carried the notes struck by Jesus—all of it the music of the God of Israel. Because the followers of Jesus were so predisposed, they could transform his defeat into triumph—a Jewish victory. Because the conclusion of exaltation fulfilled a two-hundred-year-old saga, the story was already preset to end with the transcendent metaphors of Jesus being raised, coming on the clouds, and participating in divinity as the Son of Man. At last, with stunning clarity, the pieces of the narrative fell together. Gospel.

Camera in the Tomb

We should pause here to insert a cautionary note. Only by this historical process of interpretation and reinterpretation, always "in accordance with" the Jewish interpretive tradition, was the death of Jesus turned into a positive event. At the moment of its occurring, those who loved Jesus were surely correct to perceive the crucifixion as horror pure and simple. There was no conceivable way it could have been willed by God. But in search of meaning over time, they

found it possible—then necessary—to think of Jesus' death as somehow redemptive. Tropes of sacrifice, associations with the lamb of
Passover, an economy of atonement—these are examples of structures
of thought, embedded in Jewish experience, that enabled Jesus people
to come to the startling transformation—a conviction, in John's
terms—that the "lifting up" on the cross was a "lifting up" to glory,
accomplished by God for the sake of humans.

This positive after-the-fact invention of new meaning became perverted when Christians began to imagine that God had wanted—or
needed—the crucifixion in the first place. God became reimagined,
then, as a heavenly sadist who could turn in rage against the humanity He had created, and as a heavenly legalist whose offended divinity
could be appeased only by a divine sacrifice. The redemption of the
fallen world could thus be accomplished only by using the tormented
body of His beloved son as a ransom paid—not to the devil, as the
first Christians had it,[29] but to God Himself. Critical history, which
shows how far this is from the God preached by Jesus, is the antidote
to such poisonous theology.[30]

The followers of Jesus, through the feats of interpretation we have
tracked, entered a far more spacious realm of consciousness than
mere expectation. Once the narrative jelled, their former anxiety
about the return of Jesus fell away. Time was reconfigured, and so
was space. History and nature, that is, took on different meanings.
Words, quickening what they spoke of, took on transcendent
significance—as Word. Water was holy. Bread and wine pointed beyond themselves to a nourishment that would not end. The creative I
AM of God beat as a pulse in every heart, and would not stop when
the heart itself was stilled. The Kingdom of God is *here.*

So Mark was first to give complete expression to this good news.
The author did so by rendering Jesus through his teaching, parables,
and deeds and his ultimate fate. Indeed, the arrowlike journey to that
fate gives the Gospel of Mark its structure—a road story to Jeru-

salem. Miracles and the suffering of the just were frames within which Mark drew his portraits, depending especially on the Hebrew prophets as interpretative sources. Suffering was the precondition of a better world. But, as we saw, the press of terrible events *as the author was writing* made it natural for him to offer an emphatically apocalyptic Jesus. *His* suffering was what offered hope to a decimated people.

Yet, in contrast to other apocalyptic works, like Daniel and the book of Revelation, Mark's Gospel is unrelentingly levelheaded, a story starkly told in an objective mode. The apocalypse as rendered here, especially in the blistering thirteenth chapter, is not the whole story. Mark offers more than a hint of a coming transformation of eschatological longing; he offers the *start* of the transformation. If exotic details and dramatic events are rendered, it is wholly without the usual apocalyptic appeals to fantasy. As noted, even the briefly sketched report of Jesus' Resurrection at the end of the Gospel is offered with a restrained plausibility approaching literary realism.[31] This almost journalistic understatement, offered at a time of massive social upheaval, must itself have cut through the hysteria, panic, and loss of faith that defined the lives of Mark's first readers. With what relief and wonder must the pages of this text have been copied and passed from one war-weary Jew to another. The Gospel writer, for his part, could have had no idea what that "copying and passing" would lead to—the scrutinizing and decoding of an unimaginable hyperscholarship across the centuries. Taken as belonging for all time to the open future, the Gospel was written first for a troubled present. There is no such thing as timeless faith.

Mark's purpose was threefold. The author aimed to relate the story of Jesus in a way that was essentially faithful to what, by his time, was the living tradition of the community's resources of memory, collected sayings, and interpreted scriptures. He sought to address meaningfully the actual situation of his readers, which, as we have seen, was riddled with all the anguish, fear, and despair that went with Rome's horrible war, and the consequent conflict with fellow Jews. And he wanted to offer ways to live more humanly, bravely, and compassionately in such circumstances, mainly through a call to discipleship.[32] What the author of Mark was doing, I aim to do here. Tradition, meaning, and relevance to life are my three touchstones. If my readers live in a post-Easter world, within a post-Temple religion, and in a situation defined by the physical absence of Jesus Christ—so did Mark's readers. That means we and they, for all that separates us, stand on the same ground.

But there *is* an enormous difference between twenty-first-century believers and those of the first century—and that has to do with the radically altered cosmology of which we have already taken note. What might have been possible for Mark and his readers—perhaps taking the poetic language of Daniel, for example, as descriptions of physical and metaphysical events—is impossible for me. Biology, chemistry, and physics cannot be kept at the door of this inquiry into Jesus Christ, outside, un–referred to. Like every inquiry, this one is defined by the knowledge of its own time.

But science has not changed people altogether—not even scientists. Humans are always making up myths to account for their experience, then losing hold of the fact that the myths are made up. That forgetfulness has been a bane of religion in a fact-obsessed modernity, when, because of science's own unacknowledged myths, the mythical began to be taken as trivial, or superstitious, or untrue.

But the classicist mind-set of the ancient world, what the materialists set out to overturn, was not ignorant. The idea that Christians, from a very early time, might have taken—as we would say—*literally* the mythic and poetic expressions of Resurrection accounts should give us pause today. Did the Jesus movement, and then the Church, make, in the words of one scholar, "a vast theological mistake"?[33] Or is it that, within the confines of the only worldview available to them, the assumptions they made about God's interventions in nature, time, and human awareness were wholly reasonable? Again, the point is less about what the miracles entailed than what they meant.

And speaking of miracles, if a Christian today came upon a high-tech Qumran where first-century DVDs were stored, what then? If one of the DVDs held the visual record of what unfolded across the crucial three days in front of the wide-angle lens of a camera mounted on the wall of the tomb of Jesus—the ultimate security camera—and the video recording showed no revivification of Jesus' corpse, would the Christian's faith collapse? Would a camera, for that matter, have captured *any* of the Resurrection appearances of Jesus? Of course not, since those appearances were addressed not to a machine, but to faith.[34]

Apart

"For Jesus Christ was a Jew." Bonhoeffer's watchword is the blade of purification required of Christians after the events that transformed the German pastor from witness to conspirator. This book aims to be such purification.

As is obvious by now, I am seeking, in Bonhoeffer's word, the "actual" meaning of Jesus Christ by peering through the narrow lens that Bonhoeffer held up: the Jewishness of Jesus Christ. I acknowledge here that a certain distortion follows from such a focus. But distortion in such an effort is inevitable, and all Jesus scholarship shows that. The myriad "Jesuses" put forth by a plethora of recent books and articles include the zealot, the revolutionary, the itinerant preacher, the wonder worker, the prophet, the healer, and the tribune of the end of the world. As the theologian Elisabeth Schüssler Fiorenza comments, "Scholars inescapably fashion the Historical-Jesus in their own image and likeness ... Any presentation of Jesus—scientific or otherwise—must therefore acknowledge that it is a

'reconstruction,' and open up its critical methods, rhetorical interests, and reconstructive models to critical inspection and public scru-
tiny."[35] My interest, as a believing Christian, is to expose the deep
ways—far deeper than the "Christ killer" slander—in which Christology itself has been, in a classic phrase, "the left hand of anti-
Semitism."[36] My critical method consists in measuring the effects of
beliefs on the beliefs' political and social consequences. My reconstruction aims at a retrieval of Jesus as a figure of true peace and authentic justice. The key to all of this is not to eliminate Christ the
divine, but to maintain the Jewishness of "Jesus" *and* of "Christ."

Thus, Jewishness defined our rereading of the story of Jesus of
Nazareth, and Jewishness relocated our understanding of how Jesus
came to be taken as "Christ," and even as somehow God. Jewishness
informed the acts of text-inspired interpretation (Midrash) that led
to the New Testament. Jewishness now defines the last act of the tragedy, as "Jesus people" turned into the Christian "Church," which
turned Jewishness into the dark heart of Christian hatred.

The ground of this story is Jewish refusal—*rooted in Jewishness*—
to yield to Rome. Christian memory of an overriding Roman culpability is blurred at the start (when at the very birth of Jesus, in
Matthew, Jewish Herod's slaughter of uncounted innocents is emphasized,[37] while the simultaneous, historical Roman crucifixion of
more than a thousand Jews is un–referred to) and effectively comes
to an end with the crucifixion of Jesus thirty years later. Even that
trauma is only half-remembered—a crime into which the reluctant
Pilate is said to have been pushed by a bloodthirsty crowd. But historical research tells us that there was nothing reluctant about Pilate's aggressions, or those of the Roman petty tyrants who succeeded
him across an entire century. If one were to read only what comes
down to us as the New Testament, very little of the *actuality* of social,
political, and military events of that era would come through.

We saw earlier that the catastrophic war of 68–70 was followed by further outbreaks of brute violence in 115 and 132. Hadrian's attempts to squelch Judaism—outlawing circumcision and Torah study in 117, and Sabbath observance in 129—were simply not to be tolerated by the Jews. The steady resistance of Zealots ballooned, with these blasphemous provocations, into full-blown Jewish rebellion.

The Jesus people, as we saw, were generally among those Jews who removed themselves from the suicidal confrontation with Vespasian's legions in 70, which was why, like the equally unzealous rabbis who fled to Yavne, on the coast of Palestine, they and their movement survived at all. In the decades after the destruction of Jerusalem, those Jews around the Mediterranean who revered Jesus came into a second-stage maturity as a distinct network of Jewish communities, which included a number of non-Jews, the so-called Gentiles. How precisely Gentiles attached themselves to the mainly Jewish Jesus people was contentious, as reflected earlier in the letters of Paul, but compromise toward consensus was in the making.

In the years after 70, the Gospels and other foundational texts gave expression, among Christians, to an increasingly cohesive post-Temple identity, a version of the process that the Yavne rabbis and their followers were undergoing in the same period. For all the contention between them, the two groups continued to overlap, and, even as they set off on separate paths, they influenced each other far more than later Jews and Christians would recall.[38]

Followers of Jesus were almost everywhere, but they remained concentrated in Galilee. Like other Jews, some returned to war-torn Judea after 70, and to the environs of the ruined Jerusalem. Like their ancestors, they were no more willing to forget Zion than to stop playing the harp. Still, Jesus people continued to distance themselves from the open rebellion that could be counted on to spark Rome's wrath. Most decisively, the final draft of their narrative about the life and death of Jesus, enshrined in all four canonical Gospels and completed by the early second century, insisted that Jesus had not been an enemy of Rome, despite his having been executed as precisely that.[39] This impulse, grounded in the biographical fact that Jesus was not a revolutionary Zealot, was no doubt reinforced by a simple wish to avoid being hunted down, murdered, or enslaved. With Rome's malfeasance downplayed, the dramatic roles of antagonist and archvillain in the Gospel narratives were reserved, respectively, for the Yavne progenitors (the Pharisees) and the Jewish high priests—a caste that, by the time of the writing, had ceased to exist with the Temple destruction. Alas, these portraits were the basis of what would be taken as the Gospel's anti-Jewish slant.

But Jesus people, as Jews, actually remained under constant threat from Rome. Their detachment from open rebellion did not mean that they were in any way friendly to the empire. They were appalled by its brutality. That becomes clear from the text that, after the Gospels, does more to brace the New Testament imagination than any other. The book of Revelation, appearing in the Christian Bible's order as the last book of the New Testament, brings to a fevered pitch the apocalyptic impulse that, with the book of Daniel, had early defined the understanding of Jesus as the one who would liberate Israel from its oppressors. Images, motifs, and tones found in Daniel— beasts, the Ancient One enthroned, the Son of Man on clouds— abound in Revelation, and so does the hallucinatory excess.

Also known as Apocalypse, the book was, despite its placement in the Bible, not the last of the New Testament texts to be composed. It most likely dates to the 90s, the work of an anonymous writer, probably in Asia Minor, although the text identifies the author as "John," writing on the Aegean island of Patmos.[40] It is plausible to assume that the author was a refugee from the destruction of Jerusalem, still very much feeling the threat of Roman assault and the dislocation of Jewish loss. He was writing not a wildly imagined future forecast, as Christians usually read it, but a savage account of what

Jews and Jewish Christians were undergoing at the time. Its central motif is a destroyed "heavenly" Jerusalem—with the actual destruction of the earthly Jerusalem informing its power.[41]

The time in which the author wrote was firmly within the decade in which the Gospels of Matthew and Luke, drawing heavily on Mark, were also written. Yet the Gospels give us a very different Jesus from Revelation's. While Revelation portrays the imminent return of a victorious Christ that, as we have seen, had centered the hope of Jesus people for decades, the ideological as well as geographic diversity of the movement is on display in the way these texts differ. Where the Gospels of Luke and Matthew and, later, John, adapting to the clear fact that Jesus had *not* returned, downplay apocalyptic longing in favor of a realized presence of the Lord *already among us*, Revelation heightens the expectation for, and the ambition of, the literal return by presenting an entirely new Jesus: the militant warrior who will lead God's avenging armies against the legions of Rome. The balance of history will be restored when Rome itself is destroyed, *quid pro quo* Jerusalem.

Unlike the impulses that had kept Jesus people on the margins of revolt, Revelation, albeit in somewhat coded language, launches a frontal attack on the greatest power on earth. Rome is the whore of Babylon, and the five "fallen" emperors who have wreaked such havoc against the Jews—Caligula, Claudius, Nero, Vespasian, and Titus— are obliquely condemned. Nero, who ordered the scapegoating of Jewish Jesus people after the great fire of Rome, is all but explicitly reviled.[42] Elaine Pagels writes of Revelation, "When John says that 'the beast that I saw was like a leopard, its feet were like a bear's and its mouth was like a lion's mouth,' he revises Daniel's vision to picture Rome as the worst empire of all."[43] Worse, that is, than the Seleucid empire that had sparked Daniel in the first place.

The martial belligerence of Revelation, though, really begins to drip with blood when this obliteration of Rome is accomplished by a vengeful army led by none other than the "Lamb who was slain."[44] But this lamb wields a sword. Unlike the Gospel of Mark, which has Jesus emphasizing, in that pointed thirteenth chapter, that the violence of the end of history will *precede* the coming of the Anointed One, Revelation describes that Messianic coming as *itself* consisting in violence. This is holy war, pure and simple. Jesus, whom the Gospels unanimously portray as one who rejected violence, is rendered in Revelation as the most brutish of warlords, and that alone is enough to suggest the extremity of the situations in which at least some of the Jesus people, presumably including "John of Patmos," had found themselves.

And, as we have seen, that extremity included pressures of conflict not only from Rome but from fellow Jews. Elaine Pagels argues that Revelation's main purpose is to defend the pure Jewishness of the Jesus movement against "the synagogue of Satan"[45]—the Gentile interlopers, as well as the Jewish Christians who dilute observance of the Law (kosher, circumcision, and so on) to accommodate those Gentiles. "When John accuses 'Balaam' and 'Jezebel' of inducing people to 'eat food sacrificed to idols and practice fornication,'" Pagels writes, "he might have in mind anything from tolerating people who engage in incest to Jews who become sexually involved with Gentiles, or, worse, marry them."[46]

However much the unchosen stresses of war and civil war accounted for Revelation's twisting of the story of Jesus, its portrait of the sword-wielding lamb amounted to a catastrophe, both in its meaning at the time and its consequences ever after. "To turn the nonviolent resistance of the slaughtered Jesus," as John Dominic Crossan writes, "into the violent warfare of the slaughtering Jesus is, for me as a Christian, to libel the body of Jesus and to blaspheme the soul of Christ."[47]

When the last episode of the three-act Roman War finally ended, in the smashing second-century return of the legions to the ruined city of Jerusalem to quash the Bar Kokhba revolt once and for all, a defining turn in the story of Jews and Jewish Jesus people was taken. The year was 135. By Hadrian's order, as we saw, the name of Jerusalem was deleted from all maps, to be banished from history. From then on, the restored—we would say ethnically cleansed—city was to be called Aelia Capitolina, honoring Hadrian's family name, Aelius, and the Capitoline Triad of gods: Jupiter, Juno, and Minerva. As noted, Hadrian ordered that a statue of himself be erected on the Temple Mount. The city, lavishly reconstructed, was repopulated with Greek-speaking pagans. Jews, including Jewish Christians, were forbidden to return.

This elimination of the Jewish center of the Jesus movement, and the final breaking of the physical link to the Jewish homeland, meant that, in the dispersed communities devoted to the memory of Jesus, the roots of Jewish memory, of Jewish interpretation, ultimately of Jewish meaning—not only of "Christ" and of "Jesus" but of "Gospel" itself—were cut. Without nourishment from those roots, the vital categories of understanding within which Jesus and the first three generations of those who followed him had lived were bound to wither. Reverence for Torah and veneration of Jesus as Lord began to seem contradictory. Gentiles who knew little or nothing of Jesus' historical Jewishness, or of the Jewish scriptural impulses that gave rise to "Christ," began to dominate the movement. When they read sacred texts that seemed to set Jesus against his own people, they could not imagine that he had been, in fact, one of those very people, fully and completely Jewish until the day he died—no, until his death was reimagined as Resurrection within a wholly Jewish context. Indeed, they hardly knew that the authors of these texts had themselves been Jews, and that crucial elements of their narrative had been drawn from Jewish Scripture.[48] As a self-consciously distinct "Church" came into being, it defined itself positively against the negative "Synagogue."

As Hellenized categories of philosophy moved thinking about Jesus from practice (love) to doctrine (creed), a theology of Christ was invented (Christology). This Hellenizing had begun to occur quite naturally as Jesus was initially preached in the towns and cities of the Mediterranean, but it accelerated exponentially once Jerusalem, the anchor, was gone. As the defining note of salvation, the "faith" of believers came to outweigh the "faithfulness" of Jesus—a momentous misunderstanding of the content of Paul's teaching.[49] Then came the world-historic mutation: the understanding of Jesus himself shifted from his being the Jewish-biblical "Son of Man," whose undefined but real divinity could be affirmed without violating the oneness of God, to his being the fully Hellenized Trinitarian "Son" of the Father, "begotten, not made, of one Being with the Father."[50]

Jews and Christians alike forgot, in sum, that Jesus Christ—raised from the dead, Son of Man and Son of God—had ever been fully Jewish. It took more than two centuries, and, with the emperor Constantine's conversion, the violence of the newly Christian state, for all of this to be accomplished—the final split between the religion of Jesus Christ and the religion that took its name from him. And always, it must once more be emphasized, against a long-established Christian amnesia: the division, fulfilling no conceivable will of God[51] and setting in motion a dynamic that would come to climax nearly two millennia later, *was the result of war.* The Roman war against Christians ended when the empire became the Church.[52] The Roman war against the Jews, what at last generated Dietrich Bonhoeffer's question, won't have ended until this history is fully reckoned with.

CHAPTER FIVE

Jesus and John

Return with us now to those thrilling days of yesteryear! From out of the past come the thundering hoofbeats of the great horse Silver! The Lone Ranger rides again!

—Introduction to *The Lone Ranger* radio show, 1933–1956

Eternal Thou

Jesus is the ultimate man alone—preaching, healing, heroically prophesying, bestowing grace and love, but always at a remove. Or so Christians think. Jesus has no real need of people, which is lucky, since everyone in his life proves to be unreliable. He has no teachers, no mentors, no true comrades. He has no lover. He lives in company, but he suffers alone. When he speaks to Mary of Magdala after his Resurrection, it is to say, "Do not hold me." Jesus is the beau ideal of modern individualism—and this is another reason his thoroughgoing participation in Israel is forgotten.

If Jesus had no need of fellowship, what need could he have of fellow Jews? This marked individualism has stamped, also, a certain kind of stoic human masculinity. Real men stand alone, and if they are seen to suffer, it is in radical isolation. Jesus is the paradigmatic male, rising above adversity and tribulation—surpassing it by sheer force of will. It helped in his case that his will was tethered to eternity.

Who was Christ *actually*? A fully integrated person, yet could Jesus have come into himself *except* as a member of a people—*except* in relationship to others? Ironically, even contemporary Jesus scholarship seeks a historical Jesus who stands "behind" the impressions of others—behind and alone. Thus, historians seek to debunk as less authentic those exact characteristics that friends and followers of Jesus reported of him, that he shared with others, and that allowed him to become who he was. Many Jesus historians assume, that is, that the mythical Jesus "behind" the texts, whether the Gospels or the epistles, is a solitary figure whom those texts, refracted through memory or mythmaking, distort. The historians' holy grail is an uninterpreted Jesus: can such a figure really exist?[1]

For our purposes, it must be emphasized that the hyperindividualism of modernity is another obstacle to an authentic sense of the Jewishness of Jesus—and therefore of his deep humanness. As a first-century male, was he really so independent? Seeing Jesus as an avatar of solitude attributes to him more than a lifestyle. It is also a moral stance. How can compassion, or love in any form, be understood as ethically central if the greatest virtue of human existence is high-minded endurance alone?

We are twenty-first-century people considering a first-century man, but our perceptions, whether knowingly or not, are inevitably colored by the seventeenth-century's hyper-elevation of the individual above the community.

The mythical "I" of Descartes was the solitary self cut off from all certainty except that arising from its own thinking. This absolutizing of one's own consciousness effectively relativized everything else, which led not only to a philosophical worldview centered solely on the perceiving self, but to an economy—*laissez-faire* capitalism—that girded the planet with structures of selfishness. In keeping with the preoccupation of this book, though, the major point here is that modern individualism, too, was called radically into question by the Holocaust, a crime abetted, at least in part, by the broad culture of amoral self-interest that marks modernity.

Ironically, the diabolical twist the Nazis brought to this question involved the total obliteration of individual identity as Jews and others were routinely deprived of all particularity, herded in masses, reduced to numbers, forced to wear badges that obscured all marks of personality but membership in the despised group. Meanwhile, those outside the targeted circle, retreating into what set them apart, found it possible *as individuals* not to care. The cult of the bystander was born. Jews were outside every community of concern—decidedly including the Church—even as every community of concern continually shrank. The Nazis sought to eliminate a targeted collective by shoring up the radical self-interest of individuals who, for survival's sake, embraced a totalizing solitude apart from all collectives, with perhaps the family—the self writ as large as it could be—being the single exception.

Multiple accounts of survival under Nazi occupation suggest how all forms of commonwealth were undermined by gnawing dread. Distrust was general. People passing one another in the streets of Europe made no contact, not even with their eyes. No one was untouched by what the Nazis did. It takes nothing from the particular responsibility of the war criminals to acknowledge that their demonic regime compromised all who were oppressed by it. This is what totalitarian systems do, and the German version implicated an entire continent in the breakdown of human solidarity. This destruction of individual identity in the course of the destruction of the group, by means of a fascist cultivation of a broader self-centeredness, was part of what led, after the war, to the corrective reaction that followed—a stalwart calling into question of the solipsism to which European culture had been reduced.

Against the lone-wolf assumptions of modernity, the idea that human life is essentially the life of *relationship* was recovered in the post-Holocaust period in part through a reignited and broad interest in the work of a Jew named Martin Buber. Born in Vienna in 1878, the same year that Germany's first anti-Semitic political party was founded, Buber was driven out of Germany as an adult, survived the war in Jerusalem, and came into his broadest influence as a postwar religious thinker confronting the moral meaning of what he called "the eclipse of God."[2] Buber did not directly take up the Holocaust as his subject, but this profoundly religious man's new preoccupation with the modern absence of God speaks volumes about that catastrophe's effect. Indeed, Buber can be understood to have been carrying to its next stage the inquiry about "religionlessness" that Bonhoeffer had begun but never pursued. No "Death of God" thinker, Buber was nevertheless one of those who dared to take the measure of the collapse of traditional God talk and faith.

But it was Buber's 1923 masterpiece, *I and Thou*, that once more broke the surface with power, taking on fresh significance after the war. That classic was now read in the wholly new context of shadows thrown by the chimneys. The Jewish Holocaust scholar Richard Rubenstein wrote, "Within Buber's thought, one can interpret the Holocaust as the most radical extension of the domain of I-It."[3] And indeed, that was how many read Buber in the late 1940s and 1950s. His elevation of relationship over isolation—solidary over solitary, in Albert Camus's formulation[4]—became a defining counterpoint for postwar existentialism. "All real living," Buber wrote, "is meeting." One consequence of this emphasis is the recognition that "the fundamental reality of human existence is to be found not in conceptual abstractions, but in concrete human relationships."[5] Not in "I think, therefore I am," but in "How are you?" But for Buber, the human encounter points beyond itself, which is its grandeur, for only by meeting fellow humans can a person meet God—"the eternal Thou."

Buber's work was controversial, with some reading him as abandoning the mediating function of religion for a direct mystical encounter with God.[6] Jews worried about the Law; Christians about the Sacraments. But they missed a crucial point. The biblical religion is emphatic in asserting that God's covenant is with the collective, and individuals find their meaning only within that collective: Buber takes such mediation for granted. The almost explosive reemergence of Buber's early book after the war shows how the centrality of relatedness he emphasized was revalorized. Far from diminishing the ancient tradition, Buber was retrieving for an unprecedented circumstance the meaning of *covenant*—whether "Old" or "New," for Jews and Christians alike. The language of the words "I and Thou" brought the sacredness of relationship back to the forefront of awareness. Therefore, "I and Thou" was a pivot, also, in the transformed perceptions of, like so much else, Jesus Christ—a lone ranger no more.

Modern individualism, then, but also an incipient postwar correction to it, are the bifocal lenses through which we see the first century. Christians might have long thought of Jesus as an isolated figure, yet the Gospels show him as essentially social— quintessentially *personal*—both in how he spent his days (eating, teaching, healing, with only exceptional times in solitary retreat) and in his purpose (establishing a movement marked by sharing, compassion—God's "Kingdom" was never seen more clearly than at the table over bread and wine). He depended on local hospitality, led a large group, and deployed them to imitate his work and sayings. The meaning of Jesus, in the movement of his life, was defined by his relationships and shaped by his interactions.

It is not too much to say that Jesus, from infancy forward, came into his "selfhood" through his relations with others—beginning with the smile he surely had from his mother. This has been potentially true of every human who ever lived, even if the word "self" comes to the modern ear with implications unknown to ancients. Indeed, scholars tell us that there was no word in ancient Latin or Greek for "self" as it is understood in contemporary usage. But something like the modern meaning was conveyed by Greek words like *"autos"* and *"nous,"* and the Delphic oracle surely spoke to the ages with its exhortation "Know thyself." Indeed, philosophy begins in the quest for just such knowledge—the self-awareness that undergirds all behavior, all choice, and the moral consciousness on which every religious impulse stands. But to the ancients, such purposeful interiority, however described, was arrived at by means of bodily encounters through which the soul became whole. And the ancients, even without the encouragement of Buber, took those encounters as an opening to encounters with the deity.[7]

Friend or Foil

Two of the Gospels, Matthew and Luke, begin, as if attuned to modern psychology and language theory, with Jesus' intimate relationship with his mother: their exchange of smiles, the babble opening to words, responsiveness to unconditional regard, for which infants—we would say now—are genetically programmed. The quality of Mary's nurturing of her son, the precondition of his growth in "wisdom and in stature,"[8] shows itself in the life he led. Mary's mothering of the babe rightly informs the great icon of the Western imagination—Madonna and child—and is enough to explain why she is venerated.

But for purposes of our rediscovery of Christ, the better starting point is proposed by the Gospels of John and Mark, from both of which the Madonna and child are absent. Instead these texts bring the story of Jesus into immediate focus not with nativity, but with his adult meeting of the character named John the Baptist. Jesus' bond with John, and then the tension between them, forms, we will see, the core of what makes faith matter. Our starting point is the recognition that the entire drama of Mark, in particular, is incited by the meeting of these two: "In those days Jesus came from Nazareth of Galilee and was baptized by John in the Jordan." Jesus came into his identity not by himself, but, first, by encountering John, in whose presence, Mark says, Jesus saw "the heavens opened." He heard God's voice declaring, "Thou art my beloved Son; with thee I am well pleased."[9] In meeting the Thou of John, Jesus met the eternal Thou of

God. What was that? Because the story comes to us encrusted with piety—a Bible story—we can hardly hear of this epiphany as something occurring in the life of a normal human being. Instead this encounter with the Holy One is remembered as the start of what set Jesus apart from the rest of us.

But is that right? Humans are set apart from other sentient beings by the act of knowing. That capacity depends on utterly material circumstances, like chemical interactions in the brain and the wiring of neurons, yet it opens into the immaterial world of consciousness. We are set apart from other animals, which share the capacity for some kind of knowledge, by *our knowledge that we know*. Dogs are aware, but humans are *self*-aware. That, too, opens into an even more expansive immateriality. This double knowing—knowing that we know—points beyond itself to an experience for which there are no intellectual or linguistic categories, but which humans have nevertheless constantly stretched to express. Brain cells may generate this realm of mind, but they fall far short of explaining it. The mind by definition leaps from gray matter to enlightenment.

The exquisite subtlety of human consciousness, in other words, can account for everything but itself. Following, in effect, a three-stage movement, *knowing* opens into *knowing that we know*, which can open, in turn, into *knowing that we are known*. Consciousness leans toward some kind of—what to call it?—primal consciousness that includes all consciousness in itself. Religion puts the name of God on that transcendent knower, whom Jesus recognized as "Father."

From this point of the story on, Jesus, a Galilean nobody no longer, will preach that everyone is known in this way, held in just such unconditional positive regard—and that everyone has the right to call God "Father." As others would hear this life-changing—history-changing—good news from Jesus, *Jesus heard it from the unlikely John*. What Jesus would become to those who later followed him, that is, John the Baptist was to him.

"In those days" is the biblical word package that points only vaguely to a crease in time. In this case, the opening phrase deflects attention away from whatever mundane stuff of life had defined Jesus' "coming from Galilee," as the texts puts it, and being "baptized by John." There is no historically reliable information about what led Jesus to John, or about how long the two were together. The assumption Christians make is that the encounter was brief, and almost staged. It's as if John were standing on the shady side of an oasis when Jesus happened by. John is a Jewish preacher, effectively rallying his listeners to a life of repentance. But now a sudden inspiration comes over John and he is moved, almost against his will, to yield his own messianic ambition in favor of this stranger. A veteran actor who'd signed on as the leading man is ambushed by the director, and abruptly relegated to the role of sidekick, when a more obscure matinee-idol-to-be comes along. A star is born.

This threshold moment in what is read as a God-written drama moves Jesus out of the anonymity of his life as a carpenter's son in Nazareth and into the "public ministry" that would efficiently set him on the perilous road to Jerusalem. Thus, John makes his appearance in this, the Gospel of Mark's first scene, already in a decidedly supporting role. Indeed, even the lines given John to speak emphasize his subsidiarity, since the showstopping words "Behold, the Lamb of God" originate not with him but with Isaiah, who spoke of the lamb led to the slaughter.[10] John's function as the lowly herald of the elevated Jesus is made crystal clear: "After me comes he who is mightier than I, the thong of whose sandals I am not worthy to stoop down and untie. I have baptized you with water; but he will baptize you with the Holy Spirit."[11]

But this account is all *too* sparse, and, given the importance of John *in relationship* to Jesus, it cries out for elaboration. In Mark, Jesus moves promptly on from the encounter: "The Spirit immediately drove him out into the wilderness." Only a single verse further on,

Jesus is shown returning from his undescribed sojourn in the wild, but the entrance is very much on cue. And the cue is what happened to the Baptist: "Now after John was arrested, Jesus came into Galilee, preaching the gospel of God, and saying, 'The time is fulfilled.'"[12] The prophet's arrest was the punctuation of the fulfillment Jesus announced. Though John the Baptist's tragic fate as a victim of the sadistic Herod—John will be beheaded—is soon passingly referred to in flashback, John disappears from the narrative.

It is not enough to have a figure of this significance—the one in whose presence Jesus first sees God—cross so briefly into and out of the story. John the Baptist has haunted the Christian imagination, but from the margin: he marks the end of the Old Testament, not the beginning of the New. Yet undergirding the symbolic—and theological—function of this eccentric man was a real person, and historians find in him a decisive clue to the meaning of the one whose sandal he pointed to. We can know with certainty almost nothing about the life of Jesus, or his associations, before his arrival on the Gospel scene as a man of about thirty, but we owe it to a full grasp of his humanness to exercise an act of informed imagination, measuring what we conjure against what scholars call the criterion of plausibility.

Historians tell us now that John the Baptist was a great and well-known figure of the time. Josephus, whose chronicles we have cited in relation to the war, took John's fame for granted. He gave John a climactic role in the story of the downfall of Herod Antipas, Rome's puppet ruler of Galilee and Perea, the region to the east of the Jordan River, down to the Dead Sea:

Antipas had married the daughter of Aretas, the King of Petra. On a journey to Rome Antipas had stayed with a half-brother "Herod," the son of King Herod and his wife, the daughter of Simon the high priest. While there, Antipas had fallen in love with his half-brother's wife, Herodias. Herodias agreed to marry Antipas after his return from Rome on condition he divorced the daughter of Aretas. Before Antipas' return from Rome, the daughter of Aretas realized what was happening and fled back to her father. As a result Aretas invaded Antipas' territory. Antipas' army was defeated which some Jews saw as divine vengeance for Antipas' execution of John the Baptist. Antipas is stated to have executed John because he feared John's teachings could lead to unrest.[13]

As the reader knows, twentieth-century New Testament scholarship was transformed with the discoveries by archaeologists—and shepherds—of ancient papyri rolled into earthenware jars and squirreled away in caves, most momentously including the already referred to Dead Sea Scrolls, found in 1947.[14] These texts laid bare the ideologies, cults, and commitments of numerous Jewish sects actively expressing opposition around the time of Jesus to Roman occupation and to the Hellenized corruptions of the collaborating rulers, like John's antagonist, Herod. The Qumran community had withdrawn into the cave-ridden hills above the Dead Sea, embracing precisely the kind of radical asceticism the Gospels associate with John the Baptist. He was no rogue apocalyptist, a solitary voice in the wilderness, in other words; rather, he was typical of a broad Jewish counterculture on the lookout for ways to separate from the inhuman—and blasphemous—milieu of occupation.

This charismatic figure's pronounced message of repentance falls on the modern ear as a familiar species of religious preaching, but John's proclamation involved, in context, a profoundly political campaign. It helps to recall again that the modern distinction between religion and politics—and the modern impulse to wall religion off from the rest of life—was unknown in the ancient world. There was no such thing as "religion," in fact—only life lived under the sovereignty of God. For Jews, it was God's sovereignty that was at stake in various political alignments, which is why forced submission to foreign power was always problematic. Without a full sense of the dispiriting effect of Roman oppression, that is, contemporary readers of the Gospel simply cannot appreciate John the Baptist's appeal.

The Baptist's stern repudiation of physical pleasure—he punished himself by wearing a hair shirt and eating wild locusts—comes to modern Christians as a spiritualized puritanism, but it was more than that. In Galilee and Judea, Roman agents, together with a collaborating aristocracy and cooperative petty landowners, all under the protective watch of Herod's henchmen—and Roman legions at the ready—operated a vast mechanism of economic exploitation, benefiting a small minority at the expense of everyone else. Imperial colonialism always squeezes treasure and blood out of those whom it dispossesses, and the chokehold on the people of Palestine in the time of Jesus was particularly savage. Peasants were thrown off land, laborers were deprived of work, artisans went unrewarded—or, if they did find employment, it was at slave wages, and even that pittance was harshly taxed. Patterns of ordinary family cohesion were disrupted, with old people badly cared for, the young deprived of hope. Many people were made destitute and homeless, and there were few, if any, prospects for betterment. Within recent memory, those who had openly protested such conditions had been efficiently—brutally—dealt with. It was to such a demoralized population that John's message of personal change by means of religious awakening rang with power: *Your repentance will bring about the intervention of God!*

There is every reason to assume that Jesus, raised in a village in Galilee that offered scant prospects for work, meaning, or respect, came of age looking for an alternative way of life. Nazareth was less than four miles from Sepphoris, a city that had been violently subdued by Roman legions around the time of Jesus' birth and lavishly transformed into a regional showplace of Hellenized style and taste. The likes of Nazareth villagers had been tossed out of Sepphoris and were not welcomed back. For a young Orthodox Jew growing up in a disenfranchised backwater close enough to whiff the ungodly aromas of affluence, but also to feel the threat of the garrison, Sepphoris would have been a goad. The bite of Greco-Roman social exclusion and emphatic manifestations of relative economic disadvantage were constant insults. *No to all of this!* The restless refusal to accept unjust things as they are that marks most young men as they come of age is plausibly what drove Jesus south, into the Jordan Valley.[15]

Historians accept as factual gospel characterizations of Jesus as itinerant, possessing nothing, effectively a beggar—probably, as we saw, an illiterate one at that. Perhaps he chose such a state of radical dispossession, but it is equally conceivable that, as a Galilean nobody, he was poor and vagrant without any choice in the matter. Historians accept that he had numerous siblings: why not picture Jesus as a young man who left home because his mouth was just one too many at a table where there was rarely enough food? In his early twenties, why wouldn't he have been drawn to the tough-minded Jordan Valley figure whose repudiations of material comfort amounted to a transforming embrace of the impoverishment to which most were condemned in any case?

What would have made John irresistible, though, was the sure certitude with which he promised an imminent overturning of the conditions of oppression, an intervention by the God of Israel, whose great deeds in behalf of His chosen people constituted the core of Jewish memory. What God had done in the past, God was about to do again. By means of his symbolic ritual with water, the Baptist offered those who heeded him a way of taking action now for the sake of this future expectation. By accepting baptism at the hands of John, therefore, the young Jesus did far more than enact a ritual. We conjecture here, but with plausibility: he joined a movement. Jesus grew in "wisdom and stature," as a committed disciple not of an over-the-hill movie star, but of the most charismatic Jew of the age.

To gain such fame, and to draw a following significant enough to be noted by Josephus, John would necessarily have been actively preaching for a substantial period of time. His community could well have had the cohesion, structure, and solidity scholars now know to associate with Qumran. Certainly, with the symbolic use of baptismal water, John's movement had its ritualized cult, probably showing the influence of the Qumran ascetics for whom washing was a sacred purification. There is no reason not to imagine that Jesus regarded John as a mentor, and even that Jesus served as an assistant to John. It is plausible, given the Gospel hints of the strong bond between them, that Jesus became one of John's intimate inner circle. From John, then, Jesus would have learned the ways of preaching that depended on the application of Torah to the current plight of Israel. Jesus at twenty-two, twenty-five, twenty-eight: this life could well have been the life of Jesus for most of a decade.[16]

The first thing to say about Jesus' relationship to John, in other words, is that Jesus, far from going through the motions of a scripted prelude to his own drama, was personally drawn to John as the solution to his own problem of absolute dispossession and the despair that threatened to come of it. John enabled Jesus to embrace his first idea of himself. John, therefore, was a source of meaning for Jesus. And the meaning was structured around John's preaching of the apocalypse.

We have seen how the Jewish air in that period was pumped full of End Time expectation. The rather desperate hope that mundane experience was soon to be interrupted by a divine intervention for the sake of restoring the ancient sovereignty of Israel should itself be taken as a signal of the failure of what might be called normal hope for a better life. The point is that, because of Rome, normal hope was impossible. Jews looked instead to the stories of their past, which—as told annually at Passover, weekly in Sabbath ritual and daily by Torah observance—amounted to a history of salvation. If God could stay the hand of Pharaoh, why not that of Caesar? If God could raise up a David once, why not again? So apocalyptic expectation could seem reasonable and realistic—a fulfillment of the promise that, so the collective tradition said, had again and again been vindicated. Given Rome's omnipotence, an expectation of God's intervention was the only alternative to the suicide of rebellion or the complicity of resignation.

Time and End Time

Twenty-first-century people find talk of an apocalyptic end of history crackpot, but it was not unusual in the ancient world—and not just among Jews. World-ending combat between forces of light and dark was a Mesopotamian idea before it was biblical, and Hellenistic thought was rife with apocalyptic myth. From oracles and sibyls all over the Mediterranean, prophecies of what we might call millennial expectation were common in Jesus' time. The word "millennial" is a clue, pointing to the decisive succession of epochs broken into thousand-year increments. Contemporary people mistakenly assume that the thousand-year motif originates with a calendar that starts at the birth of Jesus, with mad millennial fevers peaking after one thousand years in Europe's medieval dances of death and the Crusades; or, in the last decades of the next millennium, in the Thousand-Year Reich of Hitler. But the millennial idea is more complex—and ubiquitous—than the calendar sparked by Jesus. Virgil, for example, in the *Aeneid*, describes how the majority of mortals, after death, enjoy the "blessed field of Elysium, but after a thousand years" are summoned by the gods to return into the prison of their bodies.[17] The mechanism of cyclical time, too, revolves around the number 1,000.

Postmodern sophisticates of the North Atlantic nations may look back askance at primitives in the grip of one kind of millennial fever or another, yet we did not, despite such condescension, hesitate to stock up on water and cash ahead of the so-called Y2K phenomenon of the year 2000. That that much-dreaded computer glitch amounted, in the end, to nothing laid bare its subliminal irrationality. What began as a two-digit anomaly attached to the internal clocks of machines had blossomed into a full-blown metaphor for all that humans fear. A short time later came the 9/11 attacks, in 2001, a televised tower of Babel, the sky endlessly falling. The wild disproportion that marked the catastrophic American responses to that Al Qaeda attack cannot be understood apart from the primal human mind-set that fits the destruction of cities, whether New York or Jerusalem, into apocalyptic narratives. Americans, too, caught millennial fever. The United States embarked on the explicitly religious project of ending evil, and its leading thinkers spoke of the end of history.[18] More broadly, "the war to end all wars," a perennial dream of the liberal democracies, is a secular version of millennial End Time fulfillment.

Ancient imagination, speaking generally, assumed that time was a flow of cycles, an eternal return reflected among Egyptians in the tidal flow of the Nile, and among Greeks in the repetitive transits of heavenly bodies. Human experience was taken to endlessly redouble on itself, and to be, therefore, headed nowhere. In Plato's *Republic*, for example, Socrates relates the legend of Er, a story about the cyclical fate of souls turning on the "spindle of necessity," forever coming and going through oblivion and forgetfulness. In the *Aeneid*, as noted, Virgil reports the same dynamic at work in the underworld, where souls are "suspended upon the winds . . . washed through with flooding waters . . . until time comes round." It is then that souls, having drunk from the river of forgetfulness, are sent back to "the prison of their bodies" to begin the futile sojourn once again. Human happiness can be had only by way of contemplative withdrawal from *agon*, for struggle in a world defined by cycles is pointless.[19]

The Bible, from its creation story forward, proposes something very different—a linear conception of time that actually has a beginning: "In the beginning, God . . ."[20] If time starts, then time ends. The past is never repeated in the future. The future is the locus of fulfillment, so in the present, fulfillment is by design elusive. Experience is a flow from event to consequence, with *moral* events defined by human choice. This flow is called history, and while humans are actors in it, they are not characters in a play scripted by God. Their agency is decisive, which makes history purposeful. Meaning comes not from escaping history, but from engaging it. We live in a limited, conditional world. There is no escape from it—or from the "prison of the body." To be alive to this structure of time is to be ever on the lookout for its conclusion. Yet the conclusion of history, while ultimately an act of its Creator, depends in part on human struggle toward that conclusion—which is the point of responsible engagement. *Agon* is not to be escaped, but taken on.

But this very structure of experience is revelatory, for humans quickly learn that to find the meaning of anything *in time* requires an appeal to, or a gift from, something timeless. Only what is outside of time can fully account for what occurs within it. That paradox, rooted in the very structure of consciousness we touched on earlier, is inevitably unsettling. The present moment inevitably leans toward a future moment, as it breaks in. That "leaning toward" defines the posture of human awareness. Restlessness, therefore, is not to be regretted, but marshaled. Humans live *toward*. Religion speaks of this in the language of apocalyptic longing. This apocalyptic instinct is not crackpot, but normal.

The biblical view of history, still speaking generally, was epochal, with epochs understood by analogies drawn from Scripture, including the stories of individual covenants—Adam, Noah, etc.—we looked at earlier. Here we see the foundational, pre-Christian character of millennial thinking—a biblical adaptation of the common fixation on the number 1,000. One common scheme, for example, understood each of the six days of creation as corresponding to a period of one thousand years, the sum of epochs equating to the completed span of history: at six thousand years, time's up. If the biblical genealogy—all those Hebrew Scripture "begats"—suggests an arithmetic that puts the creation of Adam at more than five millennia before the time of Jesus,[21] then the End Time could indeed be understood by Jesus' contemporaries as somehow nigh. Among the scribes and interpreters of oracles, such a calculation could have had the authority of what passed for science.

We have already noted, with Daniel Boyarin, that the book of Daniel had all-trumping currency in the period just before, during, and after the lifetime of Jesus. Daniel gave interpreters the images and language with which to transform demoralization and defeat into the glorious prospect of restoration. Indeed, scholars like Boyarin, analyzing the manuscripts found in the Dead Sea caves, have recognized that, among that community of Jewish Zealots—with whom John the Baptist could well have been associated—the book of Daniel was key. Dozens of Daniel fragments were uncovered in those scrolls, suggesting that the book ranked in the Qumran library with the Psalms, Isaiah, and the Pentateuch.[22] And Daniel, above all other texts, was taken to propose an eschatological time frame that had immediate relevance. Indeed, Daniel was read as the angel Gabriel's End Time announcement:

> So he came near where I stood; and when he came, I was frightened and fell upon my face. But he said to me, "Understand, O son of man, that the vision is for the time of the end." As he was speaking to me, I fell into a deep sleep with my face to the ground; but he touched me and set me on my feet. He said, "Behold, I will make known to you what shall be at the latter end of the indignation; for it pertains to the appointed time of the end.

As for the ram which you saw with the two horns, these are the kings of Media and Persia. And the he-goat is the king of Greece; and the great horn between his eyes is the first king. As for the horn that was broken, in place of which four others arose, four kingdoms shall arise from his nation, but not with his power. And at the latter end of their rule, when the transgressors have reached their full measure, a king of bold countenance, one who understands riddles, shall arise. His power shall be great, and he shall cause fearful destruction, and shall succeed in what he does, and destroy mighty men and the people of the saints. By his cunning he shall make deceit prosper under his hand, and in his own mind he shall magnify himself. Without warning he shall destroy many; and he shall even rise up against the Prince of princes; but, by no human hand, he shall be broken. The vision of the evenings and the mornings which has been told is true."[23]

This vision is explicitly addressed by Gabriel to the "Son of Man," with whom Jesus was eventually identified, and with whom, at some point, Jesus might have identified himself. The epochs of history are plain enough here—the division of time into eras ruled by four kingdoms, including the Babylonians, the Persians, the Greeks, and, marking the end of this progression, the Romans. "When the transgressors have reached their full measure": *There* is the tolling of the bell. And if Rome was not at the full measure of its iniquity in the time of John the Baptist, when would it be?

Jesus certainly took for granted the cosmology of his time—and the time of his cosmology. Yet because he, too, was defined by the limits of the human condition, his growth in wisdom and stature was a characteristically human matter of trial and error; of mistakes made and learned from; of ideas embraced and discarded; and of the moral lapses that would have made real the need for repentance that brought him to John.

But plausibly assuming him to have been in John's company for a considerable period of time, years perhaps, he surely would have confronted the problem that apocalyptic expectation always eventually generates. John preached the vision of "the evening and the morning," but its being true assumed a dawn that refused to come. John's vision was for a time of the End, but the End kept postponing itself. The apocalyptic problem that would later bedevil the followers of Jesus must have first bedeviled John.

Jesus broke with John.[24] We do not know why, but the failure of an apocalyptic calendar would explain that turn in the story as well as anything. After what we are presuming to have been a considerable period, after an enormous investment of hope, after the onset of gnawing disappointment, Jesus moved on from the Jordan Valley commune. But this would have been no mere matter of impatience. More important, Jesus would have experienced a transformation in his belief about, in the phrase he read in Daniel, the rising of "a king of bold countenance, one who understands riddles." The riddle was time,[25] and Jesus probably left John because he adjusted what time meant.

We touched on this earlier, how an evolved thinking on apocalyptic expectation—whether within the solitary mind of Jesus or in the collective mind of the Jesus people later—defined the Christian movement from early on. This evolution amounted to a shift from *a future longed for* to *a present to be responsible for.* We saw how this shift defined a difference between the early Mark and the later Gospels, but that recast understanding can be said with significant plausibility to have begun in the tension between Jesus and John the Baptist. Precisely how that tension is defined, and to what extent Jesus clung to some kind of conviction that God would break into time-and-space reality to end Israel's dispossession, are unsettled questions, but there can be no doubt that John, with his fevered apocalypticism, stands in the Gospel as the foil in contrast to whom Jesus came into his own. Who was Jesus? He was *not* John the Baptist. He was *not* a Zealot.

John Dominic Crossan suggests that Jesus had embraced John's expectation of God's imminent intervention in history but moved on from that way of thinking. Instead of speaking of God as imminent apocalypse, Jesus began to proclaim God as already present.[26] That meant, as one scholar interprets Crossan, that "the Kingdom of God is not apocalyptic and social, but a challenge to individuals to lead a responsible, simple, radical life."[27] Other scholars, like John P. Meier, see in Jesus not a rejection of John's teaching but an adjustment in it.[28] But if the Gospels reliably report anything of these two figures, it is that there was dramatic conflict between them—conflict played out, presumably, every time Jesus donned a robe that was soft to the skin; or sat down to eat fruit and bread, drink good wine; every time he gave his warm attention to sinners; and every time he refused the role of judging moralist. In these and other ways—in deeds enacted more than in doctrines proclaimed—Jesus set his clock as much to the present as to any future; cocked his eye as much on earth as on heaven. It would be anachronistic to see, in such worldly preference of the byways and banquets of towns and villages over the unspoiled wilderness of John's self-denying retreat, a choice of "secular" over "sacred." The ancient world had its boundaries between holy and profane, boundaries carefully observed by Jews like Jesus, but our idea of secularity would have meant nothing to them.

Nevertheless, people of our so-called Secular Age, seeking Bonhoeffer's "religionless Christianity" and struggling to affirm the holiness of ordinary experience, are right to recognize in Jesus, unlike many shamans, priests, and preachers of old, a sanctifying regard for what, in our categories, has nothing to do with religion. There is ample testimony in the Gospels to tell us that it was characteristic of the historical Jesus to see God in the kindly touch, the risen bread, the fallen sparrow, the fight for justice. Asceticism was not necessary for holiness.

Crossan suggests that Jesus began to live this way only after the death of John the Baptist, but the Gospels themselves suggest that Jesus' abandonment of John came while John was alive, and that it included a harsh denigration of his former mentor as lesser than the "least" of Jesus' own followers.[29] Various New Testament texts make it plain that the Jesus people and John's remnant movement continued to regard one another as competitors.[30] Need it be emphasized again that this tension existed within a *wholly* Jewish context, and has nothing to do with a later conflict between "Christians" and "the Jews"?

After John was arrested by Herod, and after Jesus had come into a certain reputation of his own, the imprisoned John is said to have sent a pair of his followers to put the loaded question to Jesus: "Are you he who is to come, or shall we look for another?" Presumably, this question had importance for John because his own prospects were so bleak. Whatever his ambitions for his own movement had been, they were surely dashed by his experience now as a man on death row, with the executioner leering outside his cell. It is hard not to read an edge of panic into the question *Was I wrong about you?*

Jesus is shown answering directly, but not in the way John or his followers could have expected. Jesus might still have somehow expected God's saving intervention and, as Boyarin suggests, might have begun to understand himself as a Son of Man figure charged with ushering in that intervening presence of God. But his answer to John's disciples suggests that, for him, the intervention had taken on an altogether different meaning. A meaning that, alas for John, implied John's doom.

In effect, Jesus said, *Yes, I am the one who is to come—here right in front of you, but look, look:* "Go and tell John what you have seen and heard: the blind receive their sight, the lame walk, lepers are cleansed, and the deaf hear, the dead are raised up, the poor have good news preached to them."[31] To the modern ear, this sounds like a litany of "miracles," as if Jesus is claiming status as a worker of wonders. As we saw earlier, wonder workers were ubiquitous in the ancient world—figures whose deeds were interpreted, within that distant cosmos of meaning, as somehow "miraculous." Jesus can be understood—might have been understood—as such a charismatic person. But that was not at all the point of this definitive response to John's question. Rather, Jesus was citing a text that would have been well known to John and his disciples, and, as we have seen again and again in this inquiry, *the text was the point.*

Jesus was identifying himself with the prophet Isaiah, whose own identification in those very words would have been known to every Jew: "The Spirit of the Lord GOD is upon me, because the LORD has anointed me to bring good tidings to the afflicted; he has sent me to bind up the brokenhearted."[32] By invoking Isaiah in this way, Jesus was wrapping himself in the mantle of a justice-obsessed prophet, one whose preoccupation was less with the future, however imminent, than with the present condition of an oppressed and beleaguered people. Jesus had set out to make plain the distance between the injustice bedeviling almost all the people of Galilee and Judea and the call to justice that forms the heart of the Torah. *That* is what the Spirit of the Lord upon him meant. Jesus concluded his answer to John with this cryptic postscript: "And blessed is he who takes no offense at me."

Offense was in the air between John and Jesus. It was everywhere around them, and how could it not have been? Jesus called John "a prophet, and more than a prophet,"[33] but he himself invoked the greatest prophet of Israel to distinguish himself from John. Ironically, the word "prophet," in contemporary usage, is associated with the capacity to see beyond today, a knack for prediction, an obsession with tomorrow. Yet the prophet's true métier is the present, not the future. So with Jesus.

Pacifism

The tension between future and present defines the human condition, even if, in varied cultures across spans of history, conceptions of time within which present and future are understood have differed. It behooves us to constantly remember all that separates us from the ancient world and its meanings. As just noted, our divide between sacred and secular did not exist. Whatever distinctions were drawn between myth and fact are not the distinctions we draw, and the same is true of our contrast between faith and reason. Interpreters who forget the difference between postmodern assumptions and ancient ones are bound to fail. Nevertheless, whatever framework of meaning structured Jesus' thinking about time, a certain perennial set of experiences can be assumed. Human tragedy, of its essence, consists in the denigration of *what is* in the name of *what is to come*. The prophets of Israel were those who called that skewed schema into question. "Real generosity toward the future," as Camus famously put it, "lies in giving all to the present."

The prophet might have emphasized the coming of a saving act of God, but that emphasis itself was enough to transform present perceptions. The present was the point. The transformation that mattered occurred within history, not in some End Time afterlife. Whatever the future implications of a longed-for "Day of the Lord," the prophet's role, in widely varying circumstances, was always to remind the people that they were *already and still* the elect of God, and that their one duty was to act like it. Not "then," but "now."

Justice! The prophet's obsession was always with the structure of injustice imposed upon the people, even if the people had somehow become complicit in the injustice—from Hosea, for whom Pharaoh epitomized oppression, to Isaiah and Amos, who denounced the subjugation coming from Assyria, to Jeremiah, who railed against impositions by Babylonians, to Zechariah, who typified a prophetic counter to the Persian empire. And note that the context within which each prophet operated was war—just as the context within which Jesus lived was war; and as the context within which, a generation later, the Gospels and Rabbinic Judaism came into being was war. The Christian memory, shaped by the war-making empire that overtook it, deletes that fact, and we have seen to what effect.

Rome's war making was the necessary and sufficient cause from start to finish: from John the Baptist's cry in the wilderness to Jesus' preaching of God's kingdom to the Jesus movement's shaping of memory, meaning, and scripture into Gospel. That Rome's occupation of Palestine should have drawn a prophet's critique was firmly within the tradition of Israel, and prophetic literature was consistently wartime literature. In line with that tradition, prudently veiled denunciations of the oppressor were always paired with an explicit call for Israel's renewed observance of the commandments of God, *for Torah was the opposite of war.* Yes, John the Baptist was a prophet, and so, picking up the mantle, was Jesus, and all of this was the measure of their prophetic meaning.

Yet John and Jesus were prophets whose horizons pointed in opposite directions. The tension between John the Baptist and Jesus is the promised key to understanding the actual Christ, the renewal of his meaning that defines the purpose of this book. That tension, understood in terms of temporality—now versus "someday"—can be understood equally in terms of geography: the opposition between the "wilderness" of the Jordan Valley to which ascetics like John withdrew, on the one hand, and, on the other, the villages of Galilee, to which a man trying to make a difference in the actual lives of villagers returned.

The message Jesus carried was stark, dramatic, and clear: God's power is addressed to the here and now, and while it is decidedly in favor of the poor, it remains permanently on offer to all. While John

was imprisoned, that is, Jesus had struck out on his own, making real
the munificence of God through his ministry of healing and curing—
however such activity occurred, or was said to have occurred. Salvation, in the way Jesus presented it, is the present experience of humane
living, decent behavior, and a physical wholeness that reflects the
moral wholeness of compassion and love. Attitude is everything.

But in this tension between Jesus and John the Baptist, we de-
tect an even deeper epiphany, the clearest signal yet of the self-
understanding Jesus had come to. The revelation comes from an
exquisitely composed juxtaposition given in the Gospel of Luke.
There Jesus' response to the question from John the Baptist, recounted in chapter 7, repeated the fabled citation from Isaiah that he
had cited in a different context in chapter 4 of the same Gospel. In
the earlier verses, Jesus had already publicly claimed Isaiah's "good
news to the poor" as his personal watchword, and then, replying to
John, he repeated it—almost exactly. And that "almost" is the point.

When Jesus, having broken with the Baptist's movement, "returned from the Jordan" to Galilee, in Luke's telling, he went straight-
away to his hometown, Nazareth. In a kind of coming-out, Jesus
presented himself at the synagogue, presumably the holy place in
which he had long received Torah instruction, become a bar mitzvah,
and come of age as an observant Jew. He took his place at the bimah.
Here is the text from Luke 4:

> And there was given to him the book of the prophet Isaiah. He
> opened the book and found the place where it was written, "The
> Spirit of the Lord is upon me, because he has anointed me to
> preach good news to the poor. He has sent me to proclaim re-
> lease to the captives and recovering of sight to the blind, to set at
> liberty those who are oppressed, to proclaim the acceptable year
> of the Lord." And he closed the book, and gave it back to the

attendant, and sat down; and the eyes of all in the synagogue were fixed on him. And he began to say to them, "Today this scripture has been fulfilled in your hearing."[34]

But look: In this reading at Nazareth, Jesus not only measured himself against the call to preach good news to the poor; he associated himself with a mission to "proclaim release to the captives" and "set at liberty those who are oppressed"—notes of his prophetic vocation that, in a later passage citing precisely the same text of Isaiah, as recounted in Luke 7, he omitted. In his response to the imprisoned John, that is, Jesus made no mention of release from prison. No mention of liberation.

Let's assume for a moment that the narrative's report of the exchange between Jesus and John's disciples is historical. "Are you he who is to come, or shall we look for another?" John would have known the text from Isaiah very well. He might have known that Jesus was already using it as a kind of overture, claiming to be its fulfillment. One imagines John in his cell, stridently interrogating the messengers: *But did he not mention the prisoners? Was there no promise of liberty to captives?* John, that is, from his prison cell, would have efficiently grasped the significance of Jesus' redaction of Isaiah.

What sort of messiah are you? was John's question. And here was the clear answer: *Not the sort who can free you from Herod's dungeon. I am not a messiah who will lead an army, storming Herod's fortress—not even to rescue you, dear friend. Nor am I a messiah who will work magic, causing the locks on your cell to fall open. No to violence. No to miracles.* If Jesus could have rescued John, he would have. But he could not do it.

When it comes to the bounded human condition, the ultimate limitation is prison, the very essence of restricted space and time. That is why incarceration universally succeeds as punishment. Jesus, however much he "fulfilled the scripture," was as much at the mercy of that limit as any person, and that limit informed his answer to John. It is impossible not to take this moment as one of enormous revelation, comparable to the moment, also defined by John the Baptist, when the skies parted and the Father was heard speaking from above. The heavens opened, but the prison bars stayed closed. Jesus could not offer to John a physical liberation.

It is well known of Jesus—and essential—that he was a figure of radical nonviolence in a hyper-violent world. Indeed, because violence was such a given then, and because it so defined the entire milieu in which Jesus lived, his rejection of violence is not equivalent to the pacifism of modern times, much less something softer. "This was not," write Richard A. Horsley and Neil Asher Silberman, "mere pacifism or meekness, but the first step in the reconciliation and renewal of the People of Israel."[35] That Jesus differs from Gandhi (as Rome differed from the British Empire) does not mean, however, that the essence of their witness is not equivalent—both morally and politically. The point for us is that, in relationship to John the Baptist came the beginning of Jesus' rejection of brute force—no matter the justification. *Here* is what makes Jesus the Prince of Peace. All that Jesus could offer to John was the invitation to change his attitude about his circumstance. All that Jesus could offer to anyone was a new way of thinking—the way of thinking he himself had come to.

Having learned from John who he was in relation to God, that is, Jesus here learned who he was in relation to Rome. From one point of view, John's peril had confronted Jesus with his own impotence. What must it have cost him to admit that, when push came to shove, he could do neither? And how could he not have been crushed at having so failed his mentor and friend? But from another point of view, wasn't this the moment of Jesus' reckoning with the different sort of mission that was his? Jesus would not resist violently for John. Therefore, he would not resist violently for himself. *No to violence.* And Jesus would not "pray" John out of prison. Whatever his "curing" amounted to, this was a definitive no to miracles. *No miracle for John. No miracle for anyone.*

The Commissioning Death

As the story then unfolds, Herod sadistically decapitates John. That savage act—John's head on a platter for Herod's dancing daughter is one of the most grotesque scenes in the entire Bible—can be taken as the generating event of Jesus' own mortal resistance to the tyranny of Rome and its puppet ruler. That there was an explicitly political meaning to John's death could not have been more obvious, and certainly Jesus saw it. Here is the account of John's death at the hands of Herod, as given by Josephus:

> Herod had put [John] to death, though he was a good man and had exhorted the Jews to live righteous lives, to practice justice toward their fellows and piety toward God, and [in] so doing join him in baptism . . . When others joined the crowds about him, because they were aroused to the highest degree by his words, Herod became alarmed. Eloquence that had so great an effect on mankind might lead to some form of sedition, for it looked as if they would be guided by John in everything they did. Herod decided it would be much better to strike first before his work led to an uprising than to wait for an upheaval, get involved in a difficult situation, and see his mistake.[36]

Having learned from John's life of being radically accepted by God here and now, Jesus learned from John's death—because it *commissioned* him—that God's acceptance meant there was nothing to fear in death, even in the tinderbox over which properly insecure petty tyrants ruled. Otherwise, Jesus would not have immediately[37] embarked on the challenge that took him into the very cockpit of anti-Jewish Roman violence. "During the months preceding his final journey," in the words of Horsley and Silberman, "Jesus initiated his movement of community renewal, dedicated to restoring reciprocity and cooperation in the spirit of the dawning of the Kingdom of God. Yet his movement of revival of village life could not become just another separatist movement, withdrawing from confrontation and seeking the shelter of obscurity in the backcountry valleys and remote mountainous areas of Galilee."[38] He had to take his message to where it could change Israel.

When word came to Jesus, a few chapters on in Luke, that Herod was out to get him, too, and that he should therefore flee, Jesus did not shrink. To those who warned him of Herod, he defiantly replied, "Go and tell that fox . . ." Note that Jesus here denigrates Herod by slapping on him the label of an unclean animal, an open challenge. He goes on to say, "Behold, I cast out demons and perform cures today and tomorrow, and the third day I finish my course. Nevertheless I must go on my way today and tomorrow and the day following; for it cannot be that a prophet should perish away from Jerusalem."[39]

Jesus *against* Jerusalem: in Christian accounting, that is how the story of this progress is often told, with its culmination in a "righteous" assault on the Temple. Jesus is remembered as having moved against the city of Jews, not the garrison of Rome. Thus, while Israel's ancient prophet tradition provides Christology with its dominant interpretive lens, the meaning of that tradition is twisted, as if Jerusalem were *only* the slayer of God's prophets; as if Israel is ontologically programmed to reject God's saving interventions, when the whole point of salvation history is that Israel, again and again, accepts those interventions. Indeed, Israel is defined by never forgetting them, and always looking out for God's saving acts again. But this Israel is lost to a Christian amnesia. The witness of the prophets in whose line Jesus stands is thus reduced to the narrowest and most negative of readings, as if the quite admirable principle of self-criticism enshrined in the prophetic tradition were instead an unrelenting indictment. Prophets were *self*-critical Jews *as* Jews. To Christians, they came to be understood as outside critics *of* Jews *against* Jews.

"Jerusalem, Jerusalem," Jesus is recalled lamenting, "killing the prophets and stoning those who are sent to you!"[40] By the time Stephen, remembered as the first Christian martyr, preaches the Gospel, well after the death of Jesus, the accusation against "the Jews" has been honed: "Which of the prophets did not your fathers persecute?"[41] As if the prophets were not themselves the fathers of Israel; were not themselves the most revered of its leaders.

Countering this classic instance of the anti-Jewish imagination, Jesus, precisely like his predecessors, was a prophet *within*, not against. His journey to Jerusalem—his *aliyah*—was made in love, even as he knew that, as the center of the Roman occupation, Jerusalem, for the likes of him, was fraught. And of course, to return to our initiating motif, all of this grief about and toward Jerusalem was sparked not by Jesus' magical foresight, but by the Gospel's *post-destruction* hindsight. Jerusalem was fraught for Jesus because, as horribly demonstrated in the year 70, it was fraught for every Jew who loved it.

Some scholars speculate that the Gospels were written to portray Jesus as a classical hero, like Achilles—courageously embarking on a course of action sure to lead to his death.[42] But speculation yields to what is known from history: Jesus' deliberate progress to Jerusalem was indeed chosen, and the significance of his journey would be clearer than ever forty years later. Jerusalem was where Jesus' conflict with the force that murdered John the Baptist would be joined. Not "Jews," but "that fox." Yet from John's beheading forward, Jesus saw death differently—that it does not overturn God's love. That revelation, if anything, would have more relevance in 70 than it had in 30.

"Thou art my beloved Son." *Thou:* the intimate form of address from God. Nothing could be more powerful, or more permanent, than that. Or more Jewish.[43] Such belovedness would form the heart of Jesus' program of resistance to Rome, the heart of the promise that would carry his movement forward into history—to the climax of the war with Rome, and beyond. Such belovedness was the revelation that would make Jesus the "Christ." But the point is that Jesus did not come to it by himself. He came to it through John.

CHAPTER SIX
Thou Art Peter

Noli timere.

—The last words of Seamus Heaney[1]

Be Not Afraid

In 1939, the Nazis occupied Kraków, Poland, and moved at once to close the city's university. Its professors were murdered. Its students, including nineteen-year-old Karol Wojtyla, were pressed into slave labor, in his case at a limestone quarry not far away. After two years, Wojtyla escaped the labor camp, and he lived out the war in hiding. At one point he eluded a Gestapo roundup by hiding in the basement of his uncle's house. He knew the horrors of the German occupation firsthand, and they remained the ground of his identity for the rest of his life.

Wojtyla then came to maturity with his city locked down by another occupying power: the Soviets. The puppet government of Poland during the Cold War was a brutal stand-in for Joseph Stalin and his successors. Wojtyla emerged as the Communist regime's most powerful antagonist when he became the archbishop of Kraków in 1964, but his resistance was just beginning. In 1978, he was elected head of the Roman Catholic Church and became Pope John Paul II.

In June 1979, brushing aside the objections of Poland's Communist government, the now white-robed Wojtyla traveled to his hometown of Kraków, where, in a field on the outskirts of the city, he celebrated Mass for anyone who would dare to come. Because open practice of religion was effectively outlawed, everyone in attendance risked, at the very least, the loss of a job or an apartment or the schooling of children—reduction to the condition of non-personhood. That was why each one in attendance had come to the field expecting that almost no one else would have dared to be there.

But look around! Wojtyla might have said. More than a million people had shown up for the Mass—twice the population of Kraków. His refrain, though, was even simpler. "Be not afraid!" he had said in his first pronouncement as pope. "Open up—no, swing wide the gates to Christ! Open up to his saving power the confines of the state, open up economic and political systems, the vast empires of culture, civilization, and development. Be not afraid!"[2] Now, in Poland, the pope declared, "The Polish pope comes here to speak. . . . He comes here to cry with a loud voice. . . . You must be strong, dearest brothers and sisters. There is no reason to be afraid!"[3]

In a fraught political context, John Paul's message was by necessity oblique, but it came through with clarity anyhow. He demonstrated his own unbreakable solidarity with the Polish people, and in doing so he invited them to reclaim their solidarity with one another. Talk of love, especially coming from preachers, is cheap. But the love John Paul II lifted up was the antidote to the rank individualism that, by isolating Poles, had enabled the regime to have its way with them.

All subjects of totalitarian systems are convinced by their very subjugation of their unworthiness. That they are enslaved convinces them that they deserve to be—a demoralization on which the tyrants depend. Idealism, nobility, courage, selflessness—these are practical impossibilities, and few if any Poles of Wojtyla's time had had open experience of such virtues. The timid throng that made its way to Wojtyla's field knew this about themselves, and, more to the point, they knew it about one another. Every person present at the Mass had reason to believe that every other was an informer, an agent of the state, ready, for survival's sake, to do the Communist government's bidding. Each one knew that of the others because—here is the essence of totalitarianism—each one knew it of himself. It was precisely to this condition that the Polish Pope spoke. *Do not be afraid of yourselves! Do not be afraid of one another!*

One of those who heard Pope John Paul preach in that field outside Kraków was an unemployed electrician who had hitched a ride from the coastal city of Gdansk. Barely more than a year later, at his home shipyard, that electrician used a souvenir pen he had bought at the pope's Mass to sign the founding charter of the illegal trade union Solidarity. He was Lech Walesa, and, having heard Wojtyla, he found it possible to act as if he were afraid no more. In Wojtyla's presence, the solidarity of subjugation—the universal shame that was the first bond of victims of the Soviet imperial system—was transformed into a solidarity of resistance. The Solidarity Walesa and his fellow workers established, and the solidarity it embodied, would lead to the nonviolent overthrow of the Communist regime in Warsaw and, ultimately, to the demise of the Soviet Union itself.[4]

Every Pole heard the echo in Pope John Paul II's refrain "Be not afraid." As the pope intended, the throng of secret Catholics recognized that exhortation as having come again and again from Jesus himself. No one goes around saying "Be not afraid" unless there are mighty things to fear, and it would have been at least implicitly apparent to the demoralized people of Poland that Jesus, in his own time, had also been addressing a throng of dispossessed and powerless victims of a brutal imperial occupation.

But the Gospel accounts give the exhortation its particular resonance. When Peter and the other apostles were terrified on open water during a storm, Jesus appeared to them, saying, "Do not be afraid." When Peter and the others cowered after seeing Jesus transfigured with Moses and Elijah, he said to them, "Rise, and have no fear." After his resurrection, Jesus said to the women, "Do not be afraid." He compared his frightened followers to sparrows, whose survival is forever so precarious, yet after whom God so lovingly looks. With such radically vulnerable creatures in mind, Jesus concluded, "Fear not, therefore."[5]

For Jesus, "Be not afraid" was not a magic refrain, a cheap exhortation akin to whistling past a graveyard. The precondition of the fearlessness he preached was the terrifyingly brutal circumstance of Rome's lethal capriciousness, and he knew about fear from his own experience—dating back to the Roman legions' rampages through the territory in which he was raised, climaxing in the cruel fate of his mentor John the Baptist. And there's the point. "Be not afraid" was corollary, for Jesus, to "You are my beloved Son"—the transcendent affirmation that came to him in John's presence. Having been spared from fear himself, Jesus understood what that release was like.

To repeat, if Jesus found it necessary to say "Be not afraid" again and again, it was because there *was* much to fear in the world he and his friends were living in. But Rome, however terror-inducing, was only part of what threatened. Indeed, the condition of totalitarian slavery presents one sort of danger, but the human condition itself, even under the best of circumstances, presents another. No one gets out of life alive. Death is, overwhelmingly, the thing to fear, and it was that fear that Rome, like every totalitarian system, could so efficiently play on. Jesus had seen that up close in the fate that befell John the Baptist, which was the occasion, as we saw, of his discovery in himself—"Tell that fox"—of the capacity to rise above it. Before long, Jesus would have the cup of death forced upon him, and, having prayed, "Let this cup pass from me," he would add decisively, "nevertheless, not as I will, but as thou wilt."[6] From disabling fear of death, above all, Jesus had been released.

Here, perhaps, is the point of the transforming affirmation having come, upon his baptism by John, from one who identified himself as "Father": "This is my beloved Son." Christians hear of this father-son image as if it is a given note on the scale of religious reference, a plunge into the warm bath of daddy love. But that this most positive assertion is understood as coming from the primordial source of life—the parent—is itself a pushback against the law of mortality, the iron legacy of death. Freud's conviction that every intuition about God is at bottom a reiteration of the power of paternity points to the awful complexity of the parent-child dynamic as the only imagined release from the limitations of time. As the offspring, propelled forward out of the past, rescues the progenitor from oblivion, the paternal blessing bestowed upon the child forces the future open with its promise of life to come. Against Freud, it is the most natural thing in the world to see in this structure of generativity not a "projection" but an analogue of its Author, whose faithfulness transcends time, and therefore death.

Again, and importantly, it was as a Jew that Jesus had come to his understanding of the Father's blessing as the trustworthy promise of life. "Be not afraid" is the most frequently repeated admonition in the Hebrew Scriptures as well, appearing more than a hundred times, from Genesis ("Fear not, Abram, I am your shield") to Exodus ("But Moses said to the people, 'Fear not, stand firm'") to Psalms ("Do not fear the terror of the night") to Isaiah ("Be strong! Fear not! Behold your God") to Jeremiah ("Fear not the king of Babylon").[7]

To preach fearlessness in the face of a brutal regime that cynically depends on the fear-ridden subservience of a broken people is a profoundly political act, as Pope John Paul II knew very well, despite his insistence that all he ever preached was religion. If there can be no surprise that, as a result, even a twentieth-century pope was targeted for political murder,[8] where is the surprise that Jesus was?

Not I, Lord

In Jesus' case, from the various accounts, it seems that his message about fear was aimed at one person more than others. We have seen how I-Thou intimacy shaped Jesus' youthful coming-of-age in relation to John the Baptist. Now, still measuring our reading of texts by the principle of plausibility, we can see that Jesus came into his maturity through a second quite particular friendship—with the fisherman Simon Peter. The Gospels' "fear not" verses feature Peter, again and again, as the one to whom Jesus was addressing himself.

We have seen how Mark unfalteringly—and unflatteringly—portrays a profoundly fallible Peter, and we assumed that the author of the text did so because he was addressing a beleaguered people for whom good news could only take the form of a message of acceptance, despite every failure. The people were afraid, with reason. And the message addressed their fear. The later Gospels continued to press that theme, and Peter continued to be central to it. Indeed, Peter emerges as the captain of trepidation—a surprising characteristic, perhaps, for a man who made his living on the sea. Ironically, as the story is told, that profession did not inure him to fear but hobbled him with it.

Peter was one of the first four whom Jesus recruited, and they were all fishermen. As such, they were figures of low social status in Galilee, but they were also practitioners of a demanding and often dangerous trade. Those who could find alternative livelihoods did so, because to be a fisherman in Galilee was to spend a good deal of time deathly afraid.

If puritanical asceticism was the nub of John the Baptist's character in resistance to which Jesus found himself, the equivalent in Peter's case was a peculiar depth of fear. In one situation after another, he was rattled. If the ever-human Jesus, as the stakes grew higher in his progress toward mortal confrontation, had to push against an inevitable anguish of his own, he had a perfect foil in one who, by all accounts, was his closest friend, and who lived submerged in anguish. What Peter saw in Jesus, meanwhile, was a man who offered an escape from his innermost dread, and one of the Gospels' most well loved miracle stories makes clear how and why a Sea of Galilee boatman might feel that way.

> And a great storm of wind arose, and the waves beat into the boat, so that the boat was already filling. But he was in the stern, asleep on the cushion; and they woke him and said to him, "Teacher, do you not care if we perish?" And he awoke and rebuked the wind, and said to the sea, "Peace! Be still!" And the wind ceased, and there was a great calm. He said to them, "Why are you afraid? Have you no faith?" And they were filled with awe, and said to one another, "Who then is this, that even wind and sea obey him?"[9]

As we saw, the author of the Gospel of Mark is traditionally identified as having been the intimate companion of Peter, and the narrative is taken to reflect the special experience of Peter. Indeed, the Gospel's anecdotes, sayings, and parables are assumed to have been drawn from Peter's own preaching, and it is easy to imagine Peter telling the tale of Jesus' bringing calm to a stormy sea as the perfect image of the astonishing inner peace that the always anxious Peter himself felt in his Lord's presence.[10]

All four of the Gospels honor Peter's primacy as one on whom Jesus depended. Yet this bears repeating: except for Judas Iscariot, no one in Jesus' circle is shown to be more feckless or unreliable than Peter. Mark's surprising portrait is carried forward by the Gospels that came later. The surprise lies in the fact that the Gospels come at a time, late in the first century, when the nascent Christian movement presumably had an institutional motive for the elevation of Peter. He had emerged as a key leader of those following Jesus, and was remembered as such. The movement had a need to valorize him. Yet these texts represent a strange sort of mythmaking—especially when taken to reflect Peter's own point of view.

If Jesus is shown to be a calm, inner-directed, yet compassionate man, with a firm sense of destiny in the service of the One whom he called Father, Peter is very much the opposite. There is something buffoonish about this character whose exuberance defines his first response in every circumstance—those houses for Moses and Elijah; that "not I, Lord" about betrayal. It was Peter who pulled out a sword in the garden of Gethsemane, as Jesus was being corralled, to slice off the ear of the man doing the arresting. After the death of Jesus, Peter leaped from a boat at the sight of a mysterious stranger on the shore (having first put his clothes *on*). The encounter that occurred then, early in the morning, brought the friendship between Jesus and Peter to its transcendent peak.

The elegant anecdote of that meeting on the beach appears only in the Gospel of John, the last of the four to be written, and, paired with the story of Peter's denying Jesus three times during the night of the crucifixion—"I do not know the man!"—the story has the aura of literary masterpiece about it, one of the greatest moral reckonings ever recounted.

Just as day was breaking, Jesus stood on the beach; yet the disciples did not know that it was Jesus. Jesus said to them, "Children, have you any fish?" They answered him, "No." He said to them, "Cast the net on the right side of the boat, and you will find some." So they cast it, and now they were not able to haul it in, for the quantity of fish. That disciple whom Jesus loved said to Peter, "It is the Lord!" When Simon Peter heard that it was the Lord, he put on his clothes, for he was stripped for work, and sprang into the sea. But the other disciples came in the boat, dragging the net full of fish, for they were not far from the land, but about a hundred yards off. When they got out on land, they saw a charcoal fire there, with fish lying on it, and bread. Jesus said to them, "Bring some of the fish that you have just caught." So Simon Peter went aboard and hauled the net ashore, full of large fish, a hundred and fifty-three of them; and although there were so many, the net was not torn. Jesus said to them, "Come and have breakfast." Now none of the disciples dared ask him, "Who are you?" They knew it was the Lord. Jesus came and took the bread and gave it to them, and so with the fish. This was now the third time that Jesus was revealed to the disciples after he was raised from the dead. When they had finished breakfast, Jesus said to Simon Peter, "Simon, son of John, do you love me more than these?" He said to him, "Yes, Lord; you know that I love you." He said to him, "Feed my lambs." A second time he said to him, "Simon, son of John, do you love me?" He said to him, "Yes, Lord; you know that I love you." He said to him, "Tend my sheep." He said to him the third time, "Simon, son of John, do you love me?" Peter was grieved because he said to him the third time, "Do you love me?" And he said to him, "Lord, you know everything; you know that I love you." Jesus said to him, "Feed my sheep."[11]

This encounter between Jesus and Peter is the ground on which the Christian church stands, and the revelation of what its faith most centrally concerns. Peter comes to this moment having epitomized not virtue, but human weakness. He had been terrified and had acted accordingly. He had drawn from Jesus that transcendent rebuke, as Satan. Finally, his role in the death of Jesus was not exceptional, but defining. His betrayal of Jesus, that is, was not incidental, but essential.

Hence, Jesus' prediction: "Truly, I say to you, this very night, before the cock crows twice, you will deny me three times."[12]

And so it played out—in the Passion narrative as rendered by all four Gospels. The threefold character of this betrayal—in the courtyard, on the porch, by the fire—makes the point that it comes from Peter's moral center. In that sense, the act is paired as an ethical twin with the coldly premeditated sellout of Jesus by Judas Iscariot, although nothing in the narrative puts Judas in a place of intimacy to compare with the way Jesus had repeatedly entrusted himself to Peter. That's what makes Peter's treason worse. Indeed, every one of the disciples abandoned Jesus, but, given Peter's intimacy with Jesus, his blatant faithlessness had to be by far the most grievous blow.

In the Gospel of Luke, the act receives this emphasis: as Peter spoke the third time, the rooster crowed, and "the Lord turned and looked at Peter. And Peter remembered the word of the Lord, how he had said to him: 'Before the cock crows today, you will deny me three times.' And he went out and wept bitterly."[13] The locked gaze between them is what did it. It is as if the two men saw a ghost standing between them—the ghost of an earlier ease, of pleasure taken together, of the quiet satisfaction from long hours on the road and the joint hauling of nets, of pointed silences, laughter, roughhousing, the stuff of friendship. Dead, all dead.

Peter Stood

The stories about Jesus are consistently centered on his openness to misfits, sexual miscreants, collaborators, and ne'er-do-wells, but the Peter story shows that moral failure is a mark of the insiders as much as of the outsiders. Human weakness is universal. Jesus knew it, and he was not put off by it. That's why his mantra was "Be not afraid."

That Jesus kept repeating those words showed his deep understanding of fear as the ground of human existence. It had been the ground of his own, which surely is why the stark confrontation with Peter's fear that day on the road to Jerusalem—"Get behind me, Satan!"—drew from Jesus such a ferocious response. Jesus still knew what fear could be and what fear could do, so when his best friend justified fear, he had to push it away. What Jesus put on display in front of his cowardly associates, in other words, was the furthest thing from condemnation. It was not even pity; it was empathy. Jesus knew where they were coming from because, driven in his youth to seek out John the Baptist, he had been there himself.

Here was the surprise: the pit of moral failure into which Peter fell was not disqualifying. After his gross treason, Peter "went outside and wept bitterly," because when Jesus looked at him just as the cock crowed, Peter saw the ghost of their love—and felt the shock of his having betrayed it. But the point of this moment in the Passion drama is *what Jesus saw.* In that locked gaze, Jesus beheld not a ghost but a man. Only a man. There was no shock in Jesus, for he saw in Peter only what he already knew was in him. Peter was his familiar friend, even in his fecklessness. He was still his friend, although at that moment Peter did not know it.

Instead of being an anomalous sort of mythmaking, this portrait of the Jesus-Peter encounter, even down to the threefold betrayal, is perfectly consonant with what Jesus had been proclaiming all along. The commonwealth of God stands upon forgiveness, but in order for it to be real, forgiveness has to be arrived at through a reckoning with the full horror of what is being forgiven. Only then can the offense be left behind. The truth will set you free, yes,[14] but only after shaking you to the core. That is why, in the Gospel of John's rendition, the three betrayals of Peter had to be reenacted through the three questions posed by Jesus on the beach. *Simon Peter, do you love me? Do you love me? But do you* really *love me?* The questions, as all but explicit reminders of his threefold mortal offense, humiliated Peter, but that humiliation alone made the love of which they were speaking authentic. The solidarity of God's commonwealth is the mutuality of failure forgiven.

Let's assume for a moment that this slant on Peter's story did indeed come from Peter himself, from his preaching, and from the author of Mark's note-taking of what Peter said as he went about speaking of Jesus. In that case, a more typical panegyric celebration of a leader's heroic virtue would have been entirely irrelevant to Peter's purpose. Whatever impulse toward self-aggrandizement he might have had—and, like all men, he'd surely have had some—Peter understood that he could not speak truly of Jesus without speaking truly of himself. That was what it meant, finally, to feed the Shepherd's sheep. And the truth was simple: all that separated Peter from the vile and suicidal Judas was that he, Peter, had lived long enough to find his offense transformed—through no merit of his own—by the loving acceptance of Jesus. The humiliated Peter was, in the same moment, the forgiven Peter.

If that was the message that this apostle carried away from his last encounter with the Lord, no wonder others soon looked to him as the movement's central figure. Perhaps as a fisherman, Peter had been the net master, or the boat master; but this authority was different. His having stood more in need of forgiveness than anyone, and his having been nevertheless forgiven, was the source of his personal power. In his own being, Peter made the promise real. And look what happened then.

The first work of what might be called Church history is the Acts of the Apostles. Originally, it was the second half of the Gospel of Luke, but it stands in the New Testament as a separate book, carrying the story of Jesus forward from Jerusalem to Rome. As such, it picks up where all four Gospels end: after the Resurrection experience of Jesus. Whatever that was, the Resurrection had not been enough to assuage his followers' anxiety, for the risen Jesus had still found it necessary to greet his friends with the words "Be not afraid."[15]

At the outset of Acts, Jesus is shown taking his final leave, memorialized in the tradition as the Ascension. Clinging to him, his followers desperately ask, "Lord, will you at this time restore the kingdom to Israel?" The life of what might be called the Church begins with this rebuking response from Jesus: "It is not for you to know times or seasons which the Father has fixed by his own authority." Jesus disappears then, and the dispirited, motley group makes its way back from Galilee to Jerusalem. They are still afraid, and they go into hiding "in the upper room."[16] After all they have been through, including, as the story is told, the triumph of Easter, the Jesus people are as much at the mercy of fear as ever.

But then what will prove to be the inciting incident of the entire Christian movement takes place. At that moment of demoralization and abandonment, as the text reports it, "Peter stood up among the brethren (the company of persons was in all about a hundred and twenty), and said, 'Brethren, the scripture had to be fulfilled, which the Holy Spirit spoke beforehand by the mouth of David, concerning Judas who was guide to those who arrested Jesus. For he was numbered among us and was allotted his share in this ministry." Peter, citing a psalm of David—"His office let another take"—goes on to preside over the election of a successor to Judas, restoring the apostolic number to twelve.[17]

But that bit of organizational staff development cloaks the real meaning of Peter's act, which becomes apparent when, business-school-like, the case is unpacked. The life of the Church begins with an explicit reference to Judas, which puts everyone in the room in the same realm of moral failure—no one more than Peter himself. Only that one thing separates him from Judas, his having been forgiven. Everyone present knows that. Peter's ethical identification with Judas, and the grace of what makes him different, is what enables him to "stand up." Indeed, supreme coward that he is, the one doing this *has* to be Peter.

No sooner has Judas been replaced among the twelve with Matthias, as the text reports, than Peter finds it possible to lead the way out of the upper room and into the streets of Jerusalem, where he "lifted up his voice." Before a vast throng, he gets right to the point:

> Men of Israel, hear these words: Jesus of Nazareth, a man attested to you by God with mighty works and wonders and signs which God did through him in your midst, as you yourselves know—this Jesus, delivered up according to the definite plan

and foreknowledge of God, you crucified and killed by the hands of lawless men. But God raised him up, having loosed the pangs of death, because it was not possible for him to be held by it. For David says concerning him, 'I saw the Lord always before me, for he is at my right hand that I may not be shaken; therefore my heart was glad and my tongue rejoiced; moreover my flesh will dwell in hope. For thou wilt not abandon my soul to Hades, nor let thy Holy One see corruption. Thou hast made known to me the ways of life; thou wilt make me full of gladness with thy presence.'"[18]

This proclamation by Peter is celebrated as the initiating act of the Christian movement—in the argot, Pentecost, the birthday of the Church. The man who had denied knowing Jesus now blatantly accuses his hearers of responsibility for Jesus' death. Leaving aside for the moment the way in which this indictment will later be twisted into a scapegoating of "the Jews" for a Roman execution, the point here is that Peter, aware of his own guilt, is prepared to announce the offense of others precisely because the burden of that offense has already been lifted. In the currency of God, judgment and mercy are sides of the same coin. Peter, as portrayed in the Gospel, had learned that from his encounter with Jesus on the beach. Unshakenness, gladness of heart, uncorrupted flesh, the permanent presence of the Lord—all of this, Peter declared on the authority of his own experience, was simply on offer to anyone who would receive it.[19]

It was the conviction of those who knew Peter that, on his own, he was simply incapable of the courage, eloquence, and hope that he displayed before the Jerusalem throng. Their certain knowledge of Peter's culpability and cowardice forced the recognition that God's Spirit had come upon him. Peter was different. That difference was the starting point of all that followed. As the text says, the people saw "the boldness of Peter," and "those who received his word were baptized, and there were added that day about three thousand souls. And they devoted themselves to the apostles' teaching and fellowship, to the breaking of the bread and the prayers."[20] The rest is history.

The faith of the Church, down to the twenty-first century, rests upon this one man's experience of Jesus.[21] The Gospel began with him. Its central proclamation, therefore, was not of a noble project of virtuous action in the name of God, but rather of a solidarity in feebleness that, once acknowledged, could be transformed into strength. And, given all the ways that the beleaguered Jesus people were faltering just then, why should that news not indeed have been heard as good?

CHAPTER SEVEN

The Real Paul

I had been reading Dante and was shaken once again
how we suffer appalling punishment for being human;
I stepped out to breathe a while in the good air.

—John F. Deane[1]

Chronology Matters

It is important to have continually in mind the chronology on which
this set of reflections stands, recalling that the reflection is itself generated by the twentieth-century genocide against the Jewish people.
While there is no *direct* line of causality between Israel's first-century
traumas and the modern horror that befell Jews, we have seen how
regarding them together within brackets of history and theology
leads to illumination. So far, our consideration has centered on the
Gospels, but the history and theology that matter were generated
even earlier by works of particular genius.

Because the Christian memory, as reworked into literature, never
really accommodated the catastrophe of what the Romans called the
Jewish War—or, rather, because that trauma took the form among
Christians of memory *denied*—the character of the Jesus movement's
foundational texts as *war* literature has never been fully reckoned
with. And the consequences of an igniting misrepresentation of
the meaning of Jesus have yet to be faced. Jesus scholarship over the
last generation—especially its fuller retrieval of his inalterable
Jewishness—has enabled the beginning of these reckonings, but they
are far from complete.

We have plausibly understood that the Gospel of Mark, composed in about 70, was a response to the crisis of the savage Roman assault against the Jews. Though the climax of that assault occurred in Jerusalem, where many hundreds of thousands were slain, the Jews to whom Mark probably wrote, Jesus people huddled in Galilee, were traumatized, too. The genocidal slaughter had eliminated the Temple priesthood and the parties associated with it, like the Sadducees, as well as the die-hard Zealots, a remnant of whom took to their redoubt caves and buttes in the hills of Judea.[2] Along with a party of fugitive Pharisees—collected, as we saw, in Yavne, near the coast, and soon to be known as the rabbis—the Jesus people were one of two main groups who had not fully thrown in with the rebellion. This was the only reason the two groups survived—the only reason, that is, that two new religions, Rabbinic Judaism and Christianity, survived to rise out of the ashes of Second Temple Judaism. But in Mark's time, during and immediately after the destruction, that future was not clear, as these two groups of Jews shared one urgent question: What is it to be a Jew without the Temple, which for the thousand years since its construction by King David's son Solomon had made the Lord God present to His people? We saw this before.

And we saw that their answers differed: the rabbis said that Torah observance and study were now the new Temple, with the synagogue the new center of Jewish life, the Sabbath table the new center of Jewish cult. The Sabbath, in Rabbi Abraham Joshua Heschel's phrase, is the "Temple in time."[3]

The other party of surviving Jews answered that now *Jesus* was the new Temple, with his crucifixion equated, by Mark, to the Temple destruction itself.[4] Indeed, it was, one plausibly assumes, the Temple's shocking disappearance that drove the author of Mark to write his Gospel just then, aiming to bring into coherent, and therefore usable, form the varied strands of faith and conviction about Jesus that had evolved over the decades since his death. Not until 70 and its trauma, that is, did the multiple meanings of Jesus begin to jell into the one meaning that would really launch the movement. The staggering loss of the holy place in which God's ineffable presence had so long been enshrined could thus be taken as the sacred inter-ruption in history that irrevocably revealed Jesus Christ as the new presence of God in Israel's midst. The Gospel was urgently needed as its proclamation.

This *context* helps us enter more fully into the text. Thus, when Mark portrays the Pharisees as Jesus' great antagonist in Galilee,[5] we should understand the main antagonism as existing not in the year 30 or so but in about 70, when the Pharisees and Jesus people were just beginning their war-induced argument over the new meaning of Jewish identity. Similarly, when Jesus' lethal antagonists in Jerusalem are identified by Mark as the priests of the Temple, the main point is that the priestly caste, at the time the author of Mark is writing, was held responsible by many surviving Jews for the catastrophe that had just befallen the Temple.[6] It was not hard to see the priests as having been collusive with the Roman petty tyrant Pontius Pilate in 30 when, as Jews away from Jerusalem could see it, the Temple estab-lishment had just foolishly, in 70, invited the Roman legions to do their worst. In such intra-Jewish tensions *actually* dating to around 70 but transferred by Mark back to 30, we find the beginning of what will evolve, once this fancied calendar is fixed as "fact," into full-blown "Christian" hatred of "Jews." But another element, coming more forcefully *after* Mark, heightened the conflict even further, and that was the Jesus movement's very practical strategy of telling its story in such a way as to deflect any further Roman persecution.

About a decade after Mark, the author of the Gospel of Luke set to work writing his account of the life of Jesus. His main source was the primordial text that the author of Mark wrote, but he needed to make adjustments to it, as he all but explicitly declares in his Gospel's opening verse.[7] As Mark's narrative was shaped in large part by the needs of those he addressed—presumably, demoralized refugees from the Roman War, centered in Galilee—so was Luke's. But there was a difference. Scholars suggest that this account of Jesus' life was written for the community of believers gathered in Rome. The author of Luke expressly addresses the work to a patron, "you, most Excellent Theophilus," a title that suggests a senior Roman official. Luke proposes a version of the Jesus saga that such a figure would find appealing. This purpose, and this readership, contrasts starkly with Mark's, and that shift influences the way the author of Luke tells the story.

A striking difference between Mark and Luke shows itself at once, for the latter author begins his account with the now much beloved nativity story: the angel Gabriel, the journey to Bethlehem, shepherds, angels, the star, the babe in the manger. The story's opening—"In those days a decree went out from Caesar Augustus"—strikes the note of the harsh conditions of an occupied people, since the imperial "enrollment" that requires Joseph and Mary to go to Bethlehem is essential to the grievously burdensome tax system that defined Rome's relationship to its colonies. Augustus, the emperor who claimed to be divine, is here set up to be the antagonist of Jesus, yet Luke, in the rest of his Gospel, will downplay that antagonism. No sooner does Jesus come into his maturity than he comes into conflict—not with Romans, but with his neighbors in the synagogue of Nazareth, who, after hearing him declare "no prophet is acceptable in his own country," aim to kill him by throwing him from a cliff. "But passing through the midst of them he went away."[8] Luke's adjustment, that is, stamps the Christian imagination with a new dread: the enemy is *within*.

God Suffers with You

As Mark is taken to represent the particular point of view of Peter, Luke is regarded as reflecting the experience of Paul, especially as the author of Luke continues the account in the second part of his work, the Acts of the Apostles. A figure named Luke is referred to in the letters of Paul several times, most notably in Colossians, where Luke is called "the beloved physician." In the Second Letter to Timothy, which shows Paul anticipating his death, he says that he is in Rome and that "only Luke is with me."[9] In Acts, the author uses "we" in describing numerous events, which is the basis for assuming that Luke was a companion of Paul. Most scholars now take for granted that Luke, whoever he was, was not writing history, a conclusion readily supported by the fanciful nativity narrative. Rather, his accounts might be compared to ideologically driven historical novels. Especially when it comes to its portrait of Paul in Acts, the Lukan narrative is valuable for dramatizing the life-changing effect that even an indirect encounter with Jesus can have.

Paul was the avatar of that kind of faith, proof that you needn't have known Jesus in the flesh to be transformed by him. All you had to have been was a Jew steeped in the End Time longing that vivified, as we saw, the "Son of Man" motif in Daniel, the most widely read Jewish text of the first century. Paul was certainly one of those Daniel-obsessed Jews.

Born about a decade after Jesus, perhaps in Tarsus, a city in present-day Turkey, Paul was remembered as "a man small of stature, with a bald head and crooked legs, in a good state of body, with eyebrows meeting and nose somewhat hooked."[10] He had his life-changing but indirect experience of Jesus in about the year 35—rendered in Acts of the Apostles as the miraculous but still indirect experience on the road to Damascus—a blinding vision of the risen Jesus that knocked him from his horse. Like Oedipus, it was in losing his sight that he saw. Over the next quarter-century, perhaps supporting himself as a tentmaker, he traveled throughout the Mediterranean world, putting on offer an apocalyptic, firmly Jewish interpretation of Jesus' meaning. That that meaning carried implications

of an identity that was not only messianic but somehow divine—
Paul, more than anyone, gave currency to the equation of "Christ"
with "Lord"—located Paul firmly within the Daniel-inspired expectation of his time, of which we took note early in this book.[11]

Indeed, in his first writing—1 Thessalonians, dated by scholars to
about 51—Paul explicitly invokes Daniel's image of the Son of Man
descending "from heaven with a cry of command, with the archan-
gel's call, and with the sound of the trumpet of God." At that point,
Paul expected this history-completing climax to occur soon, so that
he himself and his readers, too, would "be caught up together with
[the dead] in the clouds, to meet the Lord in the air, and so we shall
always be with the Lord. Therefore comfort one another with these
words."[12] Jesus Christ did not return as expected on that first ap-
pointed schedule, but Paul continued his work of rumination, elucidation, and exegesis. He adjusted his first timetable, but even with
his last letter, Romans, written a decade or more after 1 Thessalonians, Paul still envisioned the End Time restoration of Israel as "at
hand." Most momentously, he saw the End Time's much prophesied
ingathering of nations as already having begun to occur—which is
the key to his inclusive opening toward those who were not part of
Israel—the "Gentiles."[13]

We saw earlier how the postponement of messianic expectation
attached to Jesus as the Son of Man sparked doubts, which in turn
inspired further reinterpretation. More than any other figure, Paul
mined the Hebrew Scriptures for analytic keys that enabled the
transformation not only of the disciples' disappointment but even of
the ever-problematic defeat of Jesus on the cross. Building on the
Resurrection accounts that he would have heard from other Jesus
people, Paul constructed a vital theology on the idea, which—
again—was embedded in the Jewish book of Daniel. In Paul's hands,
though, the Resurrection became the central symbol of Jesus' meaning. Paul turned the primordial catastrophe of the crucifixion into a

source of salvation, a flip that unlocked a deep mystery of hope in suffering itself.

In his travels across the empire, what Paul saw everywhere he went was the suffering of its underclass. Perhaps as much as 40 percent of the population of the Roman Empire was enslaved, a mass of people that included not only laborers in huge mines and vast farms but also men who worked as accountants, physicians, and tutors, and women who were universally available sex servants.[14] War captives formed a large subset of slaves, which of course, not long after Paul's time, meant tens of thousands of Jews, taken in the Jewish War. Slaves in the Roman dominions were counted in the millions and, together with the urban poor, formed the base of a host of deracinated, hounded, lost, and invisible underlings on which the pyramid of the imperium stood. Hardship was ubiquitous, and Paul made a point of personal identification with it.[15] Not incidentally, the place where his Gospel was received with greater enthusiasm than anywhere else—Ephesus—was the main slave market outside of Rome.

If Paul's message caught fire especially among the lower classes, its simple content tells why: *God suffers with you!* Critics who denigrate this expressly Christian consolation of suffering as nothing more than a kind of cosmic therapy entirely miss not only the theological urgency of faith but also the psychological sacredness of therapy itself. Instead of undercutting belief, such dismissal actually sanctifies the unconditional positive regard of the good counselor. That all assuaging of suffering, seen from a certain angle, points to the transcendent is essential to Paul's insight. The boldness in his astounding elevation of Jesus of Nazareth to the status of Christ of God, somehow God Himself, lay in the central fact of the ignominy of what befell Jesus. Instead of denying or downplaying the crucifixion, the mode of death expressly reserved for slaves and insurrectionists, Paul made it the keystone of the structure of faith. The cross saves. This was not the crude atonement theology that would come into the Christian imagination later, but a drama of an ultimate empathy. *In Jesus, God suffers with you!*

Or, as Paul put it in his Letter to the Philippians, "Christ Jesus, though he was in the form of God, did not count equality with God a thing to cling to, but emptied himself, taking the form of a servant, being born in the likeness of men. And being found in human form he humbled himself and became obedient unto death, even death on a cross."[16] Paul's language here falls on modern ears as mere piety, a long-domesticated religious rhetoric, yet in a world where the word for "slave" was *servus*, the identification of the Holy One as "servant" would have resounded like the clap of a bell. *That* identification, Paul declared, is what changes suffering into salvation. *What God did for Jesus in turning crucifixion into Resurrection, God does for you.* After the One equal to God undergoes the worst, and lives to make himself available as your source of the same saving grace, what is left to fear? "O death, where is thy victory? O death, where is thy sting?"[17] The "Be not afraid" refrain of Jesus was given its ultimate justification in Paul.

That Paul found such clear, eloquent, and explicit language for this ingenious reinterpretation, already implicit in the Resurrection, is what earns him standing as the founder of Christianity. If suffering masses found an irresistible solace in Jesus Christ as so presented, so did others, including slave masters, Roman officials, and relatively well-off men and women who knew from their own experience that suffering defines not just servitude, but human life.

Privileged people, too, could rejoice to find themselves gathered with those who, otherwise so different, were alike "in Christ." Gathered where, as Paul put it, "there is neither Jew nor Greek, there is neither slave nor free, there is neither male nor female, for you are all one in Christ." These verses are often read by Christians as a formula of universalism, deleting all particularisms, including Jewish, but that is wrong. Note that this obliteration of distinction climaxes in

Paul's affirmation of an all-inclusive, primordial distinctiveness on which even the identity "in Christ" stands: "And if you are Christ's," he goes on to say in the next verse, "then you are Abraham's offspring, heirs according to promise."[18] *You are Jews.*

Jewishness remained the given of Paul's preaching, as the God of Israel remained the object of his worship. Jesus believers were not replacing Israel, but being brought into Israel—not metaphorically, but really. This fulfillment of the promise, and Paul's preaching of it, was widely taken in—the core meaning of End Time arrival. Communities of Jesus people were established in Paul's lifetime or shortly after in Africa, Asia Minor, Greece, Italy, Armenia, Arabia, and perhaps even India.[19] In fact, the first to be receptive to Jesus Christ in all of these places, probably including India, were groups of Jews. To Paul, and to the legions who responded to him, the murdered and risen Jesus was an ultimate revelation, first, of the ever-trustworthy promise of the God of Israel. The "faith" that Paul preached, to repeat a point made earlier, was not a characteristic of the believing individual (and therefore to be opposed to "works," much less to "Law"), but was above all the characteristic attitude of God. The key to salvation was not our faith, but God's faithfulness.

Paul and Rome

We have used the destruction of the Temple in 70 as a defining marker, and so it is important to emphasize, as we reach toward Paul's meaning, that he wrote all of his letters before that. Indeed, by the time of the Temple destruction, which set in motion the separation of "the Jews" from "Christians," Paul was dead. That is why it is absurd to imagine that he himself caused the separation. Any imagined echo in his multifaceted writing of a distinction between "the Church" and "the Synagogue" resounds anachronistically from a future that did not yet exist—a fully ruptured Israel of which Paul knew nothing.

The thirteen books that are attributed to Paul, forming the oldest part of the New Testament,[20] display a subtle, well-educated, and supremely literate mind at work. The Pauline letters show that the figure of Jesus had an astonishing and almost immediate appeal in the broadly Hellenized world of the Jewish Diaspora, including among that sizable population of Gentiles, already noted and referred to as "God fearers," who associated themselves in various places with the Jewish communities.[21] The modern assumption that Paul, as the "Apostle to the Gentiles," preached mainly to non-Jews after "the Jews" rejected him ignores the complexity of both pagan and Jewish identity in the ancient world. The confusions here belong to us, not to them.

We saw earlier how modern notions of a radically univocal monotheism blunt the subtleties—and diversity—of ancient Jewish understandings of the one God. To take another example, Hellenized Jews in the cities of the Mediterranean, including many classically educated Greek speakers, would have had little in common with Aramaic-speaking Palestinian Jews. Many of "the Jews" who criticized the Greek-speaking Paul were almost certainly backcountry Jesus people who disagreed with his theological claims for Christ.

Many pagans, meanwhile, had left behind the crude polytheism of the pantheon, with, for example, the sun deity Sol widely regarded as supreme, effectively worshipped as the only god. Pagans could be monotheists. The Jewish War notwithstanding, the ancient and doggedly defended faith of Israel, predating the primordial myth of Romulus and Remus, could have had broad appeal to such Gentiles. Indeed, the Jewish refusal to betray the Jewish God, a religious loyalty that was the well-known source of Jewish rebellion, could edify even those Romans who fought Jews. A widespread spiritual restlessness prompted many non-Jews in the Hellenized world to attend local synagogues, and the "fear" in "God fearers" implies something of what that restlessness involved. Many, perhaps most, of the

"Gentiles" to whom Paul so famously touted Christ might have half-way been Jews already. They might have been inhibited from a full embrace of Jewish identity by the strict—and culturally off-putting—requirements of halachic observance, especially the initiating ritual of circumcision. That may go a long way toward explaining the special appeal of Paul's preaching, since he saw circumcision, in particular, as not required of non-Jews for incorporation "into Christ." But even among Jews, the meaning of halachic observance was debated. The sharp distinctions that moderns draw in all these categories, sharply dividing "Jew" from "Christian," simply did not exist yet in Paul's time.

For our purposes, the thing to emphasize is that both Peter and Paul, according to the tradition, were martyred in Rome, possibly in Nero's brutal scapegoating of the Jesus people for the infamous fire in 64 C.E. Even if that Roman community of Jesus believers included numerous Gentiles who had been baptized, including God fearers, it is anachronistic to regard Nero's targeted "Christians," as the Roman historian Tacitus calls them, as independent of Judaism. The Jesus people were still an emphatically Jewish sect.[22]

A sizable Jewish community in Rome predated the time of Christ. Scholars put the city's population of Jews in the first century at something like forty to fifty thousand (out of a total Roman population that might have reached a million).[23] While a certain prestige attached to Israel's ancient character, broad opinion in the Hellenized world—as reflected, for example, in the greatest of the classical writers—generally regarded the standoffish Jews with suspicion and hostility.[24]

In Rome itself, though, they could be treated with an intermittent deference. At least since the time of Julius Caesar (reigned 49–44 B.C.E.), and probably because Jews had supported Rome against the Seleucids in Syria beginning in the Maccabean period, Jews of Rome had been granted the privilege of "living according to their ancestral laws." That meant exemptions from requirements of emperor worship, military service, and other obligations. But the Jewish community's standing in the imperial capital was regularly undercut by reactions to the restless nonconformity of first-century Palestinian Jews, who, as we have seen, took fierce religious objection to the Roman occupation of the Holy Land. Before Nero (reigned 54–68 C.E.) launched his post-conflagration persecution, for example, the emperor Claudius (reigned 41–54) expelled all Jews from Rome in 49, an event referred to in Acts.[25] Historians are unsure of the scale and cause of that expulsion, but it was surely a measure of the ever-increasing jeopardy in which first-century Jews found themselves throughout the empire. Jews returned to Rome after the death of Claudius, but their standing was made even more precarious soon enough, with the explosion of the Jewish War in the late 60s. Then, with many thousands of mobilized Romans killed or crippled in far-off Palestine, citizens of the home front had intensely personal reasons to despise the Jews. As the scale of Jewish-Roman violence escalated, the Jews of Rome became a full-fledged pariah people.

That was still true in 80 or so, when the author of Luke picked up his pen. Though the first paroxysm of the multidecade Jewish War had concluded in Jerusalem ten years before, the empire's resulting anti-Judaism was ever palpable in its capital and would have still threatened the people to whom Luke was addressed.

Indeed, the imperial authority of, first, Vespasian (reigned 69–79) and then of his son, Titus (reigned 79–81), had been sealed by their joint triumph in Palestine, where blood had run in gutters and where the carrion stench of thousands of Jewish corpses had fouled the air for years. It is hard for the Christian imagination to accommodate this, because extreme Roman violence has been so downplayed in the Christian memory, but it was the slaughtered Jews who first gave these preeminent rulers the cachet they needed to claim their authority as Augusti.

Across the vast stretch of the Roman Empire, citizens and colonized alike carried tokens—literally—of this expressly Jewish ground of imperial grandeur. Beginning in 71, by order of Vespasian, coins were struck with the engraving JUDAEA CAPTA, above the female personification of the Jewish people, a beaten woman in mourning under a palm tree, the symbol of Jerusalem. The ancient phrase *Judaea Capta* has resonance with the paradigmatically modern word *Judenrein*—"clean of Jews," in Nazi argot. For the next twenty-five years, *Judaea Capta* coins were minted in every denomination, in dozens of separate casts. The wealth of Rome was literally the vanquished Jew.

As the author of Luke was writing his Gospel to Jesus people in Rome, the discreet and careful group to whom it was addressed were witnessing the construction of Rome's first great triumphal monument, the Arch of Titus. It stands to this day, near the southeast corner of the Roman Forum, beside the ruins of the Colosseum, and it, too, like the coins, evokes modern Germany and makes one wonder what monument to Jewish humiliation would stand in Berlin today had World War II gone another way?

The emperor Domitian (reigned 81–96) ordered the Arch of Titus built in 81, in honor of his just-deceased older brother. But in order to valorize Titus, Domitian had to refer back to Jerusalem a decade before, lifting up the savage assault on the Jewish city as nothing less than one of Rome's greatest achievements. The arch's marble friezes show battle scenes from the siege of the Temple, and a victory procession in which legionaries carry loot from the Jewish War back to Rome. The center panel of the entablature features the greatest of the spoils taken from Jerusalem: the seven-branch menorah, bracketed by golden trumpets. In fact, so much gold had been looted from the Jerusalem Temple that the world market for the precious metal was flooded, and gold's value plummeted throughout the Mediterranean. In recent years, archaeologists have discovered evidence that the construction of the Colosseum itself was funded by spoils from the sacking of Jerusalem.[26]

The Arch of Titus is a marble panegyric. Below a pair of winged women, personifications of victory, Titus is shown at the reins of a four-horse chariot. The inscription reads, "The Roman Senate and People dedicate this to the divine Titus Vespasianus Augustus, son of the divine Vespasian." This grand memorializing of Jewish defeat makes clear how large the people of Israel loomed in the Roman imagination—so unlike smashed populations of the colonized elsewhere in the empire. One has to go back nearly three centuries, to Scipio's defeat of Hannibal, and the laying waste of Carthage, to find a comparable mythologizing of an adversary.[27] It is as if Rome knew in the 70s and 80s that the Jewish enemy had not in fact been vanquished, that Jewish communities in cities throughout the Mediterranean would continue their subversive rejection, precisely of such imperial divinity claims as those enshrined on the Arch of Titus, and that an even more brutal return to Jerusalem—a Carthage-like grinding of salt into its soil?—would be necessary in the coming decades. The Jews of Rome understood the precariousness of their situation, and the Arch of Titus was the monument to that vulnerability. It would remain so through the centuries.[28]

For us, the point is that, exactly as this anti-Jewish contempt was being marbleized in the great arch, the author of Luke addressed his Gospel to the Christians of Rome. There can be no surprise, therefore, that we find in his text evidence of a fresh determination to separate Jesus from "the Jews," and to insist that Jesus never violated Roman law.

In Acts, as we saw, the Lukan author has Peter stand up in the streets of Jerusalem, addressing the "Men of Israel" and laying responsibility for the death of Jesus expressly at *their* feet, not those of the Romans, whom Peter expressly exonerates.[29] Jesus had been no enemy of Rome *then*, the logic went in 80, nor are his followers enemies of Rome *now*. The Christian problem, of course, was that the single most indisputable, and unforgettable, fact of Jesus' life story was that he had been executed by Rome in a way reserved to anti-Roman insurrectionists. To overcome that datum of the past, an ingenious reinterpretation of events was required—not a theological reinterpretation, like Paul's, but a historical one. And the Gospel writers created it.

The Passion narrative of Luke outdoes the Passion narrative of Mark in underscoring how the Jewish high priests had forced a reluctant Pontius Pilate to carry out the crucifixion. Indeed, in Luke (unlike Mark), both Pilate and Herod are shown interrogating Jesus and finding him innocent of any crime. The point deserves emphasis: Herod Antipas, who sadistically murdered John the Baptist, and against whom an enraged and grieving Jesus first openly declared himself,[30] is summoned by Luke as a benign witness for Jesus' defense. Pilate, who was, in fact, later stripped of authority as prefect for Judea for being too brutal even for Rome—the Jewish sage Philo, a contemporary, accused Pilate of "wanton injuries, constantly repeated executions without trial, ceaseless and supremely grievous cruelty"—is portrayed in the Gospel as a man of tender conscience.[31] These are extreme manipulations of what scholarship establishes by now to have been among the few confirmed facts of Jesus' history.

When, in Luke, Pilate announces Herod's and his own finding of innocence to the "chief priests and the rulers and the people . . . desiring to release Jesus," those Jewish leaders nevertheless demand that Jesus be crucified. "A third time he said to them, 'Why, what evil has he done?'"[32] But Pilate's goodwill toward Jesus is bowled over by Jewish hatred. One can imagine a follower of Jesus in Rome, as the Arch of Titus is being constructed precisely to demonize the Jewish enemy, reading the Lukan account with relief. *Caesar won't bother us!* From then on, more and more Christian Gentiles would feel just such distance from the Jews whom Rome despised. By the time the

Gospel of Matthew was written, not long after Luke, the legal innocence of Jesus—along with Jewish venality—was being rendered
even more emphatically, with Matthew's added detail of Pontius Pilate's ordering a basin of water to be brought to him on his balcony
high above the crowd of Jews. "He took water and washed his hands
before the crowd, saying, 'I am innocent of this man's blood; see to it
yourselves.' And all the people answered, 'His blood be on us and on
our children!'"[33] And so it would be.

Not a Christian

We are tracking a tragedy that unfolded within the Jewish community during the Roman War, and the last verses of the Acts of the
Apostles render it with heartbreaking force. Recall that the author of
Luke and Acts structured his two-volume work as a staggered road
story: the Gospel moves from Galilee to Jerusalem, and Acts tracks
the narrative from Peter's proselytizing in Jerusalem to Paul's mis-
sionizing in Rome. The arrival of the Gospel in the imperial capital is
the signal of its triumph, a fulfillment of Jesus' last command to bring
his message "into all the world." But Acts concludes with Paul's stark
repudiation of "the local leaders of the Jews,"[34] who "see but never
perceive." Acts, that is, defines "the Jews" as Paul's enemy pure and
simple.[35] Against all the sufferings inflicted upon Paul by "the Jews,"
the author of Luke contrasts the respect and good treatment shown
him by Roman officials and soldiers.[36] Thus, Paul's last words in this
text amount to a searing judgment against the Jews:

As they disagreed among themselves, they departed, after Paul
had made this final statement: "The Holy Spirit was right in saying to your fathers through Isaiah the prophet: 'Go to this people
and say, "You shall indeed hear but never understand; and you
shall indeed see, but never perceive." For this people's heart has

grown dull; and their ears are heavy of hearing, and their eyes they have closed' . . . Let it be known to you then that this salvation of God has been sent to the Gentiles; they will listen!"

It should be emphasized here that "Luke's" Paul, a character in the historical fiction of Acts, is not to be confused with the actual Paul, who died decades before "Luke" wrote. Nowhere more so than in the Acts portrait of Paul can we see the work as literary invention. That shows, especially, in Acts' final postscript about Paul in Rome, where the Lukan author's conclusion is "And he lived there two whole years at his own expense, and welcomed all who came to him, preaching the kingdom of God and teaching about the Lord Jesus Christ quite openly and unhindered."[37] This sepia-toned portrait of a self-supporting elder living tranquilly in Rome would have advanced Luke's basic aim of shoring up amity between the Jesus movement and the empire, which an account of Paul's true fate would not have done.

Tradition dating to the early second century holds that Paul was brutally murdered in Rome by Roman officialdom, perhaps, as we saw, during that Nero-ordered persecution in 64. The tradition emphasizes that Paul was beheaded, which is why the sword is a Pauline icon. That Acts, written something like twenty years after Paul's death, cites him in the postscript as the great authority for the supersession by Gentiles of Jewish election contrasts with Paul's own words, given in his final letter, written in the early 60s. Addressed, indeed, to the same Jesus community to which the author of Luke will subsequently write, the Letter to the Romans stands as Paul's great defense of Jews against Jesus people who had begun to denigrate them. "I ask, then," he says at the start of the letter's resounding eleventh chapter, "has God rejected his people? By no means! I myself am an Israelite, a descendant of Abraham, a member of the tribe of Benjamin. God has not rejected his people whom he foreknew."

Paul cuts to the heart of the issue—what will be called Christian "re-placement" theology, the idea that since Jews rejected salvation in Je-sus, Gentiles will have it—by expressly repudiating all who deny the permanence of the covenant that God made with the people of Israel, "for the gifts and the call of God are irrevocable."[38]

In this book, we have tracked the consequences of the Christian forgetting of Roman mega-violence against the Jews that began in the late 60s, but here, perhaps, we come to one of the most significant of those consequences. Saint Paul lives in the Christian imagination as the chief sponsor of Christian contempt for Jews, the avatar of law versus grace, flesh versus spirit, works versus faith, Moses versus Je-sus, the Old Covenant versus the New. This brutal dichotomizing was attributed to Paul most influentially by Martin Luther, who used a perceived Jewish legalism, materialism, and obsession with exter-nals as stand-ins for the decadence of his nemesis, the pope. "Because the Papists, like the Jews," he wrote, "insist that anyone wishing to be saved must observe their ceremonies, they will perish like the Jews."[39] After Luther, both Protestants and Catholics read Paul as the pre-eminent tribune of Jewish corruption—a misreading that had ter-rible consequences, especially in Luther's Germany, where the *Volk* were defined in ontological opposition to *Juden*.

Paul's traumatic vision of the risen Lord on the road to Damas-cus, as we saw, is celebrated as his "conversion" from Judaism to Christianity. He famously brought the faith to non-Jews, and his ar-gument that they need not undergo the ritual circumcision that initi-ated male converts into Judaism is taken to mark the radical break between Church and Synagogue. Hence Paul's image as "Apostle to the Gentiles," leading the way in leaving the rejected Jews behind.

Nothing of that is true. Paul never "converted" to Christianity for the simple reason that, during his lifetime, there was no such thing as Christianity. When Paul appeals, as he often does, to the "Scrip-tures," he is referring only to the Jewish Scriptures, with which his readers would have been familiar only because their religious reflections, even as Jesus people, occurred wholly in the context of synagogue study. Indeed, the house assemblies of those Paul addressed would have taken place under synagogue authority.[40] There are tensions galore in Paul, but they reflect not the bifurcations of a Church-versus-Synagogue oppositionalism, but the complexities, and even paradoxes, that adhere in every human heart—and every human community. In Paul's case, these complexities adhered in a profoundly and permanently Jewish heart, and the paradoxes were a mark of the Jewish community of which he was so loyally a part. Faith in the Jew Jesus, for Paul, was an intensification of faith in the God of Israel. Faith, to repeat, was *God's* faithfulness. Paul was a Jew from start to finish—period, full stop.

Here is the point: the contrary—and typically Christian—reading of Paul's meaning is entirely colored by *unknowingly* looking back at him and his writing through a lens darkened by the destruction of the Temple in 70, an event that Paul neither experienced nor anticipated. As we have seen and seen again, that interruption in history resulted in the replacement of a multifaceted set of Judaisms—diverse parties, each with its distinct emphasis, coexisting *within* Israel—by a mutually exclusive split between the only two groups of surviving Jews. That split became increasingly defined by the either-or of an unforgiving religious polemic. Paul knew nothing of the conflict between the rabbis and the Jesus people over a post-Temple Jewish identity simply because, for him, the Temple had been the permanent center of faith for as long as he'd lived. It cannot be emphasized too much: *Paul died before the Temple was destroyed.*

As Acts makes clear, Paul (like other Jesus people of the time) never stopped worshipping at the Temple. They never stopped thinking of themselves as Jews. Paul constantly promoted the Temple even among non-Jewish adherents of the Jesus movement, regularly collecting from them the traditional Temple tithe.[41]

If Paul was in dispute with fellow Jews over the meaning of Jesus—and he was—that dispute must be understood as part of the broad diversity of belief that was a mark of the Jewish community at the time, and equally a mark of the various Jesus communities. If Paul believed that the salvation available to Jews was now available to Gentiles—and he did—it was decidedly *as a Jew* that he so believed. As the Jewish scholar Mark D. Nanos explains, "When Paul argued for Gentile inclusion in Christ without becoming Jews . . . he did not appeal to the nullification of Torah because of the supersession of Christ. He appealed instead to the inherent truth of monotheism and developed his position within the context of the Shema: 'Or is God the God of Jews only? Is He not the God of Gentiles also? Of course, for He is the One God of all.'"[42] For Paul, the Shema, affirming that the one God is the God of Israel, also affirmed—precisely because of God's oneness—that the one God is the God of all humanity. This was a profoundly Jewish affirmation.

The ancient tradition of Israel had foreseen a time—End Time—when the eyes of all humanity would be opened to the great wonder of this all-encompassing embrace by the one God. Like many Jews of his generation, Paul was convinced that the End Time had dawned. Early in this book, we emphasized the ubiquity of such Jewish expectation, especially as tied to the vision of the Son of Man so dramatically laid out in the book of Daniel. In line with that vision, Paul regarded Jesus as the Son of Man figure ushering in the End Time, when, according to *Jewish* belief, Gentiles, too, would be brought into the love of the God of Israel.[43]

Among Hellenized Jews away from Palestine, especially in communities responsive to large groups of God fearers, there was much debate over the precise requirements of circumcision for adult converts to Judaism, so not even the circumcision dispute that made Paul controversial, and that came to be seen as the decisive cause of the "parting of the ways" between Judaism and Christianity, was unique to the followers of Jesus.[44] "The Jews" who appear in Acts as the enemies of Paul, and who, in his own letters, are the object of his criticisms, may well have been less the general population of "Jews" than Jewish followers of Jesus, among whom disputes over the meaning of Law observance, the time of Christ's return, the character of Jesus' messiahship, of his divinity, and so on, were intense.[45] All of these distinctions—not only among Jews but among Jewish Jesus people—are lost to subsequent generations of Christians in the smoke of the Roman destruction of Jerusalem. Not only are the distinctions forgotten, but so is the mega-violence that swallowed them up.

That "the Jews" as such were never enemies of Paul is most emphatically realized in the fact that "for all his fulminations against the observance of Jewish Law," as the Jewish scholar Jon D. Levenson writes, "Paul never blames the Jews for the death of Jesus or ascribes the founding of the Church to God's wrath against the people of the old covenant. Indeed, he does not attribute Jesus' demise to the Jews at all—an extraordinary datum in light of the reports of the trial and execution of Jesus in the canonical Gospels."[46] There it is: the canonical Gospels, unlike the letters of Paul, came *after*—were probably occasioned by—the outbreak of the Roman War. The difference between the letters of Paul, when properly read on their own terms, and the Gospels, which initiate a stunning "Christian" polemic against the people of Jesus, is what I have dubbed the first Holocaust.

The Fate of Carthage

But the destruction of the Temple in 70 was only the beginning. The fate of Carthage did indeed await Jerusalem. The last of the canonical Gospels, John, was completed early in the second century, thirty or forty years—another full generation—after Mark began the process of converting memory into literature. By then the polemical dispute between those Jews who accepted Jesus as Messiah and those who did not had reached fever pitch—affecting subsequent memory and literature both. A signal of that heat is found in the fact that the by-then-contemptuous phrase "the Jews" (in Greek, *hoi Ioudaioi*), having appeared a total of sixteen times in the previous three Gospels, appears in John seventy-one times.[47] Inspired by such polemic, Gentile readers of the Gospel could reimagine Jesus as—no surprise—a Gentile himself. After that, Jews could not affirm the Jesus presented to them by the Church without denying the very God whom Jesus preached.

But the tension escalates further. Jesus is shown, in Mark, starting out in mortal conflict with an embodied Satan who offers bribes and "possesses" swine; in Luke, written a decade later, the enemy of Jesus is still the "evil one," but that evil is now centered in "the chief priests and officers of the Temple."[48] By the time of John, the identification of Satan with "the Jews"—the totality of the people—has become complete. The cosmic conflict between divine light and primordial darkness has become conflict, simply and tragically, with a known and ever-identifiable group. Here, in Elaine Pagels's great phrase, we have the origin of Satan: Satan is the Jews.[49]

But even this conflict is playing out mainly *within* the Jewish community—one group of Jews demonizing another. Something else has to intervene to turn this ferocious intra-Jewish enmity into something wholly *anti*-Jewish, moving its lethality to an entirely other level. Sure enough, an intervention comes. What surprise can there be when the decisive turn comes in the next outbreak of Rome's Jewish War?

Now, having seen the bare facts of the decades-long Roman War outlined early in this book, we can appreciate the world-historic consequences of all of its three phases: the Great Revolt in 70; the Mediterranean-wide Rebellion of the Exile, between 115 and 117; and the Bar Kokhba revolt in Judea, between 133 and 135. No sooner was the last of the canonical Gospels completed—John, early in the second century—than the text's standing as a signal of intra-Jewish dispute began to morph into a text serving as a charter of conflict between two recognizably separate groups—Christians against Jews. The transforming was brought to a kind of completion by what the Roman historian Cassius Dio, referring to Hadrian's war, called "a war of no slight importance nor of brief duration."

Recall that Hadrian, in 135, eradicated what was left of Jerusalem, dispersing its population, deleting its name from history, and replacing it with a pagan capital, Aelia Capitolina, centered on a temple dedicated to Jupiter. Indeed, "replacement" wholly braced the imagination of non-Jews, for, with Hadrian's program of ethnic cleansing, a Gentile voice began decisively to *replace* the Jewish one within the Jesus movement.

After all, Jerusalem and its environs, through all tribulations, had remained a center of a decidedly Jewish community of Jesus believers, and now that community was simply gone—dispersed or dead. Of the 600,000 Jews Cassius Dio says Hadrian killed in this last war, an unnumbered multitude were Jesus believers—who firmly understood both the Jewishness of Jesus and the Jewishness of the terms, rooted in Hebrew Scriptures, within which he was interpreted. With the death and dispersal of the Jerusalem Jesus community, the influence of this core of Jewish-Christian belief and practice would now be lost in a movement increasingly dominated by non-Jews.

Reading texts organized around Jesus' conflict with "the Jews," it's no wonder the Gentile Christians readily imagined him as a non-Jew like themselves. Thus, the narrative of a freely inventing, Scripture-based imagination (including the report, say, that dice were thrown for the robe of Jesus, a fictional detail lifted directly from Psalm 22) could be taken by Gentiles as a journalistic retelling of events that had actually occurred (as if Roman centurions had actually gambled at the foot of the cross). The Gospels had come into being as a kind of Bible-based interpretation and commentary akin to what Jews call

Midrash, but second-century Gentiles, increasingly cut off from Jewish influence, knew little of that. A top-to-bottom amnesia was the result.

Momentously, Christians could now read the Jewish Scriptures as mere "foreshadowing" of Christ's arrival, and when Christians read their own texts, which were coming to be regarded as sacred, they could misunderstand as future-predicting "prophecy" the images and anecdotes that the oral tradition and early writers had drawn from Hebrew Scriptures. But now those images and anecdotes were taken as "prophecy" that had been "fulfilled" in Christ. If an ancient seer had predicted that dice would be thrown for the Messiah's robe, and dice were then actually thrown for the robe of Jesus, that "proved" that Jesus was the Messiah. The flip in the Jesus movement from Jewish to Gentile domination brought with it a flip in how Gospel texts were read. Now they were read *against* the Jews, a tension that was bound to escalate as "unbelieving" Jews remained unconvinced by the "proofs" that Gentile Christians drew from Jewish texts.

Take another example: Gentile readers of the second century, who had little or no knowledge of how the Gospels had been composed, could understand virginity as an essential note of Mary's identity. Her being "overshadowed" by the Holy Spirit, in the account offered by Luke, could be taken as evidence of Jesus' divinity when, in Hellenistic mythology, miraculous births were a standard motif in making divinity claims for powerful figures. Alexander the Great's father was Zeus, for example, and, more to the point of Luke's narrative, Caesar Augustus was said to have been conceived not by a human father but by Apollo. Yet what Gentile readers would have missed is that Luke's story draws from Hebrew Scripture, especially this passage from Isaiah: "Therefore, the Lord Himself will give you a sign. Behold, the young woman shall conceive and bear a son, and she shall call his name Immanuel." In the Greek version of the

Scripture that Luke and, after him, Matthew used, the Hebrew phrase "young woman" is rendered with a word that means "virgin." But in the post-Jerusalem context, a wholly Gentile appropriation of Israel's expectation meant that Mary's virginity, though rooted in a translation anomaly, "proved" that the messianic age "foreseen" by Isaiah had come—this despite the fact that the virgin birth is mentioned in none of Paul's writings.[50]

Since radical Jewish and Jewish-Christian dispersal from Jerusalem and Judea were general consequences of Hadrian's war, the Christian center of gravity, like Judaism's, necessarily tilted toward the Diaspora. A simultaneous influx of Gentiles into the Christian movement throughout the Mediterranean was also shifting the weight. Soon, a bishop in far Anatolia would coin the term "Old Testament" to distinguish the Hebrew Scriptures from the now hallowed texts about Jesus—the "New Testament." The value-laden bipolarity of "Old Testament" and "New Testament"—"Old Covenant" and "New Covenant"—would perfectly capture the inbuilt denigration of the "Synagogue" that began to define an increasingly distinct "Church." As with "New" versus "Old," the "Church" defined itself positively by defining the "Synagogue" negatively. And it is no surprise that the same Anatolian bishop who invented the term "Old Testament" was the very bishop we noted before as having been first to slap the fateful label "deicide people" on the Jews, making them nothing less than the cosmic murderers of God.[51]

But nothing captures the Christian denigration of Jews more forcefully than what amounts to the largest single impact the Roman War against the Jews had on the Christian imagination: its permanent and perverse contempt for the Temple of Israel. The one exception Hadrian and emperors after him made to the iron rule of Jewish exclusion from Aelia Capitolina was, as we saw, to allow Jews re-admittance to the city on one day a year, Tisha B'Av, the day of mourning, when

Jews ritually bewailed the loss of the Temple. That ritual of grief remains part of the Jewish liturgical calendar to this day. Romans valued
this annual reminder of their victory over the stubborn resistance of
Jews, but to Christians, soon enough, the destruction of the Temple
took on even more significance. As we saw, Mark and other post-70
texts incorporated the trauma of the Temple's loss by imagining Jesus as
having forewarned of it, and even by thinking of Jesus himself replacing
the Temple as the locus of God's presence in the world. The Temple, in
other words, took up a position in the negative-positive bipolarity that
informed the Christian imagination: the Temple versus Jesus.

That meant that the triumph of Jesus assumed the defeat of the
Temple. Unlike Jews for whom the destruction of the Temple remained a source of bottomless grief, including even those rabbis who
saw the destruction as punishment for a Jewish failure to adequately
observe the Law, Christians could rejoice at the Temple destruction
as the occasion of—no, *proof* of—Jesus' victory over the Jews. This
was doubly true once the Gentile-dominated Church lost the capacity to read its own texts in light of their profoundly Jewish origins. Most momentously, the Gospels began to be read as if they had
been written shortly after the events reported—eyewitness accounts,
instead of a literature of reinterpretation composed a full generation
later. The real impact of the Roman War on countless Jews, including Jesus people, was deleted from memory. When the Gospels came
to be understood as dating to shortly after Jesus' death, rather than
shortly after the destruction of the Temple, Jesus was understood as
magically seeing into the future to "predict" that destruction, a capacity that itself became further proof of his divinity.[52]

Once the Church, ever seeking a safe place within the empire, had
formed the habit, in remembering the fate of Jesus, of emphasizing
Roman virtue over Jewish venality, such misremembering was compounded. If the Roman legions had done the actual work of torching
and dismantling and looting the Temple, they were understood as

having done so as nothing less than agents of God. The Romans destroyed the Temple to punish Jews for destroying Jesus. Therefore, whatever ruins remained of the Temple, on the elevated plateau in the center of Jerusalem, would be precious to Christians *as ruins*. The ruins were payback. For the centuries that Christians controlled Jerusalem, especially during the stretch between Constantine's revalorizing of the city, in 335, and the Muslim conquest of 638, the Temple Mount served as a trumpeted sacrament of Jewish defeat. The Temple Mount served, that is, as the city's garbage dump.[53]

CHAPTER EIGHT

The Women, Too

Wisdom is radiant and unfading,
and she is easily discerned by those who love her . . .
She is a breath of the power of God,
And a pure emanation of the glory of the Almighty.

—Wisdom of Solomon[1]

Misogyny

Peter and Paul were alike in being elevated, across the decades, as founding heroes of the Christian movement—ultimately, the Church. But in truth, neither man could rise in the estimate of the faithful until another figure declined, and that figure was a woman. In this case, psychological and factual confusion that so marked perceptions of the Jesus people in the years of the Roman Wars was compounded by what must be reckoned with as a certain willful misrepresentation, produced in large part by unexamined patriarchal assumptions. In the ancient world, after all, there was not the remotest idea of male-female equality.

Patriarchy was a crucial factor as a Church was being formed, with communal fellowship centered on a new hierarchy defined like the hierarchies of the time. If the turning of "the Jews" into the enemy of Jesus was in some way, and mainly, a tragic accident of history, there was a distinct manipulation of memory and interpretation about the place of women that was, by comparison, nothing if not more deliberate. And it should be emphasized here that the reason our attention turns now to women is that there is a continuity between a sanctified male chauvinism and the mechanisms of religious anti-Judaism. Contempt for women and denigration of Jews are related. Both are symptoms of the larger disease referred to earlier as oppositionalism: no positive assertion without some negative contempt.

For our purposes, the matter is even simpler, since, without a more accurate retrieval of the real place of women in the life of Jesus, there can be no recovery of Jesus Christ as he was. What we need, in fact, is a truer rendering of various figures whose names were mostly Mary. The problem is generally understood—like the problem of Christian anti-Judaism—to have begun with Paul. The charge against him regarding Judaism is, as we have seen, unfair. What of the charge about women?

Writings attributed to Paul are understood as especially denigrating toward women, and contemporary feminists have regarded him as a particular nemesis. Indeed, the most antifemale statement in the New Testament is given in the Pauline epistle 1 Timothy: "Let a woman learn in silence with all submissiveness. I permit no woman to teach or to have authority over men; she is to keep silent. For Adam was formed first, then Eve; and Adam was not deceived, but the woman was deceived and became a transgressor. Yet women will be saved through bearing children, if she continues in faith and love and holiness, with modesty."[2] Verses from other letters reflect this same view of women as made for subservience, as the source of male moral failure, and as chained to childbearing. The admonition "Wives, be subject to your husbands" appears in both Colossians and Ephesians[3] and has been the banner phrase ever since not just of household power dynamics but of spousal abuse. In the First Letter to the Corinthians one reads, "As in all the churches of the saints, the women should keep silence in the churches. For they are not permitted to speak, but should be subordinate, as even the law says."[4]

The two letters to Timothy, with the letter to Titus, are sometimes called the pastoral epistles, because they are full of practical advice from Paul to his protégés, counsel in matters of Church administration and organization. The first letter's dark admonition about women—never to admit them to leadership—has been the ground for male supremacy in the Church ever since. The trouble is, as scholars now agree, that Paul did not write the pastoral epistles, including the radioactive 1 Timothy—this despite its opening verse, which expressly attributes the letter to "Paul, an apostle of Christ Jesus by command of God our Savior and of Christ Jesus our hope."[5]

Similarly, there is a near consensus that Paul also did not write Colossians or Ephesians, both of which are notable for verses aimed at keeping women in their place. Someone coming after Paul authored these antifemale strictures, with a *post facto* claiming of Paul as the authority for their enforcement. A tip-off comes in 1 Timothy's elevation of Eve's responsibility for the Fall—the exoneration of the male, the indictment of the female as source of sin—since in other, firmly authentic, letters, Paul dramatically faults Adam as the progenitor of original sin, leaving Eve aside. "Therefore as sin came into the world through one man and death through sin," Paul writes in Romans, "death reigned from Adam forward." In 1 Corinthians, Paul contrasts the saving activity of Christ with the doom wrought by Adam: "The first man was from the earth, a man of dust; the second man is from heaven."[6] *Nowhere* in these authentic writings of Paul is the woman the originator of wickedness, but because the great apostle is yoked to this antifemale slander, it would come to dominate the moral imagination of Christians.[7]

Similarly, antifemale verses attributed to Paul even *within* letters that are authenticated as his own, like the 1 Corinthians admonition to female silence just cited, are reliably understood by scholars to be "post-Pauline interpolations," additions to or adjustments in Paul's original work by later editors and redactors. The true voice of Paul, that is, expressly—and approvingly—portrays women not as silent, but as "praying and prophesying" in Christian gatherings.[8] The interpolations and forgeries that insist on female subordination reflect, in one scholar's view, the "misogyny" of later Church leaders—perhaps as late as the mid-second century—whose policies of excluding women from positions of responsibility required such adjustments in the contrary evidence of the early texts.[9] The downfall of women was a precondition of the rise of men across the decades in which the Jesus people organized themselves along lines of power drawn not by Jesus, but by the broader Mediterranean culture. One needn't imagine Paul to have been a twenty-first-century feminist to pick up the clear signal that, for him, the state of being "in Christ" trumped all such cultural divisions and hierarchies, and that clearly shows both in how he wrote about women and in how he interacted with them.

In letters reliably sourced to Paul, and directly contradicting the norms set down in epistles or interpolations wrongly attributed to him, Paul praises numerous women as his personal partners in spreading the good news of Jesus Christ, including Junia, whom he calls an "apostle" and honors as having been "in Christ before me," and Phoebe, whom he calls a "deaconess . . . a helper of many and of myself as well," and to whom he entrusted his letter to the Romans, depending on her to deliver that, his most important work.[10] It would have been out of the question for Paul that such female co-workers should be condemned to subservient silence. Paul traveled with these women, depended on the support of female patrons, and organized numerous local communities around the hospitality of powerful women. Because first- and second-generation Christian gatherings took place in domestic settings, which, unlike the public sphere, were traditionally presided over by women, positions of authority in these "house churches" naturally went to women. Paul's authentic writings consistently reflect that. Indeed, they take the essential equality of women as a given.

Parity was the point. The women at whose tables the community gathered did not assume positions of superiority, but practiced what feminist scholar Elisabeth Schüssler Fiorenza calls a "discipleship of equality."[11] One needn't look back through a romantic haze, as to a primordial golden age, to note ample evidence that the early days of the community of the baptized were marked by a spirit of egalitarianism. That shows in the famous "neither Jew nor Greek . . . slave nor free . . . male nor female" inclusiveness in Galatians cited earlier.[12] Scholars broadly accept this defining commonality as characteristic of the first generations of the Jesus movement, a relative freedom from structures of hierarchy and dominance. This might have resulted from the spirit of *agape*, or group love, that can inform a new, enthusiastic minority faction, but the fact that the memory of Jesus of Nazareth centered the gatherings of that community remains the most decisive factor in the way it organized itself and understood itself. The community was the person of Jesus carried into the future, and Jesus took reciprocity and equality for granted.

Even allowing for the impossibility—for us—of an encounter with a historical Jesus "behind the texts," the unanimous testimony of the tradition on this point makes it more than plausible to regard Jesus himself as having been marked by a rare egalitarian spirit. We saw how his radically open table fellowship, which included a wide range of characters received with kindness, contrasted with the fierce judgmentalism of John the Baptist. Indeed, an ecumenical spirit extending to the worldly, to the flawed, to the politically compromised, and to the sexually stigmatized was what separated Jesus from his rigorously puritanical mentor. Unconditional respect marked Jesus' encounters, including—if not especially—those with women. We will see more of this below. That the Church forgot that, despite numerous Gospel passages highlighting the place of women, was a curse not just on Christendom but on Western civilization, which rose from it. Present denigrations of women—still no female priests in Roman Catholicism; still no female autonomy over reproduction; still, for that matter, no equal pay for equal work—begin here.

To dismantle such an unjust structure requires a still further reckoning with what established it in the first place.

Discipleship of Equals

So something happened in the Jesus movement to push women back into a kind of subservience, silence, and subjugation that was far more typical of gender relations in the broader Hellenized world. Paul, like Jesus, treated women as equals, but those "Pauline" letters inaccurately attributed to him, and coming decades after his death, take for granted—and seek to reinforce—a ranked, professionalized ministry of which Paul would have known nothing: "If any one aspires to the office of bishop," the author of 1 Timothy declares, "he desires a noble task." Titus cites Paul to define the bishop as one to "exhort and reprove with all authority."[13] This coming of "bishops," with power to enforce an incipient orthodoxy of belief and uniformity of practice, also suggests a movement away from the primordial egalitarianism and diversity that were marks of the churches Paul served.

The letters Paul is known to have authored never refer to the office of "bishop." There are "apostles," from the Greek for "a person sent forth" to preach; "presbyters," or local presiders; and "deacons," comparable to, say, today's community organizers. There is an extensive discourse on a priesthood, tied to sacrificial conceptions of the Eucharist, but that comes in the much later Letter to the Hebrews, for which scholars unanimously reject Pauline authorship. In the real Paul, there is found no episcopate exerting broad, transgeographical authority, yet, in Paul's name, it came.

Something changed in the fundamental structure of power in the Church—when it became the Church and was no longer the Jesus people, a widely dispersed, loosely connected aggregate of the faithful.

The "discipleship of equals," evident in the first century, morphed in the second century into the kind of hierarchy that generally structured patriarchal organizations in the Roman Empire. Indeed, the empire would soon enough serve as an organizational model for the Church, with bishops exercising a regionalized power analogous to that exercised by provincial governors, the legates responsible to the Caesars. This organizational evolution into what Schüssler Fiorenza terms a "Kyriarchy," was accompanied by a theological one, with Jesus the self-styled servant reimagined as a kind of imperial master, a politicization of his messianic title, Kyrios, "Lord."[14]

Well before that—and to make such a development of Church polity possible—Paul's female partners as partners had to be forgotten. More significant still, the woman-centered experience of Jesus, as recorded even in Gospels that themselves were written by men seeking to reassert dominance over women, was downplayed, even twisted. There are dramatic and numerous Gospel passages that show women as Jesus' responsible and valued disciples. The Syrophoenician woman who challenges Jesus—"even the dogs under the table eat the children's crumbs!"—was his teacher, making him understand that faith transcends the tribe.[15] When Jesus healed the woman who touched his garment, he made a point of saying that he did so because of her goodness, not his own.[16] Jesus presented numerous women as models of faith: the persistent widow, the watchful virgin, the widow with the mite.[17] Jesus defended women against unfair divorce practices. He affirmed the dignity of prostitutes. He discussed theology with the woman at the well, and was not put off by her being ritually unclean.[18] He lifts up Mary and Martha, sisters of his beloved friend Lazarus, as exemplars of kindness and holiness. And this is to say nothing of the women who anointed him with oil, who stayed with him to the end, and whom, of all people, he loved most. Of these, we will see more below. For now, the point is that, in one Gospel verse after another, Jesus' egalitarian respect for women is emphasized—this despite the evangelists' inbred discomfort with that respect. But over the generation that followed the composition of those texts, Jesus' propensity for relating to women as equals was, in effect, deleted from the Christian imagination. How did this happen? Why?

Most commentary on the question treats the shift in the way the Christian community understood itself as a development true to the way things are. That women were in positions of equality in the beginning of the Jesus movement because of Jesus' own example was taken at first to be normal, perhaps. Then it was exceptional. Then, over time, it was denied ever to have been that way. Wasn't such a dynamic built into the human condition, with males destined to dominate? The Church, in this view, was at the mercy of an irresistible— and proper—male-supremacist impulse, one bound to assert itself against the anomalous first instinct of the Jesus movement.

But was the development of a woman-denigrating power structure that simple? That inevitable? That ordinary? Once again, it can be illuminating to pay close attention to the chronology here. What separated the authentic Pauline epistles, with their ethos of "neither Jew nor Greek . . . slave nor free . . . male nor female," from the world of "Let a woman learn in silence with all submissiveness"? Our earlier reflection on Paul's supposed villainy in relation to the Jews suggests the answer, for, as with that misremembering, the decisive before-and-after boundary may well have been the year 70.

Paul's authentic letters come before that year (since he died in the 60s); all of the pseudo-Pauline writing, with its misogyny and hierarchy, comes after. Is it possible that the viral effects of the mega-violence of the Roman War against the Jews showed itself, once again, in the way women came to be regarded in the Christian movement? The morals and meaning of the Jesus movement in relation to "the Jews" were demonstrably corrupted by that war. Did something similar happen with regard to women?

Men at War

War stories are written by men, and, since the accounts are inevitably created by the victors, they have the purpose of valorizing male conquest. Courage, physical prowess, camaraderie, honor, self-sacrifice—these are notes of male combat saga. If brutality, or even cruelty, is recorded, it is always with a view to justification. Thucydides, the founder of Western war discourse, rarely mentions women, and when he does, they are almost always paired with children, as victims. In the Funeral Speech, as rendered by Thucydides, Pericles glorifies not only the silence *of* women, but silence *about* them, saying "the greatest glory of a woman is to be least talked about among men."[19]

Thus, war is conceived without particular attention to its effect on women. Josephus, the Roman-Jewish historian, wrote in that tradition with his account of the first phase of the Jewish War, climaxing in the ravaging of Jerusalem and the destruction of the Temple. Just as the present book attempts to correct Christian amnesia about Rome's war on Jews and its catastrophic effect on Jewish-Christian relations, so an overdue attention to the fate of females in that trauma is essential. Instead of the vague dismissal of "women and children," casualties counted in the abstract without attending to specific experience—women not even meriting their own distinct category of victimhood—can we more directly call to mind what must have befallen women during the decades of savage anti-Jewish violence, the very decades in which a major shift in Christian attitudes toward women occurred? What about the women?[20]

There are no records of an explicitly female experience of the Jerusalem siege. We know from Josephus that something like ten thousand males were crucified—that forest of crosses ringing the Temple Mount. But females were not crucified by Roman legionaries. What horror befell them, then? The answer requires no testimony, and no memory. It requires only the most rudimentary acquaintance with war itself. The tsunami of mass violence, when it crashes over women, can be lethal, but it is almost always a matter of rape.

Rape is the unspoken word when it comes to war. A coconspiracy of silence joins the perpetrator—who, beneath layers of denial, knows after the fact how shameful was his act—and the victim, whose wound extends from the physical violation to the psychological blow and the social stigma. After the storm of violence passes, no one wants to speak of what the men did to the women, and so women's fates are lumped in with children's, and reckoned with, if at all, in the abstractions of casualty numerology.

Consider this, for the era of mass media. The Western European memory of the violence of World War II includes a general sense of Soviet-inflicted mayhem in the spring of 1945 as the Red Army swept out of the east toward Berlin. Yet the brutality of the Russians, even when postwar anti-Communism might have exploited it, was downplayed in favor of the emphasis given to the wickedness of the Nazis. Here, as a corrective provided by the late historian Tony Judt, is a tally of Red Army antifemale bedlam, which postwar calculations mainly ignored: in Vienna, during three weeks in April 1945, nearly ninety thousand Austrian women were raped—and that number counts only those reported by clinics and hospitals. In the first week of May, an even larger number of women were raped in Berlin. When a leading Communist learned of the Red Army's rampage, he protested to Stalin himself. Stalin complained not of the rapes but of the man who objected to them: "Can't he understand the soldier who has gone through blood and fire and death, if he has fun with a woman or takes a trifle?"[21]

The cloak over the European memory of Soviet sexual violence did not lift until the 1990s, when the Continent was presented with a fresh outbreak of assaults against women. In 1992, Serbian security forces initiated a systematic program of ethnic cleansing in Bosnia, the centerpiece of which was the raping of Muslim women. But this war, unlike others, was closely reported by an aggressive press. With its Serb-run rape camps and blatant sex slavery, Bosnia brought war rape into the open. Gang rapes were common, and women were raped in public, often in the presence of family members. By the time that third in a succession of Balkan wars ended, in 1995,[22] two million Bosnians had been displaced, more than one hundred thousand were dead, and an officially counted twenty thousand women had been raped, most of them repeatedly and systematically—a number that certainly represents a huge undercounting. Attention drawn to this phenomenon of rape used as a method of ethnic cleansing in Bosnia led to demands that rape as such be defined, for the first time, as a war crime. That campaign was what brought the prior history of Soviet sexual violence into the light.[23]

War rape is not a matter of, in Stalin's terms, "fun with a woman" or "taking a trifle." Rather, it is the ultimate method of assault against a people. The final oppression of patriarchy consists in the fact that when an enemy soldier sexually violates a woman, the real object of attack is not the person on whom he throws himself. However much marauding soldiers feel the heat of lust, the relevant emotion is not desire, but hate, for the assault is directed not only at females, but at males. Raping "the nation's women" completes the emasculation of the nation's men. A mass dishonoring of females shames the males, rubs their faces in defeat, shows them to be incapable of their primordial duty—as protectors of "the weaker sex." The nation is not destroyed, that is, until the women are fucked.

Nor is the insult merely a matter of the transient horror of forced intercourse, because an even more drastic and lasting demonstration of the impotence of the defeated comes with impregnation, which carries the conquest forward to childbirth, a future-tense vanquishing of ethnic purity. War rape aims at war conception. In the part of Germany that the Soviets controlled in 1945–46, something like

200,000 "Russian babies" were born to German women roughly nine months after the Soviet offensive.[24]

It is safe to assume that, apart from technologies of conquest, war rape was no different in the ancient world. Indeed, it had special standing in the founding myth of Rome. Romulus, after all, had no sooner murdered his brother Remus and established his namesake city than, lacking women, he led his band against the local tribe of Sabines. The "rape of the Sabine women" defines Rome's first triumph, and the abducted Sabine "wives" gave Rome its lineage—and the European imagination one of its perennial tropes.[25] No wonder the setting loose of Roman legions struck terror in the hearts of ancients wherever the empire spread. Sexual violence was eventually outlawed in Rome—except against slaves—and by the first century it would not have been openly acknowledged as an essential mode of Roman conquest, yet that is precisely what it was. Though ancient sources, like modern ones, are mostly mute on the subject for reasons of shame and stigma, it can reasonably be assumed that rape was a savage mark of the Roman War against the Jews.

Jerusalem itself had a long history as a city under siege, and the Bible records that its women had again and again been targets of sexual violence.[26] In the Roman war that began in 68 C.E., climaxing in the assault on the holy city in 70, tens of thousands of women can be assumed to have been raped. Using the figures from the Bosnian war as a template (a five-to-one ratio of killed to raped) and taking off from the 700,000 dead we find in Josephus, one could plausibly put the number of Jewish women raped by Romans at 140,000—in the time framing the siege of Jerusalem alone. The precision of these numbers is not the point. The point is the as yet unreckoned-with scale of horror, and, whatever the total number of victims, the horror was transcendent.

As we have seen, Rome's anti-Jewish violence was intergenerational, continuing until 135. Rape—the experience of it, or the imminent fear of it—would have been a fact of life for Jewish women across decades. The accompanying tribal disgrace would inevitably have been a defining note of Jewish manhood. This level of mass trauma is quite literally unspeakable, and so it was not spoken of. Because the dishonoring of the Jewish women grotesquely shamed the Jewish men, all were locked in a prison of silence. When the exception was made to speak of war rape, the purpose would have been to humiliate, as, for example, with the widely circulated non-Christian accusation that Jesus was the offspring not of the Holy Spirit, as the Lukan narrative has it, but of an illicit union between a Palestinian girl and a Roman soldier—a union that, given the actuality of Palestinian girlhood, would certainly have been rape.

How could such cultural agony not have made an impact on general attitudes toward gender? Our question is: What happened to change the stance of Jesus people toward women, with males reasserting a spirit of domination of which Jesus, and even Paul, knew nothing, and with females, apparently, acquiescing in that change? With a high measure of plausibility, we can answer simply: The war.

Jewish-Christian relations are our larger focus, but man-woman relations are tied by the same knot, and the Christian imagination was warped in both instances by one experience. We know with certainty that before 70, going back to the lifetime of Jesus, in the year 30 or so, women were essential partners in the project of spreading his message. After 70, they were marginalized in that project—but that is only half of it. Viewed as sources of sin and shame, the quintessence of dishonor, women were repositioned as exemplars of repentance. Sorrow was the supreme female virtue. Although Paul was the one cast in the role of villain here, the more potent emblem of the transformation—a paradigmatic "bishop"—was Peter.

Peter's betrayal of Jesus was total, and he was put forward by the Gospels as the first and greatest recipient of the Lord's forgiveness. We saw that: *Simon Peter, do you love me?* Yet by the second century

Peter had been transformed from the forgiven one into the unquestioned man of power. Remembered as the first "bishop" of Rome, he stood atop the pinnacle of the newly constructed hierarchy, and, seated there—the Chair of Peter—he would come to permanently embody the Church's own imperium, the spine of which is "apostolic succession," from which women are excluded.[27] No surprise, then, that the first of two New Testament letters attributed to Peter should reprise the famous words to the wives: "Likewise you wives, be submissive to your husbands," a precise echo of the domineering we saw in other texts.[28]

Women were thus twinned with "the Jews" as the negative other against which the Church defined itself positively, a bipolarity that built upon the pairing of male potency with female submissiveness. On dispossessed Jews and subservient women the Petrine claim to transcendent power was doubly staked. Meanwhile, Peter's place as the avatar of *needed absolution received* was taken by a once respected woman who began as Jesus' most intimate—and most faithful—friend, but who ended up portrayed as an abject, sorrowful whore.

Dishonoring Her

Recall that in order for Jesus' essential conflict to be structured as having been against "the Jews" instead of against Rome, Jesus had to be removed from his Jewish milieu, as if he were not actually Jewish himself. At first, as we saw, he was understood in terms of Jewish ideas of a human Messiah who could in some way share in God's divinity (the Son of Man motif in Daniel). But then, once the post-Temple crisis struck, in 70, he was reimagined as a Law-hating rebel whose highest cause was an attack on that Temple. Ultimately, the break with Jewishness was complete when, under the ever-stronger influence of Greek abstractions, he was worshipped as equal to—"one in being with"—the one God. With this full ontological divinizing,

Jesus took on the aura of a figure apart from—and above—the human condition. Thus, Christians began to understand Jesus *over against* not only traditions of Jewish religion and culture, but over against everything human.

Human knowledge, for example, was time-bound, but the inner awareness of Jesus was assumed to extend from infinite past to eternal future. He knew what would unfold tomorrow as well as he knew what happened yesterday. That Jesus was thus conceived as unique— a man radically alone—meshed perfectly, finally, with the rigid individualism that came into its own after the Enlightenment, when individualism as such gripped the modern imagination. There can be no surprise, therefore, that even contemporary theological scholarship isolates the truth of Jesus by *contrasting* it with the convictions of those he encountered.

We have seen how, against this impulse to portray Jesus as a wholly independent isolate whose immediate communion with God removed him from any need of others, the Gospels themselves show Jesus as coming into a sense of himself only *in relationship* to those with whom he lived—especially John the Baptist, in whose presence Jesus met his heavenly Father, and Peter, the very human foil (the opposite of "infallible") in relation to whom Jesus came into a full grasp of his own meaning.

As with John the Baptist and Peter, so with the women in relationship to whom Jesus also came into his own. His solidarity with women as portrayed in the four Gospels, as already noted, is one of the most important manifestations of the *actuality* of Jesus, and scholars, especially contemporary women, have emphasized that. Yet male domination is a constant mark of the tradition within which Jesus has been understood from ancient times until today. Jesus, taken by that tradition to be the lonely hero, has long been remembered as a kind of primal monk—as if he were a vowed celibate. But that is wrong. Jesus' regard for women was not general, but quite particular. Indeed, Jesus had a particular friendship.

The canonical texts do not say that Jesus was married, but he might have been. His marital status figured in early Christian debates about sexuality, including celibacy.[29] Against the assumption that if Jesus were married the canonical Gospels would offer some indication of it stands the fact that marriage was so much to be expected of a Jewish male of his time that his being *unmarried*, much less celibate, would more likely have required some comment by the tradition. The canonical texts are silent on the question, which, by this logic, can be taken as suggesting that he was indeed married. In any case, nothing in the Scriptures suggests that, had Jesus lived, he would not have married. Pop speculation on the love life of Jesus, such as informs the work of the novelist Dan Brown, however sensational and even prurient, can therefore be a useful correction. Instead of doctrinal certitude on this question, a due acknowledgment of ignorance seems warranted.

The portrait we have of Jesus comes mainly from Gospels that are only four among many other texts that were commonly circulated in the first two centuries. The various Jesus communities around the Mediterranean captured local memories and particular slants on Jesus in numerous accounts, collections of sayings, epistles, hymns, and ritual materials that came to be regarded as sacred.[30] It was only once the Church began to centralize its organization and creed that an official list, or "canon," was set, and the other texts and materials banned. The official New Testament was not promulgated until the Council of Carthage, in 397.[31]

One need not read the story of Jesus through a feminist lens to retrieve a sense of his humane attitudes toward women. All one need do is restore women to their actual roles in his life—especially a figure named "Mary," who may—who knows?—have been his wife. If such a woman was recast in the tradition—and we will see that she was—that happened not because a Jewish patriarchal culture trumped the egalitarian spirit of Jesus. Again, Jewishness was not the point. Rather, the entire Hellenistic world took a patriarchal view for granted. It may also be that, among the besieged populations of Jews and Jewish Christians in the late first and early second centuries, the pressure to emphasize male supremacy in the struggle to survive the sexually shaming mass violence inflicted by Rome would have been more intense than ever. Instead of seeing Jesus' dogged refusal to treat women, even disgraced women, with anything less than respect *in contrast to his Jewish milieu*, it is far truer to the situation faced by Jesus people, as the Gospels were composed, to see his positive regard in contrast to a broad culture of Roman assault that expressly dishonored women.

Now we see, perhaps, why the Gospels seem to take pains to show Jesus respecting the disrespected women—the woman with the unclean flow of blood, the Samaritan outcast, the impoverished widow, the woman taken in adultery. Here is the fuller meaning of Rome's chosen emblem for Jewish humiliation—that stooped and beaten woman embossed on the *Judaea Capta* coins and in the Arch of Titus bas-reliefs. Rome's defeat of Jews is pictured as the mauling of a Jewish woman. Ironically, one of the extended negative effects of this Roman dishonoring of women seems to have shown up as the impulse among males in the Jesus movement to recast the place of women, allowing those otherwise disempowered men to subjugate women in a way that Jesus never did.

Mary of Magdala

Now we come to one woman in particular who is singled out for her special, intimate relationship with Jesus, which, according to some accounts, was physical.[32] Earlier, we cited Martin Buber's schema as decisive: "All real living is meeting. . . . The fundamental reality of human existence is to be found not in conceptual abstractions, but in concrete human relationships." If, as we have argued, John the Baptist and Peter were two pillars on which Jesus' own discovery of himself rested, a third "Thou" in relationship to whom Jesus came into his own can plausibly be understood as having been Mary of Magdala.

Mary of Magdala bears the name of a well-to-do town on the Sea of Galilee, perhaps her place of origin.[33] She was one of the women who—unlike Peter and the other men—refused to abandon Jesus on Golgotha. She is the only woman named in each of the four Gospels. What elevates her above everyone else in the Gospel story is that, as all four Gospels report, she was the first to the tomb of Jesus, and the first witness of his Resurrection.[34] The account in the Gospel of John is particularly laden with implication:

> Now on the first day of the week Mary Magdalene came to the tomb early, while it was still dark, and saw that the stone had been taken away from the tomb. So she ran, and went to Simon Peter . . . "They have taken the Lord out of the tomb, and we do not know where they have laid him."

Peter and the others rush to the tomb to see for themselves, then disperse again.

> But Mary stood weeping outside the tomb, and as she wept she stooped to look into the tomb; and she saw two angels in white, sitting where the body of Jesus had lain, one at the head and one at the feet. They said to her, "Woman, why are you weeping?" She said to them, "Because they have taken away my Lord, and I do not know where they have laid him." Saying this, she turned around and saw Jesus standing, but she did not know that it was Jesus. Jesus said to her, "Woman, why are you weeping? Whom

do you seek?" Supposing him to be the gardener, she said to him, "Sir, if you have carried him away, tell me where you have laid him, and I will take him away." Jesus said to her, "Mary." She turned and said to him in Hebrew, "Rabboni" (which means Teacher). Jesus said to her, "Do not hold me, for I have not yet ascended to the Father; but go to my brethren and say to them, I am ascending to my Father and your Father, to my God and your God." Mary Magdalene went and said to the disciples, "I have seen the Lord"; and she told them that he had said these things to her.[35]

The intimacy of this encounter is palpable, and so is the stature of this woman who can act so forthrightly in circumstances of such extremity.

In the eighth chapter of Luke, Mary of Magdala is introduced as one of those followers of Jesus who is well-off enough to provide for him and his friends "out of their means."[36] Mary of Magdala is a benefactor and a sponsor of the itinerants. She is a woman of standing and power. Yet, beginning in the second century, the image of Mary of Magdala became entirely transformed when she was conflated with another woman in the Gospel, one who has no name, no standing, no place whatsoever in the social structure—a "woman of the city," a woman of the streets. That woman's encounter with Jesus is full of implication, too. Coming in the seventh chapter of Luke, ahead of the introduction of Mary of Magdala, she appears in the Gospel as a kind of foil to the patrician woman from well-heeled Magdala. With loosened hair and ointment that emphasize her sexually charged past, the unnamed woman ministered to Jesus:

One of the Pharisees asked him to eat with him, and he went into the Pharisee's house, and took his place at table. And behold, a woman of the city, who was a sinner, when she learned that he was at table in the Pharisee's house, brought an alabaster flask of ointment, and standing behind him at his feet, weeping, she began to wet his feet with her tears, and wiped them with the hair of her head, and kissed his feet, and anointed them with the ointment. Now when the Pharisee who had invited him saw it, he said to himself, "If this man were a prophet, he would have known who and what sort of woman this is who is touching him, for she is a sinner."

Instead of condemning her, Jesus sees in the woman's physical expression a sign that "'her sins, which are many, are forgiven, for she loved much' . . . And he said to her, 'Your sins are forgiven.' . . . 'Your faith has saved you. Go in peace.'"[37]

What the "woman of the city" and Mary of Magdala have in common is an intense love for Jesus, and ointment—one the ointment of a prostitute (perfumed oil as an enhancement of sex), the other the ointment of burial (countering decomposition of the flesh). That's all. Yet, in the years after the Gospels are composed, the woman with the sordid past and the "many sins" becomes identified with the aristocratic Mary of Magdala. The acts of unpinning hair, rubbing Jesus' feet with perfumed oil, weeping, and kissing—the habitually brazen behavior of a harlot, even if repentant—become the central notes of Mary of Magdala's story. The portrait, classically combining tropes of whore and madonna, was irresistible, but it was false—a complete invention that gradually jelled as narrative across several centuries. One of the great figures of the Christian imagination—subject of some of the treasures of Western art—was a perversion. A powerful, respected woman, no doubt a threatening figure to men, was reduced to a sorrowful object of pity to whom men could feel superior—indeed, who was by trade a sinner. Essential to this reduction was her reduction to object of sexuality. This transformation unfolded over time as one after another of the aptly named Church fathers sought ways to disempower women. The first of those to be disempowered was Mary of Magdala.

Even *within* the Gospels, however, pressures to downgrade Mary's status as one worthy of special intimacy with Jesus can be seen at play. At the end of Mark, the angel at the tomb instructs Mary of Magdala and the other women to "go, tell his disciples and Peter" of the Resurrection, but the text itself, with its final words, shows Mary disobeying this instruction: "they said nothing to any one, for they were afraid."[38] By the time Luke is written, a decade or more later, the downgrading of Mary has intensified. Again at the tomb, she and the other women are instructed to carry word of the Resurrection to the men, and in this version of the story she does so. But the apostles are dismissive: "These words seemed to them an idle tale, and they did not believe them."[39]

The unreliability of the testimony of women is a common theme of patriarchal denigration. What you hear from women is idle tales, unworthy of belief. Think of Cassandra, a figure immortalized in Homer's *Iliad*, Virgil's *Aeneid*, Aeschylus's *Agamemnon*, and Shakespeare's *Troilus and Cressida*—right down to adaptations in pop culture today. Cassandra is the madwoman who is not believed. But that was not who she was in the beginning. Cassandra was a princess of Troy during Troy's war with Greece. She was present when the Greeks showed up with their gift, the Trojan horse. She alone saw the trick for what it was, and the danger it posed. While all of Troy welcomed the massive horse, Cassandra, as Virgil wrote, "cried and cursed the unhappy hour, foretold our fate; but, by the god's decree, all heard and none believed the prophecy."[40] The know-it-all Trojan men were fooled. After the fall of Troy, Cassandra was raped by one Greek, Ajax, and carried off to Greece as a captive lover by another, Agamemnon. The ultimate triumph of men comes when women are set upon one another: Cassandra was finally murdered by Agamemnon's wife.

But the point of Cassandra's story is that she saw through history's most famous ruse, the Trojan Horse. If she had been listened to, the foundational myth of our civilization would have gone another way. Yet she is remembered as the avatar of hysteria—the crazy lady not to be taken seriously.[41]

Unlike Cassandra, Mary of Magdala was not raped, but her reduction in a prurient Christian memory to the repentant whore nevertheless partakes of sexual violence. In order to understand this, we must consider how the broad ethos of sexual violence that marked the decades of the Roman War converged with the movement within the Christian community toward concentrated, hierarchical—male—power. That Peter dismissed Mary's report of the Resurrection of Jesus as "an idle tale" takes on special weight if Peter was competing with Mary for pride of place in Jesus' heart—or, rather, if years later the figure of Peter was being put forward by men as supreme authority in a movement disinclined to admit any authority whatsoever to women.

Competition between Peter and Mary as "apostles" may or may not have occurred in the years after the death of Jesus, but it certainly did in the era when memory was moving into literature, and as literature underwent its exponential expansion. The great debates among late-first- and second-century Jesus people took the form of arguments that pitted the founders one against another—none more powerfully, as suggested by various texts of the early Christian era, than Peter against Mary. Chief among these texts, in fact, is the Gospel that bears Mary's own name. The *Gospel of Mary* is one of the numerous banished early texts that archaeology has discovered and credentialed, transforming the way Jesus and his movement are understood.[42] In this Gospel, Mary is a preeminent apostle, a woman whose privileged relationship with Jesus was certainly a license for female authority in the early community of believers—not for preeminence over men, but equality with them. But even in the *Gospel of Mary* itself, that very status of women is in dispute, and Mary's antagonist is none other than Peter. This Gospel demonstrates,

however, that not even the first of the apostles can deny the authority
that comes from Mary's greater intimacy with Jesus:

> Peter said to Mary, "Sister, we know that the Savior loved you
> more than all other women. Tell us the words of the Savior that
> you remember, the things which you know that we don't because
> we haven't heard them."
>
> Mary responded, "I will teach you about what is hidden from
> you." And she began to speak these words to them.[43]

But Peter takes offense at Mary's superior knowledge of the "hidden" meaning of Jesus, and he complains to his brethren, "Did [Jesus]
choose her over us?" But one of the other apostles rebukes Peter, saying, "If the Savior considered her to be worthy, who are you to disre-
gard her?"[44]

It is no wonder that a text so clearly affirming of a woman's
authority should have disappeared in the second century, when the
Jesus movement was reorganizing itself around a restored cult of
male supremacy. Indeed, one of the main criteria for the eventual inclusion of texts in the officially approved "canon" of the New Testament was almost certainly how the text understood the place of
women's authority, which is probably why Paul's letters were revised,
but also why those texts that emphasized female leadership or femi-
nine images of God were dismissed as mere apocrypha. The *Gospel of
Mary*, therefore, is ranked with heresy, while the "misogynist" 1
Timothy is in the Bible.[45]

Not only was Mary of Magdala reinvented in this process, but so
was Peter. What had made him so revered in the first place, as we
saw earlier, was his self-acknowledged status as a man desperately in
need of forgiveness. That he had that forgiveness from the Lord himself, in that poignant threefold absolution on the beach, is what made
Peter a figure of hope for a beleaguered, demoralized, unworthy

people. His preeminence was not a matter of power given to him, but of compassion *shown* to him. All that eventually flipped. Peter's humility was turned into a point of male pride.

The transformation of Mary of Magdala, meanwhile, tells the story of the disempowering of women in the Jesus movement, beginning in an era when women were being massively dishonored wherever Jews confronted Roman power—a phenomenon that surely overlapped and influenced the re-shaping of Christian memory. No longer an apostle or trusted intimate of Jesus, Mary of Magdala was, in her meaning, turned upside down to become an icon of shame, a symbol of subservience, a woman posted at the gate to keep her sisters, especially, out of the Lord's inner circle.

If the meaning of Peter and the meaning of Mary of Magdala were upended through the years of wartime trauma, how much more so was the meaning of Jesus Christ himself. Jews, women, power, and violence—these are the lenses through which the necessary *re*-vision we have undertaken here comes into focus. To reckon with the perversions of memory and interpretation that are built into *all* human understanding is not to harbor the illusion that a "true . . . historical" Jesus can be retrieved from behind the texts; nor is it to imagine that a pure, innocent Christian movement of "love and fellowship" can be uncovered—much less *re*-covered—by removing layers of institutional corruption. No, the matter is both more complex and simpler than that. History is the record of the past seen through a succession of distorting presents. There is no such thing as history undistorted. Decisive transformations of meaning occurred, and are occurring still. That knowledge points toward the permanently incomplete encounter not with one to be fully possessed or completely known, but with one who ever beckons as a final object of desire: Christ actually.

CHAPTER NINE

Imitation of Christ

Imagination is the beginning of creation: You imagine what you desire; you will what you imagine; and at last, you create what you will.

—George Bernard Shaw[1]

Compared to Him

Let us stay with a woman—a different one. She took her happiness from, as she put it in her youth, the "mystic gripping melody of struggle, a cry for world peace and human brotherhood." If Jesus Christ was not a way to that—world peace and human brotherhood—then what good was he? That became her question, and it is ours. We will come back to it, and to her.

In this book, we have been weighing traditional understandings of Jesus Christ against the new condition of human struggle sparked by the massive interruptions of history that occurred in the middle of the twentieth century. I am hardly the first to ask this, nor will I be the last. "How can we pretend to take history with theological seriousness," wrote the Catholic scholar David Tracy, "and then ignore the Holocaust?"[2] We have bracketed the modern Holocaust with an ancient one, searching out the ways in which such traumas inevitably shape—and misshape—belief. Drawing on recent scholarship, we have made a touchstone of the Jewishness of Jesus—and the Jewishness of the interpretations that were invented for him. Taking his full humanness not only as a starting point but as an end point, too, we have nevertheless asked what it means to say that Jesus is God, knowing full well that if Jesus of Nazareth had not been understood as divine, we would never have heard of him.

Here is the irony: if Jesus was not God, he was not even Virgil, or Socrates, or Dante. His greatness cannot be measured on the scale of exceptional intelligence, imagination, or even courage. Indeed, if greatness adheres in Jesus, it does so as much because of what was made of him as because of what he was. The two things, of course, are tied together: what he was *shaped* what was made of him, beginning with those terms drawn from the book of Daniel, where, as Son of Man, he began to be understood as somehow of God. So we are by no means content to reduce Jesus to the status of an "only human" character who was posthumously—falsely—elevated to divine status by his disappointed followers, especially Saint Paul. Jesus will be honored in the next millennium, and beyond, only if he is *still* regarded as somehow divine.

We have seen how the Roman War against the Jews interrupted the evolution of the meaning of Jesus, decisively channeling that meaning away from Judaism and ultimately setting the Church against the Synagogue, which set Jesus against his own people. The dark consequences of that, unfolding across two millennia, are the ground on which this work stands. And we have resigned ourselves to the impossibility of lifting the curtain of the texts to discover behind the distortions that followed upon Roman violence an unmediated "historical Jesus." The Roman War was a history-altering interruption, changing forever the meaning of Israel, and therefore of this son of Israel.

War, too, is the ground of this work. If not for the destruction of the Temple, and then the leveling of Jerusalem—contingent events of history if ever any events were contingent—understandings of the man recognized by some Jews as the Son of Man referred to in the book of Daniel would almost surely have matured within the context of Israel, instead of in opposition to Israel. That includes the way in which the divinity of Jesus Christ came to be articulated.

That Greek philosophical categories were conscripted into Christology—ultimately leading to the construction of a Trinitarian equality between the divine persons that most Jews found incomprehensible, even blasphemous—was not preordained. The so-called parting of the ways between Judaism and Christianity was neither inevitable nor willed by God. The whole sorry story could have gone another way. To acknowledge this is in no way to suggest that the savage history that followed—the Church against the Jews—can be rolled back, or that Jesus can now be retrieved by Jews as a Messiah figure. No, what must be acknowledged is the as yet uncalculated cost of a war that Christians preferred to forget. In truth, the Roman War goes on.

But finally, having brought to the fore the grandeur of courage that is not separate from, but rather is embedded in, the fear endemic to violence, we come to this recognition: the answer to Bonhoeffer's question is Bonhoeffer himself—*his life* taken as an interpretation of Christ's actuality in the middle of the twentieth century. We remember Bonhoeffer, that is, not just as an anti-Nazi hero but as an exemplar of "discipleship," a word he used as the title of his first great book on the necessity of Christian resistance to Nazism. The German martyr was a man through whom the *actual* meaning of Jesus Christ clearly shines. That is why we started with him. But, as we saw in our portraits of those whom Jesus first called as disciples, that meaning is not cast of plaster. To Jesus, the saints whom we have considered *were not saints*, which is the revelation.

Perhaps the main point about Bonhoeffer, against the golden glow of canonization in which his memory is held, is that he was, certainly to himself, a morally compromised man. We saw that, even while he staunchly opposed racial anti-Semitism, his thinking was permanently twisted by the tradition of theological anti-Judaism. He foresaw—hoped for—the eventual conversion of Jews to Jesus. Even as he opposed Hitler in 1933, to take a more particular example, he refused to preside at the funeral of his sister's father-in-law, because the man, though a Christian convert from Judaism, had never been properly baptized, making him—theologically—still a Jew and therefore ineligible for Church obsequies. Bonhoeffer later berated himself for it, but even as Nazi thugs were assaulting Jews, he simply would not honor a Jew by commending his soul to God.[3]

When Bonhoeffer joined the conspiracy to kill Hitler, declaring himself ready to carry out the deed in person if necessary, he regarded himself as plunged in evil—a lesser evil than Hitler's, to be sure, but still evil. Tyrannicide was murder. Bonhoeffer was "an accomplice," as he said, "conscious of his guilt." His biographer, Charles Marsh, concludes, "Bonhoeffer moved within an inescapable paradox; he gave his blessings to those who conspired to murder the Führer while affirming the essential nonviolence of the gospel . . . Bonhoeffer did not try to resolve the paradox by assuming moral innocence, but accepted the paradox by incurring the guilt born out of responsible action."[4] If to himself Bonhoeffer was a sinner, who are we to say otherwise? For us, what matters is that his discipleship was rooted precisely in the thick of mortal wickedness. That complexity, not some vague ethical purity, is what makes him our interpreter of Christ *par excellence*.

The first of the interpreters, though, were the contemporaneous friends and followers of Jesus, even if they would not have called their unselfconscious initiating reaction to Jesus an "interpretation" at all. They responded to Jesus not with doctrine but with what *they* called discipleship, not with "believing" but with doing, not with theology but with imitation. Because, through the normal vicissitudes of history, doctrine and theology preempted imitation and stopped being tested against the remembered actualities of Jesus himself, the Church lost its way. Eventually, the Church embraced the very values against which Jesus defined himself, and which killed him—imperial power and the violence needed to uphold it.

Against the grain of the Church's self-aggrandizing doctrine, which denies the capacity for such betrayal,[5] the disciples remained human even after they cloaked themselves in Jesus' divinity—after they began to "live in the Holy Spirit." But in the beginning, Jesus was more to be imitated than worshipped. He was, in the Gospel's supremely simple word, to be *followed*. "Come follow me" was the first and defining invitation offered by Jesus to his disciples.[6] In fact, the German word—*Nachfolge*—that Bonhoeffer chose for his book's title, which was rendered in English as "Discipleship," is better translated as "Follow Me."[7] This following, Bonhoeffer wrote, "does not create constitutions and decrees, but brings human beings into relation with one another." In the life of the movement that takes its name from Jesus Christ, the primacy of discipleship over decree must regularly be recovered. Indeed, the generating impulse to imitate Jesus remains the Church's permanent and multifaceted principle of indictment, self-criticism, absolution, and moral renewal. Jesus is the mark on history against which Jesus people have no choice but to measure themselves.

After Schweitzer

As the Gospels lay out Jesus' story, report the words attributed to him, and dramatize the effect he had on those who met him, the core identity of Jesus shines through. Not even what might be called the "normal" corruptions of memory and interpretation, made worse by the trauma of war, obscure the palpable truth of his loving ways: *Respect for everyone he met. The preference of service over power. The rejection of violence. Israel—its Law and worship—as the primal source of meaning. The Holy One's nearness, the readiness to name the Holy One as God, and the recognition of God as Father. Forgiveness as the response to the inevitability of failure. Suffering understood as part of life. Trust as the other side of anguish. A permanent thankfulness. Communion over loneliness. Death not an end, but a beginning. At home in the absolute—and absolutely unknown—future.* These are authentic notes of the man's character, established by the earliest tradition, and making available the only "historical" Jesus we need.

The strength of the hold Jesus had on people from the start is generated by the defining paradox: his simplicity is what makes him great. The subtlest minds in Western civilization have plumbed his significance; visual, literary, and musical geniuses have brought him back to life in every generation. Yet in matters of ultimate importance, even the most ordinary—and compromised—of humans has the inborn capacity to be like Jesus. And from the start, those who fell under his spell understood that being like Jesus was the only point. Imitation was the point.

Once doctrine trumped imitation—with, for example, a convoluted Eucharistic theology of the "real presence" taking on more importance than the real experience of humans gathered at the table in his memory—the simple impulse to be like Jesus became the province of, well, simpletons. "Theology is for the elite," as Terry Eagleton characterized this view, "and mythology is for the masses."[8] On one side, a religious establishment controlled access to the so-called channels of grace—Jesus behind the barricade of clerical privilege. On another, the complications of scholarship, ever more arcane, disqualified all but initiates in the secret tongues of history and theology. The once idealized imitation of Christ was reduced to a kind of mindless devotion—period. The imitation of Christ is for dullards incapable of "right thinking" (orthodoxy) or of grasping the subtleties of historical scholarship. Bishops and professors united against the rest. *Serve the soup, bring flowers to the altar, leave the disputations to the prelates and the intellectuals.*

No. The key to the actuality of Christ is *precisely* in the imitation of Jesus. Orthodoxy and responsible scholarship must equally be measured against the mandate embodied in the received character of

Jesus. The movement he spawned drew the human imagination and the faculty of reason to new heights—pinnacles of Western civilization—yet its ground remained the defining paradox: the simplicity of Jesus is what made him great. Not a crude matter of good deeds but, as we saw again and again, a subtle matter of a certain attitude toward life.

A classic emblem of such simple greatness is found in the story of Albert Schweitzer, the German physician and Scripture scholar who brought the modern search for the historical Jesus to its first climax[9] but who, after decades, dropped his studies to embrace the work of healing the poorest of the poor in his clinic in Africa. *Scholarship, too, aims at imitation.* It may seem arbitrary, at this point in our consideration, to turn to Schweitzer as an exemplar of discipleship, yet we do so not because he—any more than Bonhoeffer—is a "saint," unlike the rest of us. We do so because the scholar-doctor represents a kind of default compromise between the skepticism toward traditional claims for Jesus that results from critical historical inquiry, and the transrational affirmation of those very claims, despite what the inquiry reveals. Schweitzer, in his own biography, that is, represents a repudiation of the divide between thinking and following—between theology and mythology, if you will. In Schweitzer, that is, another instance of the deadly oppositionalism that has undermined so much else is overcome.

The concluding words of Schweitzer's *Quest of the Historical Jesus* have had great resonance across the century, implying both the impossibility of knowing who Jesus was in the past and the necessity of maintaining him as a figure of life-changing power in the present:

He comes to us as one unknown, without a name, as of old, by the lakeside, he came to those men who knew Him not. He speaks to us in the same word: "Follow thou me." And sets us to the tasks that He has to fulfill for our time. He commands. And to those who obey, whether they be wise or simple, He will reveal Himself in the toils, the conflicts, the sufferings that they shall pass through in his fellowship, and, as an ineffable mystery, they shall learn in their own experience who he is.[10]

Motivated by what he called "reverence for life," Schweitzer was fully in tune with the political implications of this piety. Indeed, his service of the poorest of the poor was itself a forecast of the new century's most potent political revolution—the impoverished world's throwing off of the fetters of European colonialism. Schweitzer conceived his medical mission as part of that revolution precisely because it was required by the standard set by Jesus:

> If all this oppression and all this sin and shame are perpetrated under the eye of the German God, or the American God, or the British God, and if our states do not feel obliged first to lay aside their claim to be "Christian"—then the name of Jesus is blasphemed and made a mockery . . . The name of Jesus has become a curse, and our Christianity—yours and mine—has become a falsehood and a disgrace, if the crimes are not atoned for in the very place where they were instigated. For every person who committed an atrocity in Jesus' name, someone must step in to help in Jesus' name.[11]

Thus, Schweitzer paradoxically embodied the two positions of the earnest search for Jesus. He concluded that the nineteenth-century "quest" would never bridge the gap between the so-called Jesus of history and the Christ of faith, and that regardless of what could—or could not—be made of the tradition that emphasized his transcendent character as the resurrected Son of God, Jesus' real importance lay in the example he set as a figure of compassion and as a challenge to political oppression. The point was to follow the example.

Yet this was not a mere surrender of faith in the divinity of Jesus, as if he were only a do-gooder after all—whether revolutionary Zealot or kindly chap. Rather, the "imitation" Schweitzer embarked upon was a way of giving expression to the divine one's ongoing relevance to human life—a revolutionary whose meaning could not be limited to the revolution. Worship of Jesus as the second person of the Blessed Trinity was not enough, but neither was it enough to celebrate his memory as "an essentially political figure," to cite a twenty-first-century writer, "a revolutionary killed because he challenged Roman rule, who was then mysticized by his disciples and divinized by Paul of Tarsus."[12]

Across the centuries before and after Schweitzer, countless Christians have "stepped in to help in Jesus' name," from the thirteenth century's Francis of Assisi—who put care of the poor on the social agenda to this day, as the choice of the name Francis by the twenty-first-century pope *for the sake of the poor* makes crystal clear—to the seventeenth century's George Fox, who saw the witness of peace as the only response to wars of religion, to Fox's disciple Anne Hutchinson, who defied male supremacy and helped invent American democracy, to the nineteenth century's Leo Tolstoy, whose embrace of nonviolence sparked Mahatma Gandhi's and Martin Luther King Jr.'s, to the twentieth century's Brother Roger Schutz of Taizé, the ecumenical community in France that rose out of the religious ashes of World War II, to the Catholic pacifist Dorothy Day, who saw the connection between Auschwitz and Hiroshima. For each of these exemplars, "helping in Jesus' name" was more than helping—because Jesus' name was "above every name, that at the name of Jesus every knee should bow."[13] All of these imitators imitated Jesus for one reason: because he was God made man.

Quality of Suffering

During the tumultuous mid-1960s, I was a seminarian working out of a Catholic parish as a community organizer in Hell's Kitchen,

New York City. That summer, I went down to the Bowery occasionally to volunteer at St. Joseph's House, on Chrystie Street, a soup kitchen and hospitality house run by the famous Dorothy Day. It was she to whom I referred at the top of this chapter, swaying to the "mystic gripping melody of struggle, a cry for world peace and human brotherhood."[14]

Miss Day—I never called her Dorothy—was a woman in her sixties then, silver-haired and lean, always wearing long woolen skirts, ample sweaters, and stout black shoes. Once, she had been a fetching beauty, but what I saw was a stern, withholding woman who, though unfailingly kind to the guests she served on the breadline, could be surprisingly sharp with her co-workers and volunteers. Because of her reputation as a saintly rescuer of desperate people, I was in awe of her, but I also knew instinctively that she would prefer it if, like other drop-in volunteers, I kept my distance. I did. Eventually I recognized her kindness toward the men whom she fed and clothed as coming from the core of her, and her standoffishness otherwise as a mark of innate shyness, mixed with exhaustion. Her piety—she often thumbed a tattered copy of *The Imitation of Christ*, a classic of Catholic spirituality that emphasized the vanity of the world and the "royal road" of the cross[15]—should have struck me as passé, but I was moved by its evident authenticity. Yet her moral code could be ruthless. When one of her most trusted assistants announced that he and his wife were separating, she angrily told him to get out, banishing him from St. Joseph's House for being a bad Catholic. After that summer, I was purged of the impulse to think of the complicated, eccentric, and stern Dorothy Day as a saint. Yet over the next couple of years, her firm opposition to the Vietnam War, and her broad support of resisters, braced my own timid enlistment in antiwar activity, and I realized that Dorothy Day's witness had stiffened my spine. She changed my life.

The complexity of my memory of Miss Day, paired with my fuller appreciation of her accomplishment, is why I turn to her now as another example of what the imitation of Christ means. Complexity like hers included something very simple. She was born nine years before Bonhoeffer, yet she defined her life by a question about Christ's actuality. She came to faith during the Great War—the spiritual quest as a response to the twentieth century's first throes of civilizational self-destruction. When Dorothy Day started out, the coming catastrophe of anti-Jewish genocide—the jackboots, the boxcars, the camps, the crematoriums—was still unimaginable, yet war and injustice provoked her crisis of conscience. Unlike Bonhoeffer, she lived to propose an answer to the question about Christ. "If we desire to have a true understanding of His Gospels," she wrote when she was young, "we must study to conform our own life as nearly as we can to His . . . [to] follow His teachings and His manner of living."

The daughter of a journalist, she embraced her father's vocation, and it would form the backbone of her life. But no sooner had she begun her writerly career than she was interrupted—by the mass violence of World War I. Journalism seemed like thin soup when such bloody mayhem spilled across Europe, so she entered a nurses' training program in Brooklyn. The urge to respond concretely to human suffering would define her. After the war, she resumed work as a journalist, first in Chicago, then in New York. The bohemian life in Greenwich Village pulled her in—she was intimate with Eugene O'Neill. But ultimately, at twenty-eight, the scattered filings of Day's life were drawn to the magnet of Jesus, and she converted to Roman Catholicism.

During the Depression, she established a radical newspaper, *The Catholic Worker*, which sparked a social movement to feed the hungry and advocate for peace—what led to the establishment of St. Joseph's House. The *Worker* icon would be a Fritz Eichenberg woodcut of defeated men in a breadline, one of whom was the illuminated long-haired, robed figure of the Savior. For half a century, Day "studied to conform" her own life as nearly as she could to the life of Jesus. Hence that little book she so often thumbed, *The Imitation of Christ*, which gave her a defining theme. Imitating Christ was Dorothy Day's lifelong method.

"Come follow me," she heard him say. Day followed a Christ who washed the feet of his friends, whose ministry consisted in passing the food, accepting the unacceptable, turning the other cheek. That a Caesar murdered him made her distrust every Caesar. "Jesus told us," she said again and again, "that what we do to the least, we do to him." Among her books—the titles are tip-offs—were *The Long Loneliness*, *Loaves & Fishes*, and *On Pilgrimage*. But the text that mattered—our text now—was her life.

From the hospitality house she established in the Bowery in 1933, with its breadline and soup kitchen, grew a phenomenal movement that today counts more than a hundred Catholic Worker hospitality houses around the world, centers where the hungry are fed, outcasts received as guests, showers made available, peace promoted—where the imitation of Christ is a way of life.

Yes, because faith must be tested by reason, theology is necessary. To know what Christ means, we must know what he *meant*, and so critical history is necessary, too. The Church keeps a kind of memory of Jesus alive, and scholars separate memory from myth. But finally, dogma and debate are not enough. True study, in her phrase, is embodying and enacting in one's own life the example of Jesus. "We do it," Dorothy Day said, "by seeing Christ and serving Christ in friends and strangers, in everyone we come in contact with." And again: "Now it is with the voice of our contemporaries that He speaks, with the eyes of store clerks, factory workers and children that He gazes; with the hands of office workers, slum dwellers, and suburban housewives that He gives. It is with the feet of soldiers and tramps that He walks, and with the heart of anyone in need that He longs for shelter.

And giving shelter or food to anyone who asks for it, or needs it, is giving it to Christ."[16]

Dorothy Day, for all her irascibility and even rigidity, was a living example of the capacity to see more in Jesus Christ than is before our eyes, which is simultaneously a capacity to see more in every person than even the person knows is there. In all of this, Day was like those who first clicked to Jesus. He called forth a concentration of perception, a revelation that came to all who knew to pay a certain kind of attention. To live like Jesus, and to see the face of Jesus in the faces of others, was the starting point of understanding Jesus. From discipleship, that is, came definition.

Thus, Incarnation did not happen at the miraculous conception of Jesus, or at his crucifixion, or at the Resurrection. It did not happen, *pace* John, at the beginning of time. It happened in the progressive evolution of Jesus' meaning that was accomplished, first, through his choices, actions, and encounters; and, second, through later meditation on those choices, actions, and encounters conducted by people who sought to reproduce them.

Yet the simple, but mostly forgotten, fact is that there would have been no post-Resurrection recognition of Jesus as Christ, *Logos*, Word; no troubling to interpret him in Son of Man terms drawn from the book of Daniel; none of this, if the disciples had not *already* experienced some kind of transcendence in Jesus, in his life, his message, his ministry. This is what the reductive impulse of certain scholarly debunkers misses, and it is the meaning of what that certain corrective school of scholars now call the "early high Christology"— the way in which, right at the outset, Jesus was taken to be something special. The way Dorothy Day took Jesus is a more useful clue, perhaps, than the arguments of turf-protecting experts or the border-enforcing pronouncements of prelates.

The Gospels make clear that the greatness of Jesus was glimpsed in his refusal of greatness. We have already seen that paradox as defining, and it was captured in one of the earliest hymns that the followers of Jesus sang of him. "Though he was in the form of God, [he] did not count equality with God a thing to be clung to," we read in the letter Paul wrote to the first settled gathering of Christians in Europe, in the Greek city of Philippi, "but emptied himself, taking the form of a servant, being born in the likeness of men."[17] We earlier referred to these verses—written in about 60 but drawing on verses that were already in circulation by then—in relationship to Schweitzer's citation of the name of Jesus as motivating, but also in emphasizing the irresistible power of that word *servus*, or slave.

But Christ's physical degradation, an identification with the lowest of the social classes, was only part of the story. This man emptying himself of the ultimate glory was at the mercy of moral degradation, too. Against the later tradition's radical exaltation of Jesus, the earliest followers, whose memory was rooted in encounters with the man himself, took his embrace of the human condition to include participation in human sinfulness—which was the point of beginning his story with his presentation of himself to John the Baptist in repentance. Modern belief and critical disbelief both seem compelled to choose between Jesus either as *a human*, complete with sinfulness like every other human, or *as God*, uniquely immune from fallibility. But those who gave us the only portraits we have of Jesus seem not to have been torn by this contradiction, which is why their witness is so elusive.

In the Gospel of Mark, Jesus' encounter with John the Baptist is immediately followed by the simple declaration that, during forty days in the wilderness, Jesus was tempted by Satan. Tempted to what? In the Gospels of Matthew and Luke, by means of mythical invention, the answer is given. In a personified contest with Satan, Jesus was tempted to magic and to power. *Turn stones into bread; try flying from the pinnacle of the Temple; all the kingdoms of the world, and the glory of them, can be yours.*

Jesus was tempted to mere wonder working and miracles, as if he were just another ancient-world wizard. He was tempted to messianic self-anointment, a worldly kingship that could have been won only through killing. We saw that he said no to the rescue of John from prison; he would—could—provide neither a miracle nor a jailbreak. In this, Jesus had come to the recognition of what we call his pacifism. And now he said no once more, and he would do so—not just in the desert, against Satan, across forty days—again and again, throughout his public life. He said no to everyone who wanted kingly power from him, or its partner, violence.

In these temptation accounts, we have a fully human person on display—a man wrestling not with the devil but with himself. Against assumptions of a venerable status that exempted him from moral complexities of the human condition, it is crucial to acknowledge that the story has power only if the teller knows that Jesus *might* have given in to these temptations. Perhaps at times, and in some ways, he did. But that he chose not to do so in the fundamental option of his public ministry was the beginning of what drew people to him. Yes, his kingdom would be unique: a Kingdom of God.

In their very different situations more than a generation later, the Jesus people to whom the Gospels spoke were themselves being tempted, as Jesus had been. That is why the story was told to them in this form. In the thick of war-generated trauma, they were tempted to power, to magical thinking, to violence. The Gospels aimed to reassure beleaguered disciples in steadfast discipleship, helping them make the right choice.

And note that, as the Gospels tell it, no sooner had Jesus returned from his contest with Satan than he declared what he had learned: that the Spirit of the Lord upon him meant good news to the poor— Jesus being interpreted, or interpreting himself, in the decisive imagery of Isaiah. "Today this scripture has been fulfilled in your hearing."[18] That is what they saw. Service, not self-aggrandizement. Suffering, not power.

Indeed, suffering was the key as his story then played out in Jerusalem. The people around him recognized in Jesus a particular presence of the Holy One precisely in how he died.

The hymn cited by Paul in his Letter to the Philippians goes on, "And being found in human form he humbled himself and became obedient unto death, even death on a cross." First humility, and only then exaltation: "Therefore God has highly exalted him and bestowed on him the name which is above every name, that at the name of Jesus every knee should bow, in heaven and on earth and under the earth, and every tongue confess that Jesus Christ is Lord, to the glory of God the Father."[19]

That Dorothy Day, like Albert Schweitzer, constructed her imitation of Christ around suffering is a large clue here, one that points beyond itself to the starkest vision of suffering imaginable—not a narrowly Christian one. Humans are so hungry for transcendence that they have the capacity to glimpse it in the extremity of despair and misery. Not capacity. Necessity. Here we return to the recognition to which Elie Wiesel came in Auschwitz: "Where is God? Where is He?" The sight of a lynched Jewish campmate had prompted the question. Wiesel heard the voice within him answer, "Where is He? Here He is—He is hanging here on this gallows." It goes without saying by now that this is not a Christian vision, but a biblical one. God came to the people, Yahweh explained to Moses, not because He saw their sin, but because He saw their *suffering*.[20]

The Bible tells the story of power and conquest—but from the point of view of the victim. When, for purposes of social order, a community drives a scapegoat out into the wilderness, the story is usually told to dramatize what made such grim action necessary; told, that is, from the point of view of those doing the expelling. But

the Bible flips that, to affirm that God stands with those who have
been cast out, beginning, in Exodus, with the scapegoat people who
were driven out into the wilderness. That forty-year exile is echoed in
Jesus' forty-day sojourn in the desert. Yet, finally, the only way human beings can allow themselves to believe the eloquent proclamation that God throws in with those who suffer is by imagining that
God, too, suffers. "His face was so disfigured he seemed hardly human," Isaiah said of God's chosen one. "And from his appearance,
one would scarcely know he was a man."[21]

The age-old biblical intuition that God is close to the hurt and the
lost is given a particular expression in the story of Jesus, especially
because it is expressly told in terms taken from the Suffering Servant
texts of Isaiah and the Psalms. In that mystery is the single simplest
explanation of how the followers of the crucified Jesus came to understand him as divine. The Son of Man was imagined, yes, as coming in
glory, but the precondition of glory, in this account, was ignominy.
Jesus' being hurt and lost—"Let this cup pass from me!"—is essential
to the psychological mechanism that sparked in his followers first a
hope, then a conviction: that this one who suffers so is God, a vision
that transforms suffering itself. "For Christian faith, the death of
God is not a question of his disappearance. On the contrary, it is one
of the places where He is most fully present. Jesus is not Man standing in for God. He is a sign that God is incarnate in human frailty
and futility."[22]

The point is not to reconceive suffering as a source of happiness;
that is masochism, and when promoted by religious gurus it is sado-
masochism. No, what changes, in T. S. Eliot's phrase, is "the quality
of the suffering."[23] If faith enables the transition from despair to
trust, the suffering is not removed, but its meaning is changed. Or,
rather, the suffering can *have* meaning. The transformation is captured in the move Jesus is remembered as having made on Golgotha
from "My God, my God, why hast thou forsaken me?" to "Into thy

hands I commit my spirit."[24] The quality of Jesus' suffering improved. Of that transformation, Dorothy Day was a connoisseur.

The Left Cheek

The imitation of Christ was for Dorothy Day a matter of the biblical reversal—seeing the story of power not from the winner's point of view but from the loser's. Concretely, that meant serving the poor and feeding the hungry, but not only that. Taking her large clue from the Jesus who was executed as a political criminal, Day's movement combined the rescue of needy people with strident political advocacy on their behalf. Not for her was suffering something to be glorified, as if willed by God, any more than poverty was to be taken as a necessary part of the social order, for "the poor you will always have amongst you." No, suffering and poverty were to be ameliorated *and opposed*. As the word "worker" in the name of her newspaper indicates, her founding inspiration came from the *Daily Worker* and the idealism she once attached to Marxism. Day invented, in effect, a true Christian socialism.

In this, she differed from saintly figures whose devotion to the poor goes hand in hand with a quiet spirit of resignation before the social structures that impoverish them.[25] Not satisfied with endlessly pulling drowning men from the torrents rushing past, Day went upstream to see who was throwing the poor bastards into the water in the first place—and to stop it. Dorothy Day's religious faith was thus the furthest thing from the opiate that Karl Marx railed against: "Our manifesto," she declared, "is the Sermon on the Mount." As to always having the poor amongst us, "Yes," she once replied, "but we are not content that there should be so many of them. The class structure is of our making and by our consent, not God's. It is the way we have arranged it, and it is up to us to change it. So we are urging revolutionary change."[26]

But revolution of what kind? In light of the drastic perversion of the meaning of Jesus Christ that occurred during the Roman War against the Jews—poisoning Christian attitudes, as we have seen, toward Jews, women, and power—Jesus' clear rejection of violence takes on added importance. The simple eloquence of his teaching cuts across all differences of time and circumstance:

"You have heard that it was said, 'An eye for an eye and a tooth for a tooth.' But I say to you, Do not resist one who is evil. But if any one strikes you on the right cheek, turn to him the other also; and if any one would sue you and take your coat, let him have your cloak as well; and if any one forces you to go one mile, go with him two miles. Give to him who begs from you, and do not refuse him who would borrow from you. You have heard that it was said, 'You shall love your neighbor and hate your enemy.' But I say to you, Love your enemies and pray for those who persecute you, so that you may be sons of your Father who is in heaven; for he makes his sun rise on the evil and on the good, and sends rain on the just and on the unjust. For if you love those who love you, what reward have you? Do not even the tax collectors do the same? And if you salute only your brethren, what more are you doing than others? Do not even the Gentiles do the same? You, therefore, must be perfect, as your heavenly Father is perfect."[27]

The heavenly Father's perfection consisted in the unconditionality of His love, and for Jesus that love defined the opposite of the imperium of Rome. Jesus, one can plausibly assume, came to his own attitude in reaction to Rome's brutality, beginning, as we saw, with his hurt fury at the murder of John the Baptist. Jesus' deploring of violence was wholly justified by what befell not *him* so much as, decades later, his whole people. Indeed, if Jesus did have the capacity to foresee the future, wouldn't that most damnable consequence of

Roman war-making—how the traumatized Jesus people turned against "the Jews"—have itself been enough to make him repudiate the works of war from start to finish?

In imitating Christ, Dorothy Day set out to do what he did. She valued joy, but she preferred goodness. She gave up affluence, power, sensuality. She repented. She saw the agony of Christ in the poor, and she saw that Christ's agony is what redeems it—not some fake Easter uplift. She lived a life of sorrow for what our fellows suffer and what they do, and she did what she could to alleviate that suffering. Compassion: she *suffered with*. Companion: she *broke bread with*. Conspiracy: she *breathed with*. Conscience: she *knew with*. And finally, consistent with this ethic of imitation, when Dorothy Day was confronted with the advent of the atomic bomb, she understood it as an apocalyptic weapon that must be denounced.

For Dorothy Day, the pacifism of Jesus was always of the essence, but imitating it took on new urgency after 1945. Having been a founder, in 1939, of the Committee of Catholics to Fight Anti-Semitism, she was attuned to the broader meaning of the revelations, as they came, of what Hitler did to Jews in the death camps. And Hiroshima seemed to her the ultimate revelation of the meaning of violence. As the climactic catastrophes of the war showed themselves that year, the *Catholic Worker* redoubled its commitment to the cause of peace. If Auschwitz emerged as a mythic revelation of Western civilization's hidden racial dynamic of contempt for a designated other—a dynamic eventually targeting not just the Jews, but racial minorities and native peoples[28]—Hiroshima could be taken as the revelation of the end point toward which the culture had turned when it embraced the totalitarian ethos of total war. The end point was still the apocalyptic End Time, perhaps, but finally seen as fully within the bounds of history, and able to be brought about not by the intervention of a killer God, but by the action of humans. Auschwitz showed what evil humans were capable of, and Hiroshima showed with what power they could enact it. This was nothing less than a mutation in the human situation, a change that ranked, whether humans were conscious of it or not, with the prehistoric invention of the first tool, which was probably a weapon. Now the finitude of the human species was defined by its first-time capacity for species-wide suicide.

In New York during the 1950s, civil defense drills were mandatory exercises—practice runs for the dreaded nuclear attack. All citizens were required, once the sirens rang out, to huddle in designated fallout shelters until the all-clear blew. The requirement was essential to the American people's acquiescence in a runaway nuclear arms race,[29] and in the government's campaign to make nuclear war thinkable. On June 15, 1955, when the sirens sounded, Dorothy Day and a few other Catholic workers sat on the sidewalk in front of New York's City Hall. They refused to take shelter, and they refused to leave the sidewalk. Their leaflet read, "In the name of Jesus, who is God, who is love, we will not obey this order to pretend, to evacuate, to hide. We will not be drilled into fear. We do not have faith in God if we depend on the atom bomb." Day told an interviewer that her act of civil disobedience was penance for the bombing of Hiroshima by the United States. She was arrested. Every time the sirens sounded after that, she returned for the demonstration—not sheltering, and not leaving the sidewalk. She was arrested repeatedly. By 1961, more than two thousand people had joined her in the protest. Eventually, the government's passion for civil defense exercises faded, but by then Dorothy Day's status as the godmother of the American peace movement was established, with her antiwar witness during Vietnam proving crucial. Despite her long history of radical protest, deplored as much by Church authorities as by the Pentagon, she is now an officially designated "Servant of God," a candidate for Catholic sainthood.[30]

As for me, I had a last encounter with her—a different one. In 1974, she was given a social justice award by the church in Boston where I was working as a priest, a center of antiwar organizing. She came from New York by Greyhound bus, carrying a carpet satchel, her only piece of luggage. I met her at the reception held in her honor—the same gray hair, the same oversize sweater, the same stout shoes. Of course, she did not recall me from my few volunteer sessions at St. Joseph's House, but when I told her my name, she asked me to repeat it. Then, shyly, she opened her bag and withdrew a small book—not *The Imitation of Christ*. It was a thin, recently published volume of my own writing, a poor attempt to put into words the meaning for religion of the political and social upheavals of the time. The book was called *Prayer from Where We Are*.[31] "You wrote this?" she asked. I said yes. She said, "It is my spiritual reading, Father, my reading on the bus." That simple affirmation should have only pleased me, yet inwardly I shuddered, and the "Father" was what did it. I was already quietly preparing to leave the priesthood, a decision that Dorothy Day would have roundly disapproved of. In the presence of that good woman, I felt ashamed. Now, looking back, I see that in her, Christ's mercy and judgment were endlessly in conflict—a moral roughness of which she would have been fully aware. She never claimed to be a saint.

In the Cloud

The key to the actuality of Christ is *precisely* in the imitation of Jesus: the *study*, in Dorothy Day's phrase, of our life conformed to his; the *following*, as Bonhoeffer put it; what Schweitzer called the *stepping in to help in Jesus' name*. Why? Because what was revealed in Jesus— what made others eventually see him as Son of Man, Christ, *Logos*, God—was that his capacity for transcendence (transfiguration, resurrection, call it what you will) was exactly a capacity that lives in every person. Not just in those we designate as saints. That is why the profound ordinariness of transcendence as beheld in him was essential—it was ordinary enough for each one of us to match, with our fears, irascibility, vanities, and doubts; also our hopes, gifts, desires, and strengths. *Acting fully as who we are, the imitation of Christ is the way to actualize in ourselves what makes Jesus matter.*

We have problems believing that Jesus is God because we don't really know what that word "God" refers to. To renounce the divinity of Jesus, as do a corps of the new Jesus scholars—never mind the new atheists—is to attribute, paradoxically, some reality to divinity itself. Isn't it better to acknowledge an essential ignorance about what—or who—lies beyond? The intuition that Jesus is the Christ, and therefore somehow "of God," far from being the product of naïveté or superstition, can be rooted in a profoundly sophisticated grasp of the meaning of existence. It pushes past the boundaries of what is readily known and suggests that the realm out there is real.

The atheist legal scholar Ronald Dworkin pointed at that depth of awareness when he wrote, "Religion is a deep, distinct, and comprehensive worldview: it holds that inherent, objective value permeates everything, that the universe and its creatures are awe-inspiring, that human life has purpose and the universe order. A belief in a god is only one possible manifestation or consequence of that worldview."[32] Belief in Jesus as making that God available is another. Yet all of this necessarily comes cloaked in uncertainty. We earlier cited Albert Einstein's assertion that humans have the capacity for grasping "the highest wisdom and the most radiant beauty," but, because we do the grasping with "our dull faculties," we can perceive such transcendent mysteries only "in their most primitive forms."[33] Atheists and theists can meet one another in the field of limits—the limits of skepticism and the limits of faith—if they can agree to acknowledge such limits, which are parallel, even overlapping.

Believers confront an ultimate mystery: all that we know *for certain* about God is that we do not know God. Here, for Christians, is the pointed relevance of Jesus Christ, for in him we have the knowledge of God that matters. Only if we accommodate and protect some kind of belief in the divinity of Christ—as critically informed as it is true to the tradition; let's call it a postmodern faith—does Jesus Christ have a future as more than a misunderstood victim, a mere practitioner of the good deed, or, perhaps, as an avatar of rebellion. The strongest argument in favor of Christ's divinity is not from biography, what unfolded over the thirty years of his life, but from history: what believers have made of this figure across two thousand years. He is "God."

But when we assert, presumably with far less complication, that Jesus was a human being, is the matter really any clearer? We do not know with certainty what or who God is, but it is equally true, in fact, that we do not actually know *what a human is*.[34] The inability to grasp the mystery of our own meaning *as humans* defines the contemporary crisis of identity more sharply than anything. God is not the problem. We are the problem to ourselves. We see now, through the insights of science and the traumas of political conflict, that all of the traditional points of reference in relation to which humans have understood themselves have been upended.

Realities as basic as time and space are not the distinct realms they seem to be, any more than energy and matter are truly separate entities. We used to think that matter was the solid unmovable ground of being, but now we know that matter is motion. Physics tells us that what we imagine to be solid is actually mostly emptiness within which waves fluctuate. And not just physics, but metaphysics: every universal truth is perceived from a particular perspective, which can seem to undercut universality. Our ideas are not what they were. All is flux, which humans have *felt* forever. But now, because of Kant, Einstein, Wittgenstein, and their heirs, we see flux for what it is: everything. We can no longer take the measure of our world with anything like precision, because the measures themselves are always changing.

To be human, therefore, is to be on the way to becoming something else. We can see this right in front of our faces now, every time we hunch over a smartphone or save a file to the cloud: a meta-world that exists everywhere and nowhere. "Cloud computing" refers to the shift of data storage and management from the personal computer to remote servers, with individual users needing little more than a screen and a minimally powered terminal. It may seem a stretch to find in suddenly ubiquitous but profoundly mundane technologies an image of world-historic evolutionary mutation, but perhaps this is the way evolution has always worked, a "secular" process in which life's most sacred secret is embedded. Today, with the cloud, human interactions are routinely filtered through a new reality that is invisible, transnational, and beyond the control of any user. Already, all significant financial transactions around the globe now occur in the cloud. What is this? The approaching loss to far-off networks of what's called the *personal* computer may be a warning, since impersonality (of learning, knowing, thinking, relating) is what threatens. Has the Internet, which most of us embraced in all innocence, ushered in such a slyly domineering force? As individual tech users surrender both control and understanding of even our most intimate communications to that new reality, does there come a point at which its abstract supremacy takes on character and agency—something like personhood? What happens to the human project then?

In fact, this is an old question. Thinkers and dreamers have long imagined the evolution of minds into Mind. Such imagining may represent a serious misunderstanding of human awareness and *self-*awareness, and we invoke it here with a certain tentativeness, but still something is afoot in the way we humans perceive one another and ourselves, and it has been for a while now. Kierkegaard wrote of "eternal consciousness"; the French sociologist Émile Durkheim of "collective consciousness"; the British writer H. G. Wells of a "world brain"; the French philosopher Edouard Le Roy of the "noosphere"—which the Jesuit Pierre Teilhard de Chardin called a "new skin" on the earth. In the twenty-first century, humanity's leap out of the biosphere into a realm of pure cognition has become thinkable, if not yet quite feasible.[35] Science fiction writers were first to advance what might be called technological spirituality, with, say, super-machines morphing into sentient beings. Think of HAL, the computer that usurped control of the spacecraft in the Stanley Kubrick film *2001: A Space Odyssey*. Computer scientists have, in effect, made such preoccupation mundane in pursuit of artificial intelligence. The point is that an overarching, human-created but independent power dominating affairs in ways that confound all but the tiniest elite is very much within the realm of possibility, perhaps in the near term. Confronted with this new shape of the human condition, language fails. Therefore, old categories of metaphysics and mysticism are appealed to, even as esoteric metaphors are coined, all in the effort to articulate this altered state of what it means to be a thinking creature alive on the planet.

The cloud is one of those metaphors, but it carries implications of its own.[36] Clouds were an early emblem of heaven, the idealized afterlife where humans come into their reward. Indeed, we saw the image at the beginning of this book, for it was on clouds that the Son of Man was to make his appearance on the last day. One problem with the trope is the way in which the insubstantial and immaterial cloud stands in contrast to the gritty earth, as if the destiny of humans is to be freed from the bondage of the body—a techno-neoplatonism. Contempt for human corporeality is a mistake of the heavenly minded, and it shows up in the high-tech denigration of the physical brain as a "meat computer." The wish to transcend the flesh, whether in the religious glorification of angels or in an IT elevation of disembodied intelligence, is inhuman.

But the cloud carries a positive connotation, too—an invitation to value the mystery, paradox, and ambiguity that remain forever foreign to machines. An anonymous genius of the fourteenth century wrote *The Cloud of Unknowing*, in which the obscuring and elusive mist offered an image of breakthrough understanding that awareness of life's ultimate unknowability, far from being mere ignorance, is the permanent precondition of the knowledge that makes us human: "For He can well be loved, but He cannot be thought." The author's "He" here is a word for "God," but in this ingenious turn on the tradition, both "He" and "God" are words for the ineffable itself:

> By love He can be grasped and held, but by thought, neither grasped nor held. And therefore, though it may be good at times to think specifically of the kindness and excellence of God, and though this may be a light and a part of contemplation, all the same, in the work of contemplation itself, it must be cast down and covered with a cloud of forgetting. And you must step above it stoutly but deftly, with a devout and delightful stirring of love, and struggle to pierce that darkness above you; and beat on that thick cloud of unknowing with a sharp dart of longing love, and do not give up, whatever happens.[37]

This "stepping above . . . stoutly . . . deftly" can open into a realm of value and truth in which norms of certitude do not apply. Contemporary experience, with social and technical mutations on the march, is understandably threatening, but it can also be taken as an invitation to a more spacious world marked less by clinging than by letting go. The meaning of intelligence, of consciousness, and of *self*-consciousness is changing with every advance in technology, a process that continually surpasses expectation and is finally showing itself to be radically open-ended. Some version of this has been going on in the human story since the primeval ancestor chipped a stone into a blade, but in the scientific age the pace of change has momentously accelerated, and so has human awareness of this staggering phenomenon. A new world—not so brave, perhaps, yet full of promise.

Locating human meaning thoroughly within the evolutionary process, anticipating transformations into heretofore unimagined, and even post-human, manifestations of intelligent being, can seem to be the secular denigration of the human person that Galileo's inquisitors warned of, a reduction of the ancient image of man as cosmic center, and even pinnacle, of God's creation. Against such a grand pre-Copernican conception, humans must now be reckoned as mere accidents of natural selection, the random outcome of evolution, beings on the way to being something else. Humans are bits of straw blowing in the wind, in Blaise Pascal's image. Perhaps so, but with this one footnote, first provided by Pascal and referred to at the outset of this book—the footnote that makes all the difference: humans are reeds of straw *who think*. Reeds of straw *who know*. Reeds of straw *who choose*. Reeds of straw *who love*. Reeds of straw who willingly *surpass themselves*. The glory of man, more evident now than ever, is this in-built capacity for—and no other word will do—transcendence. For some, transcendence has a name.

We saw that "Son of Man" can be translated as "human being," which suggests that we all have his capacity for transcendence. Jesus Christ is the revelation of what awaits us all. The tension between his two titles—Son of Man and Son of God—is full of implication here. Jesus reveals humanity as much as he reveals divinity. Indeed, what Jesus, when taken to be Christ, reveals is that divinity abides not just in him but in all of us. Here is where the traditional faith in Jesus Christ as Lord God, far from being outmoded in the Secular Age, meshes with the postmodern recognition of history's radical fluidity. The ancient Christian expectation of a future fulfilled in being taken up into God is wholly consonant with the dawning contemporary sense of an open-ended evolution ever surpassing itself.[38] This is how we "partake," in Saint Peter's phrase, "of the divine nature."[39]

The biblical tradition asserts that God is present with special focus in Israel, and in Jesus, but first, God is present in creation. Of that holy presence, Israel is but the sign among the nations; and of that holy presence, Jesus Christ is simply the sacrament. But neither Israel nor Christ exhausts the presence of God in creation. The human person—not just Christ—is *the* creature in whom this mystery is revealed, because the human person participates in the life of creation, *and knows it.* Thus, consciousness and self-consciousness—the unbounded scope of which were not fully grasped until the Secular Age—have come to be recognized as modes of the supreme consciousness known in the tradition as "God."

The language of philosophy reduces this mystery to "being." Aristotle's *Metaphysics*, for example, is the study of "being *qua* being." Martin Heidegger gave modern expression to the idea: "Everything we talk about, everything we have in view, everything toward which we comport ourselves in any way, is being; what we are is being, and so is how we are." Humans are the beings for whom *being* is a question.[40] The word "existence" brings the notion of being down to earth somewhat, and attention to that word roots existentialism, too. Jean-Paul Sartre wrote, "Man first of all exists, encounters himself, surges up in the world—and defines himself afterwards."[41] Attention to existence is the start of self-awareness, but more, it is the precondition of "surging up"—of self-surpassing, an opening to what makes existence possible in the first place.

The language of Scripture is not to be confused with the language of philosophy, any more than with the language of science, yet the sacred texts grapple with the idea of being, too. Indeed, the verb "to be" occupies the Bible's linguistic holy of holies, providing nothing less than the name of God. It all starts with Moses, who, having received the Ten Commandments, hesitates and says to God:

> "If I come to the people of Israel and say to them, 'The God of your fathers has sent me to you,' and they ask me, 'What is his name?' what shall I say to them?" God said to Moses, "I AM

WHO I AM." And he said, "Say this to the people of Israel, 'I AM has sent me to you.'"[42]

Jesus is remembered at critical moments, as we saw, associating himself with the I AM name of God. In the Gospel of John, in tension with "the Jews," he even applies it to himself: "'Your father Abraham rejoiced that he was to see my day; he saw it and was glad.' The Jews then said to him, 'You are not yet fifty years old, and have you seen Abraham?' Jesus said to them, 'Truly, truly, I say to you, before Abraham was, I am.'" Jesus' hearers understand this phrase as the blasphemous claim to divinity it quite explicitly is, and react accordingly. "So they took up stones to throw at him; but Jesus hid himself, and went out of the temple."[43]

The I AM of God, of Jesus, is the "I am" of every person, and it consists in every person being *aware* of herself or himself. And that awareness points beyond itself. Consciousness leads to self-consciousness leads to self-transcendence. *Homo erectus* leads to *Homo sapiens* leads to *Homo sapiens sapiens*. "I know" leads to "I know that I know" leads to "I know that I am known." Here is what we mean by the *image* of God in which we humans are created.[44] "Image" and "imitation" are linguistic variations on I AM. The faculty, therefore, through which the beckoning horizon of *being* runs is the imagination—what the critic Terry Eagleton calls "a secular form for grace." In Samuel Taylor Coleridge's construction, the imagination is the repetition in human beings of the creative I AM of God.[45] For Coleridge and other Romantics, the imagination was "a Christ-like capacity of redemption and reconciliation," as Eagleton puts it, "one which mimes God's own creative power."[46] In the imagination, the creature and the Creator meet. And this opening of creature to Creator opens creatures to one another: "Virtuous conduct is founded on fellow feeling, and fellow feeling flows from imaginative sympathy."[47] Just as Jesus came progressively into the fullness of his selfhood and virtuous conduct as Son of Man—the fullness his followers came to call God—so in every person is the possibility and the promise of that same fullness. Each one's "I am" opens to I AM.

This modern formulation springs from the heart of the tradition: from Athanasius, who spoke of "deification," to John Calvin's "sanctification," to Karl Rahner's "divinization," to Pierre Teilhard de Chardin's "convergent evolution" toward the Omega Point. Humans are on the move toward God. It does not matter whether the original formulations of this faith have been hollowed out by the discoveries—or disenchantments—of modernity. "If we can no longer live the great symbols of the sacred in accordance with the original belief," Paul Ricoeur famously wrote, "we can, we modern men, aim at a second naiveté in and through criticism."[48]

Criticism, yes. That has informed our purpose throughout this book. But even more, finally, what we have come to is *imitation*. No surprise, really, since imitation, we now know, is a fundamental dynamic of being human. As infants, we come into language—and mindfulness—by imitating the sounds of those who hold us.[49] So imitation makes us human. But here we see that imitation can make us more than human, too. So we act with focus and specificity in the most trying of circumstances, through every interruption of history, with Bonhoeffer, Day, and the great *cloud* of witnesses[50]—all modeling Jesus Christ. And doing so, to repeat Ricoeur, "in accordance with the original belief," since our tradition has taught since the beginning that we *imitate* Christ because we are the *image* of God. Mindful imitation makes Christ actual.

Because God Lives

It is not as a child that I believe and confess Jesus Christ. My hosanna is born of a furnace of doubt.

—Fyodor Dostoyevsky[1]

The Future of Jesus Christ

What Jesus does tells us who he is. More, what Jesus does leads to his being "lifted up," the phrase from John. Jesus was lifted up on the cross, which was simultaneously a being lifted up "in glory" as Son of Man. "Glory" means only that we the followers of Jesus can finally see the thing clear. In the Gospel of John, the Resurrection and the crucifixion are the same thing. The followers of Jesus responded to the triumph of Easter—and in their history-shaking response lies the truest miracle—because they had already responded to the triumph of the simple goodness of Jesus well before he died. That goodness came to include his willingness to risk death, and the attitude he took toward death when he finally suffered it. Even in John, despite its assertion of Jesus as the preexisting *Logos*, there was—through successive acts of goodness—a gradual divinizing of Jesus, too. The Son of Man coming into his own.

When we proclaim, with the tradition, that Jesus is "Christ," that Jesus Christ is "risen," that Jesus Christ is "God," we know that we are not asserting scientific facts. We are offering interpretations of a bottomless mystery, ever to be plumbed, never to be mastered. And, actually, Christian believers have always had language for this imprecise, ambiguous, and unfinished faith. The Church has, despite appearances, never claimed to possess the whole truth about Jesus, for the memory of his having come is always paired with the expectation that he will come again—in fulfillment of all human longing at the end of time. "Parousia" is the technical name for this expectation; "eschatology" is another. "Son of Man," we see again, is the name this culminating figure goes by. To expect him is to believe that history is headed somewhere, and has an ultimate purpose, which gives the present meaning.

The tradition of the Second Coming of Jesus defines the fallible character of this peculiar faith, for it began with a misunderstanding. We saw that the first followers of Jesus, thinking of him in Jewish apocalyptic terms drawn from Daniel, thought he would return soon in messianic glory: we saw that Saint Paul said the longed-for return would occur within the lifetimes of his readers.[2] But they were wrong.

Still, the idea captured the essential truth of what Jesus promised—that the unfinished will be finished, ambiguities resolved. Humanity will surpass itself in something more than humanity—a something that goes by the name of God. And this expectation, whether Christians remembered it or not, permanently rooted Christianity within *Jewish* messianic hope, where it remains. Recovering that sense of Christian Jewishness, like recovering the permanent Jewishness of Jesus, defines the essential work that Christians must do in a post-Auschwitz world.

Faith in God, because of questions forced by the Secular Age, is not what it was. But in what matters most, God has never changed. For this is the God of Abraham, Isaac, and Jacob. The only God whom Jesus preached, that is, was the God of Jews. And so with Jesus' only message, which was: *The God who makes the promise keeps the promise.* The covenant is permanent, broken no more by any individual death than by the end of history, which is, after all, the

Creator's way of being in time. "In Jesus, both God's trust in man and man's response of trust in God take on their definitive human form."[3]

It has been the goal of this work to consider Jesus Christ in ways true to the classical tradition of Christian faith while simultaneously limiting assertion about him to what is plausible to a modern—or postmodern—mind. That has meant both an honest return to the foundational texts, and a reading of those texts in the light of contemporary critical understanding—and the mandates of history.

We have assumed in that reading that historical events are not the same as the narrative accounts they inspire, and that, in fact, we can know with certainty not the event but only the story told about it. Ancient peoples and societies can be perceived only through distorting lenses of present experience and bias. We distort in our tales today, but so did those who wrote the Gospels late in the first century about a man who'd lived early in that century. Therefore, our faith is as much in the process by which Jesus is remembered—called "tradition"—as in Jesus. Seen in this way, he is elusive, but elusiveness is precisely what can allow Jesus to be, again, a figure of connection among varied people and peoples—including, here, the writer and the reader. To each one, the encounter with Jesus is unique, however it occurs. That no one possesses Jesus, or fully understands him, is why the movement toward Jesus can never be made alone.

But tradition, if we can personify it, has a tendency to forget that its grasp of the mediated truth is always partial, and the effect of that forgetting is to turn partial truth into complete falsehood. Nothing occasions such distortion more pointedly than looking back on the past through the present experience of war—which is decisive both for Gospel writers and for us. Such perplexity requires a constant purification of memory and narratives of tradition. In our time, that purification has been forced by scientific cosmology, dynamic evolution, the fact of pluralism, and the sin of the Church. Because of perennial pressures and recent ones, a changed view of Jesus, it turns out, is the most authentic way of remaining faithful to Jesus.[4] This is not a surrender to "relativism" or "secularism," but rather the way to carry forward the inner meaning of classical doctrine and timeless faith. Because, finally, faith is not timeless. And, in fact, both relativism and secularism can shed light on a reexamined faith without swallowing it.

The standard of explanation throughout this book has been: What makes sense? What is plausible? But also, this work is braced by awareness that not everything can be explained. The measure of reflection and interpretation has been not the reconstruction of some "historical Jesus," but what Bonhoeffer called "discipleship." Discipleship is a commitment to the memory and presence of Jesus Christ that makes a difference in how a life is lived, driving thought and behavior week in and week out.

A Simple Faith

Here is the question, finally: Why do Christians need to believe in the Incarnation? "The point of incarnation language," the Catholic theologian Roger Haight writes, "is that Jesus is one of us, that what occurred in Jesus is the destiny of human existence itself: *et homo factus est*. Jesus is a statement, God's statement, about humanity as such."[5] Humanity is the presence of God. The presence of God, therefore, lies in what is ordinary. Not in supernatural marvels. Not in a superman with whom we have nothing actual in common. Not in saints. Not in a once-only age of miracles long ago. Not first in doctrine, scholarship, or theology—but in life. Doctrine, scholarship, and theology are essential as modes of opening up that life and its meanings, and there is no separating the life of Jesus from interpretations of it. The interpretations must always be examined, and criticized. And we endlessly conjure interpretations of our own, as here in this book.

But the *life* is our object. The life of Jesus must always weigh more than his death. And, to repeat, the revelation is in the ordinariness of that life. His teaching—his permanent Jewishness, his preference for service over power, his ever-respectful attitude toward women and others on the social margin—is available to us because his followers passed the teaching along, which continues. His encounters with beloved friends, disciples, outcasts, antagonists, and Romans, all arranged in a story that is more invention than memory, are valued as occasions of his encounter with the Holy One—but they are *typical* encounters, not supernatural ones. Again and again he turned to God, and, as the tradition says, he turned *into* God—but that, too, occurred in the most ordinary of ways. Day by day. Act by act. Choice by choice. Word by word. Ultimately "lifted up," as John says, on the cross which *was* the Resurrection. And the cross is central to this meaning not because God willed suffering but because, in Jesus, God joined in it. "The quality of the suffering," in Eliot's phrase, is changed. And that includes the extreme suffering of war.

Leaving us with? A simple Jesus. An ordinary Christ. One whom the simplest person can imitate, the most ordinary person bringing Christ once more to life—day by day, word by word, bread by bread, cup by cup. In all of that we see divinity, which, paradoxically, is what makes Jesus one of us. Whatever sort of God Jesus is understood to be, it must be the God who is like humans, not different. If that seems impossible, then what we think of God—*and of humans*—must change. This is essential to the New Testament and "the very logic of Christian faith."[6] And, finally, the truest argument—not proof—for the divinity of Jesus is in the one undenied fact of this history: that billions upon billions of ordinary human beings have found in this faith an immediate and saving experience of the real presence of God, "partaking" of God—*becoming* God. Even unto here, with these words written and read. We come to Jesus, in the end as in the beginning, only through the Jesus people.

If Christ is undiscovered now, a figure lost to many, that is in part because of scandals done in his name, by those who call out his name most loudly. In part, he remains undiscovered because of the abstractions and secrets of scholars who do not trust ordinary people with the very ordinariness of Jesus—as if the mass of believers can embrace only superstition and magic. And in part, he remains undiscovered because so much about our age has shaken us to the core, leaving us stripped of the intellectual horizon within which faith, for most of these thousands of years since Abraham, has had its resonance. Even while understanding that loss, still the conclusion of this long inquiry includes a frank criticism of contemporary culture for its ignorance of, and indifference to, the language of transcendence. The divinity of Jesus is problematic, but the blatant repudiation of the faith that constructs itself around that divinity is blind to a constellation of intellectual subtleties that have enhanced human life for two millennia. Likewise, the word "God" is problematic, but its abandonment is problematic, too.

Human life is more than material. To be rendered mute in the face of that mystery is to be less than human. And being less than human now carries dangers that simply did not exist before. Auschwitz and Hiroshima amount to the twin interruptions of history that have made this inquiry not only necessary but urgent. Auschwitz and Hiroshima, which warned not just of a capacity but of an inclination, lay bare the new actuality that confronts men and women: the dread prospect that the human species—which is *the very cosmos aware of itself*—will bring about its own extinction.

Even for those of us who still find a home among people who cannot let go of their affection for Jesus, belief is not what it was, and there is an unknowing for us as much as for any agnostic or atheist. Unbelief is now built into belief, since intelligent belief includes a self-critical and necessarily skeptical element. No Christendom, no hierarchy, no church—no Catholic Worker community, even—buttresses belief or replaces it. So each person makes the choice alone, even if the choice is *for* the solidarity of faith.

Not faith *in* Jesus Christ, precisely, but faith, at the invitation *of* Jesus, in *God*. Now we know, though, the limits of our language about God. We do not know "God" not because we are ignorant, but because "God" refers to one who, when it comes to certitude, is beyond categories of knowledge. The God to whom Jesus points is the God beyond "God." We recognize in Jesus all that we need to know about the God who otherwise remains incomprehensible. And this recognition, because it is well rooted in the past, is powerful enough to carry us into the open-ended future, even extending beyond what can be imagined.[7]

And can it be a surprise, after all of this, that one of the first to sense this necessary disenchantment with Christianity's anthropomorphic naïveté was Dietrich Bonhoeffer? Whether he fully grasped the meaning of his intuition or not, we cannot miss the implications when we read today what he wrote in prison in 1944: "The God who is with us is the God who forsakes us. The God who lets us live in the world without the working hypothesis of God is the God before whom we stand continually. Before God and with God, we live without God."[8]

We live, that is, aware of the symbolic character of all of our religious affirmations. We know that, as symbols, they are both true and untrue, which is what it is to live before God—without God. And we know that even the most precious of our symbols—including the "divinity" of Jesus—are invented. Our capacity for such invention itself points to the One who gave it to us. The Holy One who comes to us in the natural order—creation as the Creator's great self-communication. The Holy One who comes to us in ordinary experience, which becomes extraordinary only through interpretation. Like this.

So we are here less to believe in Jesus than to imitate him. We imitate him above all in nurturing the conviction that the Creator of the universe cares for us as a parent loves a child, which is the conviction, finally, that rescues meaning in an otherwise pointless cosmos. Meaning is itself how God is revealed. We saw this before: "In the beginning was Meaning, and Meaning was with God, and Meaning *was* God. . . . And Meaning became one of us."[9] Yes, meaning was present in Jesus, but only to reveal that meaning is present in creation, and meaning is present in each person. For as long as humans exist, meaning will define the human horizon, and at every human approach, that horizon will withdraw, even while still beckoning. *Follow*, it says. And as we do, the word "meaning" moves from lowercase to upper.

In Dorothy Day's chosen image, we are pilgrims of that Meaning, not possessors of it. Pilgrims *en route* toward the ever-undiscovered Christ, who is Meaning become flesh. Again and again, we grasp him, but always incompletely. We depend on what others before us have made of this mystery, which is why we are at home in the tradition, whose imperfections make our own imperfections acceptable. Therefore, with something like the impulse of erotic yearning, we continually reach for the actuality of Christ.

The pilgrim's trek of this book brings us, in the end, to a simple faith:

Jesus, the Jew from Nazareth, is a living expression of the inexpressible God. He is the Christ, Son of Man, according to the Scriptures. He is present to the world the way meaning is present in the word. Just as a word points not to itself, but to its meaning, so Jesus Christ, Son of God, points to One whom he calls Father. In that way, as one of us, he is the Word of God, whose Meaning comes clear. The Unknowable One, therefore, can be known. Because God is not an enemy, but a friend, we need not be afraid. Because God completes what God begins, death is not the end, but a beginning, wholly undefined. Because God is faithful, creation has a purpose, and its name is history. Imitators of Jesus Christ, we want mainly to be kind and true, taking heart from our dear companions on the way. And we say, with those who go before, and who come after, Amen. So may it be.

Acknowledgments

I gratefully acknowledge all who helped make this work possible, beginning with long-ago colleagues in the Paulist Fathers, the Catholic religious order that first brought me into these adventures of the Word. I think especially of Paul Lannan, Tomaso Kane, Michael McGarry, John Collins, Al Moser, and Thomas Stransky. At the Paulist Center, in Boston, my faith is sustained to this day.

I wrote this book at Suffolk University, where I am a scholar in residence. I drew essential support from Dean Kenneth Greenberg and from my faculty colleague Fred Marchant. I gratefully acknowledge them, and the whole Suffolk community.

At Harvard Divinity School, starting with a fellowship in 1997 and continuing through various associations since, I have been instructed in ways large and small. The late Krister Stendahl was a precious mentor, and Harvey Cox has been a particular inspiration. Deans William Graham and David Hempton have been generous in their support, and Professors Mark U. Edwards, Diana Eck, Karen King, Francis X. Clooney, and Kevin Madigan have taught me much. At Harvard, I have been an associate of the Manhindras Humanities Center: thanks to Homi Bhabha, Mary Halpenny-Killip, Kiku Adatto, and Michael Sandel. I drew on this book in delivering the 2014 Paul Tillich Lecture at Harvard, and thank those whose responses instructed me, especially Professors Owen Gingerich and Gerald Holton, and Wendy S. McDowell, editor of the *Harvard Divinity Bulletin*.

In 2011, I was holder of the Alonzo L. McDonald Family Chair at Emory University, where Dr. Jan Love, dean of the Candler School of Theology, offered me a most generous welcome. My Emory colleagues, especially Professors Michael S. Berger and Vernon K. Robbins, received me kindly, and I offer thanks to all at Emory who responded to the series of lectures I offered there on Jesus.

The manuscript of this book was read by Donald Cutler, Mark Edwards, Bernard Avishai, Ed Bacon, Mark Richardson, and Alexandra Marshall. They helped me make the work better, and I thank them. At Viking Press, I had the benefit of the sharp intelligence and the deep human sensitivity of a great editor, Wendy Wolf. I acknowledge my debt to her and to all at Viking who brought this book to the public. My most heartfelt thanks go to Tina Bennett of William Morris Endeavor, who was first to grasp my purpose here, and to affirm it.

In their goodness, my brothers Joe, Brian, Kevin, and Dennis and their families sustain me in the convictions with which our parents raised us. If I keep the faith, it is because of support I receive from Padraic O'Hare, David Killian, Jack Smith, Gracie Smith, Mac and Georgie Gatch, Mary and Bob Murray, Larry Kessler, Jill Kerr Conway, Mary Gordon, Christopher Lydon, and Pam and Jim Morton. All of my writing, and my life, spring from the love of my family: my wife, Alexandra Marshall; our son, Patrick Carroll; our daughter, Elizabeth Carroll; her husband, James Jenkins; and their daughter, Annie, to whom, in all happiness, I dedicate this book.

Notes

EPIGRAPH

1. Bede, *Ecclesiastical History of the English People*, Penguin Classics, trans. Leo Sherley-Price, introduction by D. H. Farmer (New York: Penguin Books, 1991). The anecdote accounts for the king's decision to allow the first Christian preaching in England.

INTRODUCTION: **Christ Actually**

1. From Geoffrey Hill, "Christmas Trees," a poem about Dietrich Bonhoeffer. In *New and Collected Poems, 1952–1992* (Boston: Houghton Mifflin, 2000).
2. Dietrich Bonhoeffer, *Letters and Papers from Prison: Dietrich Bonhoeffer Works*, vol. 8 (Minneapolis: Fortress Press, 2010), 362. I first grasped the importance of this question years ago in reading John Macquarrie's *Jesus Christ in Modern Thought* (Philadelphia: Trinity Press International, 1990), 338–422.
3. I have written of my Air Force coming-of-age elsewhere. See James Carroll, *An American Requiem: God, My Father, and the War that Came Between Us* (Boston: Houghton Mifflin, 1996) and *House of War: The Pentagon and the Disastrous Rise of American Power* (Boston: Houghton Mifflin, 2006).
4. "The release of atomic power has changed everything except our way of thinking . . . and thus we drift toward unparalleled catastrophe." Quoted in Carl Seelig, *Albert Einstein: A Documentary Biography*, trans. Mervyn Savill (London: Staples Press, 1956), 223.
5. Dietrich Bonhoeffer, *Letters and Papers from Prison*, 362–65.
6. The Second Vatican Council was a meeting of the world's Catholic bishops, convened in 1962 by Pope John XXIII. It met in Rome in four sessions over three years, and promulgated major revisions in Catholic thought and doctrine. In subsequent decades, those revisions were partly rolled back by conservative Church leaders, but the Council's reforms seeded the Catholic imagination, and may yet come to flower. See Norman Tanner, ed., *Vatican II: The Essential Texts*, introductions by Pope Benedict XVI and James Carroll (New York: Doubleday, 2012).

7. Paul Tillich, *Dynamics of Faith* (New York: Harper Perennial Classics, 2001), 111.

8. Paul Tillich, *The Courage to Be* (New Haven: Yale University Press, 1952), 185.

9. Bonhoeffer was cited as an inspiration, for example, by the British scholar J. A. T. Robinson, whose 1963 book *Honest to God* rang the opening bell of the "secular theology" craze. Hard questions about the capacity of traditional theism to stand up to numerous challenges from postmodernist thought and contemporary science were swamped by a pop-culture reduction to the absurd under the heading "God is dead." But the questions asked were serious. In America, secular theology was given its most influential expression by the Harvard theologian Harvey Cox, whose 1965 book *The Secular City* remains a milestone, helping to extend Bonhoeffer's reach. For a study of Bonhoeffer's influence on Cox and the movement he spawned, see Jess O. Hale Jr., "A Journey of Christian Human Responsibility: Harvey Cox's Appropriation of Dietrich Bonhoeffer," *Journal of Lutheran Ethics* (November 2005).

10. Three-quarters of the once devout Czech Republic are now religiously unaffiliated. Pew Research Center, "The Global Religious Landscape," Religion and Public Life Project, 2012, http://www.pewforum.org /global-religious-landscape-exec.aspx.

11. Tillich, *Dynamics of Faith*, 91.

12. Zvi Kolitz, "Yid Rakover Talks to God," *Lapham's Quarterly* 3, no. 1 (Winter 2010), 91.

13. As of 2010, 84 percent of the world's population is religiously affiliated. The Pew Research Center found that, as of 2010, there were 2.2 billion Christians (32 percent of the world's population), 1.6 billion Muslims (23 percent), 1 billion Hindus (15 percent), 400 million folk religionists (6 percent), and 14 million Jews (0.2 percent). The breakdown by region of the unaffiliated: 21 percent live in Asia-Pacific, 18 percent in Europe, and 17 percent in North America, and the large majority of the globe's religiously unaffiliated (62 percent) is in China. Pew Research Center, "The Global Religious Landscape."

14. In the name of "renewalist" pieties, Bonhoeffer himself was reimagined and reclaimed. As a man of conscience who defined his political resistance in expressly Christian terms, he became, decades after the Death of God fad had passed, a hero to a very different breed: conservative evangelicals in the United States, who drafted the German martyr into antigovernment campaigns on issues like abortion and homosexuality. See Eric Metaxas, *Bonhoeffer: Pastor, Martyr, Spy* (Nashville: Thomas Nelson,

2011). Ferdinand Schlingensiepen, a good friend of Eberhard Bethge, to whom Bonhoeffer addressed his most important letters, published a more objective biography: *Dietrich Bonhoeffer 1906–1945: Martyr, Thinker, Man of Resistance* (New York: T.T. & Clark, 2010). Bethge himself, who collected and published Bonhoeffer's letters, wrote what remains the most intimate account of his friend's life: *Dietrich Bonhoeffer: Man of Vision, Man of Courage* (Minneapolis: Fortress Press, 1970). For a 2000 edition, Bethge's book was revised and edited by Victoria J. Barnett. The most important contemporary biography of Bonhoeffer is by Charles Marsh, *Strange Glory: A Life of Dietrich Bonhoeffer* (New York: Knopf, 2014).

15. Appeals to Christian themes and disciplines are routinely made, for example, not only by conservative American politicians—the "religious right"—but also by mainstream U.S. military institutions, from the Pentagon to the military academies. See Anna Mulrine, "Too Much Religion at Military Academies? West Point Cadet Revives Charge," *Christian Science Monitor*, December 7, 2012. Many U.S. businesses centered in the Sunbelt have Jesus Christ as an icon. See Bethany Moreton, *To Serve God and Wal-Mart: The Making of Christian Free Enterprise* (Cambridge, Mass.: Harvard University Press, 2009).

16. Terry Eagleton, *Culture and the Death of God* (New Haven, Conn.: Yale University Press, 2014), 3.

17. Against Arab dictators, the decisive demonstrations in places like Cairo's Tahrir Square were regularly launched on Fridays, after crowds had been stirred up in mosques. Against Moscow, the Polish labor union Solidarity was inspired by—and partly financed by—the Polish pope, John Paul II. The democracy movement in East Germany climaxed at weekly "Peace Prayer" gatherings called by Lutheran pastors, with thousands and ultimately tens of thousands rallying at Leipzig's Nikolaikirche. Inside the Soviet Union itself, a decades-long struggle by Jews *as Jews* struck early blows against the tyranny.

18. Dietrich Bonhoeffer, "The Church and the Jewish Question," in *No Rusty Swords: Letters, Lectures and Notes 1928–1936*, ed. Edwin H. Robinson, trans. Edwin H. Robinson and John Bowden (New York: Harper and Row, 1965), 226.

19. Soon after publishing the 1933 essay, Bonhoeffer contacted the New York–based Rabbi Stephen Wise, who would prove to be one of the staunchest resisters of the Holocaust. Bonhoeffer alerted Wise to what was happening, and from then on he participated actively in drawing attention to the plight of Jews in Germany and, ultimately, in helping them escape.

20. "Dietrich Bonhoeffer," United States Holocaust Memorial Museum, http://www.ushmm.org/museum/exhibit/online/bonhoeffer/?content=5. The staff director of the Committee on Ethics, Religion and the Holocaust at the U.S. Holocaust Memorial Museum is Victoria Barnett, an expert on Bonhoeffer and coeditor of the complete works of Bonhoeffer in English. I acknowledge my debt to her.

21. Martin Luther, "On the Jews and Their Lies," Jewish Virtual Library, http://www.jewishvirtuallibrary.org/jsource/anti-semitism/Luther_on_Jews.html.

22. Dietrich Bonhoeffer, *Ethics* (New York: Touchstone, 1955), 90–91.

23. After the Italian Fascist leader Benito Mussolini met with Hitler not long before *Ethics* was written, for example, Mussolini reported on the German leader's denigrations of Catholicism by saying to his ambassador to the Holy See, "I will spare you all the idiotic things that Hitler said about Jesus Christ being of the Jewish race, etcetera." Hitler aimed to discredit the Church by emphasizing the Jewishness of Jesus, but Mussolini dismissed Hitler's pronouncement as *"sciocchezze"*—nonsense. Jesus was no Jew. Mussolini understood that the Catholic establishment regarded as ludicrous any notion that Jesus was Jewish. In fact, the wily Mussolini knew that trumpeting the absurdity of the idea could build a bridge between himself and the pope. David I. Kertzer, *The Pope and Mussolini: The Secret History of Pius XI and the Rise of Fascism in Europe* (New York: Random House, 2014), 205.

24. Martin Luther's Jew-friendly tract "That Jesus Christ Was Born a Jew" was published in 1523, when he imagined that Jews would come over to his reformed Christianity. They did not. In 1543, he published his foully anti-Semitic "On the Jews and Their Lies," venting his rage, and defining Jews as the ontological enemy of the German nation. Now Judaism was cast in such evil light that Jesus Christ could have no connection to it. The Aryan Christ was born. See Susannah Heschel, *The Aryan Jesus: Christian Theologians and the Bible in Nazi Germany* (Princeton, N.J.: Princeton University Press, 2008).

25. Stephen Jay Gould, *Rocks of Ages: Science and Religion in the Fullness of Life* (New York: Bantam, 1999), 5.

26. We should note right at the outset that there is something problematic in the use of the word "Jew" in this context, because the word overwhelmingly has its main contemporary resonance in the culture and imaginative world of Rabbinic Judaism, a particular religious form derived from the Israel of Jesus' time but decisively including elements—especially the talmudic

tradition and the traumatic collective experience of exile—of which Jesus would have known nothing. Jesus was not a Jew in the way that, say, Irving Howe was. This book will explain that. But Jesus was wholly a son of Israel in all that he did and believed, and that is our larger point. It is enough to note here that the word "Jew" has its origins in the name of the tribe of Judah, one of the sons of Jacob, who, after wrestling with the angel, took the name Israel. At first the word—*Yehudi* in Hebrew—referred to those living in the territory of the tribe of Judah, Judea. But it eventually came to be used to refer to all children of Israel. *Yehudi* is first applied to a person in the book of Esther, which dates to the fourth or third century B.C.E. It appears seventy-four times in the Hebrew Scriptures.

27. "From the 1970s onward, scholars . . . have hammered home the vital importance of seeing Jesus within and as part of the living and lively world of 1st century Palestinian Judaism. Unfortunately, the response of all too many American academics has been lip service. One need only page through the many Jesus books that enshrine the word 'Jew' in their titles . . . One finds a politically correct shift away from portraying a Jesus who attacks the Law, at least in its pharisaic interpretations, to a Jesus who attacks hierarchy, priesthood, and temple—the latter suspects being assigned the role of villain in our more enlightened age." John P. Meier, *A Marginal Jew: Rethinking the Historical Jesus*, vol. 4: *Law and Love* (New Haven, Conn.: Yale University Press, 2009), 647–48.

28. And not just modernity. Medieval and Renaissance portraiture commonly gave Jesus features characteristic more of Europeans than of Semites. See Bernard Starr, *The Ethnic Cleansing of Judaism in Medieval and Renaissance Art* (San Antonio, Texas: Omnihouse Publishing, 2013).

29. In 1965, Vatican II explicitly renounced the Christ-killer slander in *Nostra Aetate*: "What happened in His Passion cannot be blamed upon all the Jews then living, without distinction, nor against the Jews of today." But Christians, including Catholics, who read the Gospel texts uncritically are condemned to the Christ-killer trope. Latino Catholics, for example, are twice as likely as other Catholics both to take the Bible literally as the Word of God and to have negative attitudes toward Jews. The two mind-sets go hand in hand. See "Changing Faiths: Latinos and the Transformation of American Religion," Pew Research Center, Hispanic Trends Project, 2007, http://www.pewhispanic.org/2007/04/25/changing-faiths-latinos-and-the-transformation-of-american-religion; and Tom W. Smith, "Hispanic Attitudes Toward Jews," American Jewish Committee, 2007, http://www.ajc.org/atf/cf/%7B42d75369-d582-4380-8395-d25925b85eaf%7D/hispanic_

attitudes_jews_042007.pdf. In the United States, according to a poll conducted by the Anti-Defamation League in 2011, 31 percent of Americans
agreed with the statement "Jews were responsible for the death of Christ."
Evangelical Christians around the globe are more broadly given to the same
text-based anti-Jewish mind-set, even as American evangelicals are simultaneously supportive of the State of Israel. According to a 2014 ADL survey,
more than one-fourth of the world's population harbors anti-Semitic
attitudes. *ADL Global 100*, 2014, http://global100.adl.org.

30. A paradigmatic and influential work by a Jewish scholar is *Jesus of Naza-
    reth: King of the Jews,* by Paula Fredriksen (New York: Knopf, 1999).
    Another is *The Historical Jesus in Context,* by Amy-Jill Levine (Princeton,
    N.J.: Princeton University Press, 2008). The scholarly convergence is re-
    flected more broadly—for example, in Pope John Paul II's statement that
    "Jesus' human identity is determined on the basis of his bond with the
    people of Israel." Address to the Pontifical Biblical Commission, 1997.
    Levine sums the task up: "After two thousand years of ignorance, the time
    has come for church and synagogue, Jews and Christians, to understand
    our intertwined histories, to see Jesus as a Jew who made sense to other
    Jews in a Jewish context, to learn how our two traditions came to a parting
    of the ways, to recognize how misunderstandings of Jesus and Judaism
    continue even today to foster negative stereotypes and feed hate, and to
    explore how the gains in interfaith relations made over the past several
    decades can be nurtured and expanded." Amy-Jill Levine, *The Misunder-
    stood Jew: The Church and the Scandal of the Jewish Jesus* (San Francisco:
    HarperOne, 2006), 16.

31. Matthew 27:25.

32. John 1:11. A definitive elucidation of New Testament roots of European
    contempt for Jews appeared in 1948, out of the still smoldering ashes of
    the Holocaust. It was *Jesus and Israel,* by the French Jewish historian Jules
    Isaac. Pope John received Isaac in a private meeting in 1960 and accepted
    a copy of the controversial book. Isaac described the encounter as positive,
    even warm. Soon after that meeting, the pope put the Church's relation-
    ship with the Jewish people on the agenda of the Vatican Council. Hed-
    wig Wahle, "Pioneers in Jewish-Christian Dialogue: Some Known and
    Unknown Pioneers of Continental Europe," *SIDIC* (*Service International
    de Documentation Judeo-Chretienne,* English edition) 30, no. 2 (1997): 2–9.

33. John P. Meier, N. T. Wright, Paula Fredriksen, John Dominic Crossan,
    et al. We will see more of this "criterion of dissimilarity," with its origins
    in German biblical scholarship.

34. John 1:1, 1:14. "Word" is the most common translation of the Greek *Logos*, which had a long history in Hellenistic thought. We will see more of the idea later.

35. John 10:30.

36. Since Jesus was taken to be *not* Jewish, the early Church faced a critical question: "What purposes—theological, cultural, social, and political—did his circumcision serve?" Andrew S. Jacobs, *Christ Circumcised: A Study in Early Christian History and Difference* (Philadelphia: University of Pennsylvania Press, 2012), x. One common trope had it that the cutting of Jesus' foreskin was an anticipation of his crucifixion, and, consequently, purported bits of the foreskin of Jesus were favored relics in the medieval Church, companions to pieces of the True Cross. The sense of the child Jesus as victim of Jewish violence reinforced the Christ-killer myth (and surfaced unexpectedly in the twenty-first century when a German court outlawed circumcision as abusive).

37. The Dead Sea Scrolls, comprising various writings of Jewish groups dating to before, during, and shortly after the time of Jesus, have been found in caves above the Jordan River Valley in a sequence of discoveries beginning in 1947 and continuing until 2014, when nine new scrolls were discovered inside material that had been found previously. Giorgio Bernardelli, "Nine New Qumran Scrolls Discovered, *Vatican Insider*, May 26, 2014, http://vaticaninsider.lastampa.it/en/world-news/detail/articolo/qumran-qumaran-qumaran-archelogia-archeology-arqueologia-32410.

38. Deuteronomy 6:4–9.

39. "Since between 95 and 97 percent of the Jewish state was illiterate at the time of Jesus, it must be presumed that Jesus was also illiterate, that he knew, like the vast majority of his contemporaries in an oral culture, the foundational narratives, basic stories, and general expectations of his tradition, but not the exact texts, precise citations, or intricate arguments of its scribal elites." John Dominic Crossan, *Jesus: A Revolutionary Biography* (San Francisco: HarperSanFrancisco, 1994), 25–26. Other scholars assume Jesus' literacy, and even his fluency in Greek as well as Aramaic. See Chris Keith, *Jesus' Literacy: Scribal Culture & the Teacher from Galilee* (London: Bloomsbury, 2011).

40. David M. Neuhaus, "Engaging the Jewish People," *Catholic Engagement with World Religions*, ed. Karl J. Becker and Ilaria Morali (Maryknoll, N.Y.: Orbis, 2010), 396.

41. The word "kingdom" here translates the Greek *basileia*, which some scholars translate as "empire." The temptation is to offer yet another

translation, one that honors the egalitarian—decidedly nonmonarchical—attitudes of Jesus. The scholar John Cobb suggests "commonwealth," a word that implies the liberal democratic polity that might well come closer to Jesus' meaning. To him, God was *"Abba,"* after all. But seeing Jesus as a Jew of his time, immersed in the legacy of the kingdom of David and assuming "kingship" as a metaphor for God's sovereignty, makes "commonwealth" a shade too anachronistic. John B. Cobb Jr., *Spiritual Bankruptcy: A Prophetic Call to Action* (Nashville, Tenn.: Abingdon, 2010), 27.

42. "The God of the Old Testament is arguably the most unpleasant character in all fiction: jealous and proud of it; a petty, unjust, unforgiving control-freak; a vindictive, bloodthirsty ethnic cleanser; a misogynistic, homophobic, racist, infanticidal, genocidal, filicidal, pestilential, megalomaniacal, sadomasochistic, capriciously malevolent bully." Richard Dawkins, *The God Delusion* (Boston: Houghton Mifflin Harcourt, 2008), 31.

43. That Pope Francis, beginning in 2013, explicitly brought the spirit of Vatican II back into the life of the Catholic Church made apparent how thoroughly it had been stifled by the pontificates of his two predecessors, John Paul II and Benedict XVI. See my "Who Am I to Judge? A Radical Pope's First Year," *New Yorker,* December 15, 2013.

44. Take one denomination as an example. In the United States, as of 2010, fully one-third of all people raised as Catholics have left the Church. An unprecedented 10 percent of the nation's population identifies itself as "former Catholic," which makes that cohort the third largest after Catholicism itself (23 percent) and "unaffiliated" (16 percent). Pew Research Center, Religion & Public Life Project, 2013, http://religions.pewforum.org/reports.

45. Diarmaid MacCulloch, *Christianity: The First Three Thousand Years* (New York: Viking, 2010), 83.

46. Hans Küng, *Credo: The Apostles Creed Explained for Today* (Grand Rapids, Mich.: Eerdmans, 1992), 9.

CHAPTER ONE: **Personal Jesus**

1. James Joyce, *Dubliners* (West Warwick, R.I.: Merry Blacksmith Press, 2010; first published 1914), 178.

2. Raphael Lemkin, a Jewish lawyer who had fought the Nazis in Warsaw before fleeing Poland, decried "the crime without a name." He saw where Hitler's program was headed and in 1943 coined the word "genocide,"

defining it as "the destruction of a nation or an ethnic group." The word appears in his prophetic treatise *Axis Rule in Occupied Europe* (Washington, D.C.: Carnegie Endowment for International Peace, 1944). Lemkin lost nearly fifty members of his family in the Holocaust.

3. The first Jews were murdered at Auschwitz in 1941, but in 1943, with the construction of three massive crematoriums and the mechanized introduction into sealed death chambers of the cyanide gas Zyklon B, its conversion from labor camp to extermination camp was complete.

4. Bruno Bettelheim asked that question in 1960. "The Ignored Lesson of Anne Frank," *Atlantic Monthly*, November 1960.

5. Elie Wiesel, *Night* (New York: Hill & Wang, 2006), 66–68.

6. Emil Fackenheim, for example: "A Jew today is one who, except for an historical accident—Hitler's loss of the war—would have either been murdered or never born." *To Mend the World* (New York: Schocken, 1982), 295. The Shoah might have exhausted Jewish identity, but for the triumph of Zionism, with the establishment of the State of Israel, which countered the Jew-as-eternal-victim theme. "Zionism was the most fundamental revolution in Jewish life. It substituted a secular self-identity of the Jews as a nation for the traditional and Orthodox self-identity in religious terms." Shlomo Avineri, *The Making of Modern Zionism* (New York: Basic Books, 1981), 13.

7. Here is Freud's frontal assault on the faith, from 1913: "The psychoanalysis of individual human beings teaches us with quite special insistence that the god of each of them is formed in the likeness of his father, that his personal relation to God depends on his relation to his father in the flesh and oscillates and changes along with that relation—and that at bottom God is nothing other than an exalted father." Sigmund Freud, *Totem and Taboo* (Mineola, N.Y.: Dover, 1998), 126.

8. The Blessed Virgin "appeared" to three sheep-herding children near the Portuguese town of Fátima six times over the course of six months in 1917—the year, not incidentally, of the Bolshevik Revolution. She encouraged the use of the rosary in prayer, and exhorted prayers for the conversion of Russia. She was the prima donna of anti-Communism. It is supremely ironic that "Fátima" became another name for Mary, since the name first belonged to Muhammad's daughter and wife of his successor, Ali. Surely a Moorish population in Iberia, eventually expelled by Catholic rulers, was responsible for the place name.

9. Lourdes, a small town in France, was the site of the masterpiece apparition of the Blessed Virgin, who appeared more than a dozen times to a

young girl in 1858. The enthusiasm of Catholics for the Virgin equated to the competing cults of secular nationalism, a rallying to the side of the Church against anticlerical forces in France and elsewhere in Europe. France had its Napoléon, America its Lincoln, Britain its Victoria, Germany its Bismarck, Italy its Garibaldi. The Church had Our Lady of Lourdes.

10. "The fate of our times is characterized by rationalization and intellectualization and, above all, by the disenchantment of the world." Max Weber, writing in 1918. *Max Weber: Essays in Sociology*, trans. H. H. Gerth and C. Wright Mills (New York: Oxford University Press, 1946), 155.

11. Charles Taylor, *A Secular Age* (Cambridge, Mass.: Harvard University Press, 2007), 59.

12. The rosary's "Hail, Holy Queen" begins: "Hail, holy Queen, Mother of Mercy! our life, our sweetness, and our hope! To thee do we cry, poor banished children of Eve; to thee do we send up our sighs, mourning and weeping in this valley of tears."

13. The Act of Contrition: "O my God, I am heartily sorry for having offended Thee. And I detest all my sins because I dread the fires of Hell and the loss of Heaven, but most of all because they offend Thee, my God, who art all-good and deserving of all my love. I firmly resolve, with the help of Thy grace, to make amends, to sin no more, and to avoid the near occasion of sin. With Thy help, through Jesus Christ, Our Lord. Amen."

14. Saint Anselm, an eleventh-century theologian reflecting the era's juridical legalism, explained in his 1098 treatise *Cur Deus Homo* that satisfaction for Adam's *infinite* insult to God could be accomplished only by the sacrifice of an *infinite* being, one whose equality to God the Father made him ontologically eligible to pay the debt. Hence the necessity for the divinity of the Son of God, Jesus. By his crucifixion, the penal debt to God the Father was paid off. Saint Paul's metaphor of ransom paid by Christ *to Satan* was thus perverted into a kind of ransom paid *to God*. No longer metaphor, but now fact, this idea of "penal atonement" dominated Christian theology from the twelfth century on because of a simplicity that could be grasped, even if inchoately, by a child.

15. The so-called *Infancy Gospel of Thomas*, a second-century text unrelated to the noncanonical *Gospel of Thomas*, and the *Quran* both show the boy Jesus fashioning birds out of clay and bringing them to life.

16. In convening Vatican II, John XXIII surely was influenced by his own wartime experience, while serving as papal legate in Turkey, of being one of the few Catholic prelates to actively oppose the genocide. He

personally provided hundreds, perhaps thousands, of fugitive Jews with documents they needed to escape.

17. Leading us in that chorus was the Yale chaplain William Sloane Coffin. I have written about this experience in *An American Requiem: God, My Father, and the War that Came Between Us* (Boston: Houghton Mifflin, 1996).

18. For a critical unpacking of this idea of "marginal," as applied to Jesus, see John P. Meier's monumental four-volume *A Marginal Jew: Rethinking the Historical Jesus* (New York: Doubleday, 1991–2009).

19. Exodus 3:7–8.

20. James Carroll, *Constantine's Sword: The Church and the Jews, a History* (Boston: Houghton Mifflin, 2001), which was made into a documentary film in 2007; *Jerusalem, Jerusalem: How the Ancient City Ignited Our Modern World* (Boston: Houghton Mifflin, 2011).

21. John 1:1–3. I take the point from John Macquarrie, who translates these verses as, "Fundamental to everything is Meaning . . . Meaning and God are virtually identical . . ." John Macquarrie, *Jesus Christ in Modern Thought* (Philadelphia: Trinity Press International, 1990), 106.

22. Josephus, *Jewish Antiquities*, XVIII:62–64.

23. The Nicene Creed offers the fourth-century definition of Jesus as "God from God, Light from Light, True God from True God, begotten not made, consubstantial with the Father; through him all things were made."

CHAPTER TWO: The First Holocaust

1. Richard Rubenstein, *After Auschwitz: Radical Theology and Contemporary Judaism* (New York: Bobbs-Merrill, 1966), x.

2. For Rome's "Jewish War," Jack Miles uses the phrase "Roman Shoah" and draws the comparison with the "twentieth-century slaughter of the Jews of Europe." *Christ: A Crisis in the Life of God* (New York: Knopf, 2001), 109–111. I independently made the same comparison in *Constantine's Sword: The Church and the Jews, a History* (Boston: Houghton Mifflin, 2001), 89.

3. The Roman historians Josephus, Tacitus, and Cassius Dio provide estimates of Jewish dead in the three-phased war totaling more than two million. Such figures cannot be taken as precise, yet they suggest the scale of killing. We will see more of these reports.

4. Josephus says that Titus, the Roman general in charge of the siege of Jerusalem in 70, did not assault Jews of Antioch, presumably because they had yielded to Roman rule. But Jewish submission in Antioch was exceptional. See Josephus, *The Jewish War*, VII:110–11.

5. Josephus, *Jewish Antiquities*, XIV:4, 4. Josephus (37–c. 100) was a Jerusalem Jew, descended from priestly aristocrats. In the citation here, he refers to the start of the Roman occupation. When, a century later, in 66, the great rebellion against Rome began, he was a military leader in Galilee. One of dozens of Jewish fighters about to be captured, he led his men in an act of collective suicide, each one killing others, rather than surrender. Josephus was the last one alive. Instead of killing himself, he defected to Rome, claiming to have had a vision that the Roman commander, Vespasian, would become emperor. When that, in fact, occurred, Vespasian ordered him released, Josephus became a Roman citizen, took the name Titus Flavius Josephus in honor of his patrons, and began to compile his histories. For obvious reasons, his accounts cannot be read as wholly objective, but modern scholarship has essentially confirmed them.

6. Josephus, *Jewish Antiquities*, XVII:250–89.

7. Matthew 2:16–18. I am especially informed here by John Dominic Crossan, *God and Empire: Jesus Against Rome, Then and Now* (New York: HarperCollins, 2007).

8. Some scholars regard the word "occupation" for the Roman domination of Palestine as anachronistic, since the legions were mainly kept apart from the Jewish population, and Roman authority was often exercised through local petty tyrants. But police enforcement in a total tyranny can be apparently restrained, even absent, precisely because what is most "occupied" is the mind of the oppressed. When Rome chose to act, the imposition of control was swift, brutal, and complete.

9. The numbers are impossible to verify, although scholars find it plausible that hundreds of thousands of Jews rallied to the side of the rebels in Jerusalem. Paula Fredriksen, *Jesus of Nazareth: King of the Jews* (New York: Knopf, 1999), 64. E. P. Sanders, *Judaism: Practice and Belief, 63 BCE–66 CE* (Philadelphia: Trinity Press International, 1992), 127.

10. His last words were said to be "What an artist dies in me."

11. Reza Aslan's 2013 book, pointedly entitled *Zealot*, conveys its considerable punch by associating Jesus with this movement. I find much in Aslan's work to admire, but, as is clear by now, I offer a different reading of Jesus.

12. Josephus, *The Jewish War*, VI:9.3. Again, Josephus's report may be unreliable, although much in his account of the war is affirmed by twentieth-century finds like the Dead Sea Scrolls. The dead would have included those killed by Romans, and by fellow Jews in what amounted to a civil

war among the various factions in Jerusalem, as well as those who starved or died of disease.

13. The Roman historian Cassius Dio, writing most of a century after the fact, says the Jews of Judea in this period "occupied the advantageous positions in the country and strengthened them with mines and walls, in order that they might have places of refuge whenever they should be hard-pressed." "Dio Cassius, *Historia Romana*, LXIX:12–14: A Roman Account of the Bar Kokhba Revolt," in *Texts and Traditions*, ed. Lawrence H. Schiffman (Hoboken, N.J.: KTAV Publishing, 1998), 487–88.

14. Here is the account from Cassius Dio: "At Jerusalem Hadrian founded a city in place of the one which had been razed to the ground, naming it *Aelia Capitolina*, and on the site of the temple of the god he raised a new temple to Jupiter. This brought on a war of no slight importance nor of brief duration." *Historia Romana*, LXIX:12:1.

15. Numbers 24:17. The Christian historian Eusebius, writing two hundred years after the fact, maligned Bar Kokhba as a madman, and those who followed him as blind Jews, yet again responding to a false messiah. For Eusebius, Roman brutality in putting down the revolt was just retribution. *The Ecclesiastical History* IV, 6.

16. Werner Eck, "The bar Kokhba Revolt: The Roman Point of View," *Journal of Roman Studies* 89 (1999): 76–89.

17. Cassius Dio, *Historia Romana*, LXIX:12, 2.

18. *Jerusalem Talmud Ta'anit*, 4:5. http://www.jewishtreats.org/2013/07/the-second-uprising.html.

19. Cassius Dio, *Historia Romana*, LXIX:12–14.

20. Hitler killed one in every three Jews in the world, and two of every three Jews living in German-controlled Europe. Scholars suggest that the first-century Jewish population of Judea, Samaria, Galilee, and adjacent Syria would likely have ranged well above a million, perhaps as high as two or two and a half million—with perhaps another million in Egypt and a million or more elsewhere. Josephus, as noted, puts the number of Jewish dead in just the first siege of Jerusalem, in 70, at 1.1 million. Diaspora Jewish revolts between 115 and 117 in Cyprus, Egypt, Libya, and Mesopotamia resulted, according to reliable estimates, in many hundreds of thousands killed. And the put-down of the so-called Bar Kokhba revolt, beginning in 132, was even more violent, with the Roman historian Cassius Dio putting the number of Jewish dead at 580,000. Out of a total Jewish population, then, of something like four to five million, it is more

than conceivable that, across two generations, about a third of those living at any one time were killed in violence sparked by Romans.

21. Matthew 24:2.

22. Matthew 23:37.

23. John 2:19, 2:21.

24. Matthew 27:51; Mark 15:38; Luke 23:45.

25. Matthew 24:6–10. I find the juxtaposition of "text" and "context" in Ismar Schorsch, *From Text to Context: The Turn to History in Modern Judaism* (Waltham, Mass.: Brandeis University Press, 1994).

26. Matthew 24:12–14.

27. Matthew, Mark, and Luke have Jesus' "cleansing" of the Temple as the immediate cause of his arrest; John locates it at the beginning of his ministry, the source of his ongoing conflict with Jewish authorities.

28. Matthew 12:6.

29. Genesis 22.

30. Dan Bahat, *The Illustrated Atlas of Jerusalem* (Jerusalem: Carta, 1989), 38–43.

31. Exodus 31 describes the construction of the Ark of the Covenant, a chest in which to house the tablets of the Law given to Moses. It is not clear what the Ark kept in the Temple actually was.

32. As we will see, the idea of monotheism, as defining Israel's faith in the one God, confuses as much as it explains. In sum, the oneness of God is a moral principle of reconciliation, not a numerical value of ranking that would require subservience from all other religions.

33. "For thou hast no delight in sacrifice; were I to give a burnt offering, thou wouldst not be pleased. The sacrifice acceptable to God is a broken spirit; a broken and contrite heart, O God, thou wilt not despise" (Psalm 51:16–17).

34. "He has no need, like those high priests, to offer sacrifices daily, first for his own sins and then for those of the people; he did this once for all when he offered up himself" (Hebrews 7:27). For an elucidation of Jewish notions of metaphor, symbol, and sacrifice, see the work of Sidra DeKoven Ezrahi, e.g., *Booking Passage: Exile and Homecoming in the Modern Jewish Imagination* (Berkeley: University of California Press, 2000).

35. Both Rabbinic Jews and Christians regard the move away from literal blood sacrifice into the realm of metaphor as a humane progression. Jews see sacrifice as a matter of Law observance and prayer. Christians see the Eucharistic meal as an "unbloody" sacrifice. But there is a problem here. "For an understanding of sacrifice in ancient Israel, it does not matter that according to Maimonides, sacrifice was destined to be replaced by prayer.

It does not matter that according to Hebrews, sacrifice was destined to be replaced by Jesus.... Looking back at ancient Israel from the presumption of intellectual, ethical, and religious superiority is not the way ancient Israel will truly be understood." Jonathan Klawans, *Purity, Sacrifice, and the Temple* (New York: Oxford University Press, 2006), 47.

36. The practice of divide and rule showed up in Northern Ireland, where, for two centuries, London stoked conflict between local Catholics and Calvinist settlers. London's exploitation of divisions between Hindus and Muslims in India left a legacy of hatred between India and Pakistan that lasts to this day. To say nothing of the British Mandate for Palestine's legacy of hatred between Arab and Jew.

37. A scholarly consensus holds that the written New Testament is based on oral traditions that included sayings attributed to Jesus and stories about him, as well as hymns and ritualized confessions of faith. A first written document is hypothesized and referred to by scholars as "Q," for *Quelle*, the German for "source," probably compiling the sayings of Jesus and composed during the 50s. The letters of Paul were written during the 50s and early 60s, before his death in around the year 62. The first Gospel to be written was Mark, dating to around 70. The Gospels of Matthew and Luke were composed in around 80 or shortly after. John was written in around 100. Because so much depends on our understanding of it, we are noting this chronology again and again.

38. Qumran became famous when its library was discovered in caves near the Dead Sea in the 1940s and 1950s—the so-called Dead Sea Scrolls, already referred to.

39. In the anti-Jewish imagination of Christians, the "money changers" whose table Jesus overturned evoke the greed of Jews, but in the Temple, where crowds came from diverse and distant realms, currency adjustments, necessary to the purchase of offerings, would have been a service.

40. The scholar E. P. Sanders makes the point this way: "Modern scholars, both Jews and Christians, are inclined to see the Temple system as corrupt, or as detrimental to the people's welfare. We all like moral reform, and it is nice to see our spiritual ancestors as moral reformers. The first century predecessors of modern Jews and Christians (Pharisees, rabbis, Jesus and his followers) must have thought there was something wrong with common Judaism, the Judaism of the Temple." *Judaism: Practice and Belief,* 91. For an explanation of how Jesus' offense in the Temple could have been in defense of it, see Bruce Chilton, *The Temple of Jesus: His Sacrificial Program Within a Cultural History of Sacrifice* (University Park: Pennsylvania State University Press, 1992), 121–27. For Christians continuing to worship in the Temple, see Acts 2:46.

41. "The Zealots, no matter how much their struggle was against the alien Roman oppressors, were first fighting a class war against their own Jewish nobility." Richard A. Horsley and John S. Hanson, *Bandits, Prophets, and Messiahs: Popular Movements at the Time of Jesus* (Harrisburg, Pa.: Trinity Press International, 1985), 225. Josephus describes the Zealots' attacks as terrorism pure and simple. *The Jewish War*, V:10.1.

42. I first heard the phrase "wartime literature" applied to New Testament texts in conversation with Elaine Pagels. She develops the idea in her groundbreaking book *Revelations: Visions, Prophecy, and Politics in the Book of Revelation* (New York: Viking, 2012).

43. In 1644, four years before the end of the Thirty Years' War, Roger Williams of Rhode Island cut to the essential cause, publishing the declaration that "magistrates as magistrates have no power of setting up the form of a church government." Williams used the phrase "wall of separation" between church and state, which Thomas Jefferson picked up more than a century later. See John M. Barry, *Roger Williams and the Creation of the American Soul* (New York: Viking, 2012), 6. While the Thirty Years' War raged, Francis Bacon, René Descartes, and Thomas Hobbes, to name only three, were laying the intellectual groundwork for a world without the religion that had spawned such mayhem.

44. Other apocalyptic writings are 1 Enoch, Syriac Baruch, and the later New Testament book of Revelation, or Apocalypse. I am giving emphasis in this work to "wartime literature" as essential to Jewish and Christian understandings, but that is not to deny other, more positive experiences as constitutive of Jewish and Christian religious thought—the goodness of creation, God's promise of life, memory of liberation, and so on. My focus on war is not to be taken as an instance of what Salo Wittmayer Baron called "the lachrymose conception of Jewish history." On the contrary, I aim to show how this most negative of experiences generated again and again creative, life-affirming responses.

45. Daniel 6:22.

46. Daniel 12:11.

47. Daniel 12:1–2.

48. Daniel 12:13.

49. Josephus, *Jewish Antiquities*, X:11, 7.

50. Recall that Joseph puts the figure at 1.1 million. *The Jewish War*, VI:9.3.

51. John Dominic Crossan and Jonathan L. Reed, *Excavating Jesus: Beneath the Stones, Behind the Texts* (San Francisco: HarperSanFrancisco, 2001), 136.

52. Mark 13:9–13.

53. Mark 1:9.

54. The First Letter of Peter refers to "my son Mark" (1 Peter 5:13). "Mark, the disciple and interpreter of Peter, himself also handed down to us in writing what was preached by Peter." Irenaeus, *Against Heresies*, III.I. But Mark's authorship and place of writing are unresolved questions. For a discussion of both, see Adela Yarbo Collins, *Mark: A Commentary*, ed. Harold W. Attridge (Minneapolis: Fortress, 2007), 1–10.

55. "Any argument based on the identity of the Gospel writer or on the composition of the original audience must remain speculative, since both who wrote the Gospels and where the Gospels were written remain unknown. . . . In Gospel studies, scholarship proceeds according to an elegant circular argument: it determines the audience on the basis of the text, and then determines the meaning of the text on the basis of the audience." Amy-Jill Levine, *The Misunderstood Jew: The Church and the Scandal of the Jewish Jesus* (San Francisco: HarperOne, 2006), 105.

56. Mark 13:17, 13:19.

57. Mark 3:16.

58. Matthew 16:18.

59. Mark 9:4–6.

60. Mark 8:29–33.

61. Mark 14:34–41.

62. Mark 14:27–31.

63. Mark 14:66–72.

64. Mark 15:40.

65. A contemporary reckoning with this phenomenon shows in the story of Pope Francis, whose own self-described failures as a prelate during the so-called Dirty War in Argentina turned out to be the ground of his remarkable character as a pope who eschews the moralizing condemnations of his kind. When he asks, "Who am I to judge?" he is acknowledging his own sins against courage, which takes another kind of courage altogether and establishes the only moral credential that matters. See my profile of Pope Francis, "Who Am I to Judge? A Radical Pope's First Year," *New Yorker*, December 15, 2013.

66. Mark 8:34.

67. Mark 13:13.

68. Mark 13:12.

69. I acknowledge my debt to Ched Myers for this reading of Mark. "During the war . . . precisely the situation the text reflects . . . the double pressure of the Roman reconquest of Galilee and aggressive rebel recruitment . . .

Mark's community would surely have been wrestling with faltering solidarity within its ranks, the suspicion of informers . . . the betrayal of some members by others to the authorities." Ched Myers, *Binding the Strong Man: A Political Reading of Mark's Story of Jesus* (Maryknoll, N.Y.: Orbis, 1991), 419.

CHAPTER THREE: The Jewish Christ

1. The opening line of the novel *The Go-Between*, by L.P. Hartley, published in London by Hamish Hamilton in 1953. It's become a cliché, with a life apart from the book, but it captures a still-underappreciated truth.

2. John Shelby Spong offers a lucid account of this Jewish liturgical origin of the Gospel of Mark. See *Liberating the Gospels: Reading the Bible with Jewish Eyes* (San Francisco: HarperSanFrancisco, 1996), 67–86. The three Gospels—Mark and the derivative Matthew and Luke—agree that the Last Supper was the Passover meal. The Gospel of John has the meal *before* Passover, so that Jesus—more emphatically the paschal lamb in John—can be shown being crucified exactly as the lambs are being ritually slaughtered.

3. John 1:1.

4. John 1:14.

5. Mark 14:63–64.

6. Wesley J. Wildman, *Fidelity with Plausibility: Modest Christologies in the Twentieth Century* (Albany, N.Y.: SUNY Press, 1998), 147.

7. Here, for example, from the preface to the *Common English Bible*: "*Ben 'adam* (Hebrew) or *huios tou anthrōpou* (Greek) are best translated as 'human being' (rather than 'son of man') except in cases of direct address, where the CEB renders 'Human' (instead of 'Son of Man' or 'Mortal,' e.g., Ezek 2:1). When *ho huios tou anthrōpou* is used as a title for Jesus, the CEB refers to Jesus as 'the Human One.'" http://www.commonenglishbible .com/Connect/Blog/ViewBlog/tabid/209/ArticleId/13/From-Son-of-Man-to-Human-One.aspx. Daniel Boyarin drew my attention to this usage in the *Common English Bible. The Jewish Gospel: The Story of the Jewish Christ* (New York: New Press, 2012), 25–26. An example of a Jesus scholar who explores the complexities of "Son of Man" as a synonym for "human being" is John Dominic Crossan, *God and Empire: Jesus Against Rome, Then and Now* (New York: HarperOne, 2007), 125.

8. Mark 14:61–62.

9. Luke 22:70. Scholars suggest that in these texts, Jesus' blasphemy consists in his use of the term "I am," an echo of the name Yahweh applies to Himself: "I AM WHO I AM" (Exodus 3:14). We will return to this.

10. The great Catholic theologian of the twentieth century Karl Rahner observed that "the heresy of monophysitism (Jesus is God in human dress) dominates the Christian view today." "Current Problems in Christology," in *Theological Investigations*, vol. 1, trans. Cornelius Ernst (Baltimore: Helcion Press, 1961), 160. As the name suggests, Monophysitism means that there was only one (divine) nature in Jesus, against the orthodox idea that his one person was made up of two natures. Another condemned heresy was Docetism, which held that Jesus seemed human but was not. That Church authorities had to regularly and repeatedly anathematize the idea that Jesus was not really human shows how pervasive the belief was.

11. For a discussion of the traditional Jewish point of view—that divinity claims made for Jesus had to be rejected by Jews at the beginning, and must be rejected now—see Jacob Neusner, *A Rabbi Talks with Jesus: An Intermillennial Interfaith Exchange* (New York: Doubleday, 1993).

12. "No mortal thing could have been formed on the similitude of the supreme Father of the universe, but only after the pattern of the Second Deity, who is the Word of the Supreme Being, since it is fitting that the rational soul of man should bear the type of the divine Word." Philo, *Questions and Answers on Genesis*, trans. Charles Duke Yonge, Early Christian Writings, http://www.earlychristianwritings.com/yonge/book42.html, II:62. The idea here is that the Supreme Being, changeless and wholly other, could not have had direct intercourse with the corruptions of the created world, and hence the need of the second, lesser God, who is the Creator.

13. Already noted is the fact that the Court of the Gentiles was the largest section of the Jerusalem Temple. Proselytes are referred to in Matthew 23:15. In Acts, Saint Paul is shown addressing God fearers in Antioch: "Men of Israel, and you that fear God, listen" (Acts 13:16). It is plausible that many, if not most, of the "Gentiles" to whom Paul preached were, in fact, these believers already at home on the margins of Judaism.

14. Albert Einstein, "Living Philosophies," in *Living Philosophies: The Reflections of Some Eminent Men and Women of Our Time*, ed. Clifton Fadiman (New York: Doubleday, 1990), 6. Einstein went on to say, "In this sense and in this sense only, I belong in the ranks of devoutly religious men."

15. Ronald Dworkin, *Religion Without God* (Cambridge, Mass.: Harvard University Press, 2013), 6.

16. "History is an exercise of self-transcendence of the human spirit, its ability to understand the other as other. . . . The historian seeks to transcend his or her present context in order to grasp Jesus precisely as having existed in another context." Roger Haight, *Jesus: Symbol of God* (Maryknoll, N.Y.: Orbis, 1999), 58.

17. Charles Taylor asks how it was that "it was virtually impossible not to believe in God in, say, 1500 in our Western society, while in 2000 many of us find this not only easy, but even inescapable?" Part of the answer lies in another of Taylor's points: "Belief in God isn't quite the same thing in 1500 and 2000." Charles Taylor, *A Secular Age* (Cambridge, Mass.: Harvard University Press, 2007), 25, 13. For that matter, belief in God changes within the span of one person's life; it is not the same for "a six year old and a sixty year old, for someone riding the crest of ecstasy and someone crawling through despair." Bernard Lee, *Jesus and the Metaphors of God: The Christs of the New Testament* (New York: Paulist Press, 1993), 31.

18. Take one example of an ancient mind that does not conform to modern prejudices about its content: Lucretius (99–55 B.C.E.), the Roman poet who influenced Virgil and Cicero. All of his works but the poem/treatise "On the Nature of Things" are lost, but that work is momentous for attitudes recognized now as "modern." He denies that humans have any need of gods, warns against religion-inspired fear, and posits that all matter is made of tiny particles that are in constant motion. Stephen Greenblatt sees Lucretius as precursor to, and even inspiration for, the Enlightenment. See *The Swerve: How the World Became Modern* (New York: Norton, 2011). A somewhat different reading of Lucretius is implied by Charles Taylor: "It is no surprise that Lucretius was one of the inspirations for explorations in the direction of naturalism, e.g. with Hume. . . . But . . . overcoming our illusions about the Gods . . . wasn't what was needed for a humanism that could flourish in the modern context." *A Secular Age*, 27.

19. Taylor, *A Secular Age*, 58.

20. "Whereas the Church fathers and early ecumenical councils insisted on an ever more clearly defined orthodoxy, the rabbis wove together an ever more detailed orthopraxis. . . . Whereas Christians formulated creeds, Jews developed halakha, often translated as 'law,' but essentially meaning 'walking': How to walk in the world." David Neuhaus, "Engaging the Jewish People," in *Catholic Engagement with World Religions*, ed. Karl J. Becker and Ilaria Morali (Maryknoll, N.Y.: Orbis, 2010), 403.

21. Mark 12:29. The Shema can be seen to inspire the Shahada of Islam: "There is no God but God. Muhammad is the messenger of God."

22. Deuteronomy 6:4; Mark 12:29; 1 Corinthians 8:6.

23. 1 Corinthians 8:5. Paul refers to "the god of this world" in 2 Corinthians 4:4 and to "beings that by nature are no gods" in Galatians 4:8.

24. Ephesians 6:12.

25. See, for example, 1 Kings 18:24, which depicts Elijah's contest with Baal's 450 prophets: "The god who answers by fire—he is God."

26. Jeremiah, for example, declares, "For the customs of the peoples are false. A tree from the forest is cut down, and worked with an axe by the hands of a craftsman. Men deck it with silver and gold; they fasten it with hammer and nails so that it cannot move." But a few verses on, Jeremiah refers to the other gods as inferior to the Creator God. "But the LORD is the true God; he is the living God . . . Thus shall you say to them: 'The gods who did not make the heavens and the earth shall perish from the earth and from under the heavens'" (Jeremiah 10:3–4, 10:10–11).

27. "Whoever sacrifices to any god, save to the Lord only, shall be utterly destroyed" (Exodus 22:20). "For I know that the Lord is great, and that our Lord is above all gods" (Psalm 135:5).

28. Cited by Paula Fredriksen, "Mandatory Retirement: Ideas in the Study of Christian Origins Whose Time Has Come to Go," in *Israel's God and Rebecca's Children: Christology and Community in Early Judaism and Christianity: Essays in Honor of Larry W. Hurtado and Alan F. Segal*, ed. David B. Capes et al. (Waco, Texas: Baylor University Press, 2007), 37.

29. Paula Fredriksen, *Jesus of Nazareth: King of the Jews* (New York: Knopf, 1999), 37. This obliteration of the fast distinction between polytheists and monotheists points to a further breakdown—that of the radical distinction between "theists" and "atheists" themselves. The usefulness of these terms, too, is called into question by the facts that Christians and Jews, refusing to pay tribute to the gods of the pantheon, were derided as the ancient equivalent of atheists, and that when contemporary "atheists" debunk "God," they are often attacking crudely anthropomorphic theologies that many, if not most, believers have long since left behind. We will return to the contemporary quest for the God beyond "God," pursued by self-identified religious people who regard "secular humanism" more as a purification of belief than a threat to it. This quest can be seen from the starting point of religion in Paul Tillich (*Dynamics of Faith*) and from the

starting point of atheism in Ronald Dworkin (*Religion Without God*), but they are the same quest.

30. John 10:30.

31. Philippians 2:6. (The RSV renders "clung to" as "grasped.") Romans 10:13; Joel 2:32. Romans 10:6–8 shows "Christ" preexisting the birth of "Jesus." Adela Yarbro Collins comments, "Paul sometimes implied that Jesus became the son of God by his being raised from the dead. At other times he implies that Jesus, as Wisdom, is preexistent." Collins, "How on Earth Did Jesus Become a God?" in Capes, *Israel's God and Rebecca's Children*, 66. The point is that, even in Paul, the status of Jesus is ambiguous. We have here the human imagination grasping for new categories.

32. These Jewish and Christian scholars, locating claims for the divinity of Jesus far earlier in the first century than most scholars, call themselves, with tongue in cheek, "the early high Christology club." The group was cofounded by the Jewish scholar Alan F. Segal and the Christian Larry W. Hurtado. See Capes, *Israel's God and Rebecca's Children*, ix.

33. 1 Corinthians 1:2.

34. Collins, "How on Earth," 57.

35. In Acts 25:26, the term "Lord" is applied to Nero. The Roman Senate voted that the emperor Octavian "should be inscribed on a par with the gods, in the hymns." Collins, "How on Earth," 62–63.

36. The "parting of the ways" between Judaism and Christianity did not irretrievably occur until the fourth century, with the totalizing emperor Constantine and the orthodoxy-establishing Council of Nicea, whose creed was already noted. See my book *Constantine's Sword: The Church and the Jews, a History* (Boston: Houghton Mifflin, 2001), 144–50. It should be emphasized that, though some Jews and Christians are engaged today in a new joint project of uncovering commonalities between ancient Judaism and early Christianity, this is not about blurring the differences between the two faiths as they developed. Despite all parallels, the religions remain mutually exclusive—and should. The point, for Christians, is to dismantle mistaken notions that led to Christianity's self-understanding as ontologically positive over against a Jewish negative. Jews have no equivalent problem.

37. Daniel Boyarin taught for ten years in the Talmud department of Bar-Ilan University, in Israel. He is currently the Taubman Professor of Talmudic Culture at the University of California, Berkeley. His books include *A Radical Jew: Paul and the Politics of Identity* (Berkeley: University of California Press, 1994); *Dying for God: Martyrdom and the*

Making of Christianity and Judaism (Stanford, Calif.: Stanford University Press, 1999); and *Borderlines: The Partition of Judaeo-Christianity* (Philadelphia: University of Pennsylvania Press, 2004).

38. Daniel Boyarin, *The Jewish Gospels: The Story of the Jewish Christ* (New York: New Press, 2012), 6.

39. "If Jesus did not think of himself as a or the Messiah, however the term is defined, he may well have been the only one in his inner circle who did not." Amy-Jill Levine, *The Misunderstood Jew: The Church and the Scandal of the Jewish Jesus* (San Francisco: HarperOne, 2006), 85.

40. Boyarin, *The Jewish Gospels*, 6–7.

41. If Boyarin's thesis, and my taking off from it, proved to be an inadvertent back door into a new supersessionism . . . well, one thinks of William Styron, who sought to advance civil rights by writing about the slave rebellion leader Nat Turner, but wound up revivifying antiblack stereotypes.

42. Peter Schäfer, "The Jew Who Would be God," *New Republic*, May 18, 2012, http://www.newrepublic.com/article/103373/books-and-arts/magazine/jewish-gospels-christ-boyarin. Schäfer is director of the Program in Judaic Studies at Princeton.

43. "Peter Schäfer Slams Daniel Boyarin—Scholarly Brawl," *BLT*, May 31, 2012, http://bltnotjustasandwich.com/2012/05/31/peter-schfer-slams-daniel-boyarinscholarly-brawl.

44. Boyarin, *The Jewish Gospels*, 10.

45. Boyarin, *The Jewish Gospels*, 7.

46. Recall that the birth of Jesus is recounted in the Gospels of Matthew and Luke, although not in Mark, which begins with Jesus' encounter with John the Baptist, nor in the Gospel of John, which begins with the preexisting Word. Matthew and Luke offer similar accounts of the nativity, but with differences: Matthew, citing the death of Herod, has Jesus being born in 4 B.C.E., while Luke, citing the Augustan census, has him being born in 6 C.E. Matthew has the family at home in Bethlehem, while Luke has them sojourning there. Importantly, only Matthew tells the story of the Magi, their encounter with Herod, and Herod's determination to kill Jesus, culminating in the slaughter of the innocents and the flight of Jesus, Mary, and Joseph to Egypt. But in the Christian imagination, all these details come together to form one Christmas narrative.

47. Matthew 2:18.

48. Boyarin, *The Jewish Gospels*, 30–31. A classic *Christian* study of the "Son of Man" motif in the Gospel, as derived from Daniel, is found in Joachim Jeremias, *New Testament Theology: The Proclamation of Jesus* (New York:

Charles Scribner's Sons, 1971), 272. Jeremias, unlike Boyarin, sees the title referring to a future eschatological role for Jesus, not to a present ontological status for "Christ."

49. Mark 1:11; Psalm 2:7. "Son of God" "connotes divine appointment rather than divine nature." Robert H. Gundry, *Mark: A Commentary on his Apology for the Cross* (Grand Rapids, Mich.: Eerdmans, 1993), 909. In five key places, Mark uses the title "Son of God": 1:1, 1:11, 9:7, 14:61, 15:39. Always behind this phrase in Mark is the address God directed to Israel, as His chosen people. For an elucidation of "Son of God" references in Judaism, see Jon D. Levenson, *Death and Resurrection of the Beloved Son* (New Haven, Conn.: Yale University Press, 1995).

50. "Somehow" is to the point here. Compared with the rigidly defined categories of a Trinitarian godhead that come later, under the full influence of Greek philosophy, this Jewish vision may seem slippery, but it has the advantage of a built-in modesty about what humans can know of transcendence, which, by definition, transcends human knowing and language. Daniel's images are more like poetry than philosophy.

51. Boyarin, *The Jewish Gospels*, 45. This duality noted by Boyarin—divine judgment in tension with divine mercy—gives rise not only, as Boyarin says, to the "Father and the Son," but also ultimately to the tension between a merciless Old Testament God of judgment and a kindly New Testament God of love. The duality, once conceived in these terms and reified by oppositionalism, forms the structure of the Christian anti-Jewish imagination.

52. Boyarin, *The Jewish Gospels*, 39, 40.

53. Daniel 7:13–14.

54. Mark 2:9–12.

55. Jesus makes the "I am" claim even more blatantly in John: "Before Abraham was, I am" (John 8:58). We will see more of this later.

56. Mark 14:62–64.

57. Demonstrating the astounding turnabout in Christian thinking since the Second Vatican Council, Pope Francis carried the council's logic about Jews to its conclusion when, in 2013, he wrote that Christians "can never be sufficiently grateful" to Jews who "preserved their faith in God." That preserving, of course, was a matter of rejecting Christian claims. What Jews were condemned for in the past they are thanked for now. Pope Francis, "Letter to a Non-Believer," *La Repubblica*, September 4, 2013.

58. Mark 16:6.

59. Levenson, *Death and Resurrection*. Levenson shows how the sibling-rivalry motif, with the younger son usurping the elder's claim to the father's blessing, runs through the Hebrew Bible, from Cain and Abel to Isaac and Jacob. When the Church replaces Israel as the chosen people, it is acting out this Jewish pattern.

60. 1 Corinthians 15:14.

61. Kevin J. Madigan and Jon D. Levenson, *Resurrection: The Power of God for Christians and Jews* (New Haven, Conn.: Yale University Press, 2008), 219.

62. Words of the Apostles' Creed, which dates to perhaps the late second century.

63. John 2:19.

64. Madigan and Levenson, *Resurrection*, 171.

65. Daniel 12:2–3.

66. Ezekiel 37:11.

67. Isaiah 26:19.

68. 2 Kings 4:35. Madigan and Levenson, *Resurrection*, 131.

69. Madigan and Levenson, *Resurrection*, 176.

70. The so-called Jesus Seminar came to near consensus, in the 1990s, about a non-apocalyptic Jesus, with 97 percent of its fellows agreeing that "Jesus did not expect the world to end soon." David B. Gowler, *What Are They Saying About the Historical Jesus?* (New York: Paulist Press, 2007), 35. Authors who disagree and insist on Jesus as an End Time apocalyptic include N. T. Wright and E. P. Sanders. Paula Fredriksen defines the action Jesus performed in the Temple as apocalyptic: "The current Temple was soon to be destroyed (understood: not by Jesus, nor by invading armies, but by God), to cede place to the eschatological Temple (understood: not built by the hand of man) at the close of the age." *Jesus of Nazareth*, 210.

71. Jesus can seem to have been explicitly apocalyptic in, for example, a statement such as this: "I say to you, you will not have gone through all the towns of Israel before the Son of Man comes" (Matthew 10:23). But we cannot know whether those words were put into the mouth of Jesus by the writer.

72. N. T. Wright, *The New Testament and the People of God* (Minneapolis: Fortress, 1992), 102.

73. Mark 16:8.

74. This expanded version, Mark 9–20, is included in most Bibles now, but usually with brackets or notes explaining the questions about its origin.

75. Mark 1:9.

76. In the Gospel of John, the term "lifted up" refers simultaneously to the crucifixion and the Resurrection, the being hung up on the cross and the being exalted into new life. "As Moses lifted up the serpent in the wilderness, so must the Son of Man be lifted up, that whoever believes in him may have eternal life" (John 3:14–15).

77. 1 Thessalonians 4:16–18. Madigan and Levenson drew my attention to this aspect of early Christian expectation, reflected in Paul's first letter. *Resurrection*, 28.

78. Romans 13:11–12.

79. 1 Thessalonians 5:23.

80. Crossan says that, in contrast to John, Jesus preached an interior kingdom, not a restored Israel. "One enters that Kingdom by wisdom or goodness, by virtue, justice, or freedom. It is a style of life for now, rather than a hope of life for the future. This is therefore an ethical Kingdom, but it must be absolutely insisted that it could be just as eschatological as was the apocalyptic Kingdom. Its ethics could, for instance, challenge contemporary morality to its depths." *The Historical Jesus: The Life of a Mediterranean Jewish Peasant* (San Francisco: HarperSanFrancisco, 1991), 292.

81. Luke 17:20–21.

82. Matthew 11:5, 13:16–17; Luke 7:22, 10:23.

83. James D. G. Dunn, *Unity and Diversity in the New Testament* (Valley Forge, Pa.: Trinity Press International, 1993), 321. The technical name for this transformed attitude toward the End Time is "realized eschatology," an idea made popular by the twentieth-century scholar C. H. Dodd. Crossan distinguishes between "apocalyptic eschatology" and "sapiential eschatology," which shifts the transforming initiative from God's intervention to the acts of the faithful disciples. John Dominic Crossan, *The Essential Jesus: Original Sayings and Earliest Images* (San Francisco: HarperSanFrancisco, 1994), 8.

CHAPTER FOUR: **Gospel Truth**

1. Joyce Carol Oates, "The Calendar's New Clothes," *New York Times*, December 30, 1999.

2. John B. Cobb Jr. describes the succession of covenants. *Spiritual Bankruptcy: A Prophetic Call to Action* (Nashville, Tenn.: Abingdon Press, 2010), 21. The champion of historical consciousness was Friedrich Hegel, who transformed philosophy by locating it within history. Hegel understood the human person as an essentially historical being. The search for

meaning, as opposed to "truth," is a quest through time, with each person—and society—grasping its present significance only in relationship to past experience and future purpose. See Charles Taylor, *Hegel* (Cambridge, U.K.: Cambridge University Press, 1975).

3. See, for example, Bernard Lonergan, "The Transition from a Classicist World-View to Historical-Mindedness," in *A Second Collection: Papers by Bernard Lonergan, S.J.*, ed. William F. J. Ryan (Toronto: University of Toronto Press, 1996), 1–9.

4. Catholicism stopped thinking of itself as the "one true Church" (*Lumen Gentium*); embraced conscience as the defining note of salvation (*Dignitatis Humanae*); affirmed the validity of the Jewish Covenant and other religions (*Nostra Aetate*); and left Just War dominance behind to become a peace Church (*Pacem in Terris*). That these changes have been resisted by the Catholic hierarchy in subsequent years does not undo them for the vast population of Catholic people. See Norman Tanner, ed., *Vatican II: The Essential Texts*, introductions by Pope Benedict XVI and James Carroll (New York: Doubleday, 2012).

5. Quoted in John Finnis, *Religion and Public Reasons: Collected Essays* (New York: Oxford University Press, 2011), 151.

6. Ismar Schorsch, *From Text to Context: The Turn to History in Modern Judaism* (Waltham, Mass.: Brandeis University Press, 1994). Schorsch, the former chancellor of Jewish Theological Seminary, is a leading conservative thinker. Rethinking the nature of Judaism centers on the Holocaust but also involves nineteenth-century Zionism, and continues in an expressly Jewish reckoning with the establishment of the State of Israel in 1948.

7. Blaise Pascal, *Thoughts*, trans. W. F. Trotter (New York: P.F. Collier & Sons, 1910), 99.

8. Josephus, *Jewish Antiquities*, XVIII:63.

9. John Henry Newman coined the phrase "development of doctrine" in the nineteenth century, a theological adaptation of Darwin's contemporaneous idea of evolution. We are tracing here the *evolution* of faith in Jesus. In fact, since Jesus is mediated by the "development," our faith is more in the evolving medium than in him. Eventually, that medium will be known as "Church." See John Henry Newman, "An Essay on the Development of Christian Doctrine," 1909, *Newman Reader,* http://www.newmanreader.org/works/development.

10. What we know as the New Testament was not doctrinally defined until the Council of Carthage, in 397. The selection of the twenty-seven books was from among a larger number of texts. There might have been a dozen

or more "gospels." The criteria for selection was shaped by the controlling orthodoxy of the Council of Nicea (326), which was related to the imposition of imperial uniformity on the Church, after Constantine.

11. Jack Miles, *Christ: A Crisis in the Life of God* (New York: Knopf, 2001), 113.

12. There is almost no money to be made from the writing of poetry. The *New Yorker*, in 2011, typically paid about $400 for a poem. There are about 750 teaching positions for poets in American colleges. The bestselling American poet of 2011, Poet Laureate Billy Collins, sold about eighteen thousand copies of his book *Horoscopes for the Dead*, earning about $40,000. Rachel Friedman, "Livelihoods of the Poets," *New York*, December 11, 2011, http://nymag.com/news/intelligencer/topic/poetry -2011-12/?mid=nymag_press. There is no contemporary equivalent of Homer, Virgil, Plutarch, Dante, or Milton—the Enlightenment genius who marked the last of his breed.

13. I make this assertion fully aware that across the centuries, in various epochs, bloody state power enforced quite literal readings of such images, and many Church authorities to this day insist, with religious sanctions, on such literal readings.

14. N. T. Wright, *The New Testament and the People of God* (Minneapolis: Fortress, 1992), 333.

15. Wright, *The New Testament*, 334.

16. John 20:26–31.

17. "Well, toward morning the conversation turned on the Eucharist, which I, being the Catholic, was obviously supposed to defend. [Mary McCarthy] said when she was a child and received the Host, she thought of it as the Holy Ghost, He being the 'most portable' person of the Trinity; now she thought of it as a symbol and implied that it was a pretty good one. I then said, in a very shaky voice, 'Well, if it's a symbol, to hell with it.' That was all the defense I was capable of but I realize now that this is all I will ever be able to say about it, outside of a story, except that it is the center of existence for me; all the rest of life is expendable." Flannery O'Connor, *The Habit of Being* (New York: Farrar, Straus and Giroux, 1979), 125.

18. Roger Haight, *The Future of Christology* (New York: Continuum, 2005), 45. This book was, in part, Haight's defense of his earlier book *Jesus: Symbol of God* (Maryknoll, N.Y.: Orbis, 1999), which had drawn fire from Catholic authorities in significant part because of the authorities' shallow and dismissive notion of the meaning of symbol.

19. John Dominic Crossan, *A Long Way from Tipperary* (San Francisco: HarperSanFrancisco, 2000), 167.

20. All four Gospels tell of Jesus' feeding five thousand people: Matthew 14:13–21; Mark 6:31–44; Luke 9:10–17; John 6:5–15. Mark and Matthew *additionally* tell of Jesus' feeding four thousand people, in what wants to be taken as an independent event but surely wasn't: Mark 8:1–9; Matthew 15:32–39.

21. "A miracle is a violation of the laws of nature; and as a firm and unalterable experience has established these laws, the proof against a miracle, from the very nature of the fact, is as entire as any argument from experience can possibly be imagined. . . . It is no miracle that a man, seemingly in good health, should die on a sudden: because such a kind of death, though more unusual than any other, has yet been frequently observed to happen. But it is a miracle, that a dead man should come to life; because that has never been observed in any age or country." David Hume, *An Enquiry Concerning Human Understanding*, ed. L. A. Selby-Bigge (Oxford, U.K.: Clarendon, 1902), 114.

22. The "placebo effect" is one example, in which interventions with no actual drug ingredients can nevertheless bring about actual physiological effect. See, for example, Cara Feinberg, "The Placebo Phenomenon," *Harvard Magazine*, January–February 2013, http://harvardmagazine.com/2013/01/the-placebo-phenomenon.

23. See, for example, John Dominic Crossan, *God and Empire: Jesus Against Rome, Then and Now* (New York: HarperOne, 2007), 119. Crossan cites medical anthropologists to distinguish between "illness" and "disease." Disease is purely physical; illness includes the "personal, social, and cultural reactions to disease." Jesus' "miracles" affected change in the latter, not the former.

24. Jesus' acts "as healer of the physically ill, exorciser of the possessed, and dispenser of forgiveness to sinners, must be seen in the context to which they belong, namely charismatic Judaism." Geza Vermes, *Jesus the Jew: A Historian's Reading of the Gospel* (Philadelphia: Fortress, 1981), 58.

25. Matthew 11:5. I have this insight about suffering resistance from Haight, *Jesus: Symbol of God*, 8.

26. Regarding disputed readings of the Passion, two divergent Catholic scholars make the point. Raymond Brown sees the Gospels accounts, centered on the Sanhedrin and Pilate trials of Jesus, as essentially historical. *The Death of the Messiah: From Gethsemane to the Grave* (New York: Doubleday, 1994). But another scholar, Gerald Sloyan, writes, "It is impossible to conclude from the Gospels what sequence of events brought Jesus to the cross." *The Crucifixion of Jesus: History, Myth, Faith*

(Minneapolis: Fortress, 1995), 40. John Dominic Crossan goes so far as to say that the Passion story is almost wholly fictional. *Jesus: A Revolutionary Biography* (San Francisco: HarperSanFrancisco, 1994), 123–58.

27. 1 Corinthians 15:14.

28. Daniel Boyarin, *The Jewish Gospels: The Story of the Jewish Christ* (New York: New Press, 2012), 159–60.

29. "For even the Son of Man did not come to be served, but to give his life as a ransom for many" (Mark 10:45). Mark here is picking up a note of Paul's: "And you are not your own, for you are bought with a price. Therefore glorify God in your body and in your spirit, which are God's" (1 Corinthians 6:19–20). But in both cases, the one receiving payment is Satan, to whom, after the Fall, humans were in bondage.

30. An example of this perverted theology is the "substitutionary atonement" idea found in Saint Anselm's *Cur Deus Homo*, referred to earlier. Roger Haight helped me see how history rescues theology here. *Jesus: Symbol of God*, 85. For me, of course—having been that atonement-tormented child at his First Confession—the rescue is personal.

31. Ched Myers's reading of Mark informs me here. *Binding the Strong Man: A Political Reading of Mark's Story of Jesus* (Maryknoll, N.Y.: Orbis, 1991), 104.

32. Roger Haight proposes his version of these three purposes as criteria for all of Christology: "fidelity to scripture and the landmark interpretations of Jesus Christ . . . intelligibility to a present-day community . . . to empower a Christian life in the contemporary world." I have adapted these three points to Mark. Haight, *Future of Christology*, 43.

33. Wesley J. Wildman, *Fidelity with Plausibility: Modest Christologies in the Twentieth Century* (Albany, N.Y.: SUNY Press, 1998), 199.

34. I heard the late scholar Krister Stendahl offer a version of this camera analogy.

35. Elisabeth Schüssler Fiorenza, *Jesus and the Politics of Interpretation* (New York: Continuum, 2000), 6.

36. Rosemary Radford Ruether, "Christology and Jewish-Christian Relations," in *Jews and Christians After the Holocaust*, ed. Abraham J. Peck (Philadelphia: Fortress, 1982), 25.

37. Matthew 2:13–22.

38. See Peter Schäfer, *The Jewish Jesus: How Judaism and Christianity Shaped Each Other* (Princeton, N.J.: Princeton University Press, 2012).

39. Paula Fredriksen sees the fact that Jesus alone—and none of his disciples—was executed by the Romans as evidence that Jesus was not

taken as a revolutionary, even by Rome. Otherwise, members of his movement, too, would have been hunted down and killed. Rather, Fredriksen argues, Jesus was killed for being a troublemaker, one in whom the crowds, during the dangerous time of Passover, saw a focus of their discontent. It was an incipient, not actual, revolution that Rome feared. Jesus was a spark to be squelched, not a raging fire. Paula Fredriksen, *Jesus of Nazareth: King of the Jews* (New York: Knopf, 1999), 214–34.

40. "John of Patmos" is not to be taken as the author of the Gospel of John, which is usually dated to around 100. Second Peter, dated by some scholars to as late as 150, is also almost certainly later than the book of Revelation.

41. The journalistic character of Revelation is also hinted at when the seventh angel blows his trumpet "and something like a great mountain, burning with fire, was thrown into the sea; and a third of the sea became blood, a third of the living creatures in the sea died, and a third of the ships were destroyed." This refers to the eruption of Mount Vesuvius. Elaine Pagels, *Revelations: Visions, Prophecy, and Politics in the Book of Revelation* (New York: Viking, 2012), 20.

42. Nero is identified as the enemy whose "number is six hundred sixty-six." This seems an obscure reference, but it was not. Hebrew and Greek designate letters by numbers, and 666 spells out "Caesar Nero." For a discussion of contemporary understandings of "666," see Adela Yarbro Collins, *Crisis and Catharsis: The Power of the Apocalypse* (Philadelphia: Westminster Press, 1984), 13.

43. Pagels, *Revelations*, 32.

44. Revelation 5:12, 13:8.

45. Revelation 3:9.

46. Pagels, *Revelations*, 50.

47. Crossan, *God and Empire*, 224.

48. For example, the narrative was composed in part of details, like the "casting of lots" at the foot of the cross, that were drawn from Scriptures, such as Psalm 22:18, with its "They divided my garments among them and cast lots for my clothing." The origin of the "lots" was not a historical event, but an appropriation from the sacred text. When Gentiles later read of the lots, however, they assumed a historical fulfillment of a "prophecy" in the Old Testament, and they took it as self-evident proof of Jesus' status as the longed-for Jewish messiah. See James Carroll, *Constantine's Sword: The Church and the Jews, a History* (Boston: Houghton Mifflin, 2001), 122–34.

49. I owe this insight about the difference between "faith" and "faithfulness" to John Cobb, *Spiritual Bankruptcy*, 29.

50. The Nicene Creed, first promulgated, as we saw, in 325. This elevation of Jesus to full equality with God, understood as Yahweh, the Ancient One, or, in Greek terms, the Prime Mover, made any further affirmation of Jesus by Jews *as Jews* impossible.

51. The parting of the ways, while not "willed by God," enabled both traditions to develop creatively. "Had the church remained a Jewish sect, it would not have achieved its universal mission. Had Judaism given up its particularistic practices, it would have vanished from history. That the two movements eventually separated made possible the preservation of each." Amy-Jill Levine, *The Misunderstood Jew: The Church and the Scandal of the Jewish Jesus* (San Francisco: HarperOne, 2006), 84.

52. With this caveat: Once, after Constantine, the Roman emperor became the enforcer of Christian orthodoxy, and the state, especially under Theodosius, began to execute heretics, Christians continued to die at the hands of Rome by the tens of thousands. That war ended with the elimination of condemned sects like Arians, Docetists, and Nestorians.

CHAPTER FIVE: **Jesus and John**

1. See, for example, Robert W. Funk, *Honest to Jesus: Jesus for a New Millennium* (San Francisco: HarperSanFrancisco, 1996), 298. Funk is "fundamentally dissatisfied with versions of the faith that trace their origins only so far as the first believers: true faith, fundamental faith, must be related in some way directly to Jesus of Nazareth." But the reason faith abstracted from the relationships Jesus had is impossible is that the faith was alive in those relationships. For a criticism of Funk, see Jack Miles, *Christ: A Crisis in the Life of God* (New York: Knopf, 2001), 270.

2. In his 1952 book, *The Eclipse of God*, Buber wrote, "Something is taking place in the depths that as yet needs no name. Tomorrow it may happen that it will be beckoned to from the heights . . . The eclipse of the light of God is no extinction; even tomorrow that which has stepped in between [man and the eternal Thou] may give way." *The Eclipse of God: Studies in the Relation Between Philosophy and Religion* (New York: Harper & Row, 1952), 129–30.

3. Richard L. Rubenstein, "Martin Buber and the Holocaust: Some Reconsiderations," *New English Review*, November 2012, http://www

.newenglishreview.org/Richard_L._Rubenstein/Martin_Buber_and_ the_Holocaust%3A_Some_Reconsiderations.

4. The Camus short story "The Artist at Work," first published in 1957, ends with the artist having painted on the canvas a single word, which cannot be made out clearly: it is either "solidary" or "solitary." The 2007 Vintage edition offers the translation as "interdependent" or "independent." Albert Camus, *Exile and the Kingdom*, trans. Maureen Freely (New York: Vintage, 2007), 80.

5. Rubenstein, "Martin Buber," 19.

6. Richard L. Rubenstein, for example, faults Buber for neglecting both the Law in Judaism and Jesus Christ in Christianity as mediations enabling an encounter with God. Rubenstein, "Martin Buber," 7. Rubenstein seems to miss the larger point of Buber's thought: that the eternal Thou is encountered only through the mediation of the earthly Thou, which presumes human solidarity for Jews, Christians, and all others.

7. This from Paul, for example: "And we all, with unveiled face, beholding the glory of the Lord, are being changed into his likeness from one degree of glory to another; for this comes from the Lord who is the Spirit" (2 Corinthians 3:18).

8. Luke 2:52: "And Jesus increased in wisdom and in stature, and in favor with God and man"—an elegantly simple description of Jesus' life as he grew up in the household of Joseph and Mary.

9. Mark 1:11.

10. "And the Lord has laid on him the iniquity of us all. He was oppressed, and he was afflicted, yet he opened not his mouth; like a lamb that is led to the slaughter" (Isaiah 53:7–8).

11. Mark 1:8.

12. Mark 1:12, 14.

13. Josephus, *Jewish Antiquities*, XVIII:2–9. This account squares with the story of John's execution in the Gospel of Mark, although its elaboration on the broader political intrigue shows that Josephus is not dependent on Mark, and draws from other sources. Unlike a passage in which Josephus describes Jesus' death and Resurrection (the so-called Testimonium Flavianum, XVIII:3.3.), this one is regarded by scholars as wholly authentic.

14. Ancient manuscripts and papyrus scrolls were found in clay jars in caves and excavations from Egypt to Israel to Iraq to Turkey: "The Teaching" (in Greek, *Didache*) was the rule of a first-century Christian community, discovered in 1873 in a monastery in Istanbul; independent second- and

third-century texts like the *Gospel of Peter*, the *Gospel of Mary*, and the *Gospel of Thomas* were discovered in Egypt in the late 1800s; fourth-century Gnostic texts, the Nag Hammadi codices, were discovered in Egypt in 1945; and the Dead Sea Scrolls, elaborate records of a Jewish sect dating to the time of Jesus, were discovered at Qumran in 1947. John Dominic Crossan and Jonathan Reed, *Excavating Jesus: Beneath the Stones, Behind the Texts* (San Francisco: HarperSanFrancisco, 2001), 13.

15. The political and economic context within which Jesus would have come of age, summarized here, is elaborated in one of my main sources, Richard A. Horsley and Neil Asher Silberman, *The Message and the Kingdom: How Jesus and Paul Ignited a Revolution and Transformed the Ancient World* (Minneapolis: Fortress, 2002).

16. Examples of scholars who accept the image of Jesus as a young man in his twenties in John's movement are Gerd Theissen and Annette Merz, *The Historical Jesus: A Comprehensive Guide*, trans. John Bowden (Minneapolis: Fortress, 1998).

17. Virgil, *Aeneid*, trans. David Ferry (unpublished), VI, II, 761.

18. See David Frum and Richard Perle, *An End to Evil* (New York: Random House, 2003), and Francis Fukuyama, *The End of History and the Last Man* (New York: Free Press, 1992).

19. Virgil, *Aeneid*, VI, II, 719–61.

20. Genesis 1:1. See Richard Elliott Friedman, *The Hidden Book in the Bible* (San Francisco: HarperSanFrancisco, 1998). An influential study of cyclical versus linear thinking is Mircea Eliade, *The Myth of the Eternal Return: Cosmos and History*, 2nd ed., trans. William R. Trask (Princeton, N.J.: Princeton University Press, 2005; first published 1971).

21. Church fathers Jerome and Eusebius agreed that the date for Adam's creation was 5,200 years before the birth of Jesus. That date defines the Earth's chronology for many creationists to this day.

22. Walter E. Wegner, "The Book of Daniel and the Dead Sea Scrolls," lecture, University of Wisconsin, http://www.wlsessays.net/files/Wegner Daniel.pdf.

23. Daniel 8:17–26.

24. E. P. Sanders sees no break. "Jesus thought that God would soon bring about a decisive change in the world. This context is historically crucial, since it is the framework of Jesus' overall mission: it includes the man who baptized him and also his own followers." *The Historical Figure of Jesus* (London: Penguin, 1993), 8.

25. "What is time? Who can explain this easily and briefly? Who can comprehend this even in thought so as to articulate the answer in words?" Saint Augustine, *Confessions*, trans. Henry Chadwick (Oxford, U.K.: Oxford University Press, 1991), 11.17.

26. "Earlier he had received John's baptism and accepted his message of God as the imminent apocalyptic judge. But the Jordan was not just water, and to be baptized in it was to recapitulate the ancient and archetypal passage from imperial bondage to national freedom. Herod Antipas moved swiftly to execute John, there was no apocalyptic consummation, and Jesus, finding his own voice, began to speak of God not as imminent apocalypse but as present healing." John Dominic Crossan, *The Historical Jesus: The Life of a Mediterranean Jewish Peasant* (San Francisco: HarperSanFrancisco, 1991), xii.

27. Roger Haight, *Jesus: Symbol of God* (Maryknoll, N.Y.: Orbis, 1999), 70.

28. John P. Meier, *A Marginal Jew: Rethinking the Historical Jesus*, vol. II (New York: Doubleday, 1991), 154.

29. Matthew 11:11: "Truly, I say to you, among those born of women there has arisen no one greater than John the Baptist. Yet the one who is least in the kingdom of heaven is greater than he."

30. This, for example, from John 3:22–30: "After this Jesus and his disciples went into the land of Judea; there he remained with them and baptized. John also was baptizing at Ae'non near Salim, because there was much water there; and people came and were baptized. For John had not yet been put in prison. Now a discussion arose between John's disciples and a Jew over purifying. And they came to John, and said to him, 'Rabbi, he who was with you beyond the Jordan, to whom you bore witness, here he is, baptizing, and all are going to him.' John answered, 'No one can receive anything except what is given him from heaven. You yourselves bear me witness, that I said, I am not the Christ, but I have been sent before him. He who has the bride is the bridegroom; the friend of the bridegroom, who stands and hears him, rejoices greatly at the bridegroom's voice; therefore this joy of mine is now full. He must increase, but I must decrease.'" By putting these words into John the Baptist's mouth, the Gospel writer can be assumed to be attempting to quell an ongoing competition between Jesus people and John's movement.

31. Luke 7:20–22.

32. Isaiah 61:1.

33. Luke 7:26.

34. Luke 4:17–21.

35. Horsley and Silberman, *The Message and the Kingdom*, 55. I owe my understanding of the importance of the contrasting Isaiah passages in Luke to these authors.

36. Josephus, *Jewish Antiquities*, XVIII:5, 2.

37. Or almost immediately. According to Matthew's account, John's "disciples came and took the body and buried it; and they went and told Jesus. Now when Jesus heard this, he withdrew from there in a boat to a lonely place apart" (Matthew 14:12–13).

38. Horsley and Silberman, *The Message and the Kingdom*, 61.

39. Luke 13:32–33.

40. Matthew 23:37; Luke 13:34.

41. Acts 7:52.

42. See, for example, Dennis R. MacDonald, *The Homeric Epics and the Gospel of Mark* (New Haven, Conn.: Yale University Press, 2000).

43. In Hosea, Israel itself is referred to as "Son of the living God" (Hosea 1:10). In Deuteronomy, Israel is called "sons of the Lord Your God" (Deuteronomy 14:1–2). This sonship defines the chosenness of Israel. See Jon D. Levenson, "The People Israel as the Son of God," in *Death and Resurrection of the Beloved Son* (New Haven, Conn.: Yale University Press, 1995), 36–42.

CHAPTER SIX: Thou Art Peter

1. The Latin for "Be not afraid." As reported by his son. Henry McDonald, "Seamus Heaney's Last Words Were 'Noli Timere,' Son Tells Funeral," *Guardian*, September 2, 2013, http://www.theguardian.com/books/2013/sep/02/seamus-heaney-last-words-funeral.

2. Carl Bernstein and Marco Politi, *His Holiness: John Paul II and the Hidden History of Our Time* (New York: Doubleday, 1996), 182.

3. Bernstein and Politi, *His Holiness*, 232.

4. "Had the Pope chosen to turn his soft power into the hard variety, the regime might have been drowned in blood. Instead, the Pope simply led the Polish people to desert their rulers by affirming solidarity with one another. The Communists managed to hold on as despots a decade longer. But as political leaders, they were finished. Visiting his native Poland in 1979, Pope John Paul II struck what turned out to be a mortal blow to its Communist regime, to the Soviet Empire, [and] ultimately to Communism." Angelo M. Codevilla, "Political Warfare: A Set of Means for

Achieving Political Ends," in *Strategic Influence: Public Diplomacy, Counterpropaganda and Political Warfare*, ed. J. Michael Waller (Washington, D.C.: Institute of World Politics Press, 2008).

5. John 6:20; Matthew 17:7; Matthew 28:10; Matthew 10:31.

6. Matthew 26:39.

7. Genesis 15:1; Exodus 14:13; Psalm 91:5; Isaiah 35:4; Jeremiah 42:11. See also Felix Just, "Have No Fear! Do Not Be Afraid!" Catholic Resources for Bible, Liturgy, Art, and Theology, http://catholic-resources.org/Bible/HaveNoFear.htm. A Google search of "Be not afraid—Bible" generates about twenty million results. The Bible can be understood, therefore, as essentially addressed to human fear.

8. On May 13, 1981, Mehmet Ali Agca, an Islamic radical, shot John Paul II at close range in St. Peter's Square. Agca claimed that he was acting for the Bulgarian state intelligence service, which was never proved. The Vatican expressed skepticism that the Soviet KGB was behind the assassination attempt, but in 2005, documents found in East German Stasi files indicated that the KGB was indeed implicated. "1981 Attack on Pope Planned by Soviets," *Agence France-Presse*, March 30, 2005.

9. Mark 4:37–41.

10. Jens Schroter, "Gospel of Mark," in *The Blackwell Companion to the New Testament*, ed. David E. Aune (London: Blackwell, 2010), 177–78.

11. John 21:4–17.

12. Mark 14:30. Here is the account of the betrayals: "And as Peter was below in the courtyard, one of the maids of the high priest came; and seeing Peter warming himself, she looked at him, and said, 'You also were with the Nazarene, Jesus.' But he denied it, saying, 'I neither know nor understand what you mean.' And he went out into the gateway. And the maid saw him, and began again to say to the bystanders, 'This man is one of them.' But again he denied it. And after a little while again the bystanders said to Peter, 'Certainly you are one of them; for you are a Galilean.' But he began to invoke a curse on himself and to swear, 'I do not know this man of whom you speak.' And immediately the cock crowed a second time. And Peter remembered how Jesus had said to him, 'Before the cock crows twice, you will deny me three times.' And he broke down and wept" (Mark 14:66–72).

13. Luke 22:61–62.

14. John 8:31.

15. "Then Jesus said to them, 'Do not be afraid. Go and tell my brethren to go to Galilee, and there they will see me'" (Matthew 28:10).

16. Acts 1:6–13.

17. Acts 1:15–21.

18. Acts 2:22–28.

19. In an astounding reversal of tradition, the image of Peter lifted up at the start of the 2013 papal conclave was not the triumphalist "Thou Art Peter, and upon this rock I will build my church" from Matthew, but the penitential Peter from John, whom Jesus interrogates three times with "Do you love me?" In hindsight, this seemed a prediction of the election of Pope Francis, who has more in common with the forgiven Peter than with the power broker. See my "Who Am I to Judge? A Radical Pope's First Year," *New Yorker*, December 15, 2013.

20. Acts 4:13, 2:41–42.

21. This is why, for example, Jack Miles disdains the "historical Jesus" quest to "get behind" Peter and all the others to an unmediated Jesus. The mediation is the point. "A faith that confesses its origins in Peter and Paul as well as in Jesus is superior to one that would admit no source but Jesus." *Christ: A Crisis in the Life of God* (New York: Knopf, 2001), 270.

CHAPTER SEVEN: The Real Paul

1. John F. Deane, "Triduum," from *A Little Book of Hours* (Manchester, U.K.: Carcanet, 2008), 95.

2. The famous Dead Sea Scrolls, the Qumran manuscripts, already noted as having first been discovered in caves above the Jordan Rift Valley by a goatherd in 1947, are dated by scholars to a period between 200 B.C.E. and 68 C.E. That last date tells the story, for, unlike the Jesus people and the Rabbis, the Qumran Zealots, mainly Essenes, were wiped out by the Romans in the assaults that began just then. No more scroll making.

3. A. J. Heschel, *The Sabbath: Its Meaning for Modern Man* (New York: Noonday, 1997), 1.

4. The death of Jesus is said, as we saw, to occur simultaneously with the tearing of the Temple veil "from top to bottom" (Mark 15:37–38). By the time the Gospel of John is written, three decades after Mark, the identification of Jesus with the Temple was explicit: "But he spoke of the Temple of his body" (John 2:21).

5. For example, "Now when the Pharisees gathered together to him, with some of the scribes, who had come from Jerusalem, they saw that some of his disciples ate with hands defiled, that is, unwashed. (For the Pharisees, and all the Jews, do not eat unless they wash their hands, observing

the tradition of the elders; and when they come from the market place, they do not eat unless they purify themselves; and there are many other traditions which they observe, the washing of cups and pots and vessels of bronze.) And the Pharisees and the scribes asked him, 'Why do your disciples not live according to the tradition of the elders, but eat with hands defiled?' And he said to them, 'Well did Isaiah prophesy of you hypocrites, as it is written, "This people honors me with their lips, but their heart is far from me; in vain do they worship me, teaching as doctrines the precepts of men"'" (Mark 7:1–7).

6. For example, "Again the high priest asked him, 'Are you the Christ, the Son of the Blessed?' And Jesus said, 'I am; and you will see the Son of man seated at the right hand of Power, and coming with the clouds of heaven.' And the high priest tore his garments, and said, 'Why do we still need witnesses? You have heard his blasphemy. What is your decision?' And they all condemned him as deserving death" (Mark 14:61–64). This portrait of high-priest villainy, composed in about 70, can be compared to the antipriest contempt of the Zealots, who, in 68, according to Josephus, violently targeted the priestly caste and Temple officers as craven collaborators, a takeover of the Temple that sparked Vespasian's assault. John Dominic Crossan, *Who Killed Jesus? Exposing the Roots of Anti-Semitism in the Gospel Story of the Death of Jesus* (New York: HarperOne, 1996), 52.

7. "Inasmuch as many have undertaken to compile a narrative of the things which have been accomplished among us, just as they were delivered to us by those who from the beginning were eyewitnesses and ministers of the word, it seemed good to me also, having followed all things closely for some time past, to write an orderly account for you, most excellent Theophilus" (Luke 1:1–3).

8. Luke 4:2–30.

9. Colossians 4:14; 2 Timothy 4:11. The actual authorship of these two "Pauline" letters is uncertain. Second Timothy might have been written by a follower of Paul's shortly after his death. It includes this forecast of his martyrdom: "For I am already on the point of being sacrificed; the time of my departure has come. I have fought the good fight, I have finished the race, I have kept the faith. Henceforth there is laid up for me a crown of righteousness which the Lord, the righteous judge, will award me on that day: and not only to me, but also to all who have loved his appearing" (2 Timothy 4:6–8).

10. The description comes from the apocryphal *Acts of Paul*, a second-century text that is not to be taken as historically accurate.

11. Daniel Boyarin, *The Jewish Gospels: The Story of the Jewish Christ* (New York: New Press, 2012), 6–7.

12. 1 Thessalonians 4:16–18.

13. In Romans 11:25–32, Paul emphasizes that God does not revoke his promises, underscoring the permanence of the covenant with Israel. In Romans 15:4–21, Paul celebrates, in terms drawn from Isaiah, the opening of that same covenant: "Rejoice, O Gentiles, with his people."

14. The rape of a slave woman was not a crime unless she was somehow injured, and then the crime was damage to property.

15. Thirty-nine lashes, three times beaten with rods, stoned at least once, shipwrecked three times. Paul acknowledged: "weaknesses, insults, hardships, persecutions, and calamities" (2 Corinthians 12:10).

16. Philippians 2:5–8. The RSV renders "cling to" as "to be grasped." Note that Paul's reference to "servant" here is a signal of his dependence for this interpretative coup on the Suffering Servant motif of Isaiah (Isaiah 52:13–53:12).

17. 1 Corinthians 15:55.

18. Galatians 4:8, 3:28–29. This inclusive language of Paul probably derives from a baptismal formula in use among Jewish Christians in the Hellenized world. Rosemary Radford Ruether, "St. Paul, Friend or Enemy of Women?" Beliefnet, n.d., http://www.beliefnet.com/Faiths/Christianity/2004/03/St-Paul-Friend-Or-Enemy-Of-Women.aspx. See Amy-Jill Levine, *The Misunderstood Jew: The Church and the Scandal of the Jewish Jesus* (San Francisco: HarperOne, 2006), 114.

19. "By the year 100, more than 40 Christian communities existed in cities around the Mediterranean, including two in North Africa, at Alexandria and Cyrene, and several in Italy." Susan Tyler Hitchcock, *Geography of Religion: Where God Lives, Where Pilgrims Walk* (Washington, D.C.: National Geographic Press, 2004), 281. Thomas the Apostle is regarded as having brought the message of Jesus to Kerala in about 52.

20. Seven of the thirteen are assumed by scholars to have certainly been written by Paul. Scholars are divided on the authorship of the others, although a consensus holds that Colossians, Ephesians, the two letters of Timothy, and Titus were not written by Paul, and came well after his death. The first of Paul's letters, 1 Thessalonians, dates to about 51. The latest actually written by Paul, Romans, dates to about 60—although it comes first in the New Testament arrangement. When we take up the question of women below, we will see the relevance of distinguishing

between writings *attributed* to Paul and those actually written by him. Hebrews was long attributed to Paul but no longer is so, and it is rarely counted as a Pauline letter.

21. For example, Paul opens his address at the synagogue in Antioch by saying, "Brethren, sons of the family of Abraham, and those among you who fear God, to us has been sent the message of this salvation" (Acts 13:26).

22. Here is Tacitus's report, from the *Annals*, written in about 116 c.e.: "Consequently, to get rid of the report, Nero fastened the guilt and inflicted the most exquisite tortures on a class hated for their abominations, called Christians by the populace. Christus, from whom the name had its origin, suffered the extreme penalty during the reign of Tiberius at the hands of one of our procurators, Pontius Pilatus, and a most mischievous superstition, thus checked for the moment, again broke out not only in Judæa, the first source of the evil, but even in Rome, where all things hideous and shameful from every part of the world find their centre and become popular. Accordingly, an arrest was first made of all who pleaded guilty; then, upon their information, an immense multitude was convicted, not so much of the crime of firing the city, as of hatred against mankind." *Annals*, XV:44.

23. Mark D. Nanos, *The Mystery of Romans: The Jewish Context of Paul's Letter* (Minneapolis: Fortress, 1996), 50.

24. "The roster of ancient writers who expressed anti-Jewish feeling reads like a roster for a second-semester course in classics: Cicero, Tacitus, Martial, Horace, Juvenal, Persius, Cassius Dio, Marcus Aurelius, Apuleius, Ovid, Petronius, Pliny the Elder, Plutarch, Quintilian, Seneca, Suetonius." John C. Meagher, "As the Twig Was Bent: Antisemitism in Greco-Roman and Earliest Christian Time," in *Anti-Semitism and the Foundations of Christianity*, ed. Alan T. Davies (New York: Paulist Press, 2004), 6.

25. In Corinth, Paul "found a Jew named Aquila, a native of Pontus, lately come from Italy with his wife Priscilla, because Claudius had commanded all the Jews to leave Rome" (Acts 18:2).

26. Bruce Johnston, "Roman Colosseum 'Built with Gold Loot from Sack of Jerusalem Temple,'" Solomon's Temple, 2004, http://www.solomonstemple .com/2004/01/roman-colosseum-built-with-loot. The menorah on the Arch of Titus served, in 1948, as the template for the menorah on the flag of the newly established State of Israel.

27. At the climax of the Punic Wars, in 146 b.c.e., with Hannibal finally defeated by Scipio, Carthage was burned to the ground and left in rubble.

Legend has it that the Romans ruined the place forever by grinding salt into the dirt.

28. At the time of the Reformation, Pope Paul IV began the tradition, at the Arch of Titus, of requiring Rome's Jews to make an annual oath of submission. In 1821, the Arch of Titus was restored, and a panel containing this inscription was mounted on one of its pediments: "This monument, remarkable in terms of both religion and art, had weakened from age: Pius the Seventh, Supreme Pontiff . . . ordered it reinforced and preserved." Thus the pope rescued the monument that Jews despised. Jews had always refused to walk under it, but in 1948, celebrating the establishment of the State of Israel, Rome's Jews went to the Arch of Titus and walked through it—backward.

29. "This Jesus, delivered up according to the definite plan and foreknowledge of God, you crucified and killed by the hands of lawless men. . . . Jesus, whom you delivered up and denied in the presence of Pilate, when he had decided to release him" (Acts 2:22–23, 3:13–14).

30. "Go and tell that fox . . ." (Luke 13:32).

31. Crossan, *Who Killed Jesus?*, 148. Paula Fredriksen says that Tacitus, Josephus, and Philo all emphasize Pilate's character as "one of the worst" of Roman governors. *Jesus of Nazareth: King of the Jews* (New York: Knopf, 1999), 86.

32. Luke 23:13–22.

33. Matthew 27:24–25. This idea of Pilate as friendly to Jesus, and forced by "the Jews" into ordering the crucifixion, so grips the Christian imagination that the ecumenically minded Pope Francis could offhandedly reiterate it in 2013 to a mass audience in Brazil when he said, "Sometimes, we can be like Pilate, who did not have the courage to go against the tide to save Jesus' life." The "tide" referred to here, of course, is "the Jews." Lisa Wangsness, "Pope Francis Proves to Be a Pontiff of Surprises," *Boston Globe*, July 27, 2013, http://www.bostonglobe.com/metro/2013/07/26/pope-francis -proves-pontiff-surprises/BSfrY2tEAGZIXcyI2CHXsN/story.html.

34. Acts 28:17.

35. See, for example, Acts 21:27–31: "The Jews from Asia . . . seized Paul and dragged him out of the temple . . . trying to kill him." Paul was rescued from "the Jews" by Roman authorities.

36. Acts 22:24–29. See Helmut Koester, *Introduction to the New Testament*, vol. 2: *History and Literature of Early Christianity* (Philadelphia: Fortress, 1982), 323.

37. Acts 28:25–31.

38. Romans 11:1–29. While Paul's concerns in Romans "involve Jews, they are not directed toward Jews, or Jewish exclusivism ... [but toward] Christian-gentile exclusivism. In Rome, gentiles are being tempted to consider Jews excluded from God's purpose (Rom. 11): Israel has rejected the gospel; God has rejected Israel. . . . Paradoxically, these gentiles are actually guilty of the same arrogant ethnocentric exclusivism that was ascribed to that part of Israel in Rome considered stumbling: judging when they ought to be serving; boasting when they ought to be grateful." Nanos, *Mystery of Romans*, 10.

39. Martin Luther, quoted by Alice E. Eckardt, "The Reformation and the Jews," in Eugene Fisher, ed., *Interwoven Destinies: Jews and Christians Through the Ages* (New York: Paulist Press, 1993), 112. In his *Table Talk*, Luther denounced Jews and papists as "ungodly wretches ... two stockings made of one piece of cloth."

40. Nanos, *Mystery of Romans*, 31.

41. "Then Paul took the men, and the next day he purified himself with them and went into the Temple, to give notice when the days of purification would be fulfilled and the offering presented for every one of them" (Acts 21:26). In his letters, Paul shows followers of Jesus paying the Temple tithes, even Gentiles, and even from far away: 1 Corinthians 16:1–3; 2 Corinthians 1:1–9:15; Rom 15:25. See Paula Fredriksen, *Jesus of Nazareth: King of the Jews* (New York: Knopf, 1999), 36–38.

42. Nanos, *Mystery of Romans*, 338. Romans 3:29.

43. This, for example, from Isaiah: "It shall come to pass in the latter days that the mountain of the house of the LORD shall be established as the highest of the mountains, and shall be raised above the hills; and all the nations shall flow to it, and many peoples shall come, and say, 'Come, let us go up to the mountain of the LORD, to the house of the God of Jacob; that he may teach us his ways, and that we may walk in his paths.' For out of Zion shall go forth the law, and the word of the LORD from Jerusalem. He shall judge between the nations, and shall decide for many peoples; and they shall beat their swords into plowshares, and their spears into pruning hooks; nation shall not lift up sword against nation, neither shall they learn war any more" (Isaiah 2:2–4).

44. "The Greek-speaking Jews of the second temple period and the Hebrew- (and Aramaic-) speaking Jews after 70 C.E. debated the meaning of circumcision and the ritual's exact place in the conversion process." Shaye

J. D. Cohen, "Crossing the Boundary and Becoming a Jew," *Harvard Theological Review* 82, no. 1 (January 1989): 27.

45. Koester, *Introduction to the New Testament*, vol. 2, 323. John Gager, "The Parting of the Ways: A View from the Perspective of Early Christianity: 'A Christian Perspective,'" in Fisher, *Interwoven Destinies*, 65.

46. Jon D. Levenson, *Death and Resurrection of the Beloved Son* (New Haven, Conn.: Yale University Press, 1995), 230. Levenson's assertion would seem to be contradicted by 1 Thessalonians 2:14–15: "For you, brethren, became imitators of the churches of God in Christ Jesus which are in Judea; for you suffered the same things from your own countrymen as they did from the Jews, who killed both the Lord Jesus and the prophets." But these verses are taken by most scholars to be a post-Pauline interpolation, added later, because in the early 50s, when Paul wrote, there was no known persecution of "Christians" by "Jews." See Levine, *Misunderstood Jew*, 96.

47. Felix Just, "'The Jews' in the Fourth Gospel," Catholic Resources for Bible, Liturgy, Art, and Theology, http://catholic-resources.org/John/Themes-Jews.htm.

48. Luke 22:52.

49. John 8:44. For the Gospels' progression of Satan from metaphor to "the Jews," see Elaine Pagels, *Origin of Satan: How Christians Demonized Jews, Pagans, and Heretics* (New York: Vintage, 1996), 99, 104–5. I acknowledge my large debt to Pagels.

50. Luke 2:1–20; Isaiah 7:14.

51. Though the canon of the New Testament would not be formally established until the fourth century, its first draft, including a version of the Gospel of Luke and some of Paul's letters, had appeared by the middle of the second century. The term "Old Testament" was coined by Melito, bishop of Sardis (died c. 180), whom we saw earlier as originator of the phrase "deicide people."

52. "Jesus left the temple and was going away, when his disciples came to point out to him the buildings of the temple. But he answered them, 'You see all these, do you not? Truly, I say to you, there will not be left here one stone upon another, that will not be thrown down'" (Matthew 24:1–2).

53. So here can be seen the symbolic significance of the solemnly respectful visit made by Pope John Paul II to the Western Wall in 2000. For a pope to pray at the last vestige of the Temple—praying in the Jewish mode, not Christian—was implicitly to reverse this ancient denigration. Jews

recognized this meaning of the pope's act. Christians, mainly, did not. In 2014, it was repeated by Pope Francis, but now in the company of a rabbi.

CHAPTER EIGHT: The Women, Too

1. Wisdom of Solomon 6:12, 7:25.
2. 1 Timothy 2:11–15.
3. Colossians 3:18; Ephesians 5:22.
4. 1 Corinthians 14:33–34.
5. 1 Timothy 1:1. Scholars agree that this letter is wrongly attributed to Paul, although down through the centuries it has been cited with Pauline authority. See Elaine Pagels, *The Gnostic Paul: Gnostic Exegesis of the Pauline Letters* (Philadelphia: Trinity Press International, 1992). It should be noted that just because Paul himself can be excused for responsibility for these troubling antifemale texts, like those that seem excessively anti-Jewish, that takes nothing from the fact that they reside in the tradition with all the power of biblical authority—no matter who "wrote" them. See Amy-Jill Levine, *The Misunderstood Jew: The Church and the Scandal of the Jewish Jesus* (San Francisco: HarperOne, 2006), 97.
6. Romans 5:12; 1 Corinthians 15:47.
7. The tradition of the woman as originator of sin becomes lethal when, at the turn of the fifth century, Saint Augustine pairs the idea of Eve as temptress with the teaching that her sexual intercourse with Adam constituted the original sin. Through sex, humans are doomed, and the antidote to doom is the avoidance of women. Celibacy becomes the defining virtue for males.
8. 1 Corinthians 11:5.
9. "The misogyny of 1 Timothy 2:11–14." Jerome Murphy-O'Connor, "The First Letter to the Corinthians," in *The New Jerome Biblical Commentary*, ed. Raymond Edward Brown, Joseph A. Fitzmyer, and Roland E. Murphy (Englewood Cliffs, N.J.: Prentice-Hall, 1990), 811–12. Murphy-O'Connor argued that a "circle" of later antifemale misogynists wrote to dilute Paul's affirmations of equality with women. It is notable that this critical view of female "post-Pauline interpolations" comes from a scholar who, until his death in 2013, was a Catholic priest.
10. Romans 16:7, 16:1–2. See Karen L. King, "Women in Ancient Christianity: The New Discoveries," *Frontline*, "From Jesus to Christ," http://pbs.org/wgbh/pages/frontline/shows/religion/first/women.html.

11. Elisabeth Schüssler Fiorenza, *Discipleship of Equals: A Critical Feminist Ecclesiology of Liberation* (New York: Crossroad, 1993). In an earlier work, Schüssler Fiorenza affirms "a feminist hermeneutics of suspicion [which] also questions the underlying presuppositions, androcentric models, and unarticulated interests of contemporary biblical interpretations." *In Memory of Her: A Feminist Theological Reconstruction of Early Christian Origins* (New York: Crossroad, 1984), 16.

12. Galatians 4:8, 3:28–29.

13. 1 Timothy 3:1; Titus 2:15.

14. *Kyriarchy* takes off from the Greek word for "Lord." "I have coined the expression kyriarchy . . . in order to name the system of domination that goes back to antiquity and is still at work today." Elisabeth Schüssler Fiorenza, *Democratizing Biblical Studies* (Louisville, Ky.: Westminster John Knox, 2009), 11. Paul often uses the term *kyrios* to refer to Jesus, but his point of reference in doing so is Hebrew messianic expectation, not a Roman power structure.

15. Mark 7:28. See King, "Women in Ancient Christianity." King, especially, informs me here.

16. Mark 5:27.

17. Luke 18:1–8; Matthew 25:1–13; Luke 21:1–4.

18. Matthew 5:31–32; Luke 7:36–50; John 4:1–42.

19. Thucydides, *History of the Peloponnesian War*, trans. Rex Warner (New York: Penguin, 1972), 151. My attention was drawn to this passage in Pericles's funeral oration by Thomas E. J. Wiedemann, "Thucydides, Women, and the Limits of Rational Analysis," 1983, JSTOR, http://www.jstor.org/discover/10.2307/642567?uid=3739696&uid=2129&uid=2&uid=70&uid=4&uid=3739256&sid=21102412465331.

20. Such "a feminist biblical hermeneutics of remembrance" would risk uncovering "a dangerous memory that reclaims the visions and sufferings of the dead." That is, of the dead *women*. Schüssler Fiorenza, *In Memory of Her*, 19.

21. Tony Judt, *Postwar: A History of Europe Since 1945* (New York: Penguin, 2005), 20.

22. Beginning in the early 1990s, there were four distinct wars of independence, all waged against the Yugoslav government in Belgrade: in Slovenia, Croatia, Bosnia, and Kosovo.

23. Violeta Krasnic, "Women of Bosnia and Herzegovina: Twenty Years Later," Foreign Policy in Focus, April 11, 2012, http://www.fpif.org/articles/women_of_bosnia_and_herzegovina_twenty_years_later. A reckoning

with rape by Americans in World War II has also been undertaken by scholars. The scale of criminal behavior by GIs—reliable estimates put the number of their documentable rapes in France, Germany, and Britain at something like fourteen thousand—was "moderate" only by comparison with Soviet crimes. J. Robert Lilly, *Taken by Force: Rape and American G.I.s in Europe in World War II* (New York: Palgrave Macmillan, 2007). American reluctance to confront this history is suggested by the fact that this book was first published in France in 2003.

24. Judt, *Postwar*, 20. This figure says nothing about the number of abortions and miscarriages, which can be presumed to have been large.

25. The rape of the Sabine women has been rendered on canvas and in sculpture by Giambologna, Pietro da Cortona, Johann Heinrich Schönfeld, Nicolas Poussin, Peter Paul Rubens, Jacques-Louis David, John Leech, and Pablo Picasso. It is the basis for Stephen Vincent Benét's *Seven Brides for Seven Brothers*.

26. "For I will gather all the nations against Jerusalem to battle, and the city shall be taken and the houses plundered and the women ravished" (Zechariah 14:2–3). "Their infants will be dashed in pieces before their eyes; their houses will be plundered and their wives ravished" (Isaiah 13:16).

27. The Catholic Church "holds that it is not admissible to ordain women to the priesthood for very fundamental reasons: the example recorded in Sacred Scripture of Christ choosing his Apostles only from among men, the constant practice of the Church which has imitated Christ in choosing only men, and her living teaching authority which has consistently held that the exclusion of women from the priesthood is in accordance with God's plan for his Church." Pope John Paul II (citing Pope Paul VI in 1975), *Ordinatio Sacerdotalis*, 1994.

28. 1 Peter 3:1.

29. In 2012, an alleged fourth-century papyrus fragment came to light, a scrap of text that seems to suggest that Jesus was married. Referred to as the *Gospel of Jesus' Wife*, the text might have originated as early as the second century, although its authenticity is disputed. The fragment includes a reference to "Mary," followed by the words "Jesus said to them, 'My wife . . . she will be able to be my disciple . . . As for me, I dwell with her.'" Harvard professor Karen L. King, who made the fragment public, commented, "Christian tradition has long held that Jesus was not married, even though no reliable historical evidence exists to support that claim. This new gospel doesn't prove that Jesus was married, but it tells us that the whole question

only came up as part of vociferous debates about sexuality and marriage. From the very beginning, Christians disagreed about whether it was better not to marry, but it was over a century after Jesus' death before they began appealing to Jesus' marital status to support their positions." Jonathan Beasley, "HDS Scholar Announces Existence of a New Early Christian Gospel from Egypt," Harvard Divinity School, September 18, 2012, http://www.hds.harvard.edu/news-events/articles/2012/09/16/hds-scholar-announces-existence-of-new-early-christian-gospel-from-egypt.

30. Modern archaeology has uncovered such texts as the *Gospel of Peter*, the *Gospel of Thomas*, the *Gospel of the Hebrews*, and the *Gospel of Truth*. Several texts show women as subject to special revelation or as leaders, like *Dialogue of the Savior* and the *Acts of Paul and Thecla*, in which Paul sends forth a patrician woman "to go and teach the word of God." We take up another below, the *Gospel of Mary*.

31. Athanasius, the bishop of Alexandria, who died in about 373, compiled a list of twenty-seven books that he called, after Melito, the New Testament, a first formal "canonization" of Christian writings. But there were dozens more texts from which, in effect, he chose. In the interest of establishing an "orthodox" reading of Christian origins, Athanasius, in 367, ordered those other texts to be destroyed. It is almost certainly this order that prompted an anonymous monk at Nag Hammadi, Egypt, to take more than fifty other "books" and hide them in a cave in a cliff, where they were discovered in 1945. Among these books are the so-called Gnostic Gospels. Elaine Pagels, *Beyond Belief: The Secret Gospel of Thomas* (New York: Random House, 2005), 96–97.

32. Including, at least, "kissing." Karen L. King, *The Gospel of Mary of Magdala: Jesus and the First Woman Apostle* (Santa Rosa, Calif.: Polebridge, 2003), 153. I offered an early take on Mary of Magdala in my book *Practicing Catholic* (Boston: Houghton Mifflin, 2009), but now, in the light of both Roman violence and Christian anti-Judaism, I understand the denigration of this woman as an instance of the broader oppositionalism that gripped the Christian imagination.

33. Magdala may be the prosperous town that, according to Josephus, was destroyed by the Romans during the Jewish War. Josephus, *The Jewish War*, III:10.5

34. Matthew 28:9; John 20:14–18; Luke 24:13–27; Mark 16:1–7.

35. John 20:1–18.

36. Luke 8:1–3.

37. Luke 7:36–50. The anointing of Jesus' feet by a "woman with an alabaster jar" shows up in Matthew, but with differences. In Matthew, Judas is shown taking offense at the value of the ointment, so the violation is less about sex than about money (Matthew 26:6–13). In John, Jesus' friend Mary of Bethany, sister of Lazarus, is the one who anoints Jesus' feet— the act of a loving friend, not a repentant prostitute. Again Judas objects about cost, and again Jesus defends the woman: "Let her alone, let her keep it for the day of my burial. The poor you always have with you, but you do not always have me" (John 12:1–9).

38. Mark 16:8.

39. Luke 24:11.

40. Virgil, *Aeneid*, II.246–247, 341–346, 403–408. Cassandra was cursed by a scorned Apollo to always speak the truth and never be believed.

41. Even men as astute as the historians Tony Judt and Timothy Snyder misremember the importance of Cassandra, as this exchange shows. They are discussing the role of the intellectual as critic of the conventional wisdom. Snyder has just challenged Judt for his naysaying. Judt replies, "Well, you know, Cassandra has quite a reputation. It's not so bad to go down fighting as the last person to tell an unpleasant truth." Snyder: "We remember Cassandra, but no one remembers what her unpleasant truth was." Judt: "Fair enough." But her "unpleasant truth" about the Trojan Horse was momentous! Tony Judt and Timothy Snyder, *Thinking the Twentieth Century* (New York: Penguin Books, 2012), 309.

42. A papyrus document, the *Gospel of Mary*, was found in Egypt in the late nineteenth century. It dated to the fourth century but was a copy of a text dating to the middle of the second century. See King, *Gospel of Mary of Magdala*.

43. *Gospel of Mary* 6:1–4.

44. *Gospel of Mary* 10:7–9.

45. Ross S. Kraemer, "The New Testament," in *Women in Scripture*, ed. Carol Meyers (Boston: Houghton Mifflin, 2000), 21.

CHAPTER NINE: **Imitation of Christ**

1. George Bernard Shaw, *Back to Methuselah*, Part 1, Act 1 (Digireads .com, 2011; first published 1921), 7.

2. David Tracy, *Dialogue with the Other: The Intra-Religious Dialogue* (Grand Rapids, Mich.: Eerdmans, 1991), 4.

3. Bonhoeffer later wrote to his brother-in-law, "I can't think what made me behave as I did. I am tormented by the thought that I didn't do as you

asked as a matter of course." Charles Marsh, *Strange Glory: A Life of Dietrich Bonhoeffer* (New York: Knopf, 2014), 166–67.

4. Marsh, *Strange Glory*, 326, 345.

5. Protestants speak of the "inerrancy" of Scripture, which of course is belied by the Jew and female denigrations in the New Testament. Catholics speak of the "infallibility" of the pope, which is belied by—take your pick of papal sins. Inerrancy and infallibility both seek to protect the idea that the Church is a reliable custodian of the Gospel, but that reliability does not imply any kind of perfection. Christian coresponsibility for the Holocaust is the single clearest refutation of any notion that the Church as such is exempt from—or above—the human condition.

6. "And passing along by the Sea of Galilee, he saw Simon and Andrew the brother of Simon casting a net in the sea; for they were fishermen. And Jesus said to them, 'Follow me and I will make you become fishers of men.' And immediately they left their nets and followed him" (Mark 1:16–18).

7. *Nachfolge* was first published in 1937. Its English edition, appearing in 1948, was titled *The Cost of Discipleship*. "Costly grace," Bonhoeffer wrote, "confronts us as a gracious call to follow Jesus. It comes as a word of forgiveness to the broken spirit and the contrite heart. It is costly because it compels a man to submit to the yoke of Christ and follow him. It is a grace because Jesus says, 'My yoke is easy and my burden is light.'" Dietrich Bonhoeffer, *The Cost of Discipleship*, trans. R. H. Fuller (New York: Touchstone, 1995), 45.

8. Terry Eagleton's characterization of T. S. Eliot's idea. *Culture and the Death of God* (New Haven, Conn.: Yale University Press, 2014), 121.

9. Schweitzer published *The Quest of the Historical Jesus* in 1910, a book that is taken to mark the end of the so-called first quest for the historical Jesus. The second quest came after World War II, sparked by the "demythologizing" typified by the work of Rudolf Bultmann, and the third quest came in the 1980s, centered on pro-and-con criticism of the Jesus Seminar.

10. The resonance of the Schweitzer quote shows in its being cited, for example, by John Dominic Crossan, *Jesus: A Revolutionary Biography* (San Francisco: HarperSanFrancisco, 1994), 53; by Paula Fredriksen, *Jesus of Nazareth: King of the Jews* (New York: Knopf, 1999), 270; and by John S. Dunne, *Eternal Consciousness* (Notre Dame, Ind.: Notre Dame University Press, 2012), 9.

11. Albert Schweitzer, *Albert Schweitzer: Essential Writings*, ed. James Brabazon (Maryknoll, N.Y.: Orbis, 2005), 76–80.

12. This is Ross Douthat's characterization of the portrait of Jesus offered by Reza Aslan in his book *Zealot: The Life and Times of Jesus of Nazareth.* "The Return of the Jesus Wars," *New York Times*, August 3, 2013, http:// www.nytimes.com/2013/08/04/opinion/sunday/douthat-return-of-the -jesus-wars.html. It is not clear that Aslan would regard Douthat's characterization as accurate.

13. Philippians 2:9–10.

14. Dorothy Day, *From Union Square to Rome* (Silver Spring, Md.: Preservation of the Faith Press, 1938), repr. The Catholic Worker Movement, http://www.catholicworker.org/dorothyday/Reprint2.cfm?TextID=207.

15. *The Imitation of Christ* was written by Thomas à Kempis, a sixteenth-century monk, a kind of rebutter of Martin Luther. Bonhoeffer valued the book, taking "imitation" as a key idea, although he did not associate with its denigrations of the world as "vanity." Marsh, *Strange Glory*, 241, 315.

16. Dorothy Day, "Room for Christ," *Catholic Worker*, December 1945, 2.

17. Philippians 2:6–7.

18. Luke 4: 21.

19. Philippians 2:8–11.

20. "Then the LORD said, 'I have seen the affliction of my people who are in Egypt, and have heard their cry because of their taskmasters; I know their sufferings, and I have come down to deliver them out of the hand of the Egyptians'" (Exodus 3:7–8).

21. Isaiah 52:14. This is the New Living Translation. The RSV gives the verse as "His appearance was so marred, beyond human semblance, and his form beyond that of the sons of men."

22. Eagleton, *Culture and the Death of God*, 160.

23. From a letter written in 1940 to Marguerite Caetani, on the occasion of the death of her only son: "You have been much in my thoughts, and I knew that your loss would not become easier. I do not pretend that such a loss ever does; only in time, perhaps, it is simply like learning to live without one's eyesight, or crippled. One just makes do and carries on the rest of life. I don't even maintain that faith makes loss easier; it just, if I may say so, improves the quality of the suffering and makes it sometimes fruitful instead of useless." T. S. Eliot, quoted in Helen Barolini, *Their Other Side: Six American Women and the Lure of Italy* (New York: Fordham University Press, 2006), 210.

24. Matthew 27:46 repeats a line from Psalm 22. Luke 23:46.
25. Consider, for example, Christopher Hitchens's criticism of Mother Teresa, as "not a friend of the poor. She was a friend of poverty. She said that suffering was a gift from God. She spent her life opposing the only known cure for poverty, which is the empowerment of women and the emancipation of them from a livestock version of compulsory reproduction." "Mommie Dearest," *Slate*, October 20, 2003. It is not necessary to share Hitchens's contempt for Mother Teresa and like-minded charity workers to see the point that concern for the poor must be extended to opposition to what causes poverty.
26. Dorothy Day, "Our Stand," *Catholic Worker*, June 1940, and "Poverty Is to Care and Not to Care," *Catholic Worker*, April 1953.
27. Matthew 5:38–48.
28. "We want genocide to have begun and ended with Nazism," the Swedish writer Sven Lindqvist observed of European colonialism. "[But] the air he [Hitler] and all other Western people in his childhood breathed was soaked in the conviction that imperialism is a biologically necessary process, which, according to the laws of nature, leads to the inevitable destruction of the lower races. It was a conviction which had already cost millions of human lives before Hitler provided his highly personal application." *Exterminate All the Brutes* (London: Granta, 1996), 141. In hatred of the Jew, that is, lies "the origin of white Christian Europe." Edward Said, *Orientalism* (New York: Pantheon, 1979), 391.
29. In the decade of the 1950s, the American nuclear arsenal far outstripped the Soviet Union's, growing from fewer than two hundred atomic bombs to, by 1960, more than twenty thousand mostly hydrogen bombs. The Soviet arsenal in 1960 was still counted in the hundreds, although in subsequent decades Moscow would draw even in the arms race. "Table of Global Nuclear Weapons Stockpiles, 1945–2002," Natural Resources Defense Council, 2002, http://www.nrdc.org/nuclear/nudb/datab19.asp.
30. See Paul Elie's treatment of Dorothy Day in *The Life You Save May Be Your Own* (New York: Farrar, Straus and Giroux, 2004).
31. James Carroll, *Prayer from Where We Are* (Washington, D.C.: National Office of Confraternity of Christian Doctrine, 1970).
32. Ronald Dworkin, *Religion Without God* (Cambridge, Mass.: Harvard University Press, 2013), 1. Dworkin might be one of those chided by Terry Eagleton as "reluctant atheists . . . They have everything of religious faith but the substance of it." *Culture and the Death of God*, 204.

33. Albert Einstein, "Living Philosophies," in *Living Philosophies: The Reflections of Some Eminent Men and Women of Our Time*, ed. Clifton Fadiman (New York: Doubleday, 1990), 6.

34. I came to this understanding in reading John Macquarrie's masterwork, *Jesus Christ in Modern Thought* (Philadelphia: Trinity International Press, 1990), 360.

35. James Gleick, *The Information: A History, a Theory, a Flood* (New York: Pantheon, 2011). I acknowledge my debt here to Gleick.

36. "A more familiar metaphor is the cloud. All that information—all that information capacity—looms over us, not quite visible, not quite tangible, but awfully real; amorphous, spectral; hovering nearby, yet not situated in any place. Heaven must once have felt this way to the faithful." Gleick, *The Information*, chapter 14.

37. *The Cloud of Unknowing and Other Works*, trans. A. C. Spearing (New York: Penguin, 2001), 27–28.

38. "God is that-without-which-there-would-be-no-evolution-at-all; God is the atemporal undergirder and sustainer of the whole process of apparent contingency and 'randomness,' yet—we can say in the spirit of Augustine— simultaneously closer to its inner workings than it is to itself. As such, God is both 'within the process' and 'without.'" Sarah Coakley, "God and Evolution: A New Solution," *Harvard Divinity School Bulletin*, Spring/Summer 2007, 10.

39. 2 Peter 1:4. Here is how John Macquarrie makes the point: "Only if there is *in all human beings* a possibility for transcendence and a capacity for God, can there be such a possibility and capacity in the man Jesus. . . . So if there is any entity on this planet in and through which God can be present and revealed, it would be in a human person." *Jesus Christ in Modern Thought*, 381.

40. Martin Heidegger, *Being and Time*, trans. John Macquarrie and Edward Robinson (New York: Harper Perennial, 2008), 26.

41. Jean-Paul Sartre, *Existentialism Is a Humanism*, trans. Carol Macomber, (New Haven, Conn.: Yale University Press, 2007), 2.

42. Exodus 3:13–14. "I AM WHO I AM" is variously translated, as, for example, "I AM WHO CAUSES TO BE," and the meaning of this phrase is much debated. For our purposes, the biblical intuition that God's name is best given as some form of the verb "to be" is the point.

43. John 8:56–59.

44. "So God created man in his own image, in the image of God he created him" (Genesis 1:27).

45. "The primary imagination I hold to be the living Power and prime Agent of all human Perception, and as a repetition in the finite mind of the ethereal act of creation in the infinite I AM." Samuel Taylor Coleridge, *Biographia Literaria,* ed. James Engell and W. Jackson Bate (Princeton, N.J.: Princeton University Press, 1983), 304.

46. Eagleton, *Culture and the Death of God,* 101.

47. Eagleton, *Culture and the Death of God,* 101. "It is through this imaginative force that individuals become most intensely alive; yet in doing so, they also become conscious of sharing in some larger more corporate form of existence, aware that the roots of the self sink down to infinity . . . the imagination is a secular form of grace, one which seizes upon the self from some unfathomable depth beyond it . . . The subject does not fundamentally belong to itself." *Culture and the Death of God,* 101–2.

48. Paul Ricoeur, *The Rule of Metaphor: Multi-disciplinary Studies of the Creation of Meaning in Language,* trans. Robert Czerny, with Kathleen McLaughlin and John Costello (Toronto: University of Toronto Press, 1977), 318.

49. Effie Kymissis and Claire L. Poulson, "The History of Imitation in Learning Theory: The Language Acquisition Process," *Journal of the Experimental Analysis of Behavior* 54, no. 2 (September 1990): 113–27.

50. "Therefore, since we are surrounded by so great a cloud of witnesses, let us also lay aside every weight, and sin which clings so closely, and let us run with perseverance the race that is set before us" (Hebrews 12:1).

CONCLUSION: **Because God Lives**

1. Fyodor Dostoyevsky commenting on "The Legend of the Grand Inquisitor" in notes on *The Brothers Karamazov.*

2. 1 Thessalonians 4:16.

3. Edward Schillebeeckx, *Interim Report on the Books Jesus and Christ* (New York: Crossroad, 1981), 109.

4. "Surely the depths of Christian revelation are inexhaustible and always yield new convictions in new situations. Globalization and current religious dialogue and conflict have thus yielded new awareness of the implications of what has been revealed in Jesus Christ." Roger Haight, *The Future of Christology* (New York: Continuum, 2005), 159. I acknowledge a particular debt to Haight.

5. Haight, *Future of Christology,* 162.

6. "The projecting upon Jesus of a divinity that radically sets him apart from other human beings does not correspond to the New Testament and undermines the very logic of Christian faith." Haight, *Future of Christology*, 162.

7. Ernst Troeltsch: "Whatever is true, great and profound in our faith today will be so two hundred years hence, even if perhaps in quite a different form. Since we possess these religious powers of the present only in association with the present and reverenced person of Christ, we gather around him unconcerned whether in a hundred years religion will still be nourished on Jesus or will have some other center. . . . We have resolutely to grasp the divine as it presents itself to us in our time." Quoted in Wesley J. Wildman, *Fidelity with Plausibility: Modest Christologies in the Twentieth Century* (Albany, N.Y.: SUNY Press, 1998), 20. I acknowledge Wildman, whose "fidelity with plausibility" formulation nicely captures my dual commitment to classical tradition and contemporary intelligibility.

8. Bonhoeffer, *Letters and Papers from Prison* (New York: Macmillan, 1971), 360–61.

9. Recall this as a variation on the opening lines of John: "In the beginning was the Word, and the Word was with God, and the Word was God. . . . And the Word became flesh and dwelt among us" (John 1:1, 1:14).

Index